The Only Three Questions That Still Count

The Only Three Questions That Still Count

Investing by Knowing What Others Don't

Fully Revised and Updated

KEN FISHER

WITH LARA HOFFMANS

AND JENNIFER CHOU

WILEY

John Wiley & Sons, Inc.

This book is a revised edition of *The Only Three Questions That Still Count: Investing By Knowing What Others Don't* published by John Wiley & Sons, Inc., 2007

Published by John Wiley & Sons, Inc., Hoboken, New Jersey.
Published simultaneously in Canada.

Important Disclaimers: This book reflects personal opinions, viewpoints and analyses of the authors and should not be regarded as a description of advisory services provided by Fisher Investments or performance returns of any Fisher Investments client. Fisher Investments manages its clients' accounts using a variety of investment techniques and strategies not necessarily discussed in this book. Nothing in this book constitutes investment advice or any recommendation with respect to a particular country, sector, industry, security or portfolio of securities. All information is impersonal and not tailored to the circumstances or investment needs of any specific person.

Limit of Liability/Disclaimer of Warranty: While the publisher and author have used their best efforts in preparing this book, they make no representations or warranties with respect to the accuracy or completeness of the contents of this book and specifically disclaim any implied warranties of merchantability or fitness for a particular purpose. No warranty may be created or extended by sales representatives or written sales materials. The advice and strategies contained herein may not be suitable for your situation. You should consult with a professional where appropriate. Neither the publisher nor author shall be liable for any loss of profit or any other commercial damages, including but not limited to special, incidental, consequential, or other damages.

For general information on our other products and services or for technical support, please contact our Customer Care Department within the United States at (800) 762-2974, outside the United States at (317) 572-3993 or fax (317) 572-4002.

Wiley also publishes its books in a variety of electronic formats. Some content that appears in print may not be available in electronic books. For more information about Wiley products, visit our web site at www.wiley.com.

ISBN 978-1-118-11508-4; ISBN 978-1-118-22421-2 (ebk); ISBN 978-1-118-23755-7 (ebk); ISBN 978-1-118-26246-7 (ebk)

Printed in the United States of America

10 9 8 7 6 5 4 3 2 1

CONTENTS

PREFACE

Who Am I to Tell You Something That Counts?

Who am I to tell you anything, much less anything that counts? Or that there are only three questions that count and I know what they are? Why should you bother reading any of this? Why listen to me at all?

As I update this book in 2011 for its second edition, I've been in the investment industry for nearly 40 years. I founded and am CEO of what is among the world's largest independent discretionary money management firms, serving tens of thousands of high net worth individuals and an impressive roster of institutions—major corporate and public pension plans and endowments and foundations—spanning the globe. I've written *Forbes's* "Portfolio Strategy" column for over 27 years, making me the fourth longest-running columnist in *Forbes's* long history. I write regular columns in Britain and Germany. And now, I've written eight books, five of which (including this one) were national bestsellers. Along the way, and without really aiming at it, I made the *Forbes* 400 list of richest Americans.

That's a lot for one lifetime and one professional career. But I'm here to tell you the prime cumulative lesson of my long career is when it comes to investing, there are only three questions that count. And my view on that hasn't changed since I first penned this book.

In reality, there really is only one question that counts. Or, at least, only one question that *really* counts. But I don't know how to express that one question in a way you can easily use for everyday investing decisions. If broken down into three subparts, I know how.

And what is that only question that counts? Finance theory is quite clear the only rational basis for placing a market bet is if you believe somehow, some way, you know something others don't know. The only question that counts is: What do you know that others don't?

Most people don't know anything others don't. Most folks don't think they're supposed to know something others don't. We'll see why. But saying you must know something others don't isn't at all novel. Pretty much everyone who took a basic college investment class was told this, although most people conveniently forget this truism.

Without answering the question—what do you know that others don't—investing with an aim to do as well or better than the market is futile. I'll say that another way. Markets are pretty efficient at pricing all currently known information into today's prices. There is nothing new about that statement. It's an established pillar of finance theory and has been repeatedly verified over the decades. If you make market decisions based on the same information others have (or have access to), you will overall fail relative to what the markets would have rendered you on their own without any decision making on your part. If you try to outguess where the market will go or what sectors will lead and lag or what stock to buy based on what you read in newspapers or chatter about with your friends and peers—it doesn't matter how smart or well trained you are—you will sometimes be right or lucky or both, but likely more often wrong or unlucky or both, and overall do worse than if you didn't make such bets at all.

I bet you hate hearing that. But I already told you I didn't know how to express that truism as a single question in a way useful to you. What I can do is show you how to know things other people don't know.

Polling for Perfect Truth

Why is knowing something others don't so important? Financial markets are "discounters" of widely known information—whatever information we commonly have access to has already been reflected in today's prices before we can articulate our knowledge of it. See it this way—compare markets to political elections that aren't discounters of known information.

You know professional pollsters can build a sample of about 1,000 people sufficiently representative of America's voters to foresee the immediate outcome of a national election within a predictable few percentage points. That technology is mature and time-tested. You're quite used to it. When a professional poll is done the night before the election, we know within maybe three to five percentage points how the election will end. It's all based on picking the participants in the poll to be representative of total votes.

Envision if someone could build a similar sample of all the world's investors. It would include every imaginable type in just the right proportions. Institutional and retail. Growth and value fans. Small and big cap. Foreign and domestic. Whatever imaginable. Suppose the pollsters polled the sample and suppose the consensus view was the market would rise next month—big time. Could it? No, because if everyone tended to agree the market would rise next month, anyone with any buying power would buy before then. The market might rise before next month, but only a fool would wait for next month to buy. Hence, next month there would be no subsequent buying power to drive the market higher. It could fall. It could stay flat. But it couldn't rise much. This is an oversimplification, but it's a useful illustration of how whatever we agree on has already been priced into the markets by the time we can articulate it, and, therefore, it can't occur. Since investors tend to be avid information seekers, the information they have access to has already been priced into the bets they've made.

Instead, it's surprise that moves markets. It's what happens next that few previously fathomed. Another piece of news consistent with what people previously expected can't move markets much further since investors already bet that way (to the extent they were able).

Said differently: You may be smarter, wiser or better trained than the next investor, but finance theory says that isn't enough. No matter how wise you think you are, you're a fool if you think being smarter or better trained is enough to beat others based on commonly available news and information. And the aim of this book is to show how to find those things you can know that others can't.

Investing by Knowing What Others Don't

Investing is a difficult, lifetime pursuit. Just knowing the questions isn't enough. You must know what the questions really mean and how to use them. And then you must actually put them to use diligently. Over and over again! The Three Questions don't constitute a craft or a simple "Three Steps to Riches" list. It isn't some *Investing Made Easy* to-do list for beating the market. If there were such a thing, I wouldn't be writing this book and you wouldn't be reading it. Instead, I'd put it in a single *Forbes* column and you would glean all you needed to know from it. From there, you would go off and promptly become unimaginably wealthy. No, it isn't *Investing Made Easy*. Instead, it's *Investing by Knowing What Others Don't*. In fact, that's why it's my subtitle.

If you can learn how to use the Three Questions, you can learn to start making better investing decisions. And that should give you an edge over your fellow investors.

Let's think about them. Your fellow investors.

Investing Isn't a Craft

You know some folks are idiots. You don't fear competing with them. But how will you compete with serious professionals who've had serious training, are seriously smart and have scads of experience? The good news is, in my observation, even most professionals don't have much better long-term results than your average amateur investor. How so? Because, despite many of them taking that class where they learn they must know something others don't, they forget or ignore it.

Inside the typical investor's mind is the false premise investing is a craft, like carpentry or doctoring. They don't treat investing like a scientific query session, which is what I'll teach you to do. Instead, consider how they approach it. Maybe they have a few favorite information sources—cable news, a few newspapers, some blogs and/or a newsletter from their guru du jour. Maybe they have software tracking price patterns. They may have specific rules they adhere to—momentum investing, buy the dips, buy on bad news. They look for clues or signals to buy or sell. They may wait for the S&P 500 and Nasdaq to correspondingly reach certain levels and then they buy or sell or just generally panic. They clock 90-day moving averages and monitor the VIX (the S&P 500 volatility index) or some other supposed predictive market indicator. (The VIX is a statistically provable worthless forecaster, by the way—but many people use it every day, applying a wasteful mythology losing more money than it makes.) They believe investing is a craft-like skill they can learn with enough diligence and effort. They believe those who acquire the best craft skills must be the better investors.

Investors categorize themselves and develop craft skills accordingly. The wannabe value investor develops a slightly different tool kit than the wannabe growth investor. Ditto for small-cap fans versus big-cap. Or foreign versus domestic. This works perfectly in carpentry. Anyone can learn basic carpentry, though some people are more naturally gifted than others. It works well for doctoring, if you're smart enough. It works for most sports, which are craft-based. Again, some folks are naturally better at some sports than others. Accounting, dentistry, lawyering, engineering and much more—all learnable crafts, though requiring varying degrees of time commitment and physical or mental prowess.

We know learning a craft is possible because there are countless people who perform craft-based functions after adequate training and apprenticeship (necessary to craft) in high quantities within acceptable and predictable bandwidths. The ability to train an accountant to do an audit in an acceptable manner is a perfect reflection of craftsmanship. But few folks beat the market, amateur or professional. Darned few! So learning a craft obviously isn't enough to do it. Craftsmanship isn't sufficient to the task of beating markets.

Finance theory says it shouldn't be—craft won't help you—because you're supposed to know something others don't. That may excuse an amateur from failing to beat the market, but what about the pros? At a minimum, there are educational licensing requirements professionals must pass to legally advise clients. University students and doctoral candidates in investment finance spend years studying markets. They learn to analyze corporate balance sheets. They learn to calculate risk and expected return, but with widely known analytical tools like Sharpe ratios and R-squared and CAPM. And with all of this, they still can't beat the market any more often than those without a PhD.

Quite wisely, after years of study, some young wannabe professionals commit to apprenticeship by laboring under another established investor. At the knee of their chosen master, they generally learn a craft the same way a blacksmith apprenticed years ago. Some became generalists and others were specialists who made only weapons like swords and spears, while others made livery gear and plowshares. And today, you name the investing style, there are adherents, apostolic in their allegiance to the modality under which they apprenticed. Armed with degrees, certifications and apprenticeships, professional investors embark into the world, and still they overwhelmingly lag markets.

They most commonly start where entry is easiest, the way I did decades ago, rendering advice to individuals. These are your stockbrokers, financial planners and insurance and annuity salespeople. Some provide forecasts and prescriptions of their own, but those working for the big-name firms generally must kowtow to the firm's forecasts. This makes sense for the firm since it's the only way these larger institutions can maintain a semblance of control over their huge employee bases. Big firms hire a few folks with extremely prestigious schooling and extensive professional training who look and sound good for a role like *Chief Economist* or *Chief Market Strategist*—whose main responsibility is forecasting. Industry analysts then forecast in their own individual realms of experience and training. Clients of said illustrious firms, both private and institutional, get the benefit of not only their individual broker's schooling and experience, but also that of the learned, tenured bigwigs who think bigger and wig out well when needed.

So why, with all the knowledge, expertise and battle scars out there, do vastly more professional investors lag markets than beat them? These are smart people. A lot of them are very smart. Smarter than me for sure. You're probably pretty smart, too. Aren't you? You might be much smarter than me, too. But that won't make any difference on whether you can do better than me as an investor. Smarts and training are good—nothing wrong with them.

A PhD is good. But they aren't enough. And they aren't necessary. You must know something others don't and then—with that extra something—you can do better than people who are smarter than you are.

Because, Mr. Crafty, It's Not a Craft

The answer to improving your error rate isn't in perfecting a craft but in knowing something others don't.

More academic study won't do it. The most learned finance PhD knows free markets are at least pretty efficient (although they do disagree about exactly how efficient). Passing tests like the Series 6, 7, 65—or the CFA or a CIMA certification won't do it. They contain no information not known by millions of other folks and parroted in a distilled form throughout the media. More magazine subscriptions and migraines from pondering pontificating pundits won't do it. They're talking about what is known and therefore priced. And if they knew something everyone else didn't and told you via the media, instantly everyone else would know it and the new information probably would be priced almost instantly. Now, hereto, worthless! (I'll show you how to measure an exception to this later.)

You can study technical investing and buy software identifying price movement patterns. Won't do it! You can study fundamental investing and vow to buy only when P/Es are at a certain level and sell at yet another level. Won't do it! You can hire someone to do it for you who has the most designation letters after his or her name. But you won't beat the market over the long term if you treat investing like a craft.

Well, that's not quite true. If enough people try all this stuff, some very few will get there simply by dumb luck. In the same way, if enough folks line up to flip coins, you will find someone who gets 50 heads in a row; but who that is remains a fluke. And it likely isn't you. Nor is it the basis for investing or beating markets. And you can count on that.

If investing were a craft, some type of craft (or even some combination of crafts) would have demonstrated market superiority. Someone somewhere would have figured out the right combination to keep beating markets. The right formula, no matter how complicated!

If it were a craft in the very long term, there would be a clear sense a specific craft had generated an army of disciples who did better over the very longterm than conflicting approaches. But such evidence doesn't exist. If investing were a craft, the decades wouldn't have sired thousands of investment books teaching largely contradicting craft—with gurus, pundits and seminars touting conflicting strategies. There would be a few differing strategies at most. There would be repeatability and consistency. Investing would be learnable like woodworking, masonry or medicine. Others could teach you. You could pass the skill on with efficacy. There wouldn't be so much failure. And you wouldn't have bought this book because anything I could say would be passé.

It's All Latin to Me—Starting to Think Like a Scientist

When I was a kid, if you wanted to be a scientist, they made you take Latin or Greek. I was a good student generally and took Latin, not because I wanted to be a scientist—I didn't—but because I couldn't figure out the benefit of my other options, Spanish or French. Since no one speaks Latin, I forgot almost everything immediately thereafter except the life lessons in which Latin abounds—like Caesar distinguishing himself by leading from the front of his troops, not the rear as most generals did (and do). It's maybe the most important single lesson of leadership. (One I write about more in my 2008 book, *The Ten Roads to Riches*.)

Another lesson: The word *science* derives from the Latin *scio*—to know, understand, to know how to do. Any scientist will tell you science isn't a craft; rather, it's a never-ending query session aimed at knowing. Scientists didn't wake up one day and decide to create an equation demonstrating the force exerted on all earthly objects. Instead, Newton first asked a simple question, like, "What the heck makes stuff fall down?" Galileo wasn't excommunicated for agreeing with Aristotle. He asked, "What if stars don't work like everyone says? Wouldn't that be nuts?"

Most of us would see the best scientists of all time, if we could meet them face to face, as maybe nuts. My friend Stephen Sillett, today's leading redwood scientist, changed the way scientists think about old-growth redwoods and trees in general by shooting arrows with fishing lines tied to them over the tops of 350-foot-tall giants, tying on a firmer line and free-climbing to the tops. He found life forms and structures up there no one ever knew existed. Dangling off those ropes 350 feet from terra firma is nuts. Nuts! But he asked the questions: What if there is stuff in the very tops of standing trees that isn't there when you cut them down? And if there is, would it tell you anything about the trees? In the process, he discovered much no one had ever known existed.

Why am I telling you this? Because most of what there is to know about investing doesn't exist yet and is subject to scientific inquiry and discovery. It isn't in a book and isn't finite. We just don't know it yet. We know more now about how capital markets work than we did 50 years ago but little compared to what we can know in 10, 30 and 50 years. Contrary to what the pundits and professionals will have you believe, the study of capital markets is both an art and a science—one in which theories and formulas continually evolve and are added and adjusted. We are at the beginning of a process of inquiry and discovery, not the end. Its scientific aspect is very much in its infancy.

Scientific inquiry offers opportunities ahead as we steadily learn more about how markets work than we ever imagined we could know previously. What's more, anyone can learn things now that no one knows but in a few decades will be general knowledge. Building new knowledge of how capital markets work is everyone's job, whether you accept that or not. You're part of it, whether you know it or not. By knowingly embracing it, you can know things others don't—things finance professors don't know yet. You needn't be a finance professor or have any kind of background in finance to do it. To know things others don't, you just need to think like a scientist—think freshly and be curious and open.

As a scientist, you should approach investing not with a rule set but with an open, inquisitive mind. Like any good scientist, you must learn to ask questions. Your questions will help you develop hypotheses you can test for efficacy. In the course of your scientific inquiry, if you don't get good answers to your questions, it's better to be passive than make an actionable mistake. But merely asking questions won't, by itself, help you beat the markets. The questions must be the right ones leading to an action on which a bet can be made correctly.

So, what are the right questions?

The Only Three Questions That Count

First, we need a question helping us where we see wrongly. Then we need one helping us where we don't see at all. Third, we need one helping us sense reality when our eyes aren't at all appropriate as tools.

For our first question, we must identify those things we believe that are actually false. The question is: What do I believe that is actually false? Note what you believe is probably believed by most people. In Chapter 1, I'll cover this question in detail. But if you and I think something is true, then probably most people do. If most people do, we can predict how they will bet and we can learn to bet against these beliefs at times because the market will discount them and their false truths.

Suppose you believe factor X causes result Y. Probably most people do, and we can verify most people believe it. Then when you see X happen, you know people will bet on Y happening next. But suppose you can prove in reality X doesn't cause Y at all. Now you know you can bet against Y happening while everyone else is betting it will happen. You can bet successfully against the crowd because you know something others don't. I'll show you how to do this.

Second question: What can I fathom that others find unfathomable? Here we need a process of inquiry allowing us to contemplate that which most people assume simply can't be contemplated at all. It's the essence of so-called out-of-the-box thinking. It's what made Edison and Einstein so successful but weird. They could think about how to think about the unthinkable. Think how unthinkable that is. Almost heretical! It's amazingly easier to do than most people assume, and it's a trainable skill. I'll show you how to do that in Chapter 2. Intuitively you know if no one knows what causes a particular result—let's call it result Q—and we can prove factor Z causes Q, then every time we see Z happen we can bet on Q happening more often than not because we know something others don't.

Finally, our third question: What the heck is my brain doing to mislead and misguide me now? To blindside me? Another way to ask this is: How can I out-think my brain, which normally doesn't let me think too well about markets? This is the realm of behavioral psychology. One thing you can come to know no one else can is how your individual brain works—what it does well in relation to markets and what it does badly and how to reprogram yourself to not use your brain in the ways it works worst for markets.

Few investors have spent any material time trying to understand how their own brains work. Most focus on craft, not internal deficiency. (*Note:* A craftsman wouldn't think about that at all.) You can learn how your brain works to hurt you, and when you do, you will know something almost unique since your brain is partly like other people's and partly yours uniquely. Chapter 3 covers this topic in very simple you-can-do-it lessons.

From there on, the rest of the book is simply about putting the Three Questions to work in various ways. We look at how to use the Three Questions to think about the overall market, different parts of the market and even individual stocks. We'll apply them to interest rates and currencies. We look at lots of things I've figured out over the years using the Three Questions. We also address areas I haven't figured out because there is still a lot of potential figuring to do, and you may be the person who figures these things out in the years ahead. We won't be able to cover everything, everywhere—nor is there a need for that.

I will make a lot of statements of fact you won't have heard before or think sound simply wrong, nuts and crazy. I've come to those conclusions using the Three Questions, and I'll show you how in each case. You can still disagree with me. That's ok. But if you learn how to use the Three Questions and you want to explore any area, including these, and have the time, you can do it on your own later. Forever! You can use the Three Questions to show me where I was wrong and messed up. I'd be delighted, and you should feel free to write me to show me evidence, using the Three Questions, where I'm wrong.

There are endless opportunities to discover new things in terms of what we don't know. You don't need to know everything. You need to know some things others don't know. If you learn to apply the Three Questions yourself, you'll be empowered to know things others don't for the rest of your life.

An additional note for those reading the second edition: Where I could, I updated graphs and numbers with the most recently available data. I left a few charts alone because they were fine examples of the point I made. I also replaced a few because in the intervening years, I've found a better way to make the same point. I also added commentary and a few new graphs in a few places.

Also, there's that old saying, "If I had more time, I'd write you a shorter letter." In reviewing this book to update it, I discovered many places where I could make the book more readable for you (and therefore, a better tool), not sacrifice any concepts and simply make my commentary briefer. Or maybe, some examples and anecdotes seemed particularly relevant in 2006 but much less so now.

What amazed me most in reading this was how much the basic framework of the Three Questions hasn't changed. And that's the idea. Over time, you get more knowledge, more data. Something that once worked doesn't anymore. Something that didn't work at all becomes more relevant. The world moves and changes and is dynamic, but the basic process of a disciplined scientific method shouldn't change. Which is why these are the Three Questions that *still* count.

Ken Fisher

Woodside, California

ACKNOWLEDGMENTS

Initially, when approached about doing a second edition of this book, I thought, "Why?" I like old investment books. You can learn tons from them—they tell you lots about what impacted people at a point in time, how they thought and why that's evolved. Then, too, I felt this book sufficiently evergreen that readers could still get something material out of the original 2007 version.

I still believe that, but there's a ton of data and graphs in this book. And what was interesting in updating them was how well they held up overall. After all, the past five years were far from dull. (Then again, I defy anyone to find any five-year span in capital markets that *was* dull. People tend to see the now and recent past as radically new and different—a common error I address in my 2011 book *Markets Never Forget*.) As I write in late 2011, we are now nearly three years from the bottom of a historically big bear market. And yet, the Three Questions are as valid as ever, as the updated graphs, data and commentary will show.

Once again, I pulled Lara Hoffmans from her other duties to assist me in doing first-round edits and overseeing the big task of updating data and graphs. Lara is managing editor of my firm's webzine MarketMinder and oversees a team responsible for creating client-facing content. Filling in for her while she was otherwise occupied on this task was her team of terrific writers: Todd Bliman, Amanda Williams, Elisabeth Dellinger and Naj Srinivas. Backing up Lara in other unaccountable ways are the other members of her team, Fab Ornani (whose web savvy I appreciate immeasurably), Molly Lienesch, Collin Smith, Jake Gamble, Evelyn Chea, Kris Bullard,

Thomas McEnany, Cianne McGeough, Thomas Perez and Leila Amiri, all under the guidance of Group Vice President David Eckerly.

Doing the heavy-lifting grunt work of running down all the data and updating graphs were Danielle Lynch and Jessica Wolfe. Both have contributed to books I've written in the past, and I appreciate their diligence, attention to detail and great patience with our requests to check, check and check again the data. Matt Schrader, head of my firm's Research Analytics and Production team does a great job, too, of ensuring data for this book (and for my firm) are as accurate as can be.

My team at Wiley also deserves special thanks, particularly Laura Walsh who is, as always, very professional and patient.

Updating a book is nowhere near as time consuming as writing a new one, particularly when I'm fortunate to have as talented a supporting cast as anyone in the publishing world. Assisting me as always in the business of my firm, whether I'm writing a book or not, are co-presidents Steve Triplett and Damian Ornani. Assisting in the management of my firm's portfolios are Vice Chairmen Jeff Silk and Andrew Teufel, along with William Glaser and Aaron Anderson. This group forms the smartest group of gentlemen I've ever had the pleasure of working with.

Though not instrumental in this second edition, the first edition would not be what it had been (and not be worthy of an update) without Jennifer Chou, Elizabeth Anathan, Jill Hitchcock, Greg Miramontes, David Watts, Pierson Clair, Thomas Grüner and Justin Arbuckle. Meir Statman (the Glen Klimek Professor of Finance at Santa Clara University) and Grover Wickersham also provided welcomed feedback on the first edition. Some I agreed with, some I didn't. But either way, the book was and is better for their input. And I must also thank David Pugh from Wiley, who edited this book the first time, and Jeff Herman, my agent, who first suggested seven years ago that I ought to think about doing another book.

And, finally, I must thank my wife, Sherrilyn—whose immense patience and love through the years have made our life's work possible.

1

QUESTION ONE: WHAT DO YOU BELIEVE THAT IS ACTUALLY FALSE?

If You Knew It Was Wrong, You Wouldn't Believe It

It's safe to assume if you knew something was wrong, you wouldn't believe it true in the first place. But in a world where so much of industry-applied craft has morphed into long-held mythologies, much of what everyone believes is false. This isn't any different from long ago when humanity believed the world was flat.

You needn't beat yourself up if you fall prey to false mythologies. Pretty much everyone has and does. Once you accept that, you can begin gaming everyone else with greater success.

If sorting false mythology from fact were trivial, there wouldn't be so many false truths. While this isn't trivial, it isn't impossible either. One inherent difficulty is this approach requires being skeptical about all your prior beliefs—something most humans dislike. In fact, most humans hate self-questioning and prefer spending time convincing themselves (and others) their beliefs are right. Effectively, you can't trust any conclusion you thought you knew.

To think through false mythologies, we must first ask: Why do so many people believe things that are false? And why do false truths persist—getting passed down the decades as if they were fact? It comes back to the same point: People persist in believing things that are wrong because, individually, people rarely investigate their own beliefs, particularly when what they believe makes sense intuitively—even more so when those around them agree with them.

1

As a society, we are often encouraged to challenge someone else's views, as in, "I know those @&%$#! (insert either Republicans or Democrats as you choose) are full of phony views!" But we aren't trained to challenge ourselves or to question the basic nature of the universe the way an Einstein, Edison or Newton would. Our instinct is to accept wisdom passed to us by former generations or smarter people or both. These beliefs don't require investigation because we believe certain truths are beyond our ability to challenge. Often in life, that is right. I mean, if "they" can't figure it out, how could I?

Medicine is a good example. We are correctly conditioned to go to the doctor, describe symptoms, hear prognosis and accept a prescription. Generally, that is good conditioning because medicine is an example of science and craft operating largely in parallel harmony—not perfectly because there are certainly plenty of myths among doctors—but generally because over time science modifies the craft and the craft improves. Because there are so many life examples where our conditioning serves us well, we're blind to the few areas, like capital markets, where it doesn't.

There are myriad beliefs you're likely to share with your fellow investors. These beliefs have been built into decades of literature and are among the first things people learn when they start investing and have been accepted by the biggest names around us. Who are *you* to question and challenge them?

Exactly the right person!

For example, investors categorically believe when the stock market has a high price-to-earnings ratio (P/E), it's riskier and has less upside than when it has a low P/E. Think about it casually, and it probably makes sense. A high P/E means a stock (or even the whole market) price is high—way high—compared to earnings. Get too far out on that scale, and it would seem a high P/E means a stock is vastly overpriced and likely to start falling. This belief is so widely held by so many people, seems so logical and has been a basic tenet of investing for so long that if you start proposing to your friends it's false, you will meet with overwhelming rejection, ridicule and perhaps suggestions you're morally deficient somehow.

Yet I proved statistically more than 15 years ago the P/E, no matter its level, by itself tells you nothing about market risk or return. Statistics aside, if you delve heavily into theory (as we do later), you will also learn the P/E shouldn't tell you anything about risk or return anyway. But tell that to people, including the overwhelming bulk of people who have been trained and should know better, and they will think you're crazy—a real whack-job.

The cool part comes after we accept the truth that P/Es tell you nothing about future returns by themselves—when people are freaking out, fearfully fretting over the market P/E being too high, we can bet against the market falling.

While that won't always work because something else can come along and knock the market down (we cover how to better see that later), it will work much more often than not. In the same way, if the market's P/E is low and we can sense people are optimistic because of it, we can bet against them also. The key is understanding the truth instead of the mythology. This is basic to the scientific approach.

Many false mythologies—like the P/E one—are accepted widely by the best and brightest minds and passed to the investing public through all forms of media. They don't inspire questioning from you, me or anyone. We have faith in them, like Catholics do in the Trinity and environmentalists in global warming, and they require no further proof. Holy! Sacred! No one questions these beliefs. No one offers dissenting analysis. And if you do, you're a heathen. And because there is no dissenting opinion, society feels no need to see proof of these alleged investing truisms with statistically valid data. And mythology continues.

How can it be so few demand hard evidence to support generally accepted investing wisdom? Why do investment decisions not get the scrutiny that car mechanics do? We should be at least as skeptical, if not more so, of the financial industry's pronouncements. To change the success (or lack thereof) you've had so far with investing, be skeptical. Be a cynic. Be the one to point out the emperor wears no clothes. Look around and assess what you and your fellow investors are accepting as truth. But the most important person to be skeptical of is yourself.

Long ago as I read or listened to media, I'd note things I believed were false and run off to do independent checking to prove I was right. (People love to prove they're right.) I'd gather data and do statistical analysis to prove they were wrong and I was right; and I could prove I was right to my satisfaction pretty often. (It's amazing how often people can prove they're right to their own satisfaction—the plaintiff, judge, jury and executioner all in one.) But later I realized I was doing the wrong thing. What I should have been doing was looking in the media for assertions I believed were *true* and then checking to see if they weren't really false.

Why?

If I believe the assertion is true, then probably so do many others, if not the overwhelming bulk of investors. Maybe everyone. And if we're all wrong, there's real power there. If I can prove I'm wrong and most everyone else is also wrong, then I've got some useful information. I can bet against everyone knowingly. I've got one provable form of knowing something others don't.

Suppose I believe factor X causes result Y. If I believe it, probably most other folks do, too. But if I'm wrong, most everyone else is wrong. When X happens, people will move to bet on Y happening. Suppose I can learn X doesn't cause Y. That means something else is causing Y. That means after X happens, Y happens sometimes, but it's purely random to X's existence. Now when X happens, people will still move to bet on Y happening, but I can bet against Y happening, and I'll be right more often than I'm wrong. (If I can figure out what actually causes Y, I can take a big step further, but we don't cover that step until Chapter 2 and Question Two.)

With our P/E notion, we can see one such perfect example. Say the market's P/E goes up—a lot. Normal investors notice and conclude risk has risen and future return is lower and bet against the market doing well. Sometimes stocks won't do well, but more often than not stocks will be just peachy because the P/E by itself tells you nothing about market risk and direction.

When I see a high-P/E market and fear of it, I can bet against the market falling. Sometimes, like 2000, it won't work. But more often, like 1996, 1997, 1998, 1999, 2003 and 2009, it will. I don't expect you to believe the P/E thing right now. Right now, I expect you to believe the traditional mythology about P/Es and not even be very interested in challenging it. (We get to that later in detail.) For now, I just want you to accept in your bones if you can learn an accepted mythology is actually false, you can bet against it and win more often than you lose.

Using Question One

A good way to think about successful investing is it's two-thirds not making mistakes and one-third doing something right. Hippocrates is frequently credited with the phrase, "First, do no harm," and it's a good investment principle.

To first do no harm, you must think about what you believe and ask yourself whether it's correct and factually accurate. Go crazy. Question everything you think you know. Most people hate doing this, which gives you a real advantage over them. As stated in this chapter's title, this is the first question: What do you believe that is actually false?

Asking Question One helps only if you can be honest with yourself. Many people, particularly in investing, are constitutionally incapable of contemplating they're ever wrong. They will tell you they do well and likely hoodwink themselves into believing it—but they don't. And they never subject themselves to reliable independent analysis. You must accept that you and the pundits and professionals from whom you glean information can be and probably are wrong about many basic beliefs. Me too!

Have you ever presented such a question to yourself about capital markets? Asking yourself if what you believe is actually wrong requires introspection.

As humans, we're hardwired to be overconfident. This is hardly a new development. Behavioralists will tell you our Stone Age ancestors had to be overconfident to hunt giant beasts each day armed merely with stone-tipped sticks. If they practiced introspection and came to the rational conclusion that tossing a flint-tipped branch at a buffalo was utter lunacy, they, their families and their communities would have starved. In fact, overconfidence—the belief you can do something successfully when rationality would argue otherwise—is basic to human success in most fields and necessary to our successful evolution as a species. However, it hurts tremendously when it comes to capital markets. (More on this in Chapter 3.)

Just so, investors are loath to question generally accepted knowledge. If we started doing so, we might soon realize the market exists solely to humiliate us as much as it can for as long as it can for as many dollars as it can. I refer to the market by its proper name, "The Great Humiliator" (TGH for short). I've come to accept my goal is to interact with TGH without getting humiliated too much.

TGH is an equal-opportunity humiliator. It doesn't care if you're rich or poor, black or white, tall or fat, male or female, amateur or an Olympian. It wants to humiliate everyone. It wants to humiliate me and you, too. To be frank, I think it wants to humiliate me more than it does you. You're fun to humiliate, but if you're fun, I'm more fun. I'm (probably) a more public figure than you and therefore a bigger TGH target. Think how much TGH would love to humiliate Warren Buffett. The bigger you are, the more TGH wants you. But in reality, TGH wants to get everyone and does a pretty good job at getting them all eventually. Can't be sated!

How do you, personally, give TGH the most fun? By making the most bets you can based on the same information everyone else has. How do you spoil the fun for TGH? By restricting bets you make to things you think you actually know that others don't.

Practice using Question One the same way I should have—by scanning the media for things asserted you believe. Make a list of them. They can be about single stocks, whole markets, currencies or anything. Make a list of anything influencing your decisions, whether on single stocks, asset allocation, anything.

Make note of decisions you've made not supported by data or any other information. Underneath there somewhere is something you believe—might be right or might be wrong. Be particularly wary of making a decision simply because of something you know others agree with. Highlight, underline and asterisk decisions prompted or based on common investor catechism. Ask what evidence you figured out for yourself supporting these beliefs. Is there any? For most investors, there isn't much.

Common Myths You Believe In, Too

For example, you may hold a stock with a high P/E ratio. You believe a high P/E signals an overvalued stock, so you decide to dump the stock and buy one with a lower P/E. It's a fairly rational decision you may have made countless times before, and one many people would agree is rational.

But are high P/Es bad for single stocks or the market? Have you personally checked the data? If you have asked the question, where did you find the answer? Did you look at the numbers, or did you rest easy because conventional wisdom or some big-name guru endorsed your belief?

Take another scenario. You hold a stock that does well in rising markets but badly in falling ones—a typical, highly volatile stock. However, you know the US federal government is running a growing budget deficit—not only a deficit, but a historically high deficit and one that "can't go on forever." You know federal budget deficits left unchecked are "bad for the economy" and, in turn, "bad for the stock market." All that debt caused by the deficit must be paid back by future generations, and the market will reflect that sooner or later, right? The burden of the deficit has long-term rippling implications, holding down growth and earnings. The deficit has grown to such a size you know a bear market looms eventually. In that environment, your highly volatile stock would do badly, and so you sell.

But how do you know budget deficit peaks are followed by poor stock performance? Is it true? Most folks won't ask the question or check history. If they did, they would be sanguine about stocks rather than fearful. Historically, big budget deficits in America and around the world have been followed by materially above-average stock market returns. Don't fear deficits—it is big budget surpluses that have been soon followed by bad markets.

That doesn't make intuitive sense to you. Deficits must be bad and surpluses good, right? After all, the word *deficit* has the same Latin root as *deficient*—and that must be bad. Most folks won't challenge their own beliefs on these kinds of subjects. The notion that big deficits are bad is overwhelming. Few beliefs have as much broad acceptance from professionals, nonprofessionals and folks from both ends of the political spectrum alike. A good way to get the proletariat on your side at a political rally is to vow to lower budget deficits. It's a crowd pleaser.

Here's a baker's dozen of some general beliefs you probably hold, or at least most people do. We've already covered two:

1. High-P/E markets are riskier than low P/E markets.
2. Big government budget deficits are bad.

Let's think about some more:

3. A weak US dollar is bad for stocks.
4. Rising interest rates are bad for stocks. Falling rates are good.
5. A tax cut causes more debt, which is bad for stocks.
6. Higher oil prices are bad for stocks and the economy.
7. Stocks do well when the economy does well.
8. Stock markets do better in countries with faster-growing economies than slower ones.
9. Small stocks do better than big ones.
10. Stocks of firms that grow more do better than those that don't.
11. Cheaper stocks do better than less cheap stocks.
12. Big trade deficits are bad for stock markets.
13. America has way too much debt.

They're all familiar to you. This is just a short list—a subset of a much bigger list—of views most folks believe that are partly or wholly false. For example, the notion America is way too heavily in debt is backward. As I say that, you may be shriekingly dismissive, or maybe the statement makes you mad. It challenges your belief set. If the statement makes you either dismissive or mad, you really need the rest of this book. The most standard reaction to someone stating your belief is wrong is to be dismissive and, if further confronted, to get mad.

Anger is a very good warning sign because anger is always, *always* about fear. Angry people usually don't know they're fearful. If you're dismissive or angry, you must question yourself to see how and why you concluded your belief was right in the first place. Was it mythology? Was it basic bias? Are you right or not? Sometimes the items in this list and others beyond it are part true and part false, depending on surrounding circumstances. (We look at all of these and more later on.) But the most obvious question is: Why would you believe any of these statements?

I'd say you believe myths mostly because of two facts: (1) They make common sense, and you aren't typically prone to challenge your own common sense. (2) People around you tend to agree these things are true, and you aren't prone to challenge widely held views.

Let's Prove You're Either Right or Wrong (or Really, Really Wrong)

As you attempt to debunk investor mythology using Question One, you will find three basic results. Either you were right all along (which may happen less frequently than you might have hoped), or you were wrong, or you were really, really wrong. Any of these outcomes is ok because it tells you how to bet better, later.

Let's examine more closely the instances when you're wrong. You and most of your fellow investors (amateur and professional) often believe something is causal—X happens because of Y—but in reality, there is no correlation at all. By now you're willing to embrace that can happen, or you would have stopped reading this book. The example we debunk is the aforementioned commonly held belief high-P/E stock markets are risky with subsequent below-average returns. As previously mentioned, it turns out high-P/E markets aren't predictive of poor returns—not even remotely. In fact, historically, they've led to some pretty good returns. What's more, low-P/E markets aren't predictive of good returns either.

The Mythological Correlation

Forgetting for now why the P/E myth is so easy to buy into, we know people overwhelmingly do believe high-P/E markets predict below-average returns and above-average risk.

But if it were true, you could show some form of high statistical correlation between the claimed cause and result. A statistician will say you can have high correlation between two things out of quirky luck with no causation. But the same statistician will tell you that you can't have causation without high correlation (unless you run into scientific nonlinearity, which doesn't happen in capital markets to my knowledge—but you could check on your own with the Three Questions when you're finished with this book). When a myth is widely accepted, you will find low correlations coupled with a great societal effort to demonstrate, accept and have faith in correlations that don't really exist.

Investors will root out evidence supporting their favorite myths and create justifications for their belief—factor X causes result Y—while ignoring a mountain of evidence that X doesn't cause Y at all. Now let's suppose everyone is of good intent. Still, even with the best of intentions, it's easy for people to latch onto evidence confirming their prior biases and ignore evidence contradicting their views. Looking for evidence to support your pet theory is human. Accepting evidence to the contrary is no fun at all. This is done in varying ways. One way is to look at a particular time period verifying the false belief and ignore other periods. Another is to redefine either X or Y in a bizarre way so the statistics seemingly prove the point and then generalize afterward about X and Y without the bizarre definitions. Discoveries of data supporting popular myths become popular discoveries.

Why High P/Es Tell You Nothing at All

A great example of redefining X or Y is the now-famous study by John Y. Campbell of Harvard and Robert J. Shiller of Yale.[1] Their paper didn't introduce a new idea because fear of high P/Es had been around forever. Their study merely introduced a new delivery of data confirming the view high-P/E periods are followed by below-average returns, an already widely held belief.

This was actually a better redo of a study they presented in 1996. But this 1998 publication got very popular, very fast because it supported what everyone already believed with new statistical documentation. Campbell and Shiller were and are noted academics. Inspired by the prior study, in 1996 Alan Greenspan first uttered the phrase "irrational exuberance" relative to the stock market, which reverberated around the world almost overnight and entered our lexicon permanently.

My friend and sometimes collaborator Meir Statman, the Glenn Klimek Professor of Finance at the Leavey School of Business at Santa Clara University, coauthored with me a paper not refuting their statistics, but reframing their approach more correctly with the same data—and you will see P/E levels aren't predictive at all. We basically asked Question One from beginning to end. Much of what follows stems from our paper "Cognitive Biases in Market Forecasts."[2]

In their study, Campbell and Shiller found high P/Es acted as people always thought they did, leading to below-average returns 10 years later. First, they noted the P/E at the outset of each year and subsequent annual market returns going back to 1872, which is about as far back as we have half-tolerably reliable data. Prior to the inception of the S&P 500's data in 1926, they used Cowles data, which is an imperfect but generally accepted proxy for pre-S&P 500 years. (All old databases are imperfect. Whenever you're looking at old data, there is apt to be lots wrong with it, but the Cowles data is the best we have.) Then they graphed the data points on a scatter plot and found a slightly negative trend line.

Figure 1.1 largely re-creates their hypothesis, showing P/Es from 1872 through 2010—again using S&P 500 and Cowles data.

I've included the years since their paper (and updated through 2010) to ensure our findings are relevant today. But you'd get the same basic effect if I hadn't. The negatively sloping trend line shouldn't influence you. You plainly see the scatter points aren't particularly well grouped around it. The scatter plot is, well, scattered—sort of like a shotgun blast in a mild wind.

The key issue I had with the study was Campbell and Shiller based their work on an odd definition of P/E—not one you intuitively leap to. They created a "price-smoothed earnings ratio."[3] The newly defined P/E divided the price per share by the average of *real* earnings over the prior 10 years.[4] (*Real*

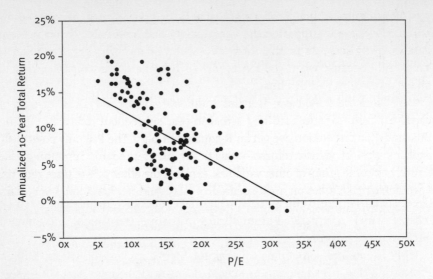

Figure 1.1   Relationship Between P/E Ratios at the Beginning of a Year and Stock Returns Over the Following Year (1872 to 2010)
Sources: Robert J. Shiller, Ibbotson Analyst, Global Financial Data, Inc., Standard & Poor's, Federal Reserve and Thomson Reuters.

means adjusted for inflation.) Fair enough, but that isn't what you think of when you think P/E, right?

But, if so, what definition of inflation would you use? I bet you would use something like the Consumer Price Index (CPI). (The CPI comes up as one of your first results when you Google "inflation.") Ironically, they chose an esoteric wholesale price index. Again, not what you might default to. So instead of what you think of as P/E, they used a 10-year rolling average based on inflation adjustments based on an inflation index most wouldn't think of. Got it?

With a normally defined P/E, as you would think of it, there isn't much of a statistical fit at all. However, Campbell and Shiller's engineered P/E gave a result consistent with what society always believed—that high P/E means low returns, high risk. And the world seemingly loved it.

In statistics, a calculation called an *R-squared* shows the relative relatedness of two variables—how much of one variable's movement is caused by the other. (It sounds complicated, but it's not—I show you how to find a correlation coefficient and an R-squared in Appendix A.) For their study, Campbell and Shiller got an R-squared of 0.40.[5] An R-squared of 0.40 implies 40% of subsequent stock returns are related to the factor being compared—in this case, their reengineered P/E. Statistically, not a bad finding (although not an overwhelming one). Though not a whopping endorsement of their theory, this finding still supports their hypothesis.

Note: Campbell and Shiller's study, tepid support or not, became wildly popular because it supported the view society had long held. If you present data violating society's myths, those data won't be met with great popularity. That's nice because when you discover the truth, the world won't be trying to take it away from you in a hurry.

By using the same basic data and traditional notions of P/Es at the start of each year from 1872 to 2010 and actual 10-year subsequent returns, updating this study for this edition, we get an R-squared of 0.25. The P/E only potentially explains 25% of 10-year returns—statistically pretty random. Something else entirely, or some group of other variables, explains the other 75% of price returns. I wouldn't make a bet on an R-squared of 0.25, and neither should you. Said another way, Campbell and Shiller's R-squared was 0.40 and ours was 0.25—so a big chunk of their result was based on how they defined P/E differently.

This myth wasn't hard to debunk. You can arrive at the same general conclusion with Google Finance and an Excel spreadsheet. When it isn't a myth and it's real, you will find you need no fancy statistical reengineering and no fancy math in your analysis.

But there's yet another issue. Even if it were valid, who cares about views of subsequent 10-year returns? Investors mainly want to know how to get positioned for this year and next, the now and the soon, not for 10 years from now. Would you really have cared what the next 10-year return was in 1996, when the next four years rose massively only to be followed by a big bear market? Would you have wanted to miss the big up years in a row, and would you have been content to hold on through the big down years? When you look at simple P/Es on a shorter-term basis, the high-P/E-is-risky thesis falls apart completely, as we shall see.

What's more, forecasting long-term stock returns is a near impossibility because stock prices in the long term are the result primarily of shifts in far-distant levels of the supply of equities, which in today's state of knowledge (or ignorance), no one knows how to address. Some of my academic friends get angry when I bring this up. But remember, when anyone gets angry, they are afraid and just can't quite put their finger on their fear. In this case, I think it's because very little real scientific work has been done analyzing shifts in supply and demand for securities. Yet, by definition, shifts in supply and demand are what determine pricing. There are great future advances to be made here, but so far, the progress is minimal despite supply and demand being basic to economics. (We get to supply and demand for securities in Chapter 7.)

For now, let's take a look at our scatter plot again, this time using normal, non-engineered P/Es and subsequent one-year returns from 1872 through 2010 (see Figure 1.2). Note we have a much shallower negative trend line, and the scatter points are even less cooperative. This is our same shotgun blast

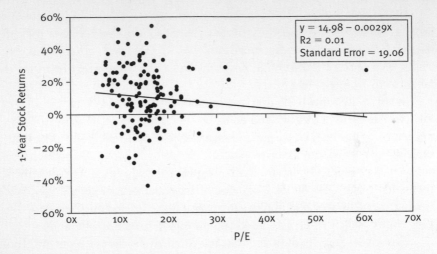

Figure 1.2   Relationship Between Annualized (Overlapping) One-Year Returns and P/E Ratios (1872 to 2005)
Sources: Ibbotson Analyst, Global Financial Data, Inc., Standard & Poor's, Federal Reserve and Thomson Reuters.

with a few stray pellets. Does this indicate any sort of correlation at all? With an R-squared of 0.01, the answer is no. If an R-squared of 0.25 is pretty random, an R-squared of 0.01 is randomness itself—pure, perfect randomness.

Finding a correlation where simply none exists is pretty creative; and simply, none exists here. To begin debunking myths on your own, you don't need a super computer and a Stephen Hawking doppelganger (that's probably illegal anyway). If you need ultra-complicated math to support the existence of a market myth, your hypothesis is probably wrong. The more jury-rigging and qualification your analysis needs, the more likely you're forcing your results to support your hypothesis. Forced results are bad science.

If Not Bad, Can They Be Good?

We have shown there's no correlation between high P/Es and poor stock results (or good ones). Even in light of such damning evidence, some may be reluctant to let go of the "high-P/E-equals-bad-stocks" doctrine. Consider this another way: It may further shock and appall you to learn years with higher P/Es had some excellent returns. Moreover, the one-year returns following the 13 highest P/E ratios weren't too shabby—some negative years, but also some big positive years. This isn't statistical but should give you pause.

Need more evidence? No complicated engineering necessary here, either. Figure 1.3 shows a basic bell curve depicting P/Es and subsequent annual market returns.

Here's how I arrived at the bell curve. We noted the broad market's P/E each January 1 going back to 1872 and ranked each year from low P/E to high P/E. Then we grouped them into intervals creating the familiar bell curve-like shape—with otherwise unrelated years falling into buckets according to their P/Es. The "normal" P/Es fall in the fat part of the bell curve, while the "high" and "low" P/Es fall on the edges.

When you note the P/E ratios for the past 139 years along with the subsequent market return, some empirical truths emerge. Most startling? Most double-digit calendar-year stock market declines—the monster drops everyone fears—occurred when P/Es were below 20, not when they were very high.

In the past 139 years, there were 20 times the US market's total return was negative more than 10%. Sixteen times—80% of those most negative years—were on the middle-to-low end of the P/E range (based on the bell curve). Fifteen (75%) happened in the fat part of the curve—on "normal" P/Es. Hardly fodder for a myth. Anyone can get these data off the Internet. Anyone can array them. It doesn't take fancy math. It just takes a little effort. But most people don't ask, so they don't try. And since they don't try, the myth still exists.

So big double-digit drops don't automatically follow high-P/E markets. But since the myth is so widely and rigidly believed, could there be some kernel of truth to it? For example, high-P/E markets must fall more often than those with low P/Es, even if they aren't the monster drops. Right? Well, no! P/Es were below 22.8 in 116 of those years, and the market finished in negative territory 32 times (27.5%).

Of those 17 years when P/Es were 22.8 or higher—the historically high end of the P/E range—the market ended down seven times (30.4%). Neither high- nor low-P/E markets did materially worse.

You've seen the data. You're henceforth unshackled from this investing old wives' tale.

Here's a simple test you can use repeatedly. Someone tells you X causes Y in America's markets—like the P/E example—and even has data to demonstrate it's true. If it's really true in America, then it must also be true in most foreign developed markets. If it isn't similarly true in most other developed Western markets, it isn't really true about capitalism and capital markets and, hence, isn't really true about America—just a chance outcome. I'll not belabor you with the data here—this book already has too many visuals—but if you take the same bell curve approach we used for America's stock market and apply it to foreign markets, the only country where low-P/E markets seemed materially better is

Figure 1.3 — 139 Years of Historical P/E Ratios and Stock Market Returns

P/E (P/E Ratio Range) — Year and Return by P/E bucket

P/E = 2.1X (Average Return 25.55%)

1918	25.55%

P/E = 9.0X (Average Return 18.73%)

Year	Return
1917	−25.24%
1978	6.44%
1921	14.60%
1949	18.06%
1979	18.35%
1919	20.67%
1982	21.48%
1951	24.55%
1924	25.70%
1950	30.58%
1980	32.27%
1975	37.25%

P/E = 12.4X (Average Return 13.69%)

Year	Return
1974	−26.54%
1920	−19.69%
1941	−11.77%
1940	−10.08%
1977	−7.41%
1981	−5.05%
1953	−1.11%
1875	2.41%
1948	5.10%
1911	5.75%
1984	6.15%
1916	8.94%
1874	9.30%
1926	11.68%
1952	18.50%
1944	19.69%
1942	21.08%
1983	22.56%
1976	23.70%
1943	25.76%
1925	29.50%
1985	31.65%
1989	31.69%
1927	37.69%
1958	43.35%
1908	44.51%
1954	52.40%

P/E = 15.9X (Average Return 8.83%)

Year	Return
1931	−43.47%
1907	−29.63%
1930	−24.97%
1903	−14.67%
1884	−13.46%
1876	−12.27%
1957	−10.84%
1913	−9.62%
1932	−8.41%
1910	−7.90%
1873	−6.56%
1914	−3.68%
1990	−3.10%
1883	−3.09%
1888	1.86%
1923	4.17%
1947	5.24%
1956	6.61%
1906	6.84%
1881	7.48%
1912	7.97%
1878	11.27%
1872	12.96%
1988	16.61%
1986	18.60%
1900	18.65%
1909	18.97%
1901	19.72%
1967	23.94%
1885	26.23%
1991	30.47%
1904	30.92%
1955	31.46%
1938	33.20%
1915	35.51%
1945	36.46%
1995	37.58%
1928	43.80%
1879	49.50%

P/E = 19.3X (Average Return 8.56%)

Year	Return
1937	−35.26%
1893	−16.00%
1973	−14.79%
1966	−10.11%
1929	−8.52%
1946	−8.18%
1877	−3.86%
1887	−2.68%
1939	−0.91%
1960	0.48%
1896	1.73%
1894	2.04%
1882	2.16%
1970	3.99%
1902	4.94%
1987	5.17%
2007	5.49%
1892	5.97%
1899	9.90%
1968	11.00%
1959	11.91%
1965	12.36%
1971	14.33%
2006	15.80%
1964	16.36%
1972	18.94%
1905	19.66%
1891	22.63%
1963	22.69%
1996	22.96%
1898	23.26%
1880	24.22%
1886	26.81%
1961	32.80%
1936	33.36%
1997	33.36%
1933	54.39%

P/E = 22.8X (Average Return 5.04%)

Year	Return
2008	−37.00%
1890	−10.16%
1962	−8.78%
1994	1.32%
2005	4.91%
1889	7.64%
1886	12.74%
2010	15.06%
1897	16.92%
1935	47.72%

P/E = 26.2X (Average Return 13.90%)

Year	Return
1934	−1.54%
1992	7.62%
1993	10.08%
2004	10.88%
1922	27.79%
1998	28.58%

P/E = 29.6X (Average Return −3.63%)

Year	Return
2001	−11.89%
1895	4.62%

P/E = 33.1X (Average Return 13.54%)

Year	Return
2000	−9.10%
1999	21.04%
2003	28.68%

P/E = 36.5X> (Average Return 2.18%)

Year	Return
2002	−22.10%
2009	26.46%

Figure 1.3 139 Years of Historical P/E Ratios and Stock Market Returns
Source: Global Financial Data, Inc.

Britain—and that is based on a few, relatively big years. Elsewhere, you get the same randomness as in America.[6] Whenever anyone tells you something works a certain way in America, a good cross-check is to see if it also works outside America. Because if it doesn't, it doesn't really work robustly in America either!

Some will say, "You must see the high-P/E problem in the right way." (*Warning:* a precursor to a reengineering attempt to support a myth, and it likely won't hold.) For example, they may agree it isn't just that a high P/E is worse than a low P/E, but when you get over a certain P/E level, the risk skyrockets, and when you get under a certain P/E, it plummets.

For example, they may assert market P/Es over 25 are bad and P/Es under 15 good and everything in between is what confuses everyone—throwing the averages off, leading you to not see things the way they would have you see them. Fair enough! That's easy to test. You take all the times when the market had a P/E over 25 and envision we sold and then bought back at some level— you pick it, I don't care what it is as long as you apply it consistently. It turns out, historically, regardless of the level picked, none really beats a long-term buy-and-hold in America.

The same is true overseas (except, again, in Britain, where you can make a weak case a low P/E has had a variety of approaches seeming to work—but only in Britain, which is probably just coincidence—and if you throw out a very few, very big years in Britain from a very long time ago, it falls apart there, too).

Suppose you sell when the market's P/E hits 22 and buy when it falls to 15. That approach lags a simple buy and hold. Suppose you change the 22 to 23. Still lags! How about dropping the 15 to 13 or raising it to 17? Still lags. What's more, there isn't a buy-and-sell approach that works overseas.

You may disbelieve all this. Great. Prove I'm wrong. To prove it, you must find a buy-and-sell rule based on simple P/E beating the market with one-, two- and three-year returns. It must work basically the same way in a handful of foreign developed markets and if you start or end your game on different dates. Try to find it. Maybe you're better than I am, but I looked and looked and can't find it in any way anyone would believe.

Every time a high-P/E market leads to very bad returns, like in 2000, 2001 and 2002, you will find a comparable number of examples where it does well, like 1997, 1998, 1999, 2003 and 2009. There is simply no basis for this myth.

Always Look at It Differently

Investors fall prey to myth because they're used to seeing investing truisms in accepted and normal ways—as they were taught. Once you start thinking even a bit differently—not in a complicated way, just differently, like graphing a bell curve or looking for the same phenomenon overseas—myths tend to fall apart. Whenever you're confirming an investing belief, try it from a fresh angle. Go crazy. Be creative. Flip things on their heads, backward and inside out. Hack them up and go over their guts. Instead of trying to be intuitive, think counterintuitively—which may turn out to be much more intuitive.

For fun, let's look at why, intuitively, high P/Es don't spell disaster for stocks. Most investors look at stocks with high P/Es and assume their prices are too high relative to the companies' earnings. If a price is proportionately much greater than earnings (so goes the thinking), the stock must be over-priced; what goes up must come down. What investors forget is the P isn't the only moving variable in the P/E.

In years following high-P/E markets, earnings often rose faster than share prices. And often after low-P/E years, we ran into unexpected rough econo-mies where earnings vanished. In fact, in 1929, the most famous market peak of all time, P/Es were low, not high, because the soon-to-disappear earnings were too high in 1929, making the P/E low.

When we buy stocks, we're buying future earnings. At some times we're willing to pay more than at others. In high-P/E markets, earnings often exceed expectations (as in 2003 and 2009), and the market prices in higher earnings before we can see them coming. Just by considering what is happening with the denominator side of the P/E—looking at it differently—you can reason for yourself why the myth is wrong.

The myth that high-P/E markets are dangerous and low-P/E markets are safe persists. But anyone with a dial-up modem and a pencil can see high-P/E years are, in themselves, not any worse than lower-P/E periods. Why does this myth persist? Because fundamentally, TGH is perverse and counterintuitive. It can be painful to accept whatever is fueling your water-cooler debates is wrong or already priced into markets. It's humbling but true.

How Would Your Grandparents Think About It?

Now I'll steal a page from Chapter 3 and focus on how our brains blindside us on the P/E issue. There's a genetic reason people fear high P/E markets. I can't prove this, but I believe it's true. And you can't disprove it. It's a pretty different way to see this dilemma. You inherited your genes and the information processor that is your brain from your parents, as did they from theirs. Your far-distant ancestors had brains adept at processing certain types of information—that which related to problems they encountered related to passing on their genes successfully. Were that not true, you and I wouldn't be here. The folks back then who didn't process information well relative to those problems don't have descendants walking the earth now.

Your brain wasn't really set up to deal with the stock market. It was set up to deal with problems of basic human survival. One problem your ancestors learned to process was heights. If they fell from greater heights, the risk of death or crippling (pretty much the same thing back then) was exponential. Higher heights increased risk. Falling from two feet is just a stumble. Falling from 10 feet isn't all that tough for a 10-year-old jumping off a roof but bone breaking for older people. Falling from 40 feet kills usually and from 400 feet always.

Folks learned well when confronted with problems appearing in a framework of heights—more height meant more risk. Greater heights meant you could fall farther—exactly how people think of P/Es. They envision higher P/Es as farther potential falls and lower P/Es as less distance to smack into the floor, so there is less smacking risk. Any time I present information to you in a form appearing as a heights framework, more height scares you and less height seems safer. If I can present the same information in a way not involving heights, your fear fades instantly. (We do that in a few moments.)

A Quick Preview of Question Three

When the market's P/E is higher than normal, most investors know it. Even those who don't know what P/E stands for can tell you "these days" the market is frighteningly overvalued. Their resulting fear of heights and concern over possibly sustaining a loss can be explained by a behavioral finance truism: People hate losses much more than they like gains.[7]

People talk about investors being risk averse, but that isn't quite right. Investors are provably loss-averse. Two pioneers in the field of behavioral finance, Daniel Kahneman and the late Amos Tversky, demonstrated and proved normal Americans (yes, you're probably pretty normal) hate losses about two and a half times as much as they like gains.[8] Investors feel the sting of a monetary loss much more intensely than they enjoy the pleasure of a gain. In your heart, you probably already knew that was true for you. And because loss is more agonizingly painful than gain is pleasant, investors will do more to avoid losses than to achieve gains.

Investors will actually adopt additional risk if they believe it can help them avoid a loss they would otherwise incur. Kahneman and Tversky described this phenomenon in what they called "prospect theory." They discovered normal investors (again, you) confuse actual risk with the *perception* of risk, all in the effort to avoid the possibility of a loss.[9] The perception (or, one could say, misconception) of possible losses long misassociated with high-P/E markets is what keeps investors fearful in what could otherwise be a relatively low-risk market environment. The same powers are at work at the bottom of a bear market. Investors are typically most fearful at the end of bear markets when risk is diminished and upside potential considerable. Investors' perceptions are just off.

Investors, particularly many who consider themselves "value investors," have had violent and near-religious reactions to this notion. Instead of practicing introspection and asking themselves Question One—What do I believe that is wrong?—they grab at any straw to disavow they're influenced by a very natural bias. In rebuttal, they claim the phenomenon occurs because ultra-high P/Es come from suppressed earnings posted at the end of a recession. Not quite. This sometimes happens, but it's far from universal. It certainly wasn't true in 1996, 1997, 1998 and 1999. To excuse that, investors say the markets are just irrational. Investors' vehemence that ultra-high P/Es must have a high risk is another aspect of the perverseness of TGH.

Upside Down and Backward If You Can

We've demonstrated how to use Question One with a well-entrenched misconception. As you strike out on your own, testing your own mythology, make sure you're thorough. A good scientist doesn't stop once he gets the answer to a question; he looks at it repeatedly from different angles.

First, be realistic about your findings. Don't jump to conclusions too fast. One might consider the previous data and create a new myth—high P/Es are predictive of above-average returns. Don't fall for that trick. The evidence here is enough to utterly decimate any wrongheaded belief about high P/Es being bad for stocks. Anything more is inconclusive. It isn't enough. It isn't overwhelming. It won't let you bet and win much more often than you lose. Ultimately, you should take away P/Es aren't, by themselves, a predictor of future results.

Furthermore, if you get just one result supporting your hypothesis, no matter how remarkable, it's happenstance, not a pattern. This is true for anything you encounter. You don't want to make a bet based on happenstance. For example, you might be tempted to conclude ultra-high P/E markets tend to be low risk and high reward. Yes, it is true ultra-high P/Es have led to some great stock returns. But there haven't been enough occurrences to make this anything more than an interesting observation and probably coincidence. As you create and test, you must test as many occurrences as you find.

We now know P/Es have no predictive power, so is the P/E good for anything? To find out, we need to steal a page again from Chapter 2 and Question Two. What can we fathom about P/Es that is hard for others to fathom? A standard trick to help you see better and see things others don't is to look at it from a different perspective. One powerful way to test your belief and results is to flip your myth on its head and see what you see then.

So take the P/E and flip it on its head. By putting the *earnings* over the *price* in this equation, you have the exact same information in a different framework—the earnings-to-price ratio, better called the *earnings yield*. This is simply the inverse of the P/E—the E/P.

Investors are used to seeing expected returns of bonds and cash quoted in yields whereas most investors are accustomed to valuing stocks by their P/Es. By inverting the P/E and looking at the earnings yield, you can compare apples to apples. What's more, you also escape the heights framework just discussed. Table 1.1 shows how to take a P/E and arrive at an earnings yield—a P/E of 20 is really a price of $20 divided by $1 of earnings. So the E/P for this is 1 divided by 20, or 5%. When you think of the relationship as an earnings yield, it compares better to interest rates (as we see later, it should), and the heights framework scaring us about P/E disappears instantly. The P/E of 20 scares you, but the earnings yield of 5% doesn't. It's pretty easy math—again, no Stephen Hawking automaton necessary.

This comparison is more rational and straightforward than determining if a stock is cheap or expensive based on P/E alone. Since stocks and bonds compete for investor dollars, the comparison of bond yields and stock earnings yields gives you something concrete for comparison. For example, if you have a market with a P/E of 20, most folks would say that seems "high." How do you think about a 5% earnings yield? If bond interest rates are 8%, the 5% earnings yield might not be attractive, but if bonds are 3%, it could be. Compare that with going bond yields now.

Before you think a stock market (or single stock) with a 5% earnings yield is inferior to, say, a 6% US Treasury bond, remember the tax treatment. The earnings yield is effectively a company's after-tax annualized cost of raising expansion capital by selling stock. What does that mean?

Since the P/E is an after-tax number, you know the E/P is an after-tax number, too. A company can get expansion capital by selling stock or issuing a corporate bond. But if it issues a corporate bond, the interest paid on that

Table 1.1 What Is an Earnings Yield?

P/E →	E/P	=	EY%
33	1/33		3%
25	1/25		4%
20	1/20		5%
15	1/15		6%
10	1/10		10%
7	1/7		14%
5	1/5		20%

bond is deductible for tax purposes against revenue. The corporate bond rate is a pretax number. The E/P is an after-tax number.

Suppose the stock has a P/E of 20 and it's an average-grade corporation, meaning a BBB corporate bond rating. As 2011 ended, it could borrow 10-year money through a bond at about 4.6%.[10] Assuming a 33% tax rate, the 4.6% cost is really 3.1% after tax. (To get the tax-adjusted equivalent, multiply the 4.6% rate by 1 minus the 33% tax rate—or 0.67.) The stock's E/P is 5%, already after tax. So it's cheaper to raise expansion capital by issuing a bond at 3.1% than selling stock at 5%. Corporate bond rates would have to rise above 7.5% to make it cheaper for that P/E 20 company to get expansion capital by selling stock. That is the firm's viewpoint.

From your viewpoint, it's somewhat different. The earnings yield needn't be above the tax-adjusted bond yield to make stocks more attractive than bonds. When you buy stocks, you do so assuming future earnings will be somewhat higher due to subsequent future growth. Stocks as a group tend to generate earnings growth over time, sometimes more, other times less. But a bond coupon is fixed. You know it has no chance of rising. If you hold it to maturity, you will get that interest rate. When you buy stocks, you're actually buying the future average earnings yield, which is likely somewhat higher than the current earnings yield. When you buy bonds, the future average bond yield is the current yield. For this reason, the current earnings yield needn't be higher than the bond yield to make stocks attractive relatively.

Interestingly, the earnings yield for the US stock market and the bond yield have historically tracked pretty close to each other—at least since 1985 (see Figure 1.4). Times when the earnings yield has been above the bond yield, it wasn't by much, but these usually marked good times to own stocks. Why? When the earnings yield is above the bond yield, stocks are typically undervalued relative to bonds. *Translation:* Stocks are relatively cheap.

Since 2002, the earnings yield has been higher than bond yields in America, so stocks have been historically very cheap—just when most folks said they weren't cheap, but high—because P/Es were above historic averages. If you had let high P/Es scare you out of stocks, you would have missed the entirety of the 2002 to 2007 bull market and the powerful initial bull market years of 2009 and 2010.

Keep in mind, this is by no means a forecasting tool. The gap was also wide during the 2008 bear market. But it is one way to assess, rationally, how firms are likelier to raise capital and whether stocks are over- or undervalued relative to bonds. Just because stocks are relatively cheap doesn't mean they must rise or that they must outperform relative to bonds. Stocks can be cheap and get cheaper still, and the reverse is true for bonds.

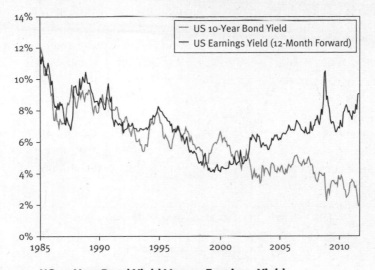

Figure 1.4   US 10-Year Bond Yield Versus Earnings Yield
Sources: Global Financial Data, Inc., Thomson Reuters.

But we aren't done yet. Remember, if something is true here, it should be true in most foreign developed countries. We can see all around the world earnings yields exceed bond yields now, and by more than in America—and that, too, is uncommon. Stocks are cheaper globally in recent years compared to long-term interest rates than they've been in a quarter century (see Figure 1.5).

When You Are Really, Really Wrong

We've talked about those myths perpetuated by investors inventing or imagining causal correlations where none exist. What about those myths so wrong the inverse is actually true? Sometimes, when you ask Question One, you discover you have been not only wrong but really, really wrong. Don't fret. Discovering you have been wrong and uncovering a reverse truth gives you yet another basis for a market bet. A powerful one because you know for certain everyone is betting on the exact opposite of what you know is likely to happen.

It may be hard for you to imagine something you and your fellow investors can get so completely wrong. But there are some myths in the misguided investor doctrine held so dearly, questioning them is almost sacrilegious. Suggesting such a belief be scrutinized, if only to confirm its veracity, would bring outrage, scandal and possible excommunication. These myths, the most sacrosanct beliefs in the investor and social catechism, those no one dares question, are sometimes ones we find to be so wrong the exact opposite holds true.

Figure 1.5   10-Year Bond Yield Versus Earnings Yield
Sources: Global Financial Data, Inc., Thomson Reuters.

The Holiest of Holies—the Federal Budget Deficit Myth

You probably believe a high federal budget deficit is bad. *Everybody* knows budget deficits are bad. How do we know? We know because everyone knows. Duh! Pundits, politicians, patriots, perverts, poker partners, your parents, your pet parakeet and worst of all, Sean Penn, Brad Pitt and Dolly Parton. Everyone! More important, everyone *believes* it. There is absolutely no reason to question this belief. I mean, how do you question Sean Penn and Brad Pitt? Which makes this sacredly held myth a great candidate for Question One. What do you believe that is wrong? Better yet, reframe and flip it on its head and ask yourself the reverse.

Is a high federal budget deficit good—and good for stocks?

Ask that question too loudly and someone may come after you with a butterfly net and commit you to a nice, safe, padded cell. Believing a budget deficit is bad is part of our collective Western-world wisdom and culture—nay, our civic duty. As stated earlier, *deficit* has the same Latin root as *deficient*. Why question something believed for thousands of years? Because it's wrong!

We are taught as children to regard debt as bad, more debt as worse and a lot of debt as downright immoral. Right after we finished making paper turkeys for Thanksgiving, we got a cookie, some apple juice, a lecture on the immorality of debt and then naptime.

As a society, we're morally opposed to debt. We haven't evolved too far from our Puritan forefathers in this regard. And deficits make more debt. Abhorring a budget deficit isn't just an American sentiment. Other inhabitants of Western developed nations fret as we do over deficits. In many places, more so! Come to think of if, they fret over ours, too—more than theirs.

Is any of this anxiety deserved? Looking at the past 20 or so years, America has run a federal budget surplus in just four years. During the budget surplus of the late 1990s, the stock market peaked, leading to a bear market and the start of a recession. That recession was fairly short-lived and shallow, but the bear market persisted three years and was huge. Clearly, the budget surplus didn't lead to outstanding stock returns. If there is no empirical evidence supporting the hypothesis (yes, Virginia, it's just a hypothesis) that budget deficits are bad for stocks, could the opposite be true?

It appears so. Figure 1.6 shows the federal budget balance going back to 1947 as a percent of annual gross domestic product (GDP). Anything above the horizontal line is a budget surplus; anything below is a deficit. We've noted relative peaks and troughs. The counterintuitive truth is stock market returns following periodic deficit extremes have been much higher on average than surplus peaks or even decreasing deficits.

Table 1.2 shows subsequent price returns after surpluses and deficits. Look at the 12-month subsequent returns after budget surpluses and compare

Table 1.2   Stock Returns Following Budget Balance Extremes

Surplus Peaks		Subsequent S&P 500 Price Return		
Date		12 Month	24 Month	36 Month
Q4 1947	Annualized	−0.7%	4.7%	10.1%
	Cumulative	−0.7%	9.5%	33.4%
Q1 1951	Annualized	13.9%	8.7%	8.0%
	Cumulative	13.9%	18.2%	25.9%
Q1 1956	Annualized	−9.0%	−6.8%	4.6%
	Cumulative	−9.0%	−13.2%	14.4%
Q1 1960	Annualized	17.6%	12.1%	6.4%
	Cumulative	17.6%	25.7%	20.3%
Q1 1969	Annualized	−11.7%	−0.6%	1.8%
	Cumulative	−11.7%	−1.2%	5.6%
Q4 1973	Annualized	−29.7%	−3.8%	3.3%
	Cumulative	−29.7%	−7.5%	10.2%
Q2 1979	Annualized	11.0%	12.9%	2.1%
	Cumulative	11.0%	27.5%	6.5%
Q1 1989	Annualized	15.3%	12.8%	11.0%
	Cumulative	15.3%	27.2%	36.9%
Q1 2000	Annualized	−22.6%	−12.5%	−17.3%
	Cumulative	−22.6%	−23.4%	−43.4%
Q4 2006	Annualized	3.5%	−20.2%	−7.7%
	Cumulative	3.5%	−36.3%	−21.4%
Average	**Annualized**	**−1.2%**	**0.7%**	**2.2%**
Average	**Cumulative**	**−1.2%**	**2.6%**	**8.8%**

Source: Bureau of Economic Analysis, Global Financial Data, Inc., S&P 500 price index as of 11/30/2011.

with the returns after the deficits. Which world do you want to be living in? The one with the average return of 16.7% or the one with the average return of –1.2%? Now look out over 36-month returns. Those appalling deficits get you an average cumulative return of 27.1% compared with 8.8% from the surpluses.

Deficit Peaks		Subsequent S&P 500 Price Return		
Date		12 Month	24 Month	36 Month
Q1 1950	Annualized	23.8%	18.7%	13.5%
	Cumulative	23.8%	41.0%	46.3%
Q1 1954	Annualized	35.8%	34.1%	17.9%
	Cumulative	35.8%	80.0%	63.7%
Q2 1958	Annualized	29.2%	12.2%	12.6%
	Cumulative	29.2%	25.8%	42.9%
Q2 1967	Annualized	9.9%	3.8%	−7.1%
	Cumulative	9.9%	7.8%	−19.8%
Q2 1971	Annualized	7.5%	2.3%	−4.8%
	Cumulative	7.5%	4.6%	−13.7%
Q2 1975	Annualized	9.5%	2.7%	0.1%
	Cumulative	9.5%	5.6%	0.4%
Q4 1982	Annualized	17.3%	9.0%	14.5%
	Cumulative	17.3%	18.9%	50.2%
Q3 1992	Annualized	9.8%	5.2%	11.8%
	Cumulative	9.8%	10.7%	39.9%
Q3 2003	Annualized	11.9%	11.1%	10.3%
	Cumulative	11.9%	23.4%	34.1%
Q2 2009	Annualized	12.1%	19.9%	??
	Cumulative	12.1%	43.7%	??
Average	**Annualized**	**16.7%**	**11.9%**	**7.7%**
Average	**Cumulative**	**16.7%**	**26.1%**	**27.1%**

The plain truth is, since 1947, if an investor had purchased stocks at federal budget deficit extremes, he or she would have seen one-, two-, and three-year returns much higher on average than if purchased at high budget surplus periods. Buying in the aftermath of budget surpluses would have rendered materially below-average returns.

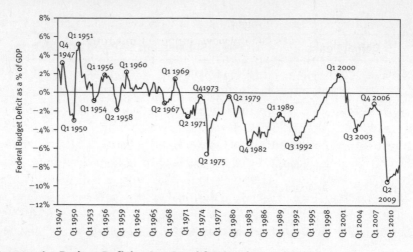

Figure 1.6   Budget Deficits Are Good for Stocks
Source: **White House, Bureau of Economic Analysis.**

If you're beginning to think perhaps budget surpluses aren't the best thing to happen to stocks, you're getting it. If you suspect the wry hand of TGH, you're also getting it. Budget surpluses aren't a panacea. They historically lead to bad markets. Don't wish for them.

This may not make sense at first blush. Conventional wisdom depicts a deficit as some sort of gigantic anchor, holding down the economy and ramming debt down its over-indebted throat. As consumers, we're careful to not overdraw our checking accounts and believe the government should do the same. Many politicians will have you believe deficits must be reduced, and now. There are no politicians saying more debt is good (although there are often politicians advocating tax cuts, which can cause a similar effect).

Let's Kill the Bloodsuckers

If you don't know the origin of the word *politics,* let me enlighten you. The word *politics* comes from the Greek *poli,* meaning "many," and *tics,* meaning "small bloodsucking creatures." Unless a poli-tic stands up and announces, "I routinely lie, cheat and steal to help my career and care nothing about you, whoever you are," you should take anything he says with a grain of salt.

People have some difficulty with this. You know you dislike any poli-tic saying things ideologically you dislike. And you know he is dishonest, a slimeball and someone if whom your daughter planned to marry, you would instead seek a cult deprogrammer to protect her. What you have difficulty accepting is

when another poli-tic says things you like and believe in, that he or she is simply lying. Of course, that's just my view. Suppose I'm wrong.

Poli-tics, overwhelmingly, aren't students of capital markets. More than
anything else they tend to be lawyers (some exceptions—like Presidents
Eisenhower, Carter, Reagan and Bush. Or even Arnold Schwarzenegger).
Don't look to them to be experts in finance or economics. They may be honest enough until they become Beltway blowhards, but they still aren't experts
on markets and economics and will never use the Three Questions. Poli-tics
never think about when they're wrong, how to fathom what others can't
fathom and how to see when their brains are misguiding them. Poli-tics
couldn't use the Three Questions if they had to. (Perhaps I've been bombas-
tic for comedy's sake in the past few paragraphs, but you'll be a better
investor and sleep better at night if you tune out approximately 97% of what
poli-tics say.)

That budget deficits are good for stocks isn't a lucky fluke. Economically,
it makes sense if you can get yourself to think about debt and deficits correctly. (We cover that in Chapter 6.) For now, suppose budget deficits really are
good for stocks in America and surpluses really are bad. If that is true, we
ought to be able to see it happening close to the same way in other developed
Western nations. That trick is a really nifty one most folks never use. And we
do see it overseas.

In other developed nations (as I demonstrate for you in Chapter 6), budget deficits have preceded good stock market returns and surpluses have preceded gloomier times. This isn't a socioeconomic-political statement. All we
are doing is looking at cold hard facts and encouraging you to do the same.
Folks who are hamstrung by bias are plagued with misconception and can't
see the truth even when it's right there in front of them. Instead, always ask if
what you believe is actually false.

What About Those Other Deficits?

The federal budget deficit isn't the only deficit boogeyman getting investors'
knickers knotted. As soon as I tell you the budget deficit isn't bad for stocks,
your reaction may be dismissal, anger and then a framework shift—that other
deficits, like the trade deficit, must be bad. You've heard it so often. You've also
heard it's bad for the dollar.

We look at such assertions in both Chapters 6 and 7, where I show these
two forms of deficits aren't bad for stocks or the dollar. I mention this here as
another version of something everyone believes that is false. Note you've
heard it, accepted it, believed it was true, winced every time a new record trade

deficit number was announced but never stopped to ask, "I know I believe it's bad; but is it really, and how would I check?" Because you know in your heart, if everyone is wrong, and trade deficits aren't bad for the stock market and the dollar, it would be tremendously bullish because that would be one less thing to fret that to most folks is a huge burden. And that is something you can know others don't.

It's All Relatively Relative

Part of the reason investors freak out about deficits—budget, trade and otherwise—is they forget to think relatively (a cognitive error). They hear we have an estimated $500 billion trade deficit (as of the end of 2010).[11] "Holy cow! That's a lot of moo-laa!" they think. "Five hundred billion??? I don't have five hundred billion. Not even Bill Gates has that much." News editors and talking heads lambaste whomever they think is responsible, using words like "record breaking," "staggering" and "irresponsible" to describe the deficit's size. Well, of course it sounds high. But is it? Are our perceptions right?

To see this correctly, we must scale. We must look at our trade deficit as a percentage of our overall economy. If you think $500 billion is a lot, what do you think about $14.5 trillion? That's the comparable size of America's GDP (also at year-end 2010).[12] As a percentage of our national income, the trade deficit is a mere 3.4%. What's more, as a historical average, it's nothing to sweat about either.

The media won't mention the trade deficit as a percentage of GDP, however, because they assume you're rational and won't get exercised over a trade deficit that is 3.4% of our overall income.

This doesn't work just with deficits. Anytime the media tries to scare you with huge numbers, think about it relatively—think *scale*.

Question Everything You Know

Success in investing requires you to question everything you think you know—particularly those things you think you really, really know. Using Question One properly gives you discipline to start preventing some basic errors. The ability to just avoid mistakes is key to successful investing. As you examine mythology and begin discovering faulty logic, don't simply correct it once and forget about it. Investing is an applied science, not a craft. If you get a validated answer to a hypothesis, don't assume you can apply the results always and everywhere and get the same result. TGH is an ever-changing opponent requiring constant re-testing of hypotheses.

Knowing big federal budget deficits don't necessarily signal bad times ahead and may in fact signal the reverse is fairly shocking, though undeniably true. Someday, in some future universe, the investing public may relinquish this myth and realize the whole world has been wrong on this point. Should that occur, you will have lost your edge. Then you will no longer know something others don't. When everyone knows federal budget deficits are to be cheered not jeered, the market will efficiently price it in. By using Question One and constantly retesting your investing doctrine, you won't fall prey to such an event, implausible though it is.

You may say (and it's a great thing to say), "But if you tell me in this book the market's P/E has nothing to do with future returns and big budget deficits are bullish not bearish, won't the whole world know? And then won't it stop working?" If the world embraces these truths, then because the market is a discounter of all widely known information, these truths would become priced into markets and knowing them wouldn't give you an edge. They wouldn't work because you wouldn't know anything others don't widely know.

But that didn't happen after I first published this book in 2007. Most of the myths in this book persist. I bet it doesn't happen in 2012 either. I'll bet most folks who read Chapter 1 will think the notions expressed about P/Es and deficits are so screwy, they ignore them completely and fall back on the mythologies. That would be comfortable and easy. Most investors will never see this book, and of those buying it, half won't read it. Of those who do, many won't get past this chapter in disgust. They will reject the truth, prefer mythology and see me as silly. I hope they do because when I see them see me as silly and wrong, I know I will be able to use these truisms for a long time. If they adopt most of these truisms, I'll need to come up with new ones to know something others don't.

Whereas the Campbell-Shiller paper was rapidly embraced and quickly became globally famous and popular because it supported the standard mythology, evidence contradicting market mythologies fortunately tends to be about as noticed as a rock thrown into a lake—a minor ripple followed by near-instant absence from societal memory. This isn't the first time I've written about the high P/E myth. I first started 15 years ago. I'll bet it is as prevalent 5 and 10 years from now as it is today, and you can still make gameable bets on it. But of course, I could be wrong and then you move onto the next myth. That's life.

The real benefit of Question One is it allows you to know something others don't know by knowing where you otherwise would have been wrong but thought you were right. Once you master the skill of doing this, you can improve yourself forever with it. You can keep learning things others don't know while reducing your own propensity to make mistakes.

Discovering new investing truths is a coincidental result of asking Question One—a lucky accident. If you're purposefully seeking what no one else knows, you must also learn to use and apply Question Two: What can you fathom that others find unfathomable? Even contemplating such a thing seems pretty unfathomable to most people, but that is exactly what we start doing if you simply turn the page and continue to Chapter 2.

2 QUESTION TWO: WHAT CAN YOU FATHOM THAT OTHERS FIND UNFATHOMABLE?

Fathoming the Unfathomable

Fathoming the unfathomable by definition seems unfathomable, so most folks don't try. However, like Question One, it doesn't require any additional scholarship, genetic superiority or magical superhero powers. All you need is Question Two: What can I see that others can't? The more you ask, the more you can see. Since the only basis for a market bet is knowing something others don't, this question can provide the second basis for a bet. Go ahead and ask yourself: What do I know that others don't? At this point, your answer may be, "Well . . . nothing." It's most people's immediate reaction.

Don't be discouraged. You won't be bombarded with Question Twos like you are with Question Ones. We get bombarded with investing nonsense daily. Discovering something others don't know isn't a "Eureka!" moment. It's not the apple falling on Newton's head. It's what happened afterward when Newton asked, "I wonder what the heck made that happen?" and contemplated what forces, natural or sinister, could be at play. It's the reflection in a quiet room away from the incessant market and media noise when you wonder if factor Q could possibly cause result Y when everyone else is yammering on about X causing Y.

The world is busy insisting high P/Es cause poor stock prices (wrong—usually), debt is bad for stocks (wrong), you shouldn't fight the Fed (wrong about half) and high trade deficits cause a weak dollar (wrong, wrong, wrong).

31

But to know something others don't, you tune out the noise and wonder—if everything everyone insists moves currencies doesn't, I wonder what actually does? (We go there in Chapter 7.) And if I shouldn't fight the Fed, is it possible the yield curve can tell me anything at all about stocks? Or must I just look at it differently somehow? I wonder? Wondering is wonderful.

Wondering Is Wonderful

Suppose no one has a clue what causes result Y. If everyone knows no one knows what causes Y, then probably almost no one is willing to think about what causes Y because they will believe it a waste of time. In our contemporary world, in America and more so elsewhere, if something is seen as unfathomable, normal people will treat it as a complete untouchable. These areas are especially ripe for inquiry because they are so virginal.

Misapplication of Question Two can lead you to waste time plowing through common media sources for clues. Through the miracle of mass production and electronics, pretty much all media is everywhere and all around us—constantly. Your investment edge won't present itself in a ready-to-use format in a front-page news story in any publication or in an evening news program or blog or e-mail newsletter. No matter how buried a news item or how insignificant a blog, we live in a fast-moving world. Your "news" edge almost certainly will be snatched from you before you've found it.

Don't despair; you can still use all that widespread noise to help you find something no one else knows. All it requires is fighting eons of behavioral conditioning. Here's how.

Ignore the Rock in the Bushes

Thousands of years ago, our ancestors grouped together for security against other tribes and giant fanged beasts. When darkness fell, they gathered around campfires for warmth, protection and the occasional grilled mammoth burger. By the glowing campfire, they regaled each other with stories of the hunt and mythological tales, carrying their culture to younger generations. On a nice night, warm and mammoth-gorged, they could feel a real sense of security and well-being and envision a beckoning future.

Suddenly, in the dark, a loud and unexplained mammalian noise sliced through their sense of security. Instantly and instinctually, they all looked toward the source of that noise—in the bushes—and prepared for what could be threatening and ugly. An attacking rival tribe, perhaps, or a lion or a stampeding wildebeest herd. Every ear and eye correctly focused on the noise to maximize the human power to identify and, if possible, overcome the threat.

If you were from another tribe and led a warring group wanting to attack this camp, what would you do? To be clever, you might throw a stone or create some other ruckus that distracts the camp—then attack from a different direction. Of course, a stampeding herd wouldn't do that. But for the camp, in case of a planned attack from clever marauders, a more evolved military-like response would be to have some folks look away from the noise, into the darkness elsewhere, to spot any surprise marauder threat.

The problem? Unless well organized, no group of people behaves that way. You hear a noise in the darkness and you turn toward it. Go camping sometime and see. Your instinctual reaction isn't to turn away from the noise, but toward it. In Stone Age days, that instinct protected lives from the most common natural forces. From tens of thousands of years of evolution, we are mentally hardwired to turn toward the noise, face it as a group and instinctually presume our ability to immediately unite our tribal eyes and ears and react.

I suspect some readers may be tempted to say, "Not me! I'm smarter than that. I'd look in the other direction. I wouldn't be fooled." The next time you hear an unexpected noise, check what your instinctual reaction is. I near guarantee you'll look to the noise. If you don't, you're really, really weird. The person who most thinks he won't is most certainly the person turning to the noise fastest. The rare bird that doesn't face the noise doesn't think about it. To know what your fellow investors don't know, you must look anywhere but where everyone else is looking. You must train yourself to stop looking toward the noise. Instead, note whenever everyone is looking one direction, whether you hear a noise or not, you should look away—where they're not.

Discounting the Media Machine and Advanced Fad Avoidance

You may be tempted to ignore the media altogether since what you hear or read is likely wrong or already discounted into current prices. There is some rationality to that view, but it's wrong. By all means, don't avoid mass media—it's your friend and ally on your quest to invest by knowing what others don't. The media is a discounting machine—you must read (watch, listen to) the media to know what everyone else is focused on so you know exactly what you can ignore and look away from to focus elsewhere.

Whatever they're fretting, you likely needn't because they're doing it for you—a service—and you don't even have to pay them for it. Such a simple concept is very hard for tribal-oriented humans to get. But anyone can train themselves to do it.

For example, I've already told you the collective histrionics regarding the so-called budget and trade deficits are typically misguided. You may not believe it, but I've told you. You also know pretty much everyone misinterprets high P/Es. (We debunk more ubiquitous myths in later chapters, but you get the idea.) Paying attention to what the media covers and consequently discarding what is irrelevant will prevent you from being trampled by herd mentality and let you begin fathoming new paths.

Avoiding being trampled by the herd sounds easy enough—look where they are stampeding and get the heck out of the way. However, if it were easy, it wouldn't be called "herd mentality." It would be called "calm, noncompelling, no pressure here, join us as we run over this cliff if you please, if not, no problem" mentality. Remember when your mom asked if you'd jump off a bridge just because cool-kid Jimmy did it? Of course you wouldn't jump, but you might buy small-cap stocks at the wrong time if your poker group pokes enough fun at you for not having done it when they did.

My March 1995 *Forbes* column, "Advanced Fad Avoidance," described how best to avoid getting swept away with the herd. It's still good advice, so I'll repeat the four steps to fad avoidance here:

1. *If most folks you know agree with you on a price move or some event's impact, don't take this as confirmation you are right. It is a warning;* **you are wrong.** *Being right requires aloneness and willingness to let others see you as maybe nuts.*

Still very true. And lots of people think I'm nuts. It's ok if people think you're nuts. It doesn't hurt. With the evolution of the Internet and blogs, I've become used to people reading my articles and columns and writing scathing criticisms of me. (Of course, sometimes they're right, and that would be when I'm wrong, but either way, what they think of me isn't any of my business.) I've trained myself to ignore what anyone who I don't already know very well thinks about me or my work. If my wife is upset at me, I take it seriously. She knows me and my strengths and weaknesses and desires my well-being. Family, friends, associates! Other than that, if you're upset at me and don't like something I've said, feel free to criticize, but know you will run into an emotional desert. You can train yourself to have that same emotional desert, too. What most people think about you is none of your business; and if they think you're nuts, it might be good.

2. *If you read or hear about some investment idea or significant event more than once in the media, it won't work. By the time several commentators have thought and written about it, even new news is too old.*

Even more true today. The Internet has multiplied the venues and speed at which news travels. Now everything moves faster and gets discounted into pricing faster. Compounding the discounting speed, which has been increasing for decades, traders trade 24 hours a day, fully five and a half days a week around the globe. It used to be evening news didn't sneak up on you until morning. Now, not only does news move across the Internet at night, but someone somewhere is trading extensively while you snooze.

3. *The older an argument is, the less power it has. So, for example, inflation fears may have moved markets in 1994, but sometime early in 1995 that view will run out of steam.*

Every year's hot fear is likely obsolete the next year. It's the new thing no one expected that has the herd stampeding around your village, not last year's noise. To think better about this—take any issue and consider when you first heard about it. The older it is, the more certain it won't affect you much. The older it is, the more certain everyone has had multiple opportunities to discount the price fully. Here is the best single example I can remember. Recall people expected all computers to break down on January 1, 2000, because of a supposed widespread glitch in everyone's software. The Y2K scare was ubiquitous, and in the fall of 1999, it scared lots of folks out of stocks. I devoted my October 18, 1999, *Forbes* column, entitled "Greater Fools," to why Y2K wouldn't hurt stocks. I said then: "Y2K is the most widely hyped 'disaster' in modern history. It is well documented: The only folks who aren't familiar with it are in the upper Amazon basins, rapidly fleeing the rest of humanity. I need not define Y2K for you to know exactly what I'm referencing. My July 6, 1998, column detailed why Y2K could not hurt the stock market." Because it was an old argument and well discounted, the S&P 500 in 1999 had a back-end rise during the supposed crisis with a total return for the year of 21%.[1] Using this simple rule, anyone could have known Y2K wouldn't bite. Fear of Y2K was bullish. But few knew because they couldn't get themselves to embrace the rule. (If you care to read my two Y2K columns, they are in Appendixes B and C.)

4. *Any category of security that was hot in the last five years won't be in the next five years, and vice versa.*

Still true—though the actual number of years matters less. Things can be hot for a long time, but they won't be hot forever. And yet, investors still fall prey to this one. Energy in 1980. Tech in 2000. You can play this game endlessly. That they were hot in the last five doesn't mean they will be the coldest in the next five or even necessarily cold at all, but no category stays hot forever. And if one did one day, it would be a double warning to seek safer and higher future returning turf elsewhere.

Follow these four steps whenever you are presented with an investment decision, and you'll be better armed to ignore the noise and see what others find unseeable.

Investment Professionals—Professional Discounters

Another great source of discounted information are investment professionals—stockbrokers, financial planners, CPAs, CFAs, etc. Precious few have access to any information their peers or even a client with a fast modem doesn't have. Whatever they focus on, you shouldn't waste time on. If they're writing about it, focus elsewhere.

Universities teach largely the same curriculum to their students in finance and economics. They're teaching pretty much from the same playbook. They're supposed to. The textbooks, methodologies and theories taught are widely available; they contain little many tens of thousands of others can't read, learn and thereby discount into markets. Decades of students have learned all this and been trained to think in these ways with the curriculum as their guide. It is basic to the craft.

Every bit of what is taught is known by so many people that the curriculum, while fine, offers nothing others don't know. It offers nothing as a way to process information that isn't already in prices by the actions of the very large number of market participants who use the curriculum as the glasses through which they see the world. It's the way they were taught to see the world. Hence, it's in pricing. One very hard fact for craftsmen to accept is the curriculum itself is widely known and, hence, discounted into pricing.

There is nothing wrong with learning it, but it doesn't teach you something others don't know. If professionals as a group have the same education, look at the same information and interpret it largely the same way, where is their edge? What unique information do they think they have? The answer is most often: none. This is why, along with the media, professionals are useful in figuring out what information is priced and can be safely set aside.

Friends Don't Let Friends Be Contrarians

The media is generally wrong. Professionals likely don't have an edge because they're looking at the same widely known information everyone else has. Following the herd is fraught with peril. Does this mean you should do the exact opposite of what you hear from pundits and professionals? Should you become a classic contrarian?

Absolutely not. No, no and no!

I'm frequently called a contrarian. But I'm not—not as that term is generally used. Of course, I've been called far worse and will be, but the contrarian label happens to be wrong. Contrarianism has become increasingly popular in recent decades, rendering it priced by the market just as much as the consensus view. We are all contrarians now and none of us are. Being contrarian will get you about as far in the long term as being wholly influenced in your investment decisions by the *New York Times* and the nightly news.

The word *contrarian* implies going against the crowd—if folks are bullish, a classic contrarian becomes bearish, and vice versa. If everyone thinks electing a given politician is good for stocks, the contrarian sees it as bad. Technically, a contrarian correctly knows what everyone assumes will happen likely won't but *wrongly* assumes the exact reverse will happen.

Let's wade further into this. The market is a pretty efficient discounter of all known information, so, as we stated multiple times, if people tend to agree something will happen to markets, it typically won't—something else likely happens instead. But that doesn't mean the something else that happens is the exact reverse.

Suppose most folks agree the market will go up. That doesn't mean it will go down. It might, but it might also go nowhere, which would also make everyone wrong. Or it might go up, but a lot more than anyone expects. That, too, would make everyone wrong. Over history, all those things have happened and in about equal proportions.

If you're a classic contrarian and correctly see most folks agree the market will go up, so you bet it will go down, and then it goes up but much more than most folks expected, you end up the most wrong guy in town. Being a contrarian is better than betting with the crowd, but not much and will still have you being right something on the shy side of one time in three.

Think of this like a compass. The consensus thinks the market will go north. Contrarians think it will go south. But it could just as well go east or west—or northeast or southwest—making the crowd wrong and the contrarians wrong and the discounting mechanism work. Because those other outcomes are less expected than the contrarian position, they actually happen more often.

The key is to remember something else typically happens than what the consensus expects, but not necessarily the reverse. True contrarians these days aren't much more right than consensus followers. It is surprise that shifts demand, which drives prices. The problem is the surprise could come from any direction.

Patterns, Patterns Everywhere

To know something others don't, you must focus away from the noise. Ask what you can come to know that others can't. But how can you know about a thing you don't know?

There are patterns to be discovered everywhere. Granted, many are simply meaningless. But there is so much out there we haven't discovered yet, people will make new capital markets discoveries for many decades to come. There is no reason you shouldn't find your share. If you seek them out, there are many patterns you can discover on your own before the rest of the investing world becomes aware. And there is your edge—your basis for a market bet.

Essentially, you seek one of two things when asking Question Two. First, you want a pattern—some sort of correlation—between two or more variables people generally think are wholly unrelated. Second, you're looking for a pattern many people see but disregard, deride or misinterpret. We show you two such examples here (and more in later chapters).

The Shocking Truth About Yield Curves

You can't turn on the news without hearing about interest rates. Yet, despite all the attention interest rates garner, many miss a remarkable pattern and life lesson.

Before we delve into remarkable patterns and causal correlation, let's clear the air regarding interest rates. Interest rates determine the cost to borrow, either short term or long term. They also determine the yield investors can get in return for locking up their liquid assets for a predetermined time period.

How often have you either heard or read, "Interest rates are falling," or, "The Fed is raising interest rates" or some such news regarding interest rates (rates, plural)?

Folks tend to mix up the rates monopoly-controlled by a country's central bank—in America, the Federal Reserve, aka the "Fed"—and market-set rates.

If America's Fed feels it should reduce or increase money supply, one tactic is to raise or lower, respectively, the federal funds target rate. The Federal Open Market Committee (FOMC) meets eight times yearly to discuss if it should raise, lower or stay the fed funds rate (also sometimes referred to as the *overnight rate* or the *short rate*) and how much the rate should move, if at all.

The short rate is that at which banks lend to each other and drives the interest rate banks pay you for deposits (savings accounts and certificates of deposit [CDs]). This is the rate (singular) investors mean to imply when they talk about the Fed monkeying around with rates.

Rates on US Treasurys and all other bond rates aren't set by the Fed, the government, the president or an evil conspiracy. Those rates are set by global market forces. (As a point of trivia, in the industry, the 10-year US Treasury rate is sometimes referred to as the *long rate*.) In our contemporary global economy, traders reach across country lines to trade bonds in a global, free and open market.

Make no mistake—though investors blather about "rates falling" and "rates rising" and "the Fed raising rates"—the Fed-controlled short rate and all other rates—Treasurys, other sovereign debt, corporate bonds, municipal bonds, etc.—move independently of each other, sometimes in the same direction and other times in opposing directions.

Let's say that again differently. Sometimes when the Fed raises the fed funds rate, other rates rise, too. Other times they fall. More often, they do a mix of things—differing maturities on different types of bonds move up or down or stay flat to varying degrees. That is true in America and everywhere else.

For those very new to this topic, the difference between the shortest-term Treasury bill (which is a very short-term rate, not the "short rate") and varying longer-rate maturities can be plotted visually on a graph resulting in a yield curve. (The same can be done with any other form of bonds, as long as they're the same type and credit quality—you can do corporate bond yield curves, muni-bond yield curves, etc.) The vertical axis plots interest rates from zero at the bottom to higher rates up top. The horizontal axis plots time from now at the left to longer-term maturities stretching out to the right, with the far right being 10 or 30 years into the future. A typical yield curve can look something like the hypothetical one in Figure 2.1.

Shorter-term rates usually tend to be lower than longer-term rates, while longer-term rates tend to be higher in return for taking the additional risk of locking money away for longer periods. When short-term rates are lower, the curve slopes upward and is *positive*. Sometimes, rarely, shorter-term rates are actually higher than long-term rates. When this happens, our graph slopes downward to the right and is *inverted*. Still rare, but less so than an inverted yield curve, is when rates are all at about the same level—this is referred to as *flat*.

The Interest Rate Brouhaha

You may have heard an age-old mythology phrased "Don't fight the Fed," which is meant to prompt you to sell stocks when the Fed raises the short rate. Nonsense—on average, stocks have done perfectly fine when the Fed raised

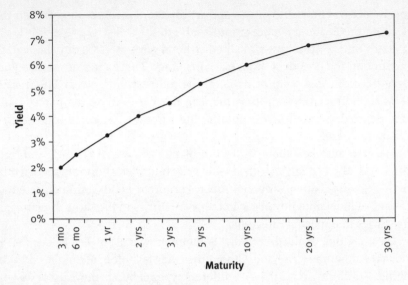

Figure 2.1   Hypothetical Yield Curve

the short rate—although not always. But nothing is "always" one way or the other. Figure 2.2 shows some recent periods of a rising fed funds rate and subsequent S&P 500 returns.

What you can see is the S&P 500 and a rising fed funds rate correlate pretty closely at times. I wouldn't take that to mean anything—the stock market is generally more positive than negative, so there is no surprise here. And sometimes the market was more positive than at others. But because positive markets have followed a rising short rate, "don't fight the Fed" is rendered one of those Question One myths you should ignore. This isn't to say a rising short rate is any kind of a bull or bear market indicator—but neither is a dropping short rate. There is no credible, consistent link between the short rate moving any direction and bull or bear markets.

What are Fed-fighting fans missing? The first step in asking a successful Question Two is setting aside any unproductive fretting about concerns that don't matter. Anyone can Google the FOMC or go to the website (http://www.federalreserve.gov/fomc/#calendars) and see when they're meeting. What's more, the FOMC under both Greenspan and Bernanke has become ever more transparent about when it plans to lower or raise the fed funds rate and by nearly exactly how much. The Fed raising the rate a quarter of a point, or even half a point, is hardly a market-moving event when the Fed has been talking about the planned pace of rate moves for months.

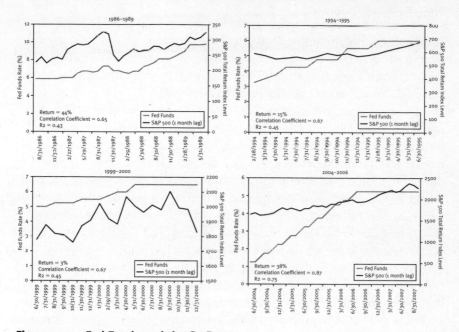

Figure 2.2 Fed Funds and the S&P 500
Source: Global Financial Data, Inc.

Instead of focusing on short rate movements, focus on the yield curve. Most investors will tell you a positive yield curve is good and an inverted one is bad. That's more or less true. The yield curve is normally positively sloped. A truly inverted yield curve is rare and has a reputation for being bearish.

But right now, you're thinking about yield curves incorrectly, and it can hurt you. Before we can discover something new, let's check if what we believe about yield curves is correct with Question One. Is it true an inverted yield curve is a harbinger of doom? The answer is—it depends on what you mean by "yield curve," or more specifically, where.

One problem behind the yield curve—I won't call it a myth so much as a misunderstanding—is folks tend to lump recessions and bear markets together. They're not the same things. You can have a bear market without a recession, and vice versa, though they do tend to come together because the stock market will price in dour sentiment and falling earnings caused by a recession. But it doesn't always (e.g., if the recession is long feared and well priced).

A moment for two definitions: A *bear market* is a prolonged stock market downturn exceeding 20% or so. (The difference between a bear market and a correction is magnitude and duration—a correction being much shorter lived, only months, and usually under 20% or so.) By contrast, a *recession* is generally defined as two consecutive quarters of negative GDP growth, but it's tough to know if you're in a recession while it's happening since GDP numbers get heavily restated afterward.

Two mildly negative quarters of GDP can be difficult to feel as they occur. Recessions usually aren't labeled recessions until long after they've started—sometimes not until after they're over. For example, the 1973 to 1974 bear market was followed immediately by a recession that was steep and pervasive throughout 1974, extending into 1975. It was one of the biggest of the post–World War II era yet wasn't recognized as having happened until 1975. Meanwhile, in September 1974, President Ford and his economic advisors were still calling for tax hikes to slow the economy and fight inflation. That's because no one knew we were in a recession.

While I was pretty darned young at the time, I remember the period very well. For me it was a strange time. What I remember was all the people I talked to in 1974 thought the economy was strong, when later we'd learn it had been declining all year. In many ways, I wasn't very sensitive or plugged in that year. My wife and I had just lost our young daughter. I was pretty well shattered and capable of working only part time for about six months. I didn't trust myself to have a good view of what was happening with the economy, so I spent a lot of time asking others what they thought was going on. Without intending to, I did a pretty good job of polling a big cross-section of investors and business-people. Pretty much no one knew in 1974 we were already long in recession. I don't think much of anyone saw it as a recession until 1975, and by then, it was mostly over—and that was a huge one. It was heavily masked by the high level of inflation then—for many firms, revenues remained strong as unit volume shrank. Still, if few saw it, note how few would see a mild economic decline.

The official measure of recession comes from the National Bureau of Economic Research (NBER; www.nber.com). Their definition captures more data, though one prominent data point is GDP, and more accurately characterizes an economic contraction. The NBER characterizes a recession thusly:

> The NBER does not define a recession in terms of two consecutive quarters of decline in real GDP. Rather, a recession is a significant decline in economic activity spread across the economy, lasting more than a few months, normally visible in real GDP, real income, employment, industrial production and wholesale-retail sales.[2]

Historically, a steep yield curve suggests an environment in which financial institutions can lend profitably, and lending is an important driver of future economic activity. However, an inverted yield curve creates a disincentive for banks to lend, thereby reducing liquidity (remember this for later in this chapter), and it's a fairly reliable predictor of recessions.

But whether an inverted yield curve causes a bear market or not depends on whether the related bad news is priced into the market. For example, in 1998 we had a flattening yield curve here in America that had people in a collective tizzy. Fear of an upcoming inverted yield curve ran rampant. That, along with the Russian ruble crisis and the Long-Term Capital Management crisis, was widely expected to drive stocks down, long and hard. We had a big midyear correction but no bear market—the S&P 500 finished 1998 up 29%.[3] Fear of a flattening yield curve was so prevalent it lost its power to create a major decline.

Fast forward to 2000 when the yield curve actually did invert. This time, nobody paid heed. Instead, folks were lauding the "new economy" and saying, "Earnings don't matter" and "It's different this time," as they rushed off to parties celebrating the launch of dot-com stocks. Among other things, the recent memory of 1998 may have convinced them inverted yield curves didn't matter. In 2000, the yield curve, because it wasn't widely noted and feared—the tribe was looking elsewhere—was a good harbinger of economic weakness and peaking Tech stock prices that led to a three-year bear market. If everyone is talking about it, dreading it and stocking up on canned goods because of it, then the inverted yield curve has likely lost some of its bearish oomph. If everyone skips about singing, "Tra-la-la! It's different this time," as in early 2000, then an inverted yield curve can devastate stocks.

Even with that clarified, people still see yield curves incorrectly. It's important we see them correctly because of the economic conditions an inverted yield curve implies. You think about interest rates here in America and the yield curve they engender. Why wouldn't you think about US interest rates? What other interest rates would you consider? The Question Two I'm about to share can be recast over and over again into other problem-solving contexts where it works just as well. So here goes.

Question Two: Is there a yield curve more important than America's? You've probably never thought to ask yourself that question. Why on earth would you? What could possibly be more important than America? Particularly to Americans!

After all, when we look at US yield curves from 30, 50 and 100 years ago, we can see some pretty compelling long-standing evidence they can signal how healthy the economy is. Everyone knows that (or at least, plenty of folks believe it—including most reporters, which means pretty much everyone). It's widely accepted America's yield curve matters and is a somewhat reliable indicator of good and bad economic times ahead. Whenever the short rate has been above long-term rates, banks became disinterested in lending as aggressively. And that's less good. Thirty years ago when America's yield curve inverted, the only way for a bank to make money lending was to lend to a worse credit risk at a higher rate than the bank's borrowing costs. This was and is risky, and banks dislike doing it. In fact, the riskier the customer they need to profitably lend, the less they like it and don't want to do it. In the days of yore, America's yield curve and its camber mattered. A lot! Of course, in those days most folks didn't know the yield curve mattered.

Think Globally, Think Better

Fast forward to now—we have not just national banks, but fully global banks, a wide array of derivatives and financial futures for hedging and electronics allowing instant access to precise accounting and trade information globally. Now money flows fairly freely across borders. A global bank can borrow in one country and lend in another and hedge its currency risk all as fast as you can read this sentence. I can borrow money from an investment bank that got it from a syndicate of insurance firms in Europe that crossed the money through global banks, and I may never know the source was overseas. To me, as the borrower, it's just money.

Decades back—in a world of national banks, minimal high-volume electronics for accounting and trading, no material hedging instruments and fixed instead of flexible currency prices—it was the national yield curve that mattered. No more! Global tendencies prevail over local ones in every country, including America, the greatest country in the world. Foreign interest rates and yield curves provide or deny liquidity heavily impacting our own. They also determine the cost effectiveness of using leverage as a means to snap up both domestic and foreign assets.

The analysis of any country's yield curve—even a country as massive as America—has become less meaningful. The right way to think about this now, something I fathomed no one had ever written about before I first did, is the GDP-weighted global yield curve. The global yield curve is representative of worldwide lending conditions. In today's world, if the global yield curve says one thing and America's says another, go with the global. America's or any other single stock market will subordinate to the global curve.

Figure 2.3 shows the global yield curve as of September 2011. The reason it's important? If a bank can borrow more cheaply in one country and lend

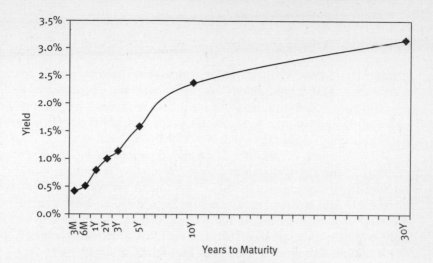

Figure 2.3   Global Yield Curve, September 2011
Sources: International Monetary Fund, World Economic Outlook Database, September 2011; Global Financial Data, Inc.; Bloomberg Finance, L.P. Yield calculations exclude Greece.

more profitably in another, it will. Everybody, including banks and their customers, likes cheap money. Note this illustration is based on the global yield curve being GDP weighted. It makes sense intuitively that a country with a larger GDP would have greater impact on the global yield curve.

In constructing the GDP-weighted yield curve, first I made a list of the countries included in the MSCI World Index. I didn't use the full list of ACWI countries because the developed nations' GDPs dwarf those of the emerging nations, so their interest rates would barely register—and accurate data on some emerging nations is devilishly tough to come by. Then I input the latest GDP for each of the countries. The GDP for all of these countries can be found at the web site for the International Monetary Fund (IMF; www .imf.org). My list looked something like this:

Country	GDP ($ in Billions)	GDP Weight (%)
Country A	50	14.3
Country B	50	14.3
Country C	250	71.4
Total	**350**	

As Global as You Can Get

In measuring global markets, the best indexes we have currently are those built by MSCI, Inc. All MSCI indexes are properly constructed—in other words, market-capitalization and float weighted—but the two we focus on most are the MSCI World Index and MSCI All Country World Index (the World Index and ACWI for brevity's sake).

The World Index represents 24 developed nations including America, Britain, Australia, Germany and Japan. I frequently refer to the World Index when discussing market history because it provides ample historical data—and having data to measure helps decipher history. More important, it is comprehensive, and each constituent is weighted by its *float*—i.e., its market liquidity. That is, a stock has little market effect if it's not trading actively. One example is Berkshire Hathaway, which isn't included in the World Index or the S&P 500 because it's so seldom traded relative to other stocks.

As a proxy for the *total* global market, another good choice is the ACWI as it also includes emerging nations. Currently, 45 countries make the cut—the stocks in the World Index plus Mexico, Brazil, China, India and so on. Because there is limited history and little data for the Emerging Markets, it's less useful than the World Index for measuring performance history. But it's a well-constructed index and an excellent proxy for the global market.

To find more information on these indexes and track historical performance, go to www.msci.com.

Clearly, that is all hypothetical information, and a shorter list for illustration's sake, but you get the idea. To get each country's appropriate GDP weight, sum for the total world GDP and divide for each country.

Next, input the short-term and long-term interest rates. (Here I show the 3-month and the 10-year rates.) I have access to some great data sources letting me compile interest rates quickly, but anyone can find this information for free on any good financial website.

Country	GDP ($ in Billions)	GDP Weight (%)	Rate 3-Month	10-Year
Country A	50	14.3	3.25	6.5
Country B	50	14.3	2.5	7.2
Country C	250	71.4	4.5	4.25
Total	**350**			

That part is just data entry. Now I subtract the 3-month rate from the 10-year rate to get the spread. A positive spread means a positive yield curve, and a negative spread means an inverted curve.

Country	GDP ($ in Billions)	GDP Weight (%)	Rate 3-Month	10-Year	Spread
Country A	50	14.3	3.25	6.5	3.25
Country B	50	14.3	2.5	7.2	4.70
Country C	250	71.4	4.5	4.25	−0.25
Total	350				

Note Country C actually has a negative spread, meaning its yield curve has inverted slightly. And Country C has a massive relative GDP. Does this spell doom for Country C? We aren't done yet. Next, multiply each country's spread by the appropriate GDP weight, and sum up the column for the global yield curve spread, as shown here:

Country	GDP ($ in Billions)	GDP Weight (%)	Rate 3-Month	10-Year	Spread	GDP-Weighted Spread
Country A	50	14.3	3.25	6.5	3.25	0.46
Country B	50	14.3	2.5	7.2	4.70	0.67
Country C	250	71.4	4.5	4.25	−0.25	−0.18
Total	350					0.95

Though Country C has a negative yield curve, the global yield curve is still positively sloped—the 10-year is above the 3-month. The global yield curve spread is 0.95—a spread from low to high of almost exactly 1%. You can imagine Country C, with a much bigger GDP than its friends on this imaginary index, is a country like the United States. The other countries' yield curves matter, too, even to a country as big as Country C.

If credit conditions are suboptimal for Country C's banks and institutions, they can borrow in other countries without feeling much of a slowdown, which is not what they would have done decades ago. (You can use the same methodology to calculate the global short-term and long-term rates if you want to create an actual global yield curve. Just multiply each country's interest rate by its GDP weighting, then sum up for the global rate. In our hypothetical example, the global 3-month rate is 4.04 and the 10-year rate is 4.99.)

Subtracting the shorter-term rate, you still arrive at the same yield curve spread of 0.95.)

Therefore, an inverted US yield curve by itself is no basis for immediate panic. Rather, you must look at what global rates and the global curve are doing. An inverted yield curve in a single nation when the global curve is positive might be a reason to underweight that country. But it's no sure-fire reason to get globally bearish, not by a long shot. The global yield curve is a more useful leading indicator for stocks and the global economy than any single country's curve.

Figure 2.4 shows the spread between *global* short-term rates and *global* long-term rates since 1985—another way of depicting the relative steepness of the global yield curve. Anything above 0% is a positive yield curve and anything below is inverted. The higher the line, the greater the spread between short-term and long-term rates and hence, the steeper the curve.

Note the global yield curve inverted in 1989, signaling the oncoming recession (a global recession, by the way). It also got very flat at the end of 2000 and early in 2007—both ahead of global recessions. Recall, at points in 2005 and 2006, the US yield curve was very flat or even inverted, depending on how you measured. Inverted! But in 2005 and 2006, the global yield curve

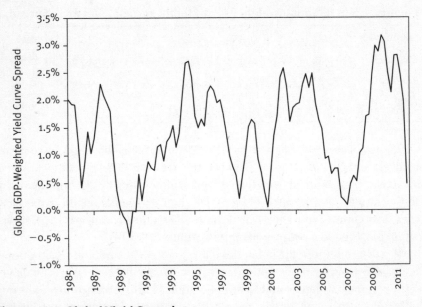

Figure 2.4   Global Yield Spread
Sources: Global Financial Data, Inc.; International Monetary Fund, MSCI World monetary zones.

was still positive—and there was no US or global recession then. Interestingly, US stocks rose 4.9% and 15.8% in 2005 and 2006, respectively, lagging world stocks both years, which rose 9.5% and 20.1%.[4] Such an outcome wouldn't surprise you if you knew the US had inverted but the world had not.

If the global yield curve is inverted or flat, be cognizant of what that could mean looking forward. Whether positive or inverted, it should be more important to your global view than any single-nation yield curve.

To my knowledge, until I did it, no one ever constructed a GDP-weighted global yield curve to summarize global credit conditions. This is a simple and perfect example of a Question Two—fathoming what is unfathomable to most people: The global, not national, yield curve is more important today. And yet fathoming what is unfathomable to most people isn't complicated, prohibitively theoretical or hard to grasp. It's actually pretty darned basic and simple.

One really neat point mentioned earlier is you can extend this principle to many other phenomena. It's the global budget deficit that matters (or doesn't) to global GDP and markets. It's the global level of inflation that will drive inflation in America and elsewhere. You can use the same methodology I just described to create a GDP-weighted global money supply and watch its growth. Why? Because it's global money creation that will drive global inflation, not what any single country does. You know you worry about trade deficits and current account deficits. By definition, these simply disappear on a global level, but we cover how to think about that later. You can apply global thinking to so many things that the age-old but seldom-applied notion of "Think global, act local" is a truly valuable saw—one way ahead of its time.

What the Yield Curve Is Trying to Tell You

Now you're thinking about yield curves correctly and can begin looking for other remarkable patterns and another basis for a market bet. Another Question Two: What is it the yield curve can tell you about stocks no one else knows? By now, you know (or you should know if you don't) all investment styles cycle in and out of favor. We talk more about why in later chapters, but you've probably seen something akin to Figure 2.5, which shows changes in leadership among equity sizes and styles.

What Figure 2.5 shows is no one size or style leads for all time. More noticeably, no predictable pattern exists to indicate which size or style will lead next. If you buy the previous year's winner, you very often end up with this year's loser—except for an unusual lengthy period of leadership in the late 1990s for large-cap US stocks. Of course, you were then rewarded for your

Figure 2.5 is a full-page "quilt" chart (rotated) showing annual total returns by asset class/style, ranked from highest to lowest within each year from 1991 through 2010.

Rank	1991	1992	1993	1994	1995	1996	1997	1998	1999	2000	2001	2002	2003	2004	2005	2006	2007	2008	2009	2010
1	Russell 2000 Growth 51.2%	Russell 2000 Value 29.1%	MSCI EAFE 32.6%	MSCI EAFE 7.8%	S&P/Citi Growth 39.4%	S&P/Citi Growth 33.5%	S&P/Citi Growth 33.5%	S&P/Citi Growth 42.0%	Russell 2000 Growth 43.1%	Russell 2000 Value 22.8%	Russell 2000 Value 14.0%	Barclays Agg 10.3%	Russell 2000 Growth 48.5%	Russell 2000 Value 22.2%	MSCI EAFE 13.5%	MSCI EAFE 26.3%	MSCI EAFE 11.2%	Barclays Agg 5.2%	S&P/Citi Growth 34.4%	Russell 2000 Growth 29.1%
2	Russell 2000 46.0%	Russell 2000 18.4%	Russell 2000 Value 18.9%	S&P/Citi Growth 3.9%	S&P 500 Index 37.6%	S&P/Citi Value 23.9%	S&P 500 Index 33.4%	S&P 500 Index 28.6%	S&P/Citi Growth 28.2%	Barclays Agg 11.6%	Barclays Agg 8.4%	Russell 2000 Value −11.4%	Russell 2000 47.3%	MSCI EAFE 20.2%	S&P/Citi Value 9.3%	Russell 2000 Value 23.5%	S&P/Citi Growth 10.3%	Russell 2000 −28.9%	Russell 2000 Growth 34.5%	Russell 2000 26.9%
3	Russell 2000 Value 41.7%	S&P/Citi Value 9.5%	Russell 2000 16.6%	S&P 500 Index 1.3%	S&P/Citi Value 37.0%	S&P 500 Index 23.0%	Russell 2000 Value 31.5%	MSCI EAFE 20.0%	MSCI EAFE 27.0%	S&P/Citi Value 6.5%	Russell 2000 2.5%	MSCI EAFE −15.9%	Russell 2000 Value 46.0%	Russell 2000 18.3%	S&P 500 Index 4.9%	S&P/Citi Value 19.7%	Russell 2000 Growth 7.1%	Russell 2000 Growth −33.8%	MSCI EAFE 31.8%	Russell 2000 Value 24.5%
4	S&P 500 Index 30.5%	Russell 2000 Growth 7.8%	S&P/Citi Value 10.1%	S&P/Citi Value −0.6%	Russell 2000 Growth 31.0%	Russell 2000 Value 21.4%	Russell 2000 22.4%	S&P/Citi Value 16.3%	Russell 2000 21.3%	Russell 2000 −3.0%	Russell 2000 Growth −9.2%	S&P/Citi Value −16.2%	MSCI EAFE 38.6%	S&P/Citi Value 15.3%	Russell 2000 Value 4.7%	Russell 2000 18.4%	Barclays Agg 7.0%	S&P 500 Index −37.0%	Russell 2000 27.2%	S&P/Citi Value 17.1%
5	S&P/Citi Value 22.2%	S&P 500 Index 7.6%	S&P 500 Index 10.1%	Russell 2000 −1.8%	Russell 2000 28.5%	Russell 2000 16.5%	Russell 2000 Growth 12.9%	Barclays Agg 8.7%	S&P 500 Index 21.0%	S&P 500 Index −9.1%	S&P/Citi Value −9.6%	Russell 2000 −20.5%	S&P/Citi Value 31.6%	Russell 2000 Growth 14.3%	Russell 2000 4.6%	S&P 500 Index 15.8%	S&P 500 Index 5.5%	S&P/Citi Growth −35.3%	S&P 500 Index 26.5%	S&P 500 Index 15.1%
6	Barclays Agg 16.0%	Barclays Agg 7.4%	Barclays Agg 9.8%	Russell 2000 Growth −2.4%	Russell 2000 Value 25.7%	Russell 2000 Growth 11.3%	Barclays Agg 9.7%	Russell 2000 −2.5%	S&P/Citi Value 4.7%	MSCI EAFE −14.2%	S&P 500 Index −11.9%	S&P 500 Index −22.1%	S&P 500 Index 28.7%	S&P 500 Index 10.9%	Russell 2000 Growth 4.2%	Russell 2000 Growth 13.3%	S&P/Citi Value 1.9%	Russell 2000 Value −38.9%	S&P/Citi Value 21.6%	S&P/Citi Growth 14.1%
7	MSCI EAFE 12.1%	S&P/Citi Growth 4.0%	Russell 2000 Growth −3.1%	Barclays Agg −2.9%	Barclays Agg 18.5%	MSCI EAFE 6.0%	MSCI EAFE 1.8%	Russell 2000 Value −6.5%	Barclays Agg −0.8%	S&P/Citi Growth −22.2%	S&P/Citi Growth −19.3%	S&P/Citi Growth −28.0%	S&P/Citi Growth 26.0%	S&P/Citi Growth 6.3%	Barclays Agg 2.4%	S&P/Citi Growth 11.0%	Russell 2000 −1.6%	S&P/Citi Value −38.9%	Russell 2000 Value 20.6%	MSCI EAFE 7.8%
8		MSCI EAFE −12.2%	S&P/Citi Growth 1.7%		MSCI EAFE 11.2%	Barclays Agg 3.6%			Russell 2000 Value −1.5%	Russell 2000 Growth −22.4%	MSCI EAFE −21.4%	Russell 2000 Growth −30.3%	Barclays Agg 4.1%	Barclays Agg 4.3%	S&P/Citi Growth 1.2%	Barclays Agg 4.3%	Russell 2000 Value −9.8%	MSCI EAFE −43.4%	Barclays Agg 5.9%	Barclays Agg 6.6%

Figure 2.5   No Style Is Best for All Time
Source: Thomson Reuters.[5]

heat chasing with a long period of miserable performance starting in 2000 (as I said, styles pretty much are never hot for 10 years).

If a pattern existed indicating when to change equity categories, how could all the smart people who've been investing through all these years have missed it?

Pretty easily.

Figure 2.6 is similar to Figure 2.4—demonstrating not the global yield curve but its spread between the short-term and long-term rates. But Figure 2.6 adds on top relative performance of value versus growth stocks. For example, in 1987—after the yield curve steepened significantly to nearly two and a half percentage points of spread—value stocks assumed leadership and outperformed growth for the rest of the decade by an impressive 28%. Then the yield curve flattened and inverted, and growth took over leadership until the yield curve steepened again. The pattern repeats itself—sometimes with longer periods of leadership and even more decisive outperformance—55% and 76%! Investors who fret over not fighting the Fed or worry about interest rates being too high or too low miss this remarkable pattern.

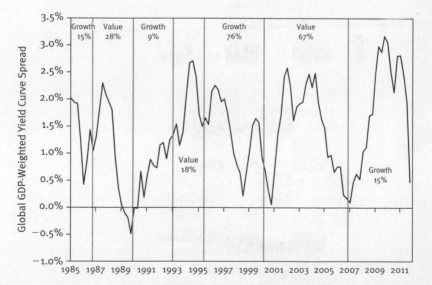

Figure 2.6   Global Growth and Value Performance Relative to Global Yield Curve Position
Sources: **Global Financial Data, Inc.; International Monetary Fund; Thomson Reuters, MSCI World Growth Index, MSCI World Value Index, all net returns.**

Figure 2.6 demonstrates that, generally, when the global yield curve is at its widest, that tends to be a period when value outperforms. Value tends to start outperforming *before* the peak is reached because stocks move first. (After all, the market is a discounter.) It's not perfect because no one thing is a silver bullet and capital markets are intensely complex. In fact, the pattern falls apart a bit in the period starting in 2007.

Based on the yield curve, you might expect value to outperform—the spread between short and long rates got very wide globally. However, this period included the 2008 credit crisis and bear market—which hit Financials stocks severely. Financials stocks tend to be value-oriented, so their big underperformance helped drag down value overall. Ignoring Financials' performance, during this period, value actually did outperform by 4.9%.[6] But if you could have predicted Financials' huge underperformance and the bear market, you likely wouldn't have needed the value-growth trade-off to do well during this period. Again, recall no one thing is a perfect predictor moving forward—even if it's worked well and consistently in the past.

However, the fundamentals behind when and why value wants to outperform relative to growth and vice versa haven't changed (more on that in a bit). So if you could know when the yield curve wanted to get very steep, that could be a good time to favor value stocks. And if you knew the yield curve wanted to flatten, that would be a strong reason to favor growth.

What's more, the difference in performance between the styles can be significant. Plus, the periods tend to last for awhile, so you needn't time this perfectly (which would be near impossible to do anyway.) But you need the global yield curve to see this right.

Unless you've been to a seminar given by me or my firm, you've probably never seen yield curve spread and performance of value and growth stocks overlaid this way. Nobody sees this pattern, and yet, the relationship is remarkable. And for good reason.

You see the connection between a yield curve spike and value outperforming, and a flattening or flat yield curve and growth taking over leadership most of the time—but so what? As said before, there are many existing patterns that don't necessarily mean anything. Before you go off half cocked and make serious portfolio changes based on a pattern, you must check your pattern for causality. Without a *causal* correlation, you have no basis for a bet. If something is causal—if something happens *because* of something else— then they're always correlated to some degree. But two correlated variables won't always be causal. When you took statistics in school, they told you high correlation doesn't necessarily mean causality, but causality does mean high correlation. The essence of a Question Two is looking first for high correlations and then seeing if you can justify causality tied to simple economics.

GROWTH AND VALUE—WHAT'S THE DIFFERENCE?

What's growth? What's value? How do you know?

First, neither growth nor value as a category is provably better or has much different risk characteristics over ultra-long periods. But they cycle in and out of favor.

Pretty much everyone agrees growth stocks have higher P/Es and value stocks lower. But higher or lower than what? Some professionals pick an arbitrary level and stick with it. In my view, it's better to be guided by your benchmark (the index you compare yourself to). Find the forward P/E of your benchmark. Stocks with a higher P/E than the benchmark will have more growth characteristics. Stocks with a lower P/E will have more value characteristics. Stocks close to the benchmark P/E are basically, for you, style neutral. Keep that in mind because your benchmark's average P/E will bounce around a bit. The more of a growth bias you want, the higher you need your portfolio's average P/E to be relative to your benchmark's P/E. Same for value but in reverse. And there may very well be times when you want to be essentially style neutral.

It's also important to remember some companies may temporarily have no earnings and no P/E. For these, you need some other metric like the price-to-book ratio or the price-to-sales ratio. You can use the same methodology with either of these ratios and find similar results.

Two events can show correlation by accident or coincidence (by definition, the same thing). This is the gambler's fallacy in reverse—every time you flip a coin, you have a 50/50 chance of getting heads, no matter if the previous 100 flips resulted in heads. Just because you have evidence of Y happening with some regularity after you observe Q a number of times, you can't bet it will happen again, no more than you have better odds the 101st flip is tails.

If Y follows Q often but you can't sort out good economics behind the correlation, go back to the drawing board. There might be something else happening when you observe Q that is really causing Y, and you must figure out what the mystery variable is (X, perhaps?) before you start placing bets. Or you might simply have found a statistical freak. Statistics can be freaky. If you have correlation without causality, you have nothing. Your discoveries must make basic, economic sense before they're useful.

What if you measure Q seeming to cause Y, and, what's more, it makes sense? But you observe Q leading to Y only 70% or 80% of the time. Should you abandon this tool? No way! In investing, 100% correlation never happens.

There are so many market pressures, so many moving maybes—if you wait for 100% correlation, you'll never make a market bet. If something is correlated 70% of the time, that's huge. You can worry about the other 30% later. Often in life, Y is caused 70% by Q and 30% by X or X+L and is simply multifactorial. Still, a 70% correlation with good causality is great. If you could bet steadily winning 70% of the time, you would blow away all professional investors in no time. All! If you can show Q causes Y with some regularity and it makes economic sense—when no one else has a clue what causes Y—you have found something big.

So, does the change in yield curve spread correlating to whether value or growth leads the market link to any basic economics? Absolutely! It stems from how corporations raise capital and how much incentive banks have to lend that capital.

Banking's core business is and has always been borrowing short-term money as the basis on which it makes long-term loans. In the industry vernacular, it's "borrowing short and lending long." The difference between the short rate and the long rates is effectively the bank's gross operating profit margin on the next loan it makes. The steeper the curve, the greater the profit banks can reap on lending. As the curve flattens, banks make less of a profit on the next loan. If the curve goes inverted, banks don't feel much incentive to lend at all, which is why an inverted curve can be so bearish. Recall, banks must seek riskier loans to make a profit in this environment, and banks don't like writing loans likely to default. The yield curve spread determines banking system propensity or eagerness to lend.

If you're a bank CEO faced with a steep yield curve and have any sense at all, you want to encourage your loan officers to lend. When the curve gets very steep, they get very eager. When it gets very flat, they get less eager. It isn't any more complicated than that in figuring out eagerness to lend.

Value companies raise capital, by and large, through the use of debt. They leverage themselves to acquire other companies, build a plant, expand their product line, increase their marketing reach or what-have-you. When the yield curve is steep and banks have an additional incentive to lend, they're more prone to lend to value companies (we see why in a moment), and value companies and their stockholders typically benefit.

On the flip side, growth companies raise capital, by and large, through the issuance of new stock. They can borrow money, too, and do, but they can also issue stock, and it's usually cheaper for them to do so (again, we see why soon). When the yield curve flattens, banks have less incentive to lend because their profit margin gets skinnier on the next loan—or disappears entirely—but investment bankers still have a terrific incentive to help growth companies issue new stock because initial public offerings (IPOs) and new stock issuances are supremely profitable for them. Consequently, in this environment, value companies typically begin to fall out of favor and growth takes over leadership. The growth companies now have ample opportunities to raise capital to fuel higher earnings just when the value companies can't raise capital as easily.

On the Flip Side, Let's Flip It

Again, when you can't fathom something, reframing or flipping it around so you see it differently often helps. Let's flip P/Es to see this right. You know growth stocks typically have higher P/Es than value stocks, by definition. And they tend to have loftier public images as great firms. Suppose some growth stock has a P/E of 50 and some value stock has a P/E of 5. You know the P/E of 50 is really $50 of price divided by $1 of earnings and the P/E of 5 is $5 of price divided by $1 of earnings. Now flip them into an E/P and you have the *earnings yield* (discussed in Chapter 1). The 50 flipped becomes 2%. If the company's accounting is accurate and its earnings are stable, that 2% is effectively its after-tax cost (remember, the P/E was after tax, so the E/P is, too) of raising expansion capital by selling stock—a low cost compared to borrowing long-term debt at corporate bond rates. The company with the P/E of 5 has an E/P of 20%—a very high after-tax cost of raising expansion capital compared to borrowing long-term debt through bonds.

Said again: The growth company will be prone, whenever it can, to raise expansion capital cheaply by selling stock. The value company won't; it will want to get expansion capital by borrowing money to the extent it can.

Let's flip and reframe again. Instead of being a corporate borrower or stock issuer, you are a bank loan officer. You've got four loan customers:

1. Microsoft, a famous big-cap growth company
2. Ford, a famous big-cap value company
3. Geewhizatronics, a not-famous small-cap growth company
4. Local County Cement, a not-famous small-cap value stock

These four are your only customers, and each has borrowed the same amount from you. Pretend these loans were issued so you could call them back in, forcing the borrower to pay them off whenever you want. One day, your bank president comes in and tells you it's no longer profitable for the bank to have so many loans. He tells you to pull in 25% of your loan base by cutting off one of your customers—your choice. Who do you cut off?

Well, you don't cut off Microsoft, generally regarded as one of the world's greatest companies. If you did, all the good old boys at the Loan Officers' Club would laugh at you. You don't much want to cut off Ford either. It isn't quite up to Microsoft's image for quality, but it's a pretty big name. Cut off Gee-whizatronics? Nah. It's small, but it's rumored to be growing fast. Maybe it will be the next Microsoft! If you cut it off, again, folks will laugh at you when (if?) Geewhiz actually whizzes.

The one you cut off is small-cap value Local County Cement. Doggy, stodgy, been-there-forever—but if construction dries up, its profits do, too. No seeming growth potential. This decision is easy. You keep Microsoft, Ford and Geewhizatronics and cut off Local County Cement. The good old boys won't laugh at you for that.

In effect, what have we done? We've deprived capital from the value side, primarily smaller value, though you were tempted to ding the big boy—Ford (and maybe you will next time)—but not growth. Local County Cement had been planning to expand but now must scrap those plans, and, hence, its stock tanks. Looking forward, it can be nothing but defensive and must live mainly from cash flow without access to any expansion capital other than what it produces through profits.

Meanwhile, growth stocks can get expansion capital by selling stock since they have high P/Es—low E/Ps. They keep growing and looking good to investors. In fact, the high P/E firm can grow right then and there, if it wants, by selling some cheap stock and launching the expansion into cement that Local County Cement previously intended, eating its lunch.

Flip It Again

Fast forward three years. You've been living happily with your three loan customers, but one day, your boss walks in and says the lending environment has become much more profitable, and he needs you to expand your loan portfolio. The yield curve is really steep, and the bank will make fat gross operating profit margins on the next loan you make. "So go out there and make a loan, Johnson," he orders you. "My name isn't Johnson," you mutter to yourself, but nonetheless, you call Microsoft. It doesn't want to borrow any more because it just floated some stock. Ford has already borrowed beyond what a drunken sailor on leave could consume and is figuratively lying unconscious on the factory floor. Geewhizatronics just laughs at you because it's planning an upcoming stock offering at 1,200 times future earnings and doesn't want to be seen talking to a banker for fear it could hurt its offering.

And suddenly you get this weird idea. There was that local cement company: Local County Cement. You call and offer to lend them money. The CEO falls out of his chair because no one has spoken to him in years. He calls downstairs to the CFO's basement office and says, "Ed! Remember those expansion plans we put on the back shelf a few years ago? Dust 'em off, and get 'em up here. There's some crazy banker wants to lend us money, and suddenly we can grow just like we're Geewhizatronics."

Actually, Local County Cement probably won't grow like Geewhizatronics might, but it can become more growth-like with financing than without it. Hence, the swing in the yield curve determines when the bank lends to Local County Cement and when it won't and when the stock will be priced more like a growth company or more like dead meat—or old, cold concrete.

This hypothetical anecdote shows the simple economics behind why shifts in the global yield curve, which reflect banking system propensity to lend, define when growth stocks and value stocks want to alternate in leading and lagging the market. Pretty simple.

Now you have a correlation pattern supported by economics—very fundamental. What's more, your fellow investors aren't thinking about how the yield curve impacts corporations in their quest for capital and how that, in turn, impacts market returns. They're probably not even thinking about the yield curve correctly to begin with.

The answer to this Question Two gives you a rational basis for a market bet—understanding when growth and value are likelier to cycle in and out of favor. Keep an eye on global rates—they're a powerful guide.

The Presidential Term Cycle

How changes in yield curve spread impact the growth versus value trade-off is easy to see with data and makes sense. No advanced degree in finance or statistics required—just publicly available data and an Excel spreadsheet, or even some graph paper. As we learned in Chapter 1, if you need fancy engineered equations, your hypothesis is probably wrong.

But what if you discover a pattern that is tough to prove with data though it makes tremendous sense? And what if the pattern is fairly predictable? Here's an example. Table 2.1 shows presidents going back to 1925 and the subsequent annual returns on the S&P 500 (which go back to 1926). By splitting the first two years of the presidential term from the last two years, you can see, for the most part, the last two years of the presidential cycle tend to be positive.

Take a pencil and draw a line through 1929 to 1932. You will remember these years as the beginning of the Great Depression, a period unlikely to be

Table 2.1   Presidential Term Anomaly

President	Party	First Year		Second Year		Third Year		Fourth Year	
Coolidge	R	1925	N/A	1926	11.7%	1927	37.7%	1928	43.8%
Hoover	R	1929	−8.5%	1930	−25.0%	1931	−43.5%	1932	−8.4%
FDR—1st	D	1933	54.4%	1934	−1.5%	1935	47.7%	1936	32.8%
FDR—2nd	D	1937	−35.3%	1938	33.2%	1939	−0.9%	1940	−10.1%
FDR—3rd	D	1941	−11.8%	1942	21.1%	1943	25.8%	1944	19.7%
FDR/Truman	D	1945	36.5%	1946	−8.2%	1947	5.2%	1948	5.1%
Truman	D	1949	18.1%	1950	30.6%	1951	24.6%	1952	18.5%
Ike—1st	R	1953	−1.1%	1954	52.4%	1955	31.5%	1956	6.6%
Ike—2nd	R	1957	−10.8%	1958	43.3%	1959	11.9%	1960	0.5%
Kennedy/Johnson	D	1961	26.8%	1962	−8.8%	1963	22.7%	1964	16.4%
Johnson	D	1965	12.4%	1966	−10.1%	1967	23.9%	1968	11.0%
Nixon	R	1969	−8.5%	1970	4.0%	1971	14.3%	1972	18.9%
Nixon/Ford	R	1973	−14.8%	1974	−26.5%	1975	37.3%	1976	23.7%
Carter	D	1977	−7.4%	1978	6.4%	1979	18.4%	1980	32.3%
Reagan—1st	R	1981	−5.1%	1982	21.5%	1983	22.5%	1984	6.2%
Reagan—2nd	R	1985	31.6%	1986	18.6%	1987	5.2%	1988	16.6%
Bush, GHW	R	1989	31.7%	1990	−3.1%	1991	30.5%	1992	7.6%
Clinton—1st	D	1993	10.1%	1994	1.3%	1995	37.6%	1996	23.0%
Clinton—2nd	D	1997	33.4%	1998	28.6%	1999	21.0%	2000	−9.1%
Bush, GW—1st	R	2001	−11.9%	2002	−22.1%	2003	28.7%	2004	10.9%
Bush, GW—2nd	R	2005	4.9%	2006	15.8%	2007	5.5%	2008	−37.0%
Obama—1st	D	2009	26.5%	2010	15.1%	2011	2.1%	2012	—
Average			8.1%		9.0%		18.6%		10.9%

Sources: Global Financial Data, Inc., S&P 500 Total Return Index from 12/31/1925 to 12/31/2011.

repeated anytime soon due to extensive banking and market reform and much knowledge we didn't have back then about how economies and central banking work. Otherwise, you get only four other negative years in the back halves of presidents' terms. Negative a scant 0.4%, 1939 wasn't such a bad year. Even 1940 was negative just 10.1%—down but not down huge. Plus, those years being negative ought not shock you since the market was discounting the beginning of World War II.

The year 2000 was pretty odd as well—after the terrific bull run of the 1990s, we experienced the Tech bubble bursting—plus, late in the year, there was a near-constitutional crisis surrounding the presidential election.

Interestingly, a lot of people remember 2000 as the "first time" we had a president elected who didn't win the popular vote. Except we often have a president elected without a majority of the popular vote. And Al Gore, despite media commentary to the contrary, didn't win a majority of the popular vote in 2000—he carried 48%.[7] Bill Clinton never did because of minority candidates like Ross Perot and later Ralph Nader.[8] Abraham Lincoln didn't win a majority of the 1860 popular vote—he only got 39.8%.[9] But he did in 1864 with 55%.[10] What people mean is Al Gore got more votes than George Bush. Neither won a majority of the popular vote in 2000, and they are in good company with John Kennedy in 1960 and Richard Nixon in 1968.[11]

Gore did win the most popular votes but didn't win the Electoral College—which is the end game. That launched us into uncharted territory to determine the election's outcome as Gore challenged the Florida vote in court for its precious electoral votes. The challenge created uncertainty and increased the weirdness of year-end 2000. Markets hate uncertainty. To show you the effect of that, on September 1, 2000, the S&P 500 was up 4.3% for the year.[12] The negative year was likely heavily influenced by election uncertainty in the last quarter.

And then there was the 2008 credit crunch—exacerbated (or perhaps caused) by a hugely problematic and thankfully now-repealed accounting rule (FAS 157—"fair value" accounting) and the government's haphazard response through that year. What we can say is, barring events of epic proportions, the back halves of presidential terms are historically periods when the stock market hasn't wanted to have negative returns. It's also obvious, as you look at these data, that the third year of a president's term has been the best—most uniformly positive with the highest average returns.

Knowing this can alleviate some anxiety as you attempt to forecast. You should be otherwise slightly biased toward bullish in the last two years in an election cycle. By contrast, market risk tends to concentrate in the first two years of a president's term, where yet another pattern emerges. When you do get a negative year in the first half, you usually (although not always) tend to get only one. If the first year is negative, the second year is usually not, and vice versa. While you do occasionally get two positive years in the first half, two negatives in a row are rare. Again, ignore 1929 and 1930 as Great Depression years and therefore an anomaly. You also get a second negative year during Nixon's truncated second term, but that was a pretty darned weird time, too.

THE GREAT DEPRESSION

It's important to note our Great Depression was part of a global great depression, and most historians miss that point endlessly. What you normally hear is the Great Depression was punishment rained on the United States for the Fed's banking missteps, individual and corporate greedy excesses and Hoover's commitment to a laissez-faire government. While a great many mistakes were made in America, economic historians tend to paint our Great Depression as if it weren't part of a bigger, and therefore largely unavoidable, global phenomenon.

For a whole series of discussions on the Great Depression as global phenomenon, see my second book, *The Wall Street Waltz*.

You might find this bit of forecasting technology an assault on your intelligence. "Why, it's patently absurd and overtly simplistic," you might say. It is simple, and that's why it's so great. This pattern isn't hidden away, cloaked in mystery. It's right out there, in the open, plain and easy to see. You've probably already heard of the presidential term cycle—it is a term that is well known and typically censured as voodoo (although no one uses it like I'm prescribing, in my view). If everyone thought it a nifty tool, it would have become priced into the market and lost all its power. As long as folks continue to sneer at it, you know you have an edge.

Nobody Can Predict What a Genuine Phony Will Do

Strong trends not commonly observed or accepted are powerful. Even so, this one is a little hard to prove with raw data statistically—calendar years don't work that way. But it makes tremendous economic sense. The market dislikes nothing so much as uncertainty; and a new president, even a newly reelected president, presents the market with tremendous uncertainty. Among poli-tics, the president is the Big Tic—the one who ultimately knows how to tic off the fewest people while getting elected and tic off the most afterward. If a poli-tic is a phony, one capable of winning a presidential election is a genuine and most capable phony. Nobody can predict what a genuine phony will do next.

George W. Bush thoughtfully violated a basic rule in 2002 all presidents have known—their party almost always loses some relative power to the opposition party in Congress during the midterm elections. Bush was the first Republican president in more than 100 years to have his party gain seats in the midterms. And since a president knows his party is likely to lose relative power to the opposition in the midterms, the most onerous legislation he would hope to pass—the hardest to get through Congress, the landmark of his presidency—he must try to get passed in the *first* two years. If he can't get it legislated then, he certainly wouldn't be able to do so in the back half of his term.

The biggest and ugliest attempts at redistribution of wealth, property rights and regulatory status (which is also property rights) almost always have occurred in the first half of presidents' terms.

Fundamental to capitalism itself and capital markets stability is faith in the stability of property rights. We often take property rights for granted because America has the best, most perfected and most stable system of property rights in the world's history. It is a key part, going back to George Mason's fundamental force on the founding fathers, leading to America being so great a nation. Anything threatening the sanctity of property rights raises risk aversion and scares the heck out of capital markets.

In the first year of his term, a president is in his honeymoon, eager to spend the political capital he earned during the campaign. Rosy-cheeked, with a sparkle in his eye and his shiny family at his side, the new guy usually shoots out the gate trying to get his toughest stuff passed—this being the infamous first 100 days of a president's term when he lays out his agenda. The threat of those shifts in property rights or wealth redistribution historically have led to higher risk aversion and the first halves of presidents' terms being perfect loam for bear markets to propagate in. Hence, the first half of a president's term is generally marked with a busy legislative calendar and a disproportionate number of our bear markets. This doesn't mean the president's proposed legislation succeeds, mind you, but that he makes a go of it. And there is the risk he gets his agenda passed, and markets don't like that risk.

Remember after Bill Clinton's 1992 election, he raised taxes in 1993, though he had promised in his campaign to cut taxes—and then in 1994, he threatened to nationalize health care (a shift in property rights). All typical first-half politico-tomfoolery of a genuine phony. With President Obama, the big agenda items happened in the front half. The back half, as I write, has been relatively very quiet. This is typical. Other times, as with President G.W. Bush, there was never a material legislative agenda proposed at all—not for either term. When there is, it's the grist of a disproportionate amount of our bear markets.

Any new proposed legislation implies potential change and a reapportionment of your money and property rights. No matter what the government decides to do, no matter how wonderful the new programs may sound, no matter how incontrovertible the benefit is—new legislation means money and rights get shifted around. Low-cost prescriptions for the poor and elderly! Who could see that as bad? Stiffer penalties for society's worst offenders— pedophiles, rapists and puppy stranglers? Sign me up! Free ponies for all children? You'd have to be a monster to oppose that! Whatever it is, Uncle Sam takes money or rights from one group, fusses around with them and passes whatever is left to yet another group.

We already know we hate losses more than we like gains. The group on the losing end of the transfer hates losing much more than those on the winning end of the transfer like winning. Those not party to the transfer watch it transpire and think they've just seen a mugging. Markets view redistribution of wealth or property rights like witnessing a mugging. It causes fear beyond the size of the action itself because it makes all witnesses realize they could be mugged next. Consequently, the market can be weak somewhere in the first two years because the market doesn't like politically forced change.

By the third and fourth years, we know our president. He may be a politic, and we may dislike him, but he is our time-proven bloodsucker. There's not much left to surprise—we think we know what he's up to, what his agenda is and how capable he is of getting anything done (or not, and sometimes *not* is a pretty good thing in a world that doesn't like forced political change). Moreover, presidents tend to avoid any potentially controversial legislation in the back half of their terms because either they are trying to get reelected themselves or they're just tired and hanging on, which is often true in a president's seventh and eighth years.

A particularly good poli-tic will hang back in his third year, get little done and at election time blame his administration's ineffectiveness on poli-tics from the opposing party. "I could have gotten you the free ponies I promised," he might intone, "had it not been for those uncooperative senators from that other damned party who opposed me! So get rid of those losers, vote for these other guys who support me and next time, I'll get you your free ponies." Quiet legislative years lead to happier markets. (They almost never lead to free ponies.)

We're not done with presidential terms yet. Ask yourself: What else is going on no one notices or lends any credence? We know the first two years are where most of the market risk will likely be. Is there anything particularly remarkable about the first half of a *second* term for a reelected president? Ignoring all the first and the single presidential terms, see what patterns you can find in Table 2.2.

Again, you tend not to get two negatives in a row, except for that screwy Nixon. But when you don't get a negative year, you tend to get a big positive year. Positive years in the first two years of a reelected president's term have

Table 2.2 Incumbents Uninhibited

Won Re-Election

2nd Term Election Year	President	Party	1st Year of Second Term S&P 500		2nd Year of Second Term S&P 500	
1904	Roosevelt, T.	R	1905	19.7%	1906	6.8%
1916	Wilson	D	1917	−25.2%	1918	25.6%
1924	Coolidge	R	1925	29.5%	1926	11.7%
1936	Roosevelt, F.	D	1937	−35.3%	1938	33.2%
1948	Truman	D	1949	18.1%	1950	30.6%
1956	Eisenhower	R	1957	−10.8%	1958	43.3%
1964	Johnson	D	1965	12.4%	1966	−10.1%
1972	Nixon/Ford	R	1973	−14.8%	1974	−26.5%
1984	Reagan	R	1985	31.6%	1986	18.6%
1996	Clinton	D	1997	33.4%	1998	28.6%
2004	Bush, GW	R	2005	4.9%	2006	15.8%

Source: Global Financial Data, Inc., S&P 500 total return.

averaged 21% and 24% respectively[13]—big booming, positive years. These years typically are either negative or up big—extreme one way or the other—sort of barbell-like returns. Being on the right side of the market is more important and most keen in its impact during these years. This is a good example of looking beyond averages into what makes up the averages. The historic averages of first and second years of presidents' terms are below average. But within those averages, you get a very wide spread between nasty years and pretty great years. Averages can be very deceiving. (Technically, Teddy Roosevelt wasn't really reelected in 1904 since he wasn't elected in the first place—same for Truman in 1948 and Johnson in 1964. But I'm not really sure that matters to the phenomenon—all were the second terms of poli-tics we already knew.)

Should you abandon all other forecasting efforts and let your political calendar be your one determining factor in your allocation of stocks, bonds and cash? No! Beyond super silly! While the presidential term cycle is a trend and makes absolute socioeconomic sense, keep in mind there are many other market forces at work, including all the ones outside of America. For example, the US markets correlate to foreign markets in our increasingly globalized economy. Foreign forces can and will impact America. Never assume you've found the one silver bullet.

To summarize, market risk trends higher in the first half of presidents' terms. The back half tends to be positive with the third year most positive. In the front half when it isn't negative, it tends to be up big and particularly so in second terms (though that didn't happen in 2005 and 2006, it certainly did in 2009 and 2010). What's more, the tendency for non-negative years to be up big makes sense. Apprehension about political risk fading away can lead to elation, causing big positive years.

Interestingly, as 2010 ended, a lot of folks started mentioning that 2011 being Obama's "third year" would be a bullish force. Which made me skeptical—suddenly a wave of folks believing in this technology could sap it of power. That (among other reasons) led me to forecast 2011 markets would be volatile but end overall flattish. In my January 26, 2011, *Forbes* column I said:

> My research now shows there are too many optimists out there. That's bearish! But wait, the research indicates that there are also too many pessimists lingering about—many longtime, heels-dug-in doomers—as well as newly converted acrophobics. They are fearful mostly because of the last two years' heady rise. That's bullish. It's a standoff between gloomers and bulls—a barbelled sentiment bifurcation. I've regularly referred to the market as "The Great Humiliator," a nearly all-powerful spiritual entity existing solely to humiliate as many people as possible for as many dollars as possible for as long as possible. It's after you and me and your aged aunt. It now accomplishes its goal best by

frustrating bulls and bears alike in a year where the stock market ends up or down just by a hair.

And that's just what happened. US and world stocks ended exceedingly flat for the full year, with lots of volatility along the way. My guess is 2011 being flat sapped belief in this pattern, which actually makes it powerful again. Not a silver bullet—nothing is. But a useful tool once again.

Something like this is a simple example of fathoming something others can't or won't fathom. But if for whatever reason others start widely fathoming it, it won't work as well because it will be discounted into pricing. (For still more ways to use the presidential term anomaly, see my 2010 book, *Debunkery*, and my 2011 book, *Markets Never Forget*.)

Test and Test Again

You may be surprised I'm sharing with you, in this chapter and others, any of what I've come to believe I know that others don't. Why give it away if I think I know something giving me an edge? Now, lots of people will know what I know, meaning it will soon be priced into markets and therefore not work anymore, right?

Maybe, maybe not. I've been talking and writing about presidential term cycles for a long time, and every time I do, someone looks for a giant butterfly net to haul me away. Just like my views on high P/Es. People think I'm a kook for believing this works, which is how I know this little bit of technology still is powerful. The same is true for most other examples I share in this book. Once I've found something that works, I continually test it to make sure it hasn't become priced. Once I believe I've fathomed something new, I look to see if others can or will fathom it. One way I test it is by giving it away. The more people think it's nuts, the more they don't fathom what I find fathomable and the more I know it likely still works. If they start embracing it, thinking it's good and not nuts, then it's less powerful. Maybe becomes obsolete. When an unfathomable becomes widely fathomable, it's time to abandon it and fathom new unfathomable truths.

The goal with Question Two is to know something now that might be common knowledge in 3 or 30 years. Once everyone knows your new piece of reality, it will no longer be useful to you. So test it. Ask your friends and colleagues if they were aware shifts in the yield curve signal a change in style leadership. Ask if there is any truth to the presidential term cycle. As long as the response is a blank look, a "What?" or "That's crazy!" or an even better "You're crazy!" you still have a basis for a bet.

I give away some—not all—of the findings I've had over the years so I know what I can safely continue using and what has outlived its usefulness. Far too many of my peers stick to repeating what they learned at the knee of their mentors and wonder why they can't beat the market. Winning at investing requires constant innovation and constant testing.

Now you can use Question One to free yourself from blindness and Question Two to fathom the unfathomable. However, none of this will keep you from persisting in your old investing errors if you can't control your brain. Investing is inherently counterintuitive. You can remind yourself of that all you like, but your cranial command center rebels. In a fight between you and your brain, your unruly brain will win—unless you learn how to ask Question Three. Next chapter!

3 QUESTION THREE: WHAT THE HECK IS MY BRAIN DOING TO BLINDSIDE ME NOW?

It's Not Your Fault—Blame Evolution

One of the first things we learn about finance is: "Buy low, sell high." In the movie *Trading Places,* when Eddie Murphy and Dan Aykroyd prepare to corner the orange juice market (illegally and implausibly but comically), you can tell the scriptwriter was casting about for something finance-sounding to say. So Dan tells Eddie, "Buy low, sell high." What more advice do you need, really?

We all know the goal, but more often than not, we end up doing the opposite. How hard can this be? Buy when stuff is priced low; sell when it's priced high. It's not rocket science. And yet this problem is ageless and endless. Investors routinely buy and sell precisely backward. For evidence, look at Figure 3.1 showing fund flows—the amount of money going into and out of equity mutual funds each month—in the period just before and after the 2000 Tech peak.

Inflows for stock mutual funds were highest during February 2000[1]—a good time to get out of stocks—at the peak of an ensuing three-year bear market. Fast forward to 2002, and the reverse is true. Huge numbers of folks bailed from funds in July[2]—a fantastic time for stocks—just before a new bull market. Here is evidence of investors buying high and selling low en masse. These weren't a few deranged outliers; this shows widespread groupthink—a frenzied mob lumbering in and out of the market precisely backward.

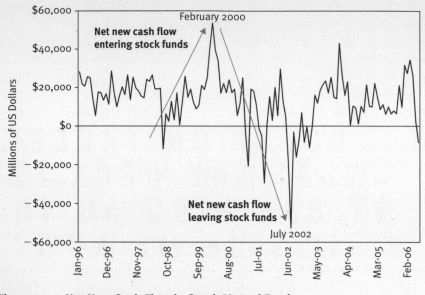

Figure 3.1   Net New Cash Flow in Stock Mutual Funds
Source: **Investment Company Institute.**

No one intends to buy high and sell low. That would be stupid. So why do so many of us end up doing the stupid? There are many convenient scapegoats. Following the 2000 to 2002 bear, folks blamed crooked CEOs and accounting fraud—like Enron, MCI and the rest. After the 2007 to 2009 bear market, it was greedy bankers, too much debt, Freddie Mac and Fannie Mae. Or it's rotten politicians. Or some social cause you hate. Or or or. There's always a convenient scapegoat.

Stop pointing your finger at everyone else. If you want to know what causes your investments to fare worse than you'd like, look in the mirror. Better yet, get a CT scan done. Your biggest investing enemy is your brain. Even more precisely, your biggest enemy is the cerebral evolution that formed your brain to be largely focused on keeping you alive in the face of starvation, treachery and woolly, fanged beasts.

To survive as a species, our brains evolved with specific goals in mind—primarily, bodily survival in a primitive world. The easy ability to buy good food at the local supermarket or bistro and live relatively free from fear of instant death or dismemberment at the claws of predatory beasts is relatively new to human development—an advancement still in its infancy. Humans spent most of their evolution as hunter-gatherers, traveling in nomadic bands, hunting wild animals, foraging for often spoiled foods, finding mates to perpetuate the species (which is a lot more enticing than investing in stocks), avoiding predators and seeking shelter. These are the tasks our brains evolved for—to keep us fed, warm, dry and safe from wild beasts.

Think of our Stone Age ancestors and how their survival struggle impacts how we behave now. Our ancestors' friends were their tribesmen (and women)—people they could trust. Their enemies were other tribes, rampaging beasts and the dark things they couldn't understand. So they banded together for protection and lit fires to keep the dark (and the dark things) away. Recall our example of the noise outside the campfire—the same cognitive processes kept our ancestors alive and served them well for tens of thousands of years. It's only been a short time since they've caused us to make errors and then only in limited realms, largely offset by other, more common life realms where they don't hurt us to this day.

Even with technology and the complexity of modern society, most of this preordained wiring remains intact. Prewiring as a concept is somewhat controversial among psychologists. Evolutionary psychology is sometimes equated with pop-culture thinking by critics. I'll not attempt to retread the literature on evolutionary psychology here. For an introduction to this area, try *How the Mind Works* by Steven Pinker of Harvard (Norton, 1997). It covers a lot of turf fast. But I'm firmly convinced most of our shortcomings in seeing markets correctly stem from cranial hardwiring derived from many eons of evolution and are so fixed in our brains we can't escape them. Because we can't find people from 25,000 years ago to scrutinize now, we can never prove or disprove much of this. But based on studying what has and hasn't been proved and what is reasonable to me, I believe if you simply restrict your thinking about psychology to how we think about markets, you will see evolutionary psychology and hardwiring are very basic.

Our brains are so structured that when information comes in a form our brains are hardwired to receive well, we process it correctly, easily and quickly. When information comes to our brains in a form or framework our brain isn't hardwired to process well, we are often simply blind to it. And that's because our brains are hardwired by evolution to take certain types of inputs down defined paths and not elsewhere. You have already seen some of that with the P/E and E/P trade-off. But you see it throughout this book, recurring in phenomenon after phenomenon. While behavioral finance is not based on evolutionary psychology, many discoveries paralleling evolutionary psychology have been uncovered in the past 35 years in behavioral finance.

Behavioral Finance

Behavioral finance is still a relatively new field of study intersecting the fields of finance and human behavioral psychology. Advocates strive to expand our existing knowledge of how markets work but, more important, how our minds work in relation to risk and markets. Until recently, the study of finance focused primarily on tools of investing, including statistics, history, theory and market mechanics. Does category X typically generate higher or lower returns than category Y? How should a portfolio theoretically be constructed? What is the right way to think of diversification? How do indexes like this compare to indexes like that? What is the best measure of volatility? For mean variance optimization schemes, should we use variance or covariance? All fine, but basically all issues of mechanics, history, statistics and theory in one form or another.

Scholarly finance textbooks written in the 1990s don't differ much from those written in the 1970s. They address new technology, regulations and products, sure, but they're mainly about the tools of investing. Traditional finance notions derive from traditional notions of economics—that humans in aggregate act rationally, markets are efficient or at least semi-efficient and individuals acting irrationally can be ignored. The nut job in the straitjacket has been identified and locked away and doesn't impact markets—in the traditional view.

By contrast, behavioral finance assumes quirky behavior—or the person standard finance might view as a nut job—is pretty common. Irrationality is assumed to be potential behavior. Investors are presumed to behave in ways that sometimes seem irrational. Behavorialists try to discover the "why."

I think this is always easiest seen when you accept evolutionary notions that we're still influenced by our Stone Age ancestors. It's true—our modern skulls contain Stone Age brains. Investors aren't rational automatons; they are humans and regularly behave in crazy ways when making financial decisions. And that is because our brains weren't set up to do this stuff. Our brains were set up to do survival stuff from a long time ago.

If we can understand why people behave as they do, we can better understand how markets work and bet better based on what we know about human behavior. If you can understand your brain better, you can understand how to better control yourself so you can begin avoiding many of the typical mistakes investors make and begin lowering your error rate. For this, you need Question Three. Before you take any market action, stop and ask: What the heck is my brain doing to mess me up? To make me blind now? To make me see and feel the situation exactly wrong and backward? After all, the market is nothing more than millions of people behaving like, well, cavemen. If you can unravel this code and understand your own decision-making process better, you can conquer your caveman brain and get humiliated less by TGH—that is the goal.

It's not your fault your brain suffers cavemanisms. Our minds are conditioned to biases making us do dumb things that seem really smart at the time. Questions One and Two are intended to give you a framework for finding gameable bets. But those two questions are nothing if your brain runs ruinous. Hence, you need Question Three.

At one level, you're very, very smart. Your brain is an amazing pattern recognizer if information is fed to it even partly correctly. If information is fed to it incorrectly, you can't see a pattern at all. Most readers will have received some version of this goofy email:

> fi yuo cna raed tihs, yuo hvae a sgtrane mnid too. Cna yuo raed tihs?
> i cdnuolt blveiee taht I cluod aulaclty uesdnatnrd waht I was rdanieg. The phaonmneal pweor of the hmuan mnid! It dseno't mtaetr in waht oerdr the ltteres in a wrod are, the olny iproamtnt tihng is talht the frsit and lsat ltteer be in the rghit pclae. The rset can be a taotl mses and you can sitll raed it whotuit a pboerlm. Azanmig huh? yaeh and I awlyas tghuhot slpeling was ipmorantt!

And most readers can probably read it. It's a perfect "eaxpmle" of your brain being able to receive information well if delivered well. In this case, you don't even need it to be all that well delivered to be able to get it pretty easily. But often, if correct information is delivered exactly wrong, you can't see it at all.

Our earlier P/E examples are perfect in this regard. Maybe you've struggled with P/Es forever without them making much sense to you. But by turning the P/E into an E/P like an interest rate—your after-tax return on owning the whole business—it makes sense. A P/E of 8 is a 12.5% return, which beats the heck out of a 6% pre-tax bond. Your brain gets that easily. The issue is knowing when your brain sees well and when it's actually hurting your ability to see reality.

The Great Humiliator

It all goes back to TGH.

TGH has endless ways to humiliate us. Bull market tops are typically marked by intense and comforting euphoria. Investors are never so enthusiastic about stocks as when pretty much every single person who might ever buy a stock has already done so and there is basically no place left for stocks to go but down. Even worse, market tops usually roll and churn. They don't announce themselves with a sudden drop, like a correction. Everyone looks for some announcement-like effect showing a bull market is over, but that almost never happens. There is an age-old but almost universally true statement nearly no one can accept: "Bull markets die with a whimper, not with a bang." There isn't a dramatic spike top to bull markets if the historic measure is calculated correctly. Bear market bottoms are different only in form. TGH just confuses us differently. Bottoms are often violent and sharp, freaking everyone out so enough folks finally dump their stocks. Just when folks who first got into stocks at the peak abandon them from fatigue, stocks take off sharply, leaving the messes and the masses in the dust. "It's just a bear market correction," pundits will say. (I show in my 2011 book, *Markets Never Forget*, that the media routinely disbelieves a new bull market—sometimes for years.) There is always a small universe of pundits that's bearish at the top (and probably consistently for the three previous years) and receives accolades for it and then remains bearish at the bottom. No one notices that for years as people keep listening to them, fighting the last war. The potential for TGH to suck you in, chew you up and spit you out is nearly infinite.

Don't think TGH rests on its laurels in between peaks and troughs. During the normal course of a bull or bear market, the market can correct multiple times—that is, go briefly opposite to its longer-term trend by 10% to 20% or more. During the 1998 correction (mentioned in Chapter 2), the US market spiked downward nearly 20% over only six weeks from July 17 to August 31.[3] That can terrify. And though corrections that size are fairly normal in bull markets, few remember or recognize one when next it happens. Corrections have investors dumping stocks just in time for the market to recover and move to higher prices. Like in 1998! The market's year-to-date return was only at break-even late in the fall.[4] Yet by year-end, it was up 28.6%.[5] The correction disappeared as fast as it came. TGH is fast.

The market needn't move nearly enough to qualify as a true correction to have seemingly rational, intelligent human beings utterly terrified. Even professional investors, trained over time to turn a tough shoulder toward normal market volatility, will still regularly ask if a drop of a few percentage points over a few weeks augurs a bear market, recession, the Apocalypse or even Paris Hilton being nominated to the Federal Reserve Board of Governors. No, a drop of a few percentage points is what TGH calls Tuesday.

Cracking the Stone Age Code—Pride and Regret

Admitting you have a problem is the first step to recovery. But you won't know you have a problem unless you ask Question Three: What the heck is my brain doing to blindside me now? You can and will get multiple answers when you ask how your brain affects you. Some fall in the realm of your spouse, mother or psychologist. The only ones concerning us here involve market behavior. Most investing errors result from cognitive errors, the most common of which we cover here.

Look! Me Kill Huge Beast! Me Very Skilled!

As mentioned in Chapter 1, behavioralists have shown normal Americans (we'll assume you're normal) hate losses about two and a half times as much as they like gains.[6] A 25% gain feels about as good as a 10% loss feels bad. Said otherwise, if you gain 10% over here and lose 10% over there, you feel like you're behind. Therefore, people typically exert more effort to avoid pain than achieve gain. This is commonly known as loss aversion, sometimes referred to as *myopic loss aversion,* intimating shortsightedness and an overactive reaction to short-term movements. It explains many investing errors. At root, myopic loss aversion and the mistakes it leads to are about two things—*pride* and *regret.*

Our Stone Age information processors learned to do what is called "accumulating pride" and "shunning regret" as matters of survival. Imagine two hunters returning to camp at dusk. One carries a gazelle. The other has nothing but some broken spears that missed their marks.

The hunter with the gazelle thrills the camp with his entrance. That night he tells the tribe the story about how he skillfully and masterfully hunted and brought down the mighty beast. He talks about his deftness in forming the spear and how his spears are particularly deadly. He talks about the signs he interpreted leading him to the grazing gazelles. He details his physical prowess in accurately launching his spear into the gazelle with deadly finality. He accumulates *pride.* It feels good and motivates him to eagerly go out to hunt again and again so he can continue to experience that prideful high. And that is good for the tribe because it needs this young man to kill high-powered, animal-based protein that went a long way in those days toward separating those whose genes were passed on from those whose genes weren't.

The other young hunter, the one with no gazelle, has a different story to tell. It wasn't his fault he didn't bag a gazelle. He has skill in spear-making and experience in tracking beasts, too. But on this particular day, a bolt of lightning scattered the gazelles moments before he could aim. Or maybe someone borrowed his spears so they weren't sharp enough. Or maybe there were lions roaming in his hunting ground. Or the wind was wrong. He fabricates seemingly plausible excuses so he can rise the next morning and try again. He *shuns regret.* In so doing, his campmates let him hunt the next day as well; their belief in his story motivates him to try, try again. His tribe needs him to hunt, too. Maybe he really was just unlucky that day. Even if he is a terrible hunter, he may stumble across an injured animal. Maybe tomorrow he will come across a gazelle just after it has been killed by a wild dog. Either way, it's worth it if protein accumulation is possible.

Accumulating pride when successful and shunning regret when failing motivate both hunters to keep trying. Both of these tendencies are good for the tribe. Their tribe's very survival depends on their willingness to make repeated forays. The successful hunter hunts again and again. The unsuccessful hunter hunts again too.

Many sources say investors are motivated by greed and fear. Behavioralists would disagree and suggest investors, and through them markets, aren't driven by greed and fear, but by humanity's drive to accumulate pride and shun regret. It just comes out as greed and fear.

Pride is a mental process associating success with skill and repeatability—the hunter who bagged a gazelle believed he wasn't lucky. He believed himself masterful. More important, he believed he could repeat it. By writing this book, I too am displaying pride accumulated over a career span where I don't want to believe it was all just luck—that I was the guy flipping way too many heads for way too long. Who wants to believe that? The natural tendency of humans is to want to think success was because of skill and repeatability, not luck.

Think about your own behavior after buying a stock that went up. Maybe it went up a lot. Did you pump your fist in the air? Did you congratulate yourself? Did you brag about it to your colleagues, spouse and father-in-law? More important, did your success make you feel like you could do it again? "I bought it. It went up. I'm smart. Want to see me do it again?" Just like the hunter.

Regret is a process of denying responsibility for failure—attributing it not to lack of skill but usually to bad luck or victimization. The gazelle-less hunter isn't a bad hunter. He is just the hapless victim of poor circumstances. He'll kill a gazelle next time. "I bought it. It went down. The broker sold it to me. He's the problem." Or, "I bought it. It went down. The CEO was a crook." There are many ways to do bad luck and victimization. "I wouldn't have bought it if my wife hadn't been ragging on me that morning." The mindset isn't, "I bought it, it went down, I don't know how to do this so I better not do it again." Or, "I better work on this so I can get better."

If the hunters didn't accumulate pride and shun regret, they would have become despondent over failure. They would have given up hunting giant beasts as a fool's errand. Their brains had to function this way to forage enough food to pass on their genes. It was a motivational tool. If a hunter became beset by regret and ultimately depressed, those benefiting from his future potentially lucky hunting would have starved and died, and that isn't such a good way to perpetuate the species. Accumulating pride and shunning regret were basic to our ancestors' survival. They were necessary then, and we still do it—motivating ourselves to keep trying.

But in modern times, these behaviors cause investing mistakes. Suppose Bill owns a stock that rises 40%. Bill was smart to have chosen such a stock. He is a savvy stock picker, and he believes he can do it again—he accumulates pride.

Then his stock drops 10%. He feels the loss about two and a half times as much as the gain and disregards the fact that overall he is still up 26%. The sudden drop causes pain he wants to avoid, so he shuns regret. He believes he was just unlucky on this 10% drop because previous pride accumulation convinces him he can and will succeed overall. He considers selling while he can. He concludes the stock will fall further and loses sight of his long-term goals, focusing only on the short term, and acts to minimize potential short-term pain. He sells the stock and protects his ego for another day of hunting. But the stock bounces back and goes to new highs. He chooses to ignore that because acknowledging it would cause too much pain and ignoring it shuns regret nicely.

Regret causes Bill to avoid pain by taking action—selling at a temporary relative low point. Pride prevents him from analyzing his behavior accurately, so he is doomed to repeat this vicious cycle. Loss aversion causes investors to buy high and sell low—not a great strategy.

Throwing Spears—Overconfidence

Another Stone Age behavior leading to investing errors is *overconfidence*. One behavioral lesson learned in recent decades is the average investor is markedly overconfident. He believes he has greater skill than he really possesses. This is parallel to the notion that 75% of drivers believe they're above-average drivers. Overconfidence stems directly from accumulating pride and shunning regret over time. If Stone Age hunters weren't nearly crazed with overconfidence, they would never attempt felling massive beasts with sticks tipped with a stone. They needed to fell those beasts or they would starve. (Or be vegetarians—which was effectively the same thing.)

For ancient hunter-gatherers, life was short and food was scarce. Consider recent findings regarding Kennewick man—who lived roughly 9,000 years ago in what is now Washington state. Scientists discovered a spear head embedded in his hip. It wasn't a death blow; this was a healed wound. He also apparently had multiple healed broken bones and other wounds.[7] Life was tough for Kennewick man and his cohorts in 7000 BC. But it paid to take big risks—one big kill could mean a month's protein for the tribe. Our ingrained survival instincts urge us to take risks—we frequently choose "fight" over "flight" when facing insurmountable odds.

Investors by definition are overconfident when assuming they know more than they do—or when overestimating their skill level. Reading *The Wall Street Journal* and a handful of blogs and newsletters every day doesn't make anyone an investing expert. Yet scores of otherwise intelligent people feel their ability to subscribe to and absorb common media makes them sufficient to bet and win. Investing is tough. An overabundance of highly educated and experienced professionals invest as stupidly as rank amateurs. That doesn't make getting in over your head any less dangerous.

Don't mistake me. I'm not advocating you either dedicate your life to scholarly pursuit of investment knowledge or you hire a worthy professional. Quite the opposite! (Remember, all you need to succeed in investing is knowing something others don't, and for that you need only the Three Questions.) Rather, you should beware overconfidence because it leads to very serious errors—the same errors everyone else makes.

For example, overconfidence leads investors to invest in an *initial public offering* (IPO; for the neophyte, IPO alternately means "it's probably overpriced") of stock, micro-caps, hedge funds and other volatile or illiquid interests while ignoring or downplaying the associated risk. Think about how often you've heard pundits, friends or your broker describe an opportunity as the "next Microsoft." Maybe it is! But the odds are stacked against you—precious few new businesses survive, much less blossom into hot stocks.

Overconfidence may lead you to hang onto a stock, hoping it will someday bounce back, even when mountains of evidence contradict it. If you plowed your entire net worth into Level 3 at $130, and you insisted to your wife when it fell to a buck and a half that it was a great firm and would bounce back one day, you were shunning regret and displaying overconfidence.

Behavioralists note one common investor tendency is holding onto a stock hoping it gets back to "break-even"—refusing to sell until then. By refusing to sell until then, the break-even investor mentally refuses to acknowledge the loss and therefore postpones having to absorb full regret. It's human nature to think you haven't made a mistake and refuse to cut losses. No doubt, selling a stock just because its price drops is a loser's strategy. But sometimes you must admit you've erred and your money is better placed elsewhere.

Figure 3.2 shows the lagging performance of some very fine companies in the Energy sector following the Energy-led bear market of 1980. It took years, more than a decade in some cases, for prices to breakeven. The opportunity cost of hanging onto those stocks after 1980 was great. As shown in Figure 3.3, the S&P 500 greatly outpaced the beleaguered Energy companies over the subsequent 5 and, in most cases, 10 years. Try doing this with some big Tech names after the Tech bubble, and you see the same phenomenon.

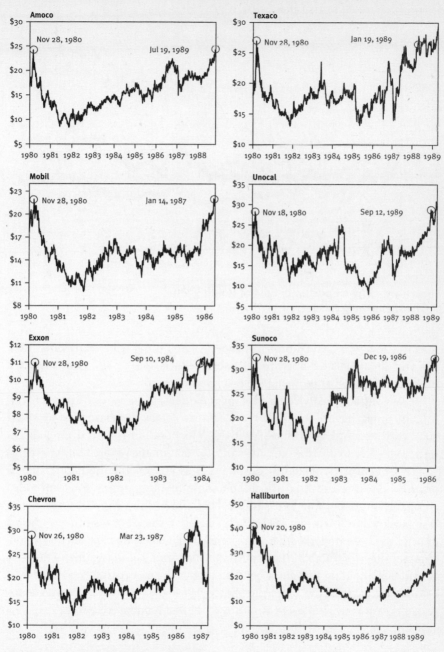

Figure 3.2   Don't Hold Your Breath
Source: Bloomberg Finance, L.P.

Figure 3.3   The Opportunity Cost of Holding On
Source: **Bloomberg Finance, L.P**

And in a few years, you'll probably see the same thing with many Financials after the Financials-led 2007 to 2009 bear. Stocks don't obey some arbitrary time line for growth—nor should you expect them to.

Overconfident individuals often own too few stocks—maybe just a hand-ful. You might have a 401(k) plan or a company stock purchase plan in which you buy your employer's stock. Many investors do. But is your overall alloca-tion to your company stock (or any stock for that matter) more than 5%? If so, you're being overconfident unless you really do know something material oth-ers don't. Most folks who do this don't know anything others don't know. No company, no matter how seemingly robust and healthy, is guaranteed not to lose stock value. Investors load up on company stock because they've heard examples where it worked because some single stock was spectacularly suc-cessful. They forget about the backfires. Investors say things like, "But I'm comfortable holding this stock because I *know* the company." You may be an astoundingly productive employee, but as fabulous as you are, your presence doesn't grant your employer immunity from market depreciation.

The Tragedy of Enron

Remember a little Houston company called Enron? The firm, embroiled in a huge fraud scandal, saw its value plummet, went bankrupt and most all employees unceremoniously found themselves out of work.

The biggest story engendered by Enron's gory, self-inflicted demise was the army of employees who found their life savings wiped out because their 401(k)s were all or mostly in Enron. Nice, upstanding folks who worked hard and penny-pinched and saved and were good, decent Texans and thought, "I know the company." Nearly overnight, these unfortunate souls found the value of their retirement savings decimated.

The real Enron tragedy wasn't that so many lost almost everything. The tragedy was it was utterly preventable. Whatever evil may have lurked in the hearts of Ken Lay, Andrew Fastow and Jeff Skilling, it's never a wise idea to plow everything, or most everything, into one stock.

If the employees followed my rule of thumb of having no more than 5% of your portfolio in any single stock, the Enron disaster would have downgraded from apocalyptic to minor bummer. Yes, employees would have become unemployed. Yes, they would have been simultaneously seeking work in a worse work world, competing with their former colleagues all sporting relatively similar resumes. Yes, they would have lost money. But this is all less humiliating if one has a 401(k) and net worth still relatively intact—decreased by one small stock's implosion instead of one huge one.

Enron did match employee 401(k) cash contributions with Enron stock[8]—but even more reason for employees to never buy another nickel's worth of Enron. Overconfidence is to blame. Not Ken Lay. Not Jeff Skilling. Yes, for other things, but not for that. And in the years since, they've all gotten their comeuppance.

But no matter the degree and severity of their crime, they didn't hold a gun to anyone's head and force them not to diversify their retirement savings. The overconfidence of the Enron employees themselves, those who invested their entire liquid net worth in one stock, is to blame for the total (or near-total) loss of value of their retirement and other savings accounts. That may seem harsh, but sometimes the truth hurts. They need to absorb their regret.

See! I Told You So—Confirmation Bias

As humans, we intentionally seek those fragments of evidence supporting our pet theories and preexisting notions. We tend to ignore those contradicting our biases. With differing biases, two investors can consider the same data yet espouse two completely opposing conclusions—both swearing the data support him and not the other fellow. I've seen this all my life. What's more, almost never will either investor set out to use simple statistical techniques to demonstrate being right. Each has a bias and is overconfident, so they don't have to check and validate. Correlation coefficients? That's for the other guy.

Another easy technique to support a preset notion is seeking a big name who says the same things you believe and relying on him as an authority for why you should do what you already want to do. Whatever nutty thing someone believes, I promise there are plenty of seemingly credible authorities supporting the lunacy.

How did we get this way? Think about the Stone Age hunters again. Each hunter may be predisposed to liking a particular hunting ground. Maybe the first gazelle one hunter caught was in Gazelle Gulch to the north. He sees Gazelle Gulch as perfect for hunting. His feeling is bolstered each time he kills a gazelle there. "Yep," he thinks, "this is where it's at." He justifies times he doesn't catch a gazelle by telling himself he can't catch one every time. Over many hunting sessions, he assures himself, there will be times he must come home empty-handed. But on average (in his mind), when looking at three or four months' worth of hunting expeditions, Gazelle Gulch is tops. And if he doesn't go to other hunting grounds, he will never disprove his bias.

His hunting buddy is equally convinced Gazelle Canyon to the south is best. Both hunters hunt every day. They observe the number of times they each kill gazelles. They both run hot and cold streaks in which they each go for days having back-to-back successes or bagging nothing. And they each remain firmly convinced of their favorite area's superiority, though neither one can statistically demonstrate long-term superiority. (Stone Age folks didn't do statistics—which is why you don't naturally.) Neither hunter will have his thesis tested and therefore rejected as wrong. Doing so would be painful.

We've evolved less than you might hope. Recall the Chapter 1 example regarding the myth of high P/E ratios spelling doom for stocks. Utter unsupported nonsense—yet a near-universal belief! This is a great example of what behavioralists call *confirmation bias*—the instinct to seek out information confirming our preset notions and rejecting or overlooking contradictory evidence. Believers of the high P/E myth are quick to point out data supporting their theory, but they tend to reject contradictory evidence.

Confirmation bias is comfortably consistent with religious views throughout humanity, starting with early paganistic days up until the neo-paganism of popular contemporary environmentalism in which folks hold warm and fuzzy but deeply seated views about what is good for the environment that isn't supported by science. (By this I'm not arguing against the environment or that environmentalists don't have many points supported by science. I'm saying many of them see the arguments supporting their view and ignore perfectly valid factors contradicting them—because they *believe*. Nature worship is, of course, one of our oldest religions.)

Many myths are thus propped up by confirmation bias. It's an overwhelming part of being human. It's natural. But in markets, being natural hurts us. Confirmation bias makes us feel good—it reaffirms our conviction we are clever (overconfidence, yet again). And we like thinking we're clever. But as any doctor will tell you, things that feel good aren't necessarily good for you.

Confirmation bias perfectly explains the resilience of the "as goes January, so goes the year" myth. As each year starts, particularly if the start of the year is negative, pundits pound their "so-goes" drums. Some particularly zealous adherents go further, claiming, "As goes the first week, so goes January, so goes the year." This puts the world on notice should January happen to be a negative month. It's a great story and has that freak-out effect TV news producers love.

Years when both January and annual returns are negative provide the confirmation adherents require. The same goes for positive results, but the "so-goes" crowd seems to prefer bearish results. For example, during January 2006, which was rousingly positive, you'd be hard-pressed to find a mention of this dubious effect in the media. However, a Google search turns up plenty of mentions of the dreaded effect for January 2005, which was a negative January. By the way, overall, 2005 was positive 9.5% as measured by the MSCI World Index.[9] The so-goes adherents somehow ignore that.

How many pundits who claim "so goes" in January come back in December to issue a mea culpa when wrong? I've never seen any. And they don't have to. Years like 2005 or 2009, when the year didn't go the way January did, cause investors to *reframe*. Suddenly, you can't expect it to work every year. Rather, you must look at longer time periods, like 5, 7, 10 or 23 years. Or after the pundit retires. Here, the "so-goes" crowd rejects contradictory evidence, clings to the bias and reframes the issue by giving some new, arbitrary time frame.

Reframing is an important, hand-in-hand byproduct of confirmation bias. Behavioralists see framing as fundamental to our ability to see information correctly or incorrectly. When something is framed in ways we see well, then we can see it—jsut liek ew ddi wtih hte mssieplled praagarph. When it's framed in ways we see badly, we're blind. You shouldn't find that surprising. Few people would ever stop to ask, "How about instead of starting the 'so-goes' game in January, try playing it starting June or any other month? While we're at it, instead of thinking about the US market, let's think about some other country that moves in parallel to the United States, like Britain." I assure you, only weird people think like that, and when they do, they find no more reality within the data than in the notion January predicts annual stock returns for America.

Though year after year we're regaled with "so-goes" warnings, this myth remains wholly unsubstantiated. Anyone with an Internet connection and a functioning knowledge of Excel can figure this one out. Table 3.1 shows the power of January as an indicator for overall annual results.

Table 3.1 plots four possible outcomes since 1926: US stocks were up in both January and the full year, January was down while the year was up, January was up but the full year down and both January and the full year were down.

First, note 72% of all years are positive, regardless of what January did. A fact many have a hard time believing. Then note the most common occurrence (53%) is a positive January and positive full year. Proof January is predictive? Hardly—it's just proof stocks have been positive more than not historically. Least common, 9% of all years, is an up January followed by a down full year. But when January is down, it's a coin flip whether the year is up or down. Not predictive. Believing in this investing myth is a good symptom of a brain paralyzed by confirmation bias.

Following a Trail—Pattern Recognition and Repetition

Our ancestors—those wily hunters and gatherers and their tribesmen (and tribeswomen)—learned to recognize repeating rewards. They noted what led to their own and their neighbors' successes so they could repeat it and have yet more success. For example, they might have said, "This weapon is good for hunting, so I'll always use it," or "I never get lost when I follow this trail, so I'll keep on it," or "These berries didn't kill my neighbor, so I'll eat them." Pattern recognition and repetition was a safe, rational thing to do. Who wants to be adventurous with poisonous berries?

Table 3.1   The January Ineffect

S&P 500		January		
		Up	Down	Total
Full Year	Up	45 (53%)	16 (19%)	61 (72%)
	Down	8 (9%)	16 (19%)	24 (28%)
	Total	53 (63.1%)	32 (38%)	

Source: Global Financial Data, Inc., S&P 500 total returns, from 12/31/1925 to 12/31/2010.

Like our Stone Age ancestors, many investors still create control rules and follow them instead of assessing each individual situation. This leads to the popularity of "charting"—poring over graphs looking for predictable patterns. A cottage industry exists around "momentum investing" and "technical analysis," which claim certain formations—cup-and-handle, saucer-bottom, head-and-shoulders, deer-in-headlights (ok, I made that one up)—are predictive of a stock's future movement.

Anyone can easily see what a stock *has* done. What we want to know is what a stock *will* do. But no one can. And we can't because despite what someone may have told you, no amount of charting tells us anything about what a stock will do next other than the random occasion of serendipitous luck. Ever. End of story. Stocks are what a statistician would call "not serially correlated," which means when a stock is heading in a particular direction, the odds are 50/50 the stock continues in that direction or reverses course. For every chart you show me indicating a pattern leading to an expected result, I can show you many more where the exact same pattern leads to nothing at all. Stock price patterns by themselves are well measured to have no predictive power. Yet folks still use them.

We practice finance as a craft—using stodgy technology and iffy indicators—rather than reinventing it for modern use or creating new capital markets technology. We cling to outmoded and useless craftery because we love patterns. They feel safe, reassuring and nonpoisonous. Investors place reverence in the predictive power of a plethora of patterns—yield curves, high P/Es, moving averages, CPI, budget deficits—the list goes on. We rarely stop to ask, "What is my brain doing now to make me see something completely bassackward and hence act bassackwardly?" If an indicator (or a group of indicators) existed that could reliably predict the market, everyone would know about it (or them), and we'd all use it (or them) and we'd all be unimaginably wealthy. Since that isn't the case, and since it's only the unknown that has the power to move the market, we must get over our bias for following the known path.

20/20 Hindsight Bias and Order Preference

Hindsight bias, one result of our desire to follow a trail, is our tendency to exaggerate the quality of our foresight while conveniently forgetting our initial errors. What behavioralists call hindsight bias leaves no room for luck. Investors deceive themselves into believing they have some sort of special ability or knowledge that led to a good outcome. In hindsight, vision is always 20/20.

Hindsight bias is hard at work in an investor who claims he knew Altria would be a great stock when he bought it in January 2000 (up 352% over the next six years).[10] His stock skyrocketed as the global stock market imploded. He's a genius, of course, and credits that decision to his sheer mental acuity. What this investor forgets to mention is he bought Yahoo at $108 and sold it when it was trading at about $4 two years later. Excess pride accumulation and regret shunning go hand in hand with hindsight bias. (All these biases work together, and none lead you to make smart decisions.)

Hindsight bias also leads us to presume prior patterns persist—the stock that did well will continue being a star, and the doggy stock is a continual canine. And where there has been no action? There won't ever be. The simplest form of hindsight bias is projecting the past into the future. It's so easy, and rarely will folks argue with you when you do it.

Order preference is a manifestation of our instinct to predict and collect. For example: Many investors want each piece of their portfolio to perform well. If they are benchmarking (as you should be—managing your portfolio against the S&P 500 or MSCI World or another broad index and then regularly comparing your portfolio to it), they expect each and every stock they own to do as well or better than the benchmark. This is a natural instinct but impossible. Note in any benchmark, whatever it is, there are stocks with a very wide array of returns. To think you should have stocks without a wide array of returns means your portfolio doesn't have anything like the benchmark's diversification. And then, even if your stocks do uniformly well, it's likely only because you took a huge bet against the benchmark and got very lucky, very temporarily.

Simply said, if an investor owns, say, 60 stocks (not necessarily a bad number to own if you are investing globally), order preference makes him want each of the 60 stocks to be up as well as the entire portfolio. He forgets all that matters in finance is how the whole portfolio does. That's what impacts your net worth.

Investors suffer from order preference when they brag about the stock they bought that is up 800% but don't bother to look at how the portfolio as a whole is performing. When assessing performance, the whole is more important than the parts. This is a nearly impossible concept for most investors to get in their bones.

Imagine a portfolio containing only two $10,000 stocks. One rises 25% and the other falls 15%. The antiquated parts of our brain will tell us to regret the stock that fell. Standard finance tells us not to regret the parts—the totality did fine. Standard finance is right. The movements by themselves don't really tell us anything about the future, and we shouldn't act based on them anyway.

Think about it another way—imagine you owned an S&P index fund in a year it did great, like 1997, when it was up 33%.[11] You felt good, right? Now, imagine instead of the index, you owned 500 individual stocks. Five hundred stocks is far too many to own, by the way, but for the sake of this argument, let's pretend you did.

Among those 500 stocks, you have some down 40%, 50% and 60%.[12] Now how do you feel about your portfolio? You should feel equally as good as you did about the index fund because the 500 stocks you own are the ones in the index, appropriately weighted. It doesn't matter you had a few down 50% any more than it matters you had a few up over 150%.[13] In total, you were up 33%, which is what matters. Order preference causes you to focus on the individual parts and makes you lose sight of what is important.

The Great Humiliator's Favorite Tricks

If we were more evolved as investors, perhaps TGH would be reclassified as "The Mild Humiliator" (TMH) or even "The Softer, Gentler and Kinder Trickster" (TSGKT). Our preconditioning keeps us repeatedly humiliated by the market through psychological tendencies we fall for over and over again. Unfortunately, and as mentioned before, our biases don't work alone—they work in concert with each other, making completely nonsensical investment decisions seem rational even while we commit them. Your brain won't tell you when you're making a stupid mistake because it doesn't think the cognitive errors you make are stupid. Rather, your brain tells you the investments "just didn't work out." And then you look for something to blame it on—regret shunning.

Your only weapon is Question Three—with every decision you make, ask: What the heck is my brain doing to lead me astray this time? The more sane and rational a decision may seem, the more important it is to ask. I've given you some examples already of your brain working against you, and I give you more later in this book. You can make a list of them and keep it by your desk or nightstand. But you must keep asking yourself the question with every decision: What is my brain doing to blindside me now?

Consider the following hypothetical (though very plausible) scenario with an investor we'll call Jim. See if you've ever made similar decisions.

Let's say Jim's overall portfolio has risen 50% over the past three years. That's a pretty believable result after a few bull market years. Then a market correction hits and the portfolio drops 18% over several months. Corrections are perfectly normal in a bull market—expect one every year or two. They happen in history more years than not. Jim knows this and realizes the markets are volatile and knows markets can correct 10% to 20% in a jiffy and still move on to higher prices. He knows he has a long time horizon and short-term moves don't matter much. Even so, when it happens to him, it feels terrible. Just terrible!

First—*myopic loss aversion*. That 18% loss feels more like 45%. He's about as miserable about his short-term 18% loss as he is happy about the gains of recent years. (The more recent and the short term are the myopic part of myopic loss aversion. We tend to weigh the short term more than the long term despite the fact that eventually it's the long term we end up with.) Jim starts thinking about doing something to stop this (myopic) pain. If Jim asked himself Question Three, maybe he could have stopped the downward spiral of the rest of this scenario. He would have recognized myopic loss aversion was making him consider selling at a terrible time—in midst of what's likely a correction. Unfortunately, Jim didn't buy this book, and his Stone Age brain took over.

Next—*order preference*. He notices some of his stocks are down—way down. He overlooks that overall, even in the midst of this correction, his whole portfolio is still up over 20%. He fixates on a few of his stocks that are down over 40%. He has one, XYZ, that is down 65%. He thinks his life would be so much better if he hadn't bought XYZ. Poker buddies tell him it's probably going lower. It eats at him. He has a few stocks still up 80% or more. Those stocks are so much better. Why did he ever buy that turkey XYZ—down 65%? Why didn't he buy more of the ones up 80%?

Then—*regret shunning*. He should never have delegated these decisions to a broker since he could have done a better job if he had been paying attention.

Then—*confirmation bias* and more *regret shunning*. The last stock he picked himself immediately rose 50%. At least this XYZ isn't his fault. He wouldn't have allowed a stock to be down 65% if the decision was his alone. This is the idiot broker's fault. Jim is a smart cookie.

Followed closely by—*hindsight bias*. He *knew* XYZ was no good when the broker pitched it. He was going to pass on it and buy one currently up 140% and knew that was what he should have done. He just wasn't paying attention. He should follow his instincts more often since he tends to be right about this stuff. But then why does he feel so bad?

More *loss aversion*. If he doesn't do something soon, his wife may mistakenly think Jim is the idiot instead of the broker.

Next up—*overconfidence*. Forget that idiot broker. Though Jim has no background in finance or capital markets, he knows he can do it better. He was smart enough to get through medical school, after all. What's the difference? If you're smart, you're smart. And Jim is really, really, really smart.

Jim has had it. He can't take the pain of being down 18%, or the greater indignity of having that XYZ dog down 65%, so he sells every stock down over some arbitrary time period or maybe just every stock down more than some arbitrary amount. Two weeks later, the entire market and the stocks Jim sold finish correcting and are trading higher than before. And Jim is sitting with about 40% of his liquid net worth in cash. He tries to think about medical things and doctoring and his upcoming vacation and anything but the market.

Jim would currently be a wealthier man had he (1) asked Question Three or (2) made no decisions at all and (3) recognized his brain was trying to protect him from attack by a saber-toothed tiger, not guide him toward rational investing decisions. Meanwhile our smart doctor, in other realms a scientist, learns nothing from his cognitive mistakes as he shuns regret. "At least I didn't lose more," he tells himself. And he lives to repeat these errors and more another day.

Get Your Head Out of the Cave

Jim may not be beyond all hope. Neither are you. We suffer these behaviors, to be sure, but we aren't doomed. The way to overcome Stone Age thinking is regular and rigorous application of Question Three. After you've asked if what you believe is correct, and after you ask what you can fathom that others can't, it's imperative you pull your head out of the cave and ask whether your brain is sending you bad messages.

There are some practical things you can begin doing, right now, to help combat the more common cognitive errors. Once you learn to repeatedly ask Question Three and are suspicious you're on the brink of making a cognitive error, you can apply some of the following practices to keep yourself on this side of the millennium.

Another Flip—Accumulate Regret, Shun Pride

The Bible tells us pride goes before a fall. In capital markets, pride goes before myopic loss aversion as well as overconfidence, hindsight bias and just about everything else that is evil, including selling at the bottom. You must reverse your natural inclinations permanently. You must shun pride and accumulate regret. It's the simplest, most basic trick I know to becoming a better investor.

If you have a stock up a lot, assume you aren't a genius. Assume you're lucky, and luck can run out. If you have a stock down a lot, don't run from your regret. Accumulate regret with every loss. Live with it. Love it. Assume you weren't victimized by Enron management, greedy bankers, your stockbroker or your spouse (although I can't help you much with that last one). Assume you and only you were wrong about every down stock, and your job is to learn a lesson about why you were wrong that teaches you how to do the same thing correctly the next time. If you can embrace your regret, you will be less inclined to sell at relative low points. Remember, the idea is not to buy low and sell whenever stock prices have you freaking out.

Accumulating regret and shunning pride have many benefits. First, you can learn from your mistakes. Second, instead of becoming more overconfident, you become less confident and start seeing markets closer to the way they really are. Studies show less overconfident investors do better than more overconfident ones, and you can make yourself less overconfident over time by accumulating regret and shunning pride.

Have you ever sold a stock because it was down, bought something else and never looked back? You were glad to be rid of a dog and that was that? Maybe you didn't sell a stock, you sold the whole portfolio and bought something else—bonds, cash, an annuity—because the market as a whole scared you. Many investors do that—act emotionally and never check afterward to see if their decision made them better or worse off. And they never evolve.

Embrace your regret. Know you can and will be wrong and your decisions have consequences. This is a game in which if you're right 70% of the time, in the long run, you're a super-monster success. That means being wrong often, too. Being wrong is ok. The more you embrace your wrongness and see it as an opportunity for learning, the less wrongness you will have long term.

Don't be so busy patting yourself on the back that you "didn't lose more" to realize you have made a colossal error in selling out of the market or buying the wrong thing. Maybe that stock you sold wasn't a dog. Maybe the one you bought in its place was. Maybe the one you sold turned out to be the best-performing stock for years afterward and you pulled the trigger because you suffered from loss aversion, hindsight bias or some other simple cognitive error. Maybe the market wasn't headed for a downward spiral. Maybe it ended the year up 25% or so, but you got a cash-like return of 1.5%, lagging the market and putting a serious damper on your chances of reaching your long-term goals. Know you will be wrong again (and again and again), and take steps so when it happens you do your best to learn from your mistakes. Look for lessons to be learned from your mistakes so you make fewer of them in the future.

Question Three will prevent you from committing many crazy, irrational acts. More important, you need an all-encompassing and overriding strategy guiding every decision, and you absolutely must have a benchmark. (We discuss benchmarking and why it is vital to survival in Chapter 4.) But for now, know that a benchmark can be any well-constructed index and is your road map in portfolio construction. If your benchmark is 50% US stocks, you want to vary from 50% US stocks only if you think you know something others don't about why US stocks should do better or worse than foreign stocks. If your benchmark is 10% Energy stocks, you should be 10% Energy stocks unless you used the Three Questions to know something others don't, causing you to overweight or underweight Energy. Otherwise, you should just be passive to your benchmark. The goal is to perform similarly to your benchmark and better if you know something unique. Over time, the benchmark will get you where you need to go. Major deviations from your benchmark caused by your brain blindsiding you, like myopic loss aversion, will seriously impact your ability to get to your long-term goals.

Here's an example. In March 2000, I called the Tech cycle top pretty well—one of my better calls of the past 20 years. (More on this in Chapter 8.) My firm cut our clients' weight from slightly overweight (when Tech was a third of the US market and 25% of the world) to materially underweight. In hindsight, now I know I could have cut it even more, but I always know I could be wrong. Most particularly when I think I know something others don't, which I did then, I still know my brain is working to blindside me, so I try not to get too carried away—I don't make my bets too big. You should do that, too—always seek to know what others don't but also always know you could be wrong. If you were wrong and were bearish on Tech when it turned out to be the best-performing sector, you still participated in it to some extent and didn't lag the market too darned badly. If you were right, then you participated less in a poor-performing area and did better than the market—which is the game over time.

Accumulate regret. Shun pride. Focus on your benchmark. Only veer hugely from it when the Three Questions lead you to believe you know things others don't. That is how to beat myopic loss aversion and overconfidence. It's how to engage TGH without getting humiliated.

Less Can Be More

When combating *overconfidence,* women have a proven, distinct advantage over men. A wonderful academic study was done to see who are better investors—men or women. It was no surprise to me it found women to be much better investors with better long-term results.[14] Why? While the men were hunting boar and gazelles, women were gathering berries and grains. Picking berries doesn't require as much overconfidence as flinging stone-tipped twigs at charging beasts. Because women aren't hardwired from eons of hunter evolution to be as overconfident as men, they tend to trade less and make fewer changes to their portfolios.

In the study, both women and men tended to be wrong more than right and in the same proportions. But because men are more overconfident, they trade more often without knowing anything unique. Those extra senseless trades work against them relative to the fewer senseless trades made by women. Fewer changes can result in better performance—unless you actually do know something others don't to justify the extra trades. Maybe that's why the fairer sex lives longer. They have more money to support themselves. (I always thought it was because they presumed we men were stupid and overconfident, so they got us to do all the dangerous stuff, but I'm not really sure about that.) Of course, that is something for the gentlemen to ponder.

Something for the ladies to consider? Throughout history, essentially all of the very top, most famous and richest investors have been men. The only big-time exception was Hetty Green from the nineteenth century (see my book, *100 Minds That Made the Market,* for a cameo biography of Hetty Green). Women have almost never made it to the ranks of the very most successful investors. Why? Many women will tell you historical (or current) social bias didn't allow it or even dissuaded women from trying.

Of course, TGH doesn't care who you are. It's an equal-opportunity humiliator and is delighted to humiliate a woman as much as a man. That Hetty Green did it more than 125 years ago proves it could be done then, and many women have been in the industry these past 35 years. I'd guess, without really knowing for sure, few women historically have been among the very best investors because of the following: Women are proven less overconfident than men (as in the earlier cited research) and better investors on average than men (a point provable but still not widely accepted). Still, it's always a mistake to confuse a single incident with an average. Because women are less overconfident than men, they probably don't fare as well as the very few supremely overconfident males on the far end of the bell curve that end up being the few who are right or lucky or both. Those few men just pushed further. Still, less overconfidence means fewer unwarranted trades, and here, women have an undisputed advantage.

Any time you get ready to make a trade, use your other two Questions to make sure you aren't trading on false myths and your action is based on an advantage you reasonably believe you have over other investors. If you aren't sure your reason to trade is correct or you're in possession of unique—or uniquely framed—information, then you may be overconfident. Sometimes being passive is the most active and appropriate thing to do. Don't trade just to trade. Practice humility.

Genius? Or Lucky and Forgetful?

You're most likely to suffer *hindsight bias* after a run of luck with an individual stock, sector or even a broad market call you've made. Luck being the operative word.

A little pride shunning and regret accumulation goes far toward helping combat this bias. When you're right about a bet, your reaction shouldn't be, "I knew I was right about that." Rather, it should be, "I knew I could have been wrong, and I was probably at least partly lucky. Where was I lucky? How could I have been wrong?" Every decision you make should come with the assumption you can be wrong. If you think this way, you will take steps to ensure you're not injured too badly by bad assumptions.

Thinking about building an all-Energy portfolio? (If you're benchmarking, that would never happen, but let's pretend.) Maybe you were thinking about it somewhere in 2005 or 2006, after you saw your Exxon and ConocoPhillips and Chevron stocks appreciate in value for several years. What a genius you were for picking those stocks! You *knew* a global economic expansion following the recession, including labor reforms and a boom in China and India, would lead to increased global oil demand and, hence, higher oil stock prices. And you knew fears about higher gas prices impacting the industry and causing inflation were overblown and priced into markets anyway. In fact, you're pretty sure you told your tennis group the net of that back in 2003. They don't remember this alleged conversation, but you sure do.

Stop. Ask yourself: What if you were wrong? What if your success wasn't due to your adroit analysis of global oil consumption but rather some dumb luck? Would you want to take that big a gamble? Just because you were right once (or twice) doesn't mean you will be again. Many investors were heavily invested in Tech in 1998 and 1999 or Financials in the mid-2000s because those stocks had done well. Being grossly over-allocated in a hot sector makes you a terrific dart thrower but a risky money manager. It definitely doesn't make you a market genius.

If you were one of those people heavily invested in Tech in the 1990s (or Energy in the late 1970s or Financials in the mid-2000s or or or or), you might have been patting your back after those stocks did well for a few years. But if you were hugely over-allocated and didn't shift away when those stocks fell out of favor (as hot categories always do), you may have lost your shirt. Being *lucky* and right is no way to manage your assets. Being cautious and right more often than you're wrong is how to increase the odds you meet your long-term goals.

If you're tempted to brag you *knew* Altria would be a superstar or you *knew* Apple would go on a tear, ask yourself if you *knew* about any of the stocks that turned out to be losers. You didn't, otherwise you wouldn't have bought them. Shun that pride, accumulate regret, honor your benchmark and avoid hindsight bias.

The Whole Versus the Sum of Its Parts

On *order preference*, remember what matters most is the overall result. Nobody cares if you have a stock up 800%, and you shouldn't necessarily care if you have one that is down 80%. Your individual stocks will gyrate wildly and per-form, by and large, the way most of the stocks in their respective categories do (e.g., Tech, Health Care, large cap, value, Japan).

And most important, look at the progression of the portfolio as a whole. Learn to calculate the performance of your overall portfolio and focus less on what the individual stocks are doing (we cover the other part later).

I'm not saying you shouldn't consider how each stock does relative to its category. You should, just not pathologically too often. Watching individual stocks too often and too intently leads to serious loss aversion as well as other cognitive errors. When you look at your individual stocks, it shouldn't be to check whether they are "up or down." It shouldn't even be to check how they are doing relative to your overall portfolio. If your overall portfolio is up 25% for the year and you have some stocks that are up less than that or even down, it doesn't mean they're bad stocks. If a stock is performing similarly to others in its category, then it's doing its job. If a stock behaves wildly different from its category, that is surely cause for pause. But if an entire sector is up or down and an individual stock in it is up or down similarly, the stock is doing what it's supposed to do.

A little out- or underperformance over a month or two is probably noth-ing to even think about. But if a stock performs significantly worse or even significantly better than its peers over a longer time period, then you can start asking what makes it behave differently.

If you select stocks that are good representations of the categories in your benchmark, and those stocks then perform largely in line with their categories, then you have no need to obsess about how each one is doing

The only basis for any bet, including one stock versus its category, is rationally thinking you know something others don't while also knowing you could be wrong. That implies not being obsessive. If your portfolio in totality is performing similarly (again, not over a week or a month or a quarter—think longer term) to your benchmark, you're doing fine. Better than most investors!

Bunnies or Elephants? Always Think in Terms of Scalability!

Yet another way to combat a whole slew of cognitive errors is relative thinking. Every investing concern, every finance issue, every news item can be scaled.

Our Stone Age brethren knew a bunny rabbit was small and an elephant was big. They also knew the elephant was scary and hard to kill and it might stomp on them and the fuzzy bunny was cute and cuddly and easy to catch and delicious. Big was scary, small was tasty (and not scary). But ask the same Stone Ager if the H1 Alpha Hummer is bigger or smaller than the mammoth and he has no basis for comparison. Are we talking height? Weight? Cubic inches? Mammoth power? Coming at you or going away? Of course, Hummers didn't exist back then. (I believe Fred Flintstone drove an early model Sand Rover.)

Modern man can learn to always scale and think relatively. Still, investors rarely think in terms of scaling and relativity on investment decisions. Inability to scale is a cognitive error our caveman brains want to commit when we see big numbers. Big numbers seem scary—like a crazed, stampeding mammoth. However, scalability can make us see big numbers correctly—debt, deficit, GDP, jobs, wars, whatever. Practice scaling when you read the news. Sure, the local ABC correspondent delivers the latest dreadful news on the trade deficit being many, many billions (Egads! Hundreds of gazillion bajillions!), but does she really help you with perspective? You can do it easily by thinking about the percentage of GDP this big number represents. Better yet, global GDP. Usually, it's nothing to worry about once you start thinking relatively (we look at that in more detail in Chapter 6).

A pattern should be emerging here. Many cognitive errors can be avoided—once you recognize a brain gone haywire by using Question Three—if you shun pride, accumulate regret, use a benchmark, have a strategy, think relatively and focus on your long-term goal.

Questions One and Two can help you find gameable bets—edges your fellow investors don't have. But without Question Three, you will be adrift, subject to the powerful suggestions of a brain intent on saving you from long extinct dangers. In Chapter 9, I show you how to pull your Three Questions together and create a strategy to keep your brain disciplined, even when it most wants to stray. But first, in Chapter 4, let's talk about how the Three Questions can be used together to build ahead-of-their-time, beyond-state-of-the-art technology to beat the market. Thanks for reading on.

4 CAPITAL MARKETS TECHNOLOGY

Building and Putting Capital Markets Technology Into Practice

By now you know the Three Questions work together, helping you identify what you can know that others don't. While this book demonstrates how to debunk some common myths and uncover some surprising truths via the Three Questions, don't stop with the few examples the limited space in these pages allow. The point isn't to garner a few useful investing tidbits but to use the questions always with every decision. Stop and ask, "Why am I buying or selling this stock, sector, fund, whatever? Why do I think this is a good idea? What do I know that others don't? What do I believe that is false here? What can I fathom?" Simply asking the questions puts you ahead of most investors. Then ask, "Is my brain just messing with me?" This isn't a static how-to book. Its aim is to give you a dynamic process and a tool set to serve you for your entire investing life.

The answers to the Three Questions, either one by one or together, provide you with a new way of approaching markets—one amounting to a technology you can repeatedly test and apply. Your goal in repeatedly asking the Three Questions is to build, over time, a dynamic arsenal of *capital markets technology*. In effect, with each answer to a question, you've created new capital markets technology. Some capital markets technologies can be big game-changers. Others can be smaller, simpler tools. This book is chock full of examples of them.

We don't know much today about how capital markets work compared to what we will know in 10, 20 or 50 years. One way to know something others don't is to build capital markets technology of the future now. If you can know something now others won't know for 5, 10 or 20 years, you have a long lead. Capital markets technology will help explain parts of the investing world never before understood and, like any other piece of technology, give you a dependable, usable tool. The technology you create allows you to make more accurate forecasts and learn to make bets that are right more often than wrong. What's more, technology allows you to discover and create even more unique technology.

History as a Research Lab

If approaching investing correctly (like a scientist, not a blacksmith), you must test your capital markets technology. And there's no better laboratory for testing new technology than history. Far too many of our investing myths, the ones comprising the documented and accepted ways of thinking, are based on ideology, theoretical whim, political inclination or, worse, cognitive bias. When tested against historical data, they often simply fall apart—just like the myth about high P/Es and the misplaced fear about federal budget deficits. Proving something is true takes more rigor than proving something isn't true. To prove something isn't true, you just need to show consistently lousy correlation. History can teach us if something is beyond reasonable to expect.

If, throughout history, X wasn't tightly linked to Y, and, in fact, X is linked to a bunch of stuff other than Y, you have no basis to bet X will suddenly start causing Y consistently. Stubbornly clinging to a popular causal theory without supporting evidence is how myths become firmly entrenched in our culture. But it takes a long time, and the longer the myth runs, the less people are prone to verify its validity.

The good news is you needn't own a pricey Bloomberg terminal to have access to data. Vast quantities of neatly organized data in varying levels of granularity are available for free on any number of websites. A sampling of websites that might be useful can be found in Table 4.1.

If you can't figure out how to download or analyze the data using Excel, see the example in Chapter 1 or find a high school student to show you how. By 2011, I assume most readers are at least generally comfortable on the Internet.

That said, the data in your proof can be either quantitative or qualitative. The high-P/E myth was debunked with quantitative data. You saw how easy it was to disprove a very widely held theory using standard data by doing simple tests based on asking the questions.

Table 4.1 Data Sources

Authority	Website	Data Include
Bloomberg	www.bloomberg.com	Global stock market news and quotes, calculators, other media
Bureau of Economic Analysis	www.bea.gov	GDP, current account balance, import/export
Bureau of Labor Statistics	www.bls.gov	CPI, unemployment, productivity, inflation
Centers for Disease Control and Prevention (CDC)	www.cdc.gov	Statistics: births, deaths, health trends and statistics, demographics, etc.
Department of Commerce	www.commerce.gov	Trade conditions
The Economist	www.economist.com	World financial and economic news, current events weekly
Energy Information Administration	www.eia.doe.gov	Energy source statistics, historical data
Financial Times (UK)	www.ft.com	International stock market, business and world news
International Monetary Fund	www.imf.org	International economic and financial statistics
LexisNexis	www.lexisnexis.com	Comprehensive search engine of news, public records, information sources
Morgan Stanley Capital International	www.msci.com	MSCI indexes, data, characteristics, performance
National Bureau of Economic Research	www.nber.org	Business cycles (recession timing)
New York Stock Exchange	www.nyse.com	New York stock exchange
Organisation for Economic Co-operation and Development	www.oecd.org	International economic and trade statistics

(continued)

Table 4.1 (Continued)

Authority	Website	Data Include
Real Clear Politics	www.realclearpolitics.com	Essential political news, headlines, blogs, polls, etc.
Russell index service	www.russell.com	Russell index data, characteristics, valuations
Standard & Poor's index service	www.standardandpoors.com	S&P indexes, data, characteristics, constituents
Thomas/US Library of Congress	www.loc.gov	Legislative information
US Census Bureau	www.census.gov	Statistics by region
US Congress	www.house.gov	Representative sites, bills, laws, roll call
US Department of Defense	www.defenselink.mil	Official news, reports
US Federal Reserve	www.federalreserve.gov	Bank balance sheet, credit statistics, money stock, flow of funds
US Government Official Web Portal	www.firstgov.gov	Links to all government branches, departments, areas
US House of Representatives Office of the Clerk	clerk.house.gov	Legislative branch details, history, election statistics
US Office of Management and Budget	www.whitehouse.gov/omb	US budget
US Treasury	www.ustreas.gov	Taxes, interest rates, social security, Medicare
Wall Street Journal	www.wsj.com	International stock market, business and world news
Wilshire index service	www.wilshire.com	Wilshire stock indexes, valuations
World Health Organization (WHO)	www.who.int	Global health & burden of disease statistics, mortality, news, alerts

But what if the data are either hard to come by or measure? Can your capital markets technology be qualitative in nature? Sure, as long as you have plenty of examples to analyze and it makes economic sense. A great example is the presidential term cycle from Chapter 2. The cycle is difficult to measure numerically but thus far is still powerful. In terms of data, you can examine all the election cycles going back to 1926. It's not exactly quantitative, but there's a clear pattern with underlying fundamentals. And, of course, an important reason it works is the fundamentals aren't well understood, the pattern isn't well accepted and most often, when articulated, it's ridiculed.

But your proof must make basic economic sense. If you find a reliable pattern but don't have a good causal explanation for it, don't bet on it. Did you know every year ending in a 5 since 1926 has been positive for US stocks?[1] You might feel thus justified betting on the next 5 year. Don't! Simple numerology! There's no known economic reason why every 10th year should always be positive. For that matter, years ending in 5 since 1955 have seen more fierce land-falling hurricanes (as evidenced by the number of hurricane names retired).[2] So what? I doubt the National Oceanic and Atmospheric Administration is relying on the "year-5" theory in any way whatsoever in its forecasting. And you sure as heck can't argue heavy hurricane incidence causes years ending in 5 to have good stock markets. What we have here is a statistical anomaly—a freak of nature. The lucky guy flipping 50 heads in a row. They happen all the time, so be cautious. Again, correlation without causation is no basis for a bet.

Then again, maybe you can uncover a sound economic reason why 5 years are always positive, and that can be your personal capital markets technology. Good for you. Then you've done a Question Two and fathomed what is otherwise unfathomable to the rest of us. Fair game—if you can do it, you have the basis for a bet.

Also, once you've tested and put a new piece of capital markets technology to good use, don't become overconfident and assume you have a sure winner every time you make the same bet. Nothing is perfect or works all the time. Suppose X causes Y 70% of the time. That's pretty good. It's likely worth betting on. And yet some other thing or things cause Y 30% of the time. So while it's worth betting on X to cause Y, you will still likely be wrong 30% of the time. No one thing is perfect.

What's more, even the best capital markets technology can fade, which is why you must keep testing your hypotheses. Following are two examples of great technologies that were, in many ways, groundbreaking—but their effectiveness, at least as initially intended, has largely passed.

It's Good While It Lasts

The price-to-sales ratio (PSR; sometimes P/S) is a good example of ground-breaking capital markets technology I pioneered that was powerful in its day yet isn't so much now. I had uncovered a way no one had yet used to tell if a stock might be over- or undervalued—it became the subject of my 1984 book called *Super Stocks*. While Ben Graham made passing mention of the relationship between price and sales being potentially interesting, the first published work anywhere on the relationship was mine. I'm very proud of that—just like I am of my third-grade school report on Guatemala. But otherwise, neither is noteworthy today. Just memories.

But 30 years ago, if you could simply screen for low-PSR stocks (which wasn't easy), you could beat the market more often than not. After my book and subsequent exposure, the PSR became widely used and even, off and on, part of the required curriculum for the CFA exam. Most analytical websites include the PSR today. But as capital markets technology and a forecasting tool, the PSR has become largely priced into the market. Even a great discovery becomes obsolete with popularity and time. If it becomes popular, it loses its power. It's always time to be working on the next discovery.

For the uninitiated (in the event the name didn't give it away), the PSR tells you a stock's price relative to its per-share sales. It's just like a P/E but uses annual revenue or sales where the P/E uses earnings. A stock selling for $25 with $25 in sales per share has a PSR of 1. Pretty straightforward. This may not sound revolutionary now—like trying to imagine a time before someone said, "Hey, what would happen if we divided a stock's price by its earnings?" But when I first started writing about it, no one had done it.

For the purposes of this book, there is no need for an in-depth rehash of PSRs or my first book, *Super Stocks*. But there are a couple of points I should make. First, about the book. Reading old investment books is useful and a great way to learn the canvas of what developed in terms of capital markets technology—when, how and by whom.

Finding Earnings When There Were None

Second, anyone who plans on making money in stocks knows you want to buy a stock before it becomes "in favor." The requisite flip side is you must buy the stock when it seems *out* of favor. The trick is knowing which stock will be in favor soon while currently seeming doggy. How can you know that? That was how I got interested in PSRs initially. My early PSR evolution translates directly into how to think about developing capital markets technology.

Investors have long used P/Es to look for cheap stocks. One hundred years ago—plus! But some emerging companies may not have any earnings to report. Even established companies may be profitless during cyclical downturns and times of individual corporate crises, and those can be interesting times to consider a stock—when it's out of favor. You can't get a P/E in those scenarios because you can't divide something by zero. Sometimes a company has a P/E of 1,000 because its earnings have almost completely disappeared. Sometimes a company has a P/E of 5 because of temporarily high profit margins that can't be sustained.

But even if a firm doesn't have earnings, it still has sales (or at least it should, or it's in big trouble). This is where Question Two came into play for me decades ago—what could I fathom others couldn't? It made sense any stock with a low price relative to its previous 12-month sales would rise—if its future earnings might become large enough to make the current PSR translate into a low future P/E ratio (or in other words, a high future earnings yield). What people don't like today, they would tomorrow. How tough is that? People would eventually discover this undervalued stock was posting super revenue and fat future profit margins and was cheap—and they'd come around and drive the price up. Hence, if you were rational, you'd want to buy a stock when its price relative to the company's sales was low but didn't appear cheap based on P/E. Low relative to the market but, more important, low relative to its category and low relative to its future earnings.

When I wrote *Super Stocks*, I defined low PSR stocks as generally ones where the company's total market value was less than 75% of the company's total annual revenue. I defined high PSR stocks as ones where the market value of the company was more than three times its annual revenue.

There was the theory, but that's all it was. At the time, there were no sources citing PSRs like there are now. There were no databases. Bloomberg.com and Morningstar.com didn't exist to neatly calculate a PSR for every stock for me like they (and many other sources) do now. I extrapolated data from publicly available information and built my own data to arrive at my ratio. Back then, there was actually money to be made by compiling data because data was still scarce and expensive. Today, data is essentially free. If you're younger, you may have difficulty realizing just how hard data was to get. In 1981, I paid Goldman Sachs $20,000 for a simple one-time screen of the New York Stock Exchange (NYSE) based on current PSRs. It was that expensive for something anyone can get now for free, near instantly. Historical data had to be built by hand, which was effectively prohibitive unless you knew exactly what you wanted to do.

When I back-tested historical PSRs against subsequent stock market returns, my theory held up. I built data against several stock universes ranging from a 1970s Tech universe compiled by the former investment banking firm, Hambrecht & Quist, to general 1930s stocks based on Moody's data retrieved by hand. Stocks with lower PSRs did far and away better than those with higher ratios. Not every single time with every single stock, but enough to provide me with a reliable indicator for forecasting and a good basis for a market bet. In other words, stocks with low PSRs were superior stocks, which ultimately led to my book title.

Before I wrote *Super Stocks*, I used this nifty new technology with a fair amount of success. Effectively, my usage of PSRs propelled my career in many ways. You may again wonder why I would advertise something giving me a competitive edge in a mass-produced book. You may think I should have kept what I knew about the PSR a secret so I could have maintained my advantage. Not so! Wrong way to think.

Any advantage you have is likely temporary. Behind you, there is someone else looking for what you just found. I knew I had discovered something neat, but I hadn't done anything magical or prohibitively mathematically complicated or both. I hadn't done anything anyone else couldn't do. All I did was look at available data (hard-to-get data, but available data nonetheless) in a new way and do a little back-testing and a little linkage to fundamental theory. Other people were bound to see what I saw sooner or later. Probably sooner! So I kept putting the idea out there to see if anyone else was biting. For a while, no one was.

After I published the book, people bit, but it took a long time. For about 10 more years, I had the PSR pretty much to myself. For example, in 1997 James O'Shaughnessy wrote a best-selling book titled *What Works on Wall Street* in which he analyzed all the common ratios to see which might lead to higher subsequent returns.[3] He labeled the PSR "the King of the Value Factors," and he claimed his analysis (at the time) showed PSRs generated higher subsequent returns than any other single ratio. Jim's handwritten inscription in the copy he gave me reads, "Boy did you ever come up with a good ratio! Think how horrible us poor money managers would feel if instead of market cap, S&P had based their index on low PSR stocks." O'Shaughnessey's book propelled PSRs further into prominence, and soon, the PSR lost most of its power. It got priced.

Was I upset my innovation became widely used and therefore thoroughly priced? Not at all! I was thrilled. First, if it really was good, it was inevitable—at least this way it happened on my terms and I was ready for it. There was no way the dot-com era would arrive with all its free data without someone stumbling on the PSR and popularizing it. I got a good run from that technology and was able to see when it was time to move on. By then, I was off on other new things I'd never dreamed of when I first did the PSR. I wasn't so overconfident (a cognitive error) in the 1970s and early 1980s to assume I had out-thought all investors for all time. If the PSR was clever in the early 1980s, in a world of CP/M-based PCs with $5^1/_4$-inch floppy discs and no hard drives, the guys who created the Commodore 64 were pretty clever, too. The subsequent wave of 1980s and 1990s electronics would wipe out the world of expensive data. It would make the PSR visible to everyone. Markets evolve, and so must we.

If the PSR no longer works much, why waste ink telling you about it? First, because some people are still convinced this antiquated piece of technology still works as it did. With any ratio like this, once popularized, sometimes it works and sometimes it doesn't—just enough to keep people interested— same with the P/E, dividend yield, price to book, you name it. You can even take the most nonsensical ratios and find times when they appear to generate excess returns. Just looking at the companies with the highest cash per share will sometimes give you market-beating stocks. Looking at companies with the lowest cash per share will sometimes beat the market, too. But neither has anything to do with being able to beat the market in the long term.

Over the past 20 years or so, low-PSR stocks have been a bit less volatile than both low-P/E stocks and the market and have no long-term, risk-adjusted, excess return—now. They're priced. However, when value stocks have outperformed growth, low-PSR stocks have generally beaten both the market and value and been more volatile than the market overall. When growth stocks beat value stocks, low-PSR stocks have lagged the market and value.

What can you do with this knowledge right now—the way you've learned to think in Chapters 1 through 3? How can you use what I've told you to make rational, workable bets here and now—at least until making those bets becomes well known and popular? Let's do a Question Two. What can you fathom no one else fathoms about this? We saw in Chapter 2 how to know when growth stocks are likelier to best value stocks, and vice versa. I just told you when value stocks lead the market, PSRs have still had extra oomph relative to value but not when growth stocks lead historically. So I just told you when you're likelier to get some temporary excess return by using PSRs as a screening device. The PSR isn't a uniform tool for all seasons—it's a tool to use temporarily when incorporated with other successful capital markets technology. Your goal is to figure out when value stocks will lead the market and then incorporate low PSR stocks into your stock selection—but not when growth stocks lead the market. When growth leads the market, you want your stocks to be higher PSR stocks. And like any good capital markets technology, be sure to keep testing this in the future to ensure the relationship hasn't broken down.

The Stock Market Is Not a Ball-Peen Hammer—But It Can Hit You Hard

Briefly consider this another way: Some category of stock outperforms the market for five years. A preponderance of investors jumps on its bandwagon, doing whatever it was that was so successful in those years. But those things stop working for the next five years or so, leading investors to think they will never work again. Because investors think they won't work anymore, it's very possible for them to start working again. They're no longer discounted into pricing but simply ignored because of cognitive error. This is what happens to low PSR, low P/E, dividend yield and others. They come through long periods where they haven't worked, so they're ignored for another long period. Then, when value comes back into favor, they can and do work temporarily. Traditional craftsmen hate these kinds of very real market phenomena because they want their tools to work the same way all the time.

This further illustrates the importance of continued testing and ongoing innovation. I repeatedly tested my PSR technology before deploying it so I wouldn't be guilelessly relying on it when it became priced and useless. I gave up on it long ago as a primary tool and have since developed many other capital markets technologies because developing the next new thing is what the game is all about. But it is still a secondary tool that can be used at times.

Sure, you can use the Three Questions a few times and stumble on a thing or two others don't know. But if you don't make the Three Questions a part of your way of thinking, always, you will eventually lose any advantage you might have stumbled on.

Let's take another sidestep to Warren Buffett. A quality many miss about Mr. Buffett is his ability to morph. If you read his materials from the 1960s, he said very different things than in the 1970s and early 1980s. Early on, he was buying dirt-cheap stocks by simple statistical standards and typically smaller stocks—which would today be referred to as small-cap value (although that term didn't exist until the late 1980s). Later, he bought what he called "franchises." Then he entered a period of buying great managements of big companies and being a long-term holder—otherwise thought of as big-cap growth today—that many ascribed to the influence of my father coupled with Charlie Munger.

When Mr. Buffett was buying Coke and Gillette, you couldn't quite reconcile those activities with the kinds of things he owned two decades earlier. Then, amazingly, 12 years ago, at just the right time, he was buying smaller things dirt cheap again just as value came back into play as the twenty-first century began. While Buffett never lost the core of what he was doing or what he was looking for, he tactically morphed steadily over the decades. Trying to freeze his tactics from any decade and replicate them in the next few would never have led you to his actual actions. There's nothing wrong with that. It's as it should be. That he doesn't develop capital markets technology is just his way because—I think—he is mainly intuitive and, in that regard, very rare. But whether developing capital markets technology or being instinctual like Mr. Buffett, morphing, adapting and changing are fundamental to success. Stagnancy is failure long term. Since I don't know how to be instinctual, I rely on the Three Questions and building capital markets technology.

Forecast With Accuracy, Not Like a Professional

Another example of capital markets technology I developed is something I call sentiment-based bell curve forecasting. Like PSRs, I used it for a number of years, but this technology as I first introduced it in the 1990s is today largely priced into the market—in some applications and in some places. But in other applications and places, it still works (we get to that in a bit).

We all now know if everyone agrees some specific market move will occur, it likely won't. But let's consider why for another moment to lead us in a circuitous path to some valuable technology. Remember our analogy from the Preface about creating a representative sample of investors for a poll? You know polling technology is sufficient because it can discern within a predictable level of error the outcome of the election of a president, governor or senator just beforehand. This technology is mature. The pollsters start by building a representative sample of the actual voter world. If the sample isn't built correctly, the polls don't work; but if the sample is representative, it needn't be huge. You can forecast a big state election with a sample of just 500 people if they're picked right.

So we took our imaginary sample of investors and polled them about what they thought the market would do next month, let's call it March. And they overwhelmingly concluded the market would soar in March. So we knew it couldn't. Because if they were overwhelming in their view it would go way up, and if they were reflective of all investors as a group, then whatever buying they had to do would be completed before March began—or before it went on for long—and there would be no subsequent buying to drive stocks up. Their belief priced it in, and it couldn't occur.

Sadly, we don't have technology today letting us correctly build a sample of all investors. There are sentiment universes existing that claim to be useful this way, but they aren't. One commonly used is the so-called Investors' Intelligence data, based on newsletter writers. Another is a regular poll of members of the American Association of Individual Investors. Meir Statman and I looked at these in some detail and demonstrated they aren't predictive, despite often being used by many investors as if they were. (For this study in detail, see "Investor Sentiment and Stock Returns.")[4] These tools don't stand up to statistical analysis and are grossly lacking.

There are many reasons we don't know how to build a correct sample today. To start, individual investors have little incentive to be vocal with a pollster about their money views. Why should I tell you about my money life any more than I would tell you about my sex life? In addition, different investors use the same words for different meanings, leading to conflicting conclusions when you poll—they don't really speak a common language.

Also, individual investors are actually hesitant or incapable of being open to pollsters about who they are. There is nothing new about this. This problem was well known and documented before 1954 when Darrell Huff wrote his classic, *How to Lie With Statistics* (which is one of the best, brief, easy reads ever written, and I encourage everyone to read it).

Something can fill the gap until we figure out how to build that elusive sample. Professional investors are avid seekers of information. As a group, they have access to all the same information as other investors. But luckily, professionals are a smaller sample size, more manageable statistically and easier to categorize and sort. They're also very vocal about their views— indeed, they have incentive to vocalize. Professional investors speak in a commonly trained language, so output from them is relatively consistent, unlike individual investors. And best of all, professionals' views are more heartfelt. Because they believe in their training, they tend to hang on to their views longer.

Then, too, they tend to make very specific forecasts on index returns. And they do so all in a clump—at the start of each year. The January forecast barrage is a result of order preference (in this case insisting on certain things in a certain order for no purpose other than societal convention) and another symptom of our brains gone haywire. Good or bad, right or wrong, every year most investment institutions engage in this ritual. The wire houses have in-house economists making predictions. Fund managers have theirs. Professional money managers responsible for smaller pools might throw their hats in the ring via quarterly reports to clients. A great many big-name gurus will tell you forecasting is impossible and then proceed to tell you what they think will happen. You can't pay a blogger *not* to tell you what he thinks. Blogger pollution is ubiquitous! Everyone's got an opinion. And there's nothing wrong with that. Over the years, an increasing flow of characters make public prognostications such that now, we have a huge menu of forecasters.

But most are wrong more than right. And you already knew that.

At any point in time, a few will be right—some few because they know something and some few more because they're lucky, just like the lucky coin tosser and his 50 consecutive heads. But you don't see most of them being right more often than not. Why? Because they are avid seekers of information and collectively have access to all widely available information, what they agree on is normally already priced into the market and therefore unlikely to occur as they expect.

In the early 1990s, I wanted to see how much forecasters differed from one another. I found all the published annual forecasts I could going back as far as possible from as many sources as possible. Then I plotted the forecasts for each phenomenon and the actual subsequent return on a graph. One thing I found was the forecasts usually fell into a seemingly natural bell curve. The masses grouped in agreement in the fat part of the bell with decreasing numbers of forecasters having more extreme bullish and bearish views out to either side. In each year, there were a few outliers, but most ended up somewhere bunched around a consensus range.

Figure 4.1 shows the consensus bell curves from 1996 to 2003 and respective returns for each year (more on why we don't show past 2003 in a bit). Each number represents one professional forecaster's forecast. The middle of the bell curve is what they agree on. You can see, in every year, the actual return fell not within the consensus, but either outside the bandwidth or in a hole somewhere. In several years, one or two maybe lucky folks got it right, but they're not the same folks each year. Some years, people were bullish and the market did poorly. Some years, they were bullish and the market did much better than they forecast. In other years, the market did something weird and different than what they could agree on. This is a perfect example of why being a classic contrarian (as discussed in Chapter 2) doesn't work. The market typically does something different, not necessarily the reverse of what most people expect.

Figure 4.1 demonstrates where the forecasts were wrong and the outcomes themselves already priced. The consensus agreed on a range of outcomes— the range was what most folks believed would happen, so it couldn't. From this, I concluded a consensus was therefore somewhat gameable.

With this technology, forecasting became a matter of exclusion. I knew the consensus was unlikely to happen, so I considered both extremes and any potential holes within the consensus range. I also knew the market does only

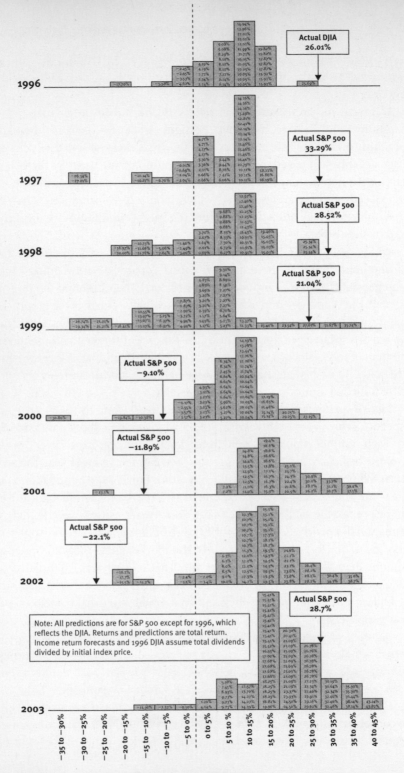

Figure 4.1 Annual Market Forecast Surveys
Sources: BusinessWeek, Fisher Investments.

one of four things each year—it can be up a lot, up a little, down a little or down a lot—just those four things (more on that in Chapter 8). So I ruled out scenarios I thought were unlikely, and my forecast was whatever market scenario seemed likeliest where there weren't other forecasters. That logic is consistent with the market being a discounter of all known information, consistent with history and an example of Question Two—fathoming something the forecasters couldn't fathom: that they, themselves, are part of the market and can be gamed collectively.

Another way to say this is you don't want to make your forecast until after year end when everyone else has, and then you want to make sure, at a minimum, you aren't forecasting what everyone else is.

For example, in 1999, the consensus was wary of Y2K and ready to capitulate after a wondrously positive decade. The consensus was indifferently bullish; most forecasters couldn't see any reasons why the market should break double digits, so I knew it could—might not, but could. A fair few were bearish with a hole on the down-a-lot side of the bell curve. There were plenty of bearish concerns being rehashed daily on the evening news, but I couldn't see anything bad on the horizon not already priced into the market, so I ruled out down a lot.

There was another hole between about 15% and 23%. I could see a number of things largely disregarded or ignored by the masses that could drive stocks up. As previously discussed in Chapter 2, I thought Y2K very likely to be a nonevent, which would be a pleasant surprise to those stockpiling canned goods and fashioning tinfoil hats. People also ignored the election cycle—1999 was the third year in Clinton's second term. You'll recall from Chapter 2—third years are rarely negative and often smashingly positive. Folks were dour on the prospects for US businesses, but I thought corporate earnings would continue to surprise to the upside. I thought it was pretty likely America's stock market would be up a lot, possibly over 20% in 1999. Hence, my *Forbes* forecast (in my December 28, 1998, column entitled "Bullish for '99") was for the S&P 500 to be up 20%. And it was—the S&P 500 finished 1999 just over 21%.[5] I was beyond lucky my 20% forecast was so close to the actual outcome—that was pure luck—but the bell curve technology I'd perfected in the mid-1990s let me see how to be on the right side of the market.

Did I pat myself on the back for getting it almost spot on in 1999? No. That would've been hindsight bias and overconfidence. My goal in forecasting isn't to get the actual number right. I don't much care about forecasting an actual return at all (but the editor of *Forbes* at the time wanted me to). It's far more important to use the Three Questions to get the market *direction* right.

Direction is far more important than magnitude. If I get the direction right and number wrong, I'm as happy as if the number is closer (more on that in Chapter 8).

Just one example for one year, but you get the idea. This technology kept me on the right side of the market throughout the late 1990s and into the early part of the next decade, helping me beat the market as it went down in 2000 and 2001. My annual *Forbes* forecasts were based on this technology year after year, and I was right and very lucky throughout those years. I waited to make my forecasts until everyone else had made theirs—I let them go first—so I could game them. Sounds great, right? And it was, for a while. But here's the dirty little secret: Just like the PSR, it doesn't work anymore. At least, not like it used to.

It worked beautifully for years, and you can see clearly it stood up to back-testing. When I described it in *Forbes* at first or wrote about it in *Research* magazine,[6] it was derided as voodoo. Starting around 2000, the voodoo epithet stopped being used. By then, others were adopting the technology or similar ones.

I felt reassured when the bell curves were initially used incorrectly as a contrarian tool. If the consensus was bullish, the early adopters were automatically bearish and vice versa. They looked at 2001 and 2002 when the consensus was gleefully bullish but the actual results were quite bearish. That further bolstered misuse by contrarians. They were using it wrong but getting lucky, which fueled them on.

But wrong and lucky is still wrong. If you used it correctly, you might have been bullish too when the consensus was. Take 1996, 1997, 1998, 1999 and even 2003. In every one of those years, the consensus was mildly bullish, falling far shy of the much more bullish results. If you had used bell curves to arrive at bearish conclusions in those years, you would have missed out on terrific returns.

Eventually, people began getting it right. I knew I was in trouble when Richard Bernstein was promoted to chief market forecaster at Merrill Lynch. Bernstein had built a very good parallel technology that had worked well looking backward at the 1990s. Meir Statman and I had also covered his data in the previously mentioned "Investor Sentiment" paper.[7] Bernstein's model demonstrated useful predictive powers historically. His becoming a bigwig foretold the impending demise of my bell curve technology working as it had before.

It worked a few years more and, lo and behold, by 2004, it stopped working altogether. By then, you could read on the Internet multiple sources mimicking or paralleling my original bell curves—still can now. Some folks actually use my old technology directly. Just like the PSR, what had once been novel became popular enough to be priced into the market and therefore obsolete. Granted, 2004 might have been a one-time fluke. But as more professional forecasters raced to adopt this technology, I knew it was doomed to not work. By 2005, it didn't.

For several years after, some material subset of forecasters gamefully watched each other as they issued forecasts, then revised their forecasts. So when they made their initial forecasts, they didn't have the gravitas and permanent intent forecasts had only a few years ago. Everyone was gaming everyone, so it was time to move on to a new game.

For US stocks, that is.

Once I'd built this technology, I discovered it worked on any freely traded market where there were sufficient forecasters making public prognostications. We used it regularly to triangulate Nasdaq, for which there were a plethora of forecasts in the 1990s, to the S&P 500. In fact, this technology partially influenced my decision to go bearish on the Tech sector in early 2000. (You can read my Tech bubble market call from my March 6, 2000, *Forbes* column titled "1980 Revisited"—re-created for you in Appendix G.) Once I saw this capital markets technology was no longer powerful for the major US indexes, we set our sights on determining if folks in other parts of the world thought to use this technology there.

And it worked well for foreign stock markets for several additional years—so long as there were enough public professional forecasts. Beyond stocks, it also continued to work for long-term interest rates inside and outside America, as well as for the biggest major currencies.

But even there, the power as a stand-alone forecasting tool has begun to break down. It happens to the best tools, which is why you must test, test, test. We still look at bell curves because, as said earlier, often things that stop working regain power if folks widely lose faith in them. But knowing what the consensus thinks is an additional data point we consider at my firm when making forward-looking forecasts.

Why Tell You Any of This?

Again, you may wonder why I opened my proverbial big mouth. Wouldn't remaining silent let me use these longer? Maybe. Maybe not. I might have gotten a few more years out of my bell curves for the US markets had I not vocalized them. But Bernstein and others were coming along anyway and would have created the same effect regardless. I knew this advantage would go away one day. Did I speed the adoption of this technology by publicizing it?

Possibly. Graphing forecasts into a bell curve format in the mid-1990s is the sort of unique research we do at my firm you don't readily see from most places. It's derivative of always asking the Three Questions.

So why give the results and discoveries away? Two reasons! First: I'm not fearful of losing one piece of technology when we're constantly innovating and know we must. We have hundreds of capital markets technologies still in use at my firm—many developed since the bell curves stopped being so powerful. And we will develop hundreds if not thousands more in the years ahead.

Second: If the world continually ridicules what I know to be good technology—like it does with the presidential term cycle material or my P/E work from a long time ago—then I learn it has legs. I know I can count on the world's cognitive bias to keep it from seeing reality, and thus, the tool remains useful. I can focus my efforts on innovating in other areas knowing this area still has legs. In my view, you can't know this until you give it away.

If bell-curve forecasting were my only arrow, maybe I would have jealously guarded that secret. But if you use the Three Questions and keep building capital markets technology, you will constantly be seeking the next thing and won't fear losing the old thing. Without the Three Questions, if I lost a tool or two, I might be forced to retire to my wife, redwoods and cats. But with the Three Questions, the next thrill is always on the tip of the next question. Constant innovation invites me to do the most fun part of asset management. And if I'm not innovating in this day and age, I don't deserve to be managing over tens of billions for other people.

Staying competitive in this game takes constant innovation, but most people dislike that or don't even get it. My view is the financial services industry overall doesn't get that. When I think about a corporate role model for my firm, I don't look to Wall Street. My corporate role models are Intel from the early 1970s, Sam Walton and Wal-Mart from the same era, Procter & Gamble for marketing and GE in terms of management. These were visionary innovators from my young adulthood. I look to Bob Noyce, co-inventor of the integrated circuit, co-founder of Intel and longtime partner of Gordon Moore.

Back in a simpler world, I got to meet and know Bob Noyce, and he blew me away. Noyce knew he and Moore could never stop moving at a time I didn't know it was necessary. While not tall (actually quite short), he was such a towering intellectual presence most folks presumed there would be no Intel of materiality after him. Here, they missed the power of the combined spirit of Bob Noyce and Gordon Moore and how each knew what they knew then about making semiconductors would be dwarfed by what innovators would soon know. Their goal was to move along Gordon Moore's learning curve faster than the next guys. What was really proprietary was their faith in the learning curve and innovation.

That role model has been ever present in my thinking since, which is why my focus is now, always has been and always will be on constant innovation. I don't want my firm to be like a Wall Street firm. I want it to be like the Intel of Noyce and Moore circa 1975. So no, when I've developed something I think is really neat, I don't mind if it gets accepted, priced into markets and subsequently rendered useless. I assume it will. That's called progress.

NEW CAPITAL MARKETS TECHNOLOGY— CONSTANT INNOVATION

For an accounting of new capital markets technology my firm has developed through the years, as well as older technologies still in use, I direct you to my newer books, including 2010's *Debunkery* and 2011's *Markets Never Forget*, both published by John Wiley & Sons.

Better Living Through Global Benchmarking

Not all capital markets technology is about forecasting. It can also be a tool to keep you disciplined. One such mature capital markets technology alive and well in my firm (to which I've already alluded) is global benchmarking. This isn't new, and I didn't invent it! We spoke about benchmarking as a cure to many Stone Age ills in Chapter 3.

You may scoff at this idea of picking an index to follow and manage against and measure yourself against as being technology. It's too simplistic and not a new concept—maybe too widely dispersed already. And anyone can do it! Yes, it is simplistic, and anyone can do it—but mostly, they don't. And if they do, they usually do it wrong. If they did use it, they would likely have more success and make fewer errors. This is why it's great. You can measure yourself against your benchmark, but more important, you should manage yourself against it.

Your inclination, like many US investors, may be to shy away from global investing, preferring to focus on the S&P 500 and US stocks and mutual funds. After all, you know America is better and are more comfortable with it. Cincinnati doesn't scare you but maybe Tampico does. Still, it remains true global thinking helps you think better about everything, including understanding America better. One prime purpose of global benchmarking is to think better.

For example, many wrongly believe they don't need to think globally or own foreign stocks because they can get the equivalent of global exposure through US firms that have heavy sales exposure overseas—through US multinationals. This widely held view is easily proven false using what you learned in Chapter 1. Now you just have to do it on your own. If US multinationals give you foreign exposure, then they should correlate tightly with foreign stocks, right? If not, you're not getting the exposure you want. But if you get a bunch of US, Japanese, German and Dutch multinationals, you will find they correlate much closer with their own countries than they do with each other. That is to say, Exxon, Coke and Ford correlate much closer to each other and the S&P 500 than they do with Sony, Toyota, Hitachi and the Morgan Stanley Topix. The correlations teach you that US multinational stocks act like US stocks and don't give you foreign exposure.

The reason, of course, is each country has cultural effects impacting its stocks beyond where the company generates its revenue. A Japanese firm has primarily Japanese employees, is centered on Japanese laws more than non-Japanese laws and primarily gets more financing from within Japan than outside Japan. But the answer remains in the correlations. This example also teaches you that until you start thinking globally, you can't really understand that about the US multinationals—which is my basic point. To understand America better today, whether through global yield curves or relations between US stocks and how they perform, you must think globally.

Xenophobes don't know and have a hard time accepting that the index you pick as your benchmark doesn't much matter if you have a very long investing horizon. Believe it or not, all correctly calculated major equity benchmarks end up in about the same place if you give them enough time—they just get there via very different paths (as I detail later). But a rational person would select a benchmark getting to that long-term equity return with the least likely volatility—for a smoother ride. Additionally, a rational person would pick the benchmark that provides the most opportunities to make market bets and win and has the most to teach using the Three Questions—and that must be the whole world, leading us back to global.

A benchmark is absolutely vital because it's your road map for your portfolio. Investing without a benchmark is like getting on an unfamiliar road in an unfamiliar state in an unfamiliar car even, meandering without a map or directions and wondering why you're getting no closer to your destination. But you aren't really sure what your destination is except you might recognize it when you see it. The benchmark, as your road map, instructs you on what to include in your portfolio, in what percentage and when.

Your Benchmark Is a Road Map for Your Long Journey

On the morning of September 11, 2001, I happened to be on a train with a group of my East Coast staff on the way from Washington, DC, to Philadelphia to conduct client seminars for local clients. Then the terrorist attacks shattered normality. From Philly, staff dispersed toward homes and families posthaste in all different directions—from New Hampshire to Florida. Unable to fly, two colleagues and I rented a van and drove west to California. We broke the speed limit whenever possible—most of the time. There are two main routes to take. We took the longer southern route through St. Louis for fear if there were more bombings, Chicago and the northern route was a more logical target—hence, we picked the road less traveled. We dropped off one fellow in St. Louis who planned to take a midnight train to his home in Dallas. We drove on in three-hour shifts, and then we stopped at a convenience station for gas, food and to switch for the next three-hour shift. We made it across America, amazingly, in 32 hours. If you really set your mind to it, nonstop, that is how long it takes.

And we never could have done it without a road map. It helped us see the southern route wasn't much longer and was maybe faster and certainly less traveled. It told us where to go and, when detoured, how to get back on track. It helped us decide which way to drive around Denver. From Denver, whether to take the northern route through Salt Lake City and the Donner Pass or the southern route through the Mojave Desert (this time, we went north). It helped us manage and plan our trip. It let us control our risk. A good stock market benchmark provides the same benefits.

The benchmark also serves as a measuring stick for performance. When you look at your portfolio each year, do you check if you were up or down and by how much? If you do, how do you know if you had a good year or a bad year? If you were up 20%, is that good? Is it still good if you find out the broad market was up 35%? If you were down 5%, is that bad? What if you were down just 5% while the market was down 25%? As you drive from Philly to San Francisco, there are simply stretches where you can beat the speed limit and stretches where you can't be anything but patient. Markets are like that.

Many investors claim their goal is to beat "the market" but fail to identify *which* market they mean and how they'll go about beating it. The market could refer to US equity markets, world equity markets, even bond markets. For a few years, myriad investors wanted to beat the Nasdaq. You cannot rationally aim to beat "the market" unless you choose a specific one to beat. The market you select will be your benchmark and drive every conscious portfolio decision you make.

Once you've selected your benchmark, you can then choose to beat it by plowing everything into one narrow stock subcategory, but the risk if you're wrong is huge. The benchmark helps you define your risk profile—how concentrated or diverse you are compared to the road map you're managing against.

Broad equity indexes like the S&P 500, the MSCI World and the MSCI ACWI make good proxies for market performance and, hence, a benchmark against which to manage and measure results. But your benchmark can be any well-constructed index—the Russell 2000 if you like small caps. Most British investors use the FTSE and Germans the DAX. Or the Nasdaq if you're a technophile. Whatever the index, you must be specific about what you compare and measure your portfolio and investing activities against. And then you must generally stick to that index for a long time.

Pick an Index, Any Index (But Don't Believe More Volatility Gets You Higher Returns)

Ten years on and another bear market later, many investors still keenly remember the Tech bubble bursting, making them fear the Nasdaq. Yes, the Nasdaq tanked in 2000, 2001 and 2002 and led the global market into a relatively long bear market. Is it therefore bad and to be avoided? The Nasdaq isn't a bad index. In fact, it's perfectly fine and well constructed. It's just very narrowly focused and, hence, more volatile. The narrower the index, the more volatile you can expect it to be over time—which is a fairly intuitive investing truth. It has very little that zigs within it to reduce total volatility when something else zags. The Tech-heavy Nasdaq will gyrate wildly with the fortune of mostly Tech and Tech alone.

But there's no reason to suffer such an intense, near-term roller-coaster ride since over long periods (like your 20, 30 or 40-year investment time horizon), all well-constructed indexes should, near the end, yield very similar returns, though traveling wildly different paths to get there. Maybe you don't believe that. I hope to convince you.

But you can accept that if all well-constructed major equity benchmarks eventually get you to about the same place, one prime concern should be how smooth the ride will be. Figure 4.2 shows a variety of indexes or benchmarks converging over time but taking different paths en route. These aren't real indexes but rather a representation of different types.

Index 4 is a volatile benchmark that vastly outperforms other major indexes at its peaks but vastly underperforms at its troughs. Think of this as any very narrow index, like the Nasdaq, or perhaps a very small country index. Index 3 lagged a bit early on but outperformed in later years—which could be

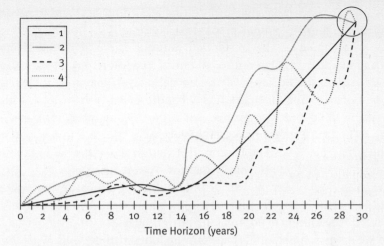

Figure 4.2 Benchmark and Time Horizon
Note: For illustrative purposes only. Not drawn to scale. Not to be interpreted as a forecast.

like a larger, developed country index. Index 2 did better early on but trailed off a bit in the past 15 years—which is somewhat similar to Japan. A rational investor would prefer the index with the lowest volatility as represented by Index 1, which arrives with the smoothest ride. The smoothest ride tends to come from the broadest benchmarks.

Currently, the broadest indexes are the globally oriented MSCI World Index, which reflects developed nations and has a long history, and the ACWI, which includes Emerging Markets (which I still prefer to call "less developed nations"—after all, some of them emerge and some of them submerge). The ACWI has a shorter history and is less useful in measuring historical data but is darned acceptable as a benchmark.

Keep in mind, even a very broad index doesn't protect you from systemic risk. When broad markets fall, a global index likely falls big, too. Huge even! But a global index does mitigate country- and sector-specific risk inherent in narrower indexes.

Risk Versus Return?

How can it be the volatile Nasdaq is likely to get you to about the same place over long periods as the S&P 500 or even the über-broad ACWI? If the Nasdaq is more volatile, you should get *more* return, right?

Many who have studied finance believe this common myth. It is conventional wisdom—wrong—and propagated commonly by infinitely educated people who should be able to see right through it but somehow can't. The notion is that to get higher return, you must take more risk, as measured by volatility, so you should have a volatile portfolio if you want to beat the market. That works over time for stocks versus bonds versus cash—which is historically where the concept originated. But within equity types, it's measurably wrong in history. This is one reason history is so beautiful as a way to test if commonly accepted wisdom is right. If it were true, Tech would have higher long-term returns than less volatile indexes—but it doesn't.

You can create a narrow, volatile index by taking almost any pure category of stocks that all move the same way in the short term. You get volatility that way, but it has nothing to do with long-term returns (as we cover in Chapter 7 when we discuss supply shifts determining long-term pricing). Were that not true, all the subsectors that make up a broad index, all being more volatile individually than the total index, would have higher returns than the index itself. But that can't be—the returns of the parts can't be different than the parts of the returns. This is a very fathomable Question Two most people can't get themselves to contemplate at all. Within equities, short-term volatility has nothing to do with long-term returns. All correctly calculated equity indexes should get you to about the same return—the equity return—if you give them a long enough period. And the ones that come out ahead don't come out ahead by much and only by serendipity or some weird shift in stock supply, likely soon reversed.

Mind you, lots of readers will have been taught what I'm telling you here is wrong. But this is a provably false assumption. History says, "It ain't so." History is beautiful.

This Question One myth persists because we don't question our assumptions and don't use history to verify if theory is real. Investors are biased toward their favorite category, and confirmation bias props up their preset notions. Many investors incorrectly assume their pet category—small-cap growth, Energy, Tech, large value, Emerging Markets, whatever it is—is inherently superior. It's provably wrong, yet precious few bother to check, which is why this is a great myth to debunk. There is absolutely no evidence any one category is permanently better. A fan of a category can show you a cut of time where that category beat the market. Pick a different starting and ending date and its dominance fades. Take a slightly different cut of the same noun and adjective and their meanings fade, too.

A data mine is when someone, intentionally or unintentionally, picks data conveniently seeming to prove their point. But if you use slightly different data or alter the time frame, the whole thing falls apart. Take the long-held myth small-cap stocks do better than big-cap stocks. Historically, there is some validity to this because since 1926, small stocks on average have done better than big-cap stocks. Most observers confuse averages with (1) what happens most often and (2) reality. We know it's a myth because if you take the data series used to prove the point, and then take the homogenous periods coming off the bottom of the four biggest bear markets (times when small caps have always done well)—1932 to 1935, 1942 to 1945, 1974 to 1976 and 2002 to 2004—and looked at the rest of history, you would see in the remaining time periods, big-cap stocks did better than small-cap stocks by a big margin. All the excess small-cap return comes from those few periods. But if you could identify the bottom of the four biggest bear markets correctly, you wouldn't need small-cap stocks to figure out how to beat the market. (Or if you took the very smallest, least liquid small caps out of the study, the whole thing falls apart again.)

My point is the supposed long-term small-cap effect touted by so many is worse than a data mine. It's a confusion pit for most observers (courtesy of TGH). Otherwise, there's simply no validity to it. Some long times, like most of the 2000s, small stocks do lead and markedly. Other times, they lag for a long time.

Said another way, if you were 35 in 1945, just back from World War II and starting to invest and thought you knew small-cap stocks did better on average than big cap, you would have gotten all the way to retirement age at 65 in 1975 and seen big cap beating small cap on average during that overall period. That's just a little too long to count on something working that gets most of its payoff rarely in history. Or say you got back from Vietnam at 25 in 1973, went through psychological counseling for five years, cut your hair and started investing in 1978 at age 30—for the next 20-plus years, big-cap stocks did better on average than small caps (although for the first few years, you would have done well and absorbed some confirmation bias). A quarter century is a long, long time to wait for averages to revert.

Pick your time period carefully, and you can seem to prove a lot of things. But despite most investors having longer time horizons than they think they have, darned few can afford to be wrong for a full quarter of a century. You can combat that by not concentrating all in one size, style, sector, you name it.

If one category was demonstrably better than all the others, we'd all know it by now and invest our money in it; all other equity categories would go away. We're all subject to capitalism. Stock prices are determined by supply and demand. And no one index, size, style or category is best forever. None. And you don't have 25 years to wait for the next time category X leads the market.

Global Thinking Equals Better Thinking

It should make sense the more you spread your exposure globally, the more you spread your risk. No country leads consistently, and no one knows with certainty who the next leader will be. Table 4.2 illustrates the changing leadership of country performance from year to year. The opportunity cost of not diversifying across geographic lines can be huge. Instead of fearing the unfamiliar, you should fear missing large opportunities to be had abroad. And you should fear your own country of origin may be where the roughest risk resides next.

If you aren't comfortable picking individual foreign stocks, you can easily get global exposure through a low-cost index fund or an exchange-traded fund (ETF). The MSCI EAFE, reflecting the developed foreign markets, has been widely available as an inexpensive index fund for years. Using such an investment vehicle spreads your risk, getting you needed foreign exposure while being otherwise completely passive.

Note: I'm generally not a fan of mutual funds or index funds (as I wrote in a *Forbes* column reproduced in Appendix D). They're usually far too expensive and eliminate too many tax benefits for high net worth investors. But if you have a smaller kitty to work with, they can help you get the diversification you need. And if you don't know anything others don't, passiveness is always appropriate.

If you do go the mutual fund route, be sure to buy a sufficiently broad fund or a collection of funds. Also, remember to check the expense ratios. Many funds are very expensive. Diversifying your portfolio globally is smart, but not if fees eat all the benefit.

Truly, you need not fear foreign investing. Many foreign stocks can be purchased easily with US dollars in the form of American depositary receipts (ADRs). What's more, you need only check your fridge, medicine cabinet, closet, workbench or garage (or heck, maybe your employer) to find plenty of familiar names from foreign lands.

Never Say Dow

I keep saying your benchmark should be a "well-constructed" index, but what's a "poorly constructed" index? Say hello to the Dow Jones Industrial Average, a very poorly constructed index indeed.

Many investors live and die by the Dow Jones Industrial Average, frequently referred to reverently as "the Dow." Investors assume the Dow is a reliable market indicator, but in reality, the Dow is poorly constructed, tells little and should never be used as a benchmark. I haven't paid any attention to the Dow in

Table 4.2 Leadership Keeps Shifting—Top Five Performing Stock Markets Since 1990

Year	#1		#2		#3		#4		#5		US return
1990	Greece	90.4%	UK	10.3%	Hong Kong	09.2%	Austria	06.7%	Norway	01.1%	–02.1%
1991	Hong Kong	49.5%	Australia	35.6%	USA	31.3%	Singapore	25.0%	New Zealand	20.8%	31.3%
1992	Hong Kong	32.3%	Switzerland	18.1%	USA	07.4%	Singapore	06.3%	Netherlands	03.4%	07.4%
1993	Hong Kong	116.7%	Finland	83.2%	New Zealand	70.0%	Singapore	68.0%	Switzerland	46.7%	10.1%
1994	Finland	52.5%	Norway	24.1%	Japan	21.6%	Sweden	18.8%	Ireland	14.5%	02.0%
1995	Switzerland	45.0%	USA	38.2%	Sweden	34.1%	Spain	31.2%	Netherlands	28.9%	38.2%
1996	Spain	41.3%	Sweden	38.0%	Portugal	36.4%	Finland	34.7%	Hong Kong	33.1%	24.1%
1997	Portugal	47.4%	Switzerland	44.8%	Italy	36.4%	Greece	36.2%	Denmark	35.0%	34.1%
1998	Finland	122.6%	Greece	78.1%	Belgium	68.7%	Italy	53.2%	Spain	50.6%	30.7%
1999	Finland	153.3%	Singapore	99.4%	Sweden	80.6%	Japan	61.8%	Hong Kong	59.5%	22.4%
2000	Switzerland	06.4%	Canada	5.6%	Denmark	03.7%	Norway	–00.4%	Italy	–00.8%	–12.5%
2001	New Zealand	09.5%	Australia	02.7%	Ireland	–02.7%	Austria	–05.0%	Belgium	–10.2%	–12.0%
2002	New Zealand	26.1%	Austria	17.3%	Australia	–00.3%	Italy	–06.3%	Norway	–06.7%	–22.7%
2003	Greece	69.5%	Sweden	66.1%	Germany	64.8%	Spain	59.2%	Austria	57.8%	29.1%
2004	Austria	72.3%	Norway	54.5%	Greece	46.1%	Belgium	44.9%	Ireland	43.1%	10.7%
2005	Canada	28.9%	Norway	25.7%	Japan	25.6%	Denmark	25.3%	Austria	25.2%	05.7%
2006	Spain	50.2%	Portugal	48.4%	Ireland	47.6%	Singapore	46.7%	Norway	46.3%	15.3%
2007	Finland	50.1%	Hong Kong	41.2%	Germany	35.9%	Greece	32.9%	Norway	32.4%	06.0%
2008	Japan	–29.1%	Switzerland	–29.9%	USA	–37.1%	Spain	–40.1%	France	–42.7%	–37.1%
2009	Norway	88.6%	Australia	76.8%	Singapore	74.0%	Sweden	65.9%	Hong Kong	60.2%	27.1%
2010	Sweden	34.8%	Denmark	31.1%	Hong Kong	23.2%	Singapore	22.2%	Canada	21.2%	15.4%

Source: Thomson Reuters, individual country returns from 12/31/1989 to 12/31/2010.[8]

decades and can't even tell you its absolute level because I trained myself (as titled in my November 19, 1999, *Forbes* column) to "Never Say Dow."

My advice to you is you will see markets better if you train yourself to ignore the Dow for the rest of your life as well. The only time to ever say Dow is when you're referring to a publishing company, a chemical company or an Asian philosophy (spelled Tao). But *never* use the Dow Jones Industrial Average.

First, but not most important, the Dow is comprised of only 30 big stocks—hardly a fair and total representation of US markets. Then, those few Dow stocks are picked arbitrarily. Some get taken over and drop out. Others are dropped out and replaced by the Dow committee doing the picking. (They picked Coca-Cola but not Pepsi. Microsoft but not Apple, though Apple is 75% larger by market cap. Then they picked both Merck and Pfizer. Why? No idea.)[9] It has maintained its stature in the popular press mainly for sentimental and cultural reasons—the same type of reasons allowing market myths to persist for multiple decades. (That its sponsor also owns the *Wall Street Journal* and *Barron's* doesn't hurt either.)

But its biggest deficiency is it's a *price-weighted* index. Never pay attention to price-weighted indexes—any, ever. Let me say that again for emphasis. Never pay attention to any price-weighted index.

Consider, as I update in 2011, Caterpillar has three times more potential impact on the Dow's outcome than Microsoft, though Microsoft is three times bigger by market cap.[10] Why does a vastly bigger stock have materially less impact? Welcome to price-weighting.

The higher the price per share of a stock in a "price-weighted" index like the Dow (and Japan's NIKKEI—by the way, don't use it either—another very misleading price-weighted index), the more impact it has relative to other stocks in the index. In a price-weighted index, a $100 stock has 10 times the future impact on the index as a $10 stock, even though the $10 stock can be from a firm worth vastly more and much bigger by any standard. Madness.

Price-weighted indexes are inherently problematic because if a stock splits, its weight in the index also splits. The overall level of the index hasn't been affected, but the split reduced the impact of that stock relative to the index's other stocks. You don't want to believe that—most people don't—but it's true. The reverse is also true—if a stock does a reverse split, as rarely happens (meaning you get one share for every two you owned previously, as an example), the stock's weight in the index doubles.

Stock splits and reverse splits are purely cosmetic and don't impact a company's market capitalization or dividends, investors' net worth or any other form of real economics—not at all. However, stock splits absolutely affect which stocks have impact and power within a price-weighted index. Unless you can predict stock splits, and there has never yet been a technology capable of it, you don't have a rational basis for predicting a price-weighted index for even a year or two at a crack—even if you could perfectly predict the price performance of every single stock in the index. That's a fact. In some years, the Dow would have done 10% better or worse than it actually did depending on which stocks in the index could have ended up splitting or not. I don't mean 11% instead of 10%. I mean 20% instead of 10%.

Mathematically, year by year, the Dow's value is quite technically purely random depending on which stocks split and when. In any year, if the split stocks do worse than the stocks that don't split, the index does better than the average stock. If the stocks that split do better than the stocks that didn't split, the index does worse than the average return of the stocks.

Crazy, right? Said alternately, if the high-priced-per-share stocks beat the low-priced-per-share stocks, then the Dow does better than the economic returns of its stocks. Conversely, if the low-priced-per-share stocks do better than the high-priced-per-share stocks, then the Dow does worse than its stocks.

You've heard the Dow has a thing called the "divisor" to adjust for splits. Let's truly alter your sense of reality. When a stock in the Dow splits, Dow Jones and Company does adjust the "divisor"—just like with any price-weighted index. This divisor keeps the level of the overall Dow constant from before the change to afterward so it's cosmetically seamless. That is, changing the divisor makes the split not affect the overall level of the Dow (allegedly) as the split occurs. The divisor is continually adjusted, but it still can't keep the Dow from its steady march away from reality.

The Two-Stock Index

Here is an easy demonstration why price-weighted indexes are to be shunned and you should wholly disregard the Dow. We're creating a price-weighted index made up of just two stocks—ABC and XYZ—each initially worth $100 per share. For simplicity, they both have the same overall market value, and every other quantitative feature about them is identical. To get the initial index value, we simply add the prices of ABC and XYZ together, divide by the total number of stocks (2) and get $100. So our Two-Index starts out at 100. Straightforward! You didn't even need a calculator for that.

On Monday, ABC is up 10% to $110 and XYZ is down 10% to $90. Add 110 to 90 and you get 200, divide by 2 (our initial divisor) and you still get $100, which makes sense because the 10% move in each perfectly offsets. Again, easy math! Nothing weird—yet. Later Monday, they reverse and are both at $100 again and the index remains at 100.

But wait!

On Tuesday, ABC announces a 100-for-1 stock split. Mind you, most splits are usually on the order of 2-for-1 or 3-for-1, but for the sake of example, clarity and insanity (since price-weighted indexes are insane), it's easier to use extreme numbers. ABC now trades at $1 per share, though the overall value of the company remains unchanged. Nothing changes for shareholders, either. If a shareholder earlier had 100 shares of ABC at $100, now he has 10,000 shares each worth $1—and in both cases owns $10,000 of ABC. ABC sells for $1. XYZ is still $100. Add the two together and you get $101. Divide by 2 and now you get $50.50.

But wait, that isn't right. That won't work. We know the index must remain at 100 because nothing changed but the split. Time for a divisor adjustment! Just what the Dow would do. Instead of dividing by 2, like we did initially, now we ask, "What number, divided into 101, gives us 100?" Simple algebra—the answer is 1.01. So we set the new divisor at 1.01, just about half of what it was before the split, and our index remains at 100, and we're fat, dumb and happy.

On Wednesday, ABC rises 10% again and XYZ falls 10%. But instead of the index remaining unchanged as it should and as it did before the split, now it changes markedly. ABC is now $1.10. XYZ is now $90. Add them together and you get $91.10. Divide by our new divisor of 1.01 and you get an index value of $90.20. What the . . . ? The index fell nearly 10% for no reason other than the two stocks in the index had identical but reverse percentage moves. How can that be?

Welcome to the dirty little secret reality of price-weighted indexes. While the economic returns of the companies haven't changed one iota since the index's creation, the index itself has—markedly. If the companies are worth the same, they should have identical impacts on the index, but this is impossible with any price-weighted index—even the most holy Dow.

Said again: In any year, if the split stocks do worse than the stocks that don't split, the index does better than the average stock. If the stocks that split do better than the stocks that didn't split, the index does worse than the average return of the stocks.

I'm always amazed, with most professionals focused on craftsmanship, how few of them in their training ever took a course in construction of indexes—which are always craft-like. Almost none! Hard to figure why. For those of you who would like a further, easy-to-self-learn tutorial on index construction, I recommend Chapter 5 of Frank Reilly's *Investment Analysis and Portfolio Management* (Dryden Press, 1996). It's one of my favorite investment textbooks. And Frank is one of my favorite academics and a very nice guy.

A well-constructed index is market-capitalization weighted, which means companies worth more actually weigh more heavily in the index. Apple, with its behemoth market capitalization of $370 billion, has much more impact on the S&P 500 and the ACWI than Caterpillar with its market cap of around $60 billion.[11] As it should. Few would argue a bigger stock shouldn't be more impactful on the index.

Never Maximize Return

So benchmarking should be based on market capitalization-weighted indexes. What's more, as mentioned earlier, this specific capital markets technology—global benchmarking—is intended not to forecast returns but to keep you on your path and to force you to think globally. It's the essence of conquering your Stone Age brain and gaining self-control to help you master Question Three.

Even after selecting an appropriate benchmark, many investors end up hurting themselves by trying to maximize return. They want to see big positive returns each and every year—hit home runs—and forget to check what the benchmark is doing as a way to control risk. Tied to order preference, they disregard the importance of *relative return* versus *absolute return* in a preference for absolute return. And in doing so, they forget about risk completely.

Relative return is the return realized relative to your chosen benchmark. For instance, if your portfolio returns 5% in a year, you may think it's a rather poor showing. But if your benchmark is up 3%, you beat the market by 2%, which is very good and better than most do on average. Likewise, you might feel pretty good if your portfolio returns 15% in a year. But if the benchmark did 30%, you lagged by a very big 15%. Making up a lag that big if your aim is to get market-like returns on average is tough—you'd have to beat the market by an average 1% for the next 15 years!

Usually, your focus should be on relative return—how you did versus your benchmark—rather than absolute return. Why? Because we already know if you can do a little better than the market over the long term, you do better than almost all investors—it's that simple. Even just matching the market is a feat most investors fail at long term—even professionals.

Beating the market (whatever your chosen market is) is a noble goal but very tough. Doable but tough. But instead of focusing on whacking the ball out the park each and every year, a better goal might be to aim to be benchmark-like. If your benchmark is up 20% over a year, you had a great year if you met it or beat it by a little bit with returns of 21% or 23%.

Why is such a narrow margin great? See it this way. If your benchmark is up 20% and you're up 40%, you may be elated and think you're a genius. (Beware pride accumulation, overconfidence and hindsight bias!) However, if you take a bet big enough to beat your benchmark by 20%—ask yourself, "What if I was wrong?" Answer: If you were wrong with that same bet, you would have likely lagged the benchmark by 20%. If the benchmark was up 20% and you were flat for the year, you wouldn't feel so smart anymore.

Remember the good discipline control mechanism talked about in Chapter 3: Don't aim to beat your benchmark by much more than you are comfortable lagging it. Why? You can and will be wrong. Often! And if you are more wrong than right in a year, you'll likely lag. That's ok, and you should expect it. It doesn't much harm you long term, as long as you use your benchmark to control risk.

If you do beat your benchmark by 30%, you can do a joy dance to the luck gods, but don't try to repeat it. That's likely much too much risk for your long-term goals, and you probably should figure out how and why you did it, or next time you may be on the negative end of the spread. Those who swing for the fences regularly strike out much more than average. Try to maximize return, and you may end up maximizing losses. Nobody likes that.

This means, usually, if your benchmark is down, you will be down, too (we look at the one exception a bit later). If your benchmark is down 10% in a year and you're down a bit more or less, you had a fine year. Your benchmark was slightly negative. It happens. It's reality and you can't do anything about it.

For now, start thinking about relative return and not absolute return. Do a good job managing risk and you'll likely get better results than you do now. Portfolio management is all about controlling risks, not about hitting home runs. Do a poor job by taking on too much or too little risk and you'll be surprised how quickly you can do lasting harm to your chances of achieving your long-term goals.

The Greatest Risk of All

Most investors focus on risk that is felt as near-term volatility. However, in the long run, the greatest risk you take as an investor is benchmark risk. *Benchmark risk* is how much you differ from your benchmark, for good or bad. If you have an all-equity benchmark because you need long-term market-like returns to reach your goal but think you're being safe and conservative by holding large allocations of cash and bonds most of the time, that's huge benchmark risk and potentially very damaging to your long-term goal. It just isn't the volatility risk you're thinking about. You're betting that, in the long term, stocks do worse than cash and bonds, which is a very long-shot prediction and historically backward.

Consider the risk of needing to average 8% a year (over a long time period, of course) to get the growth needed to support your desired retirement lifestyle and getting only 4% or 5% instead because you held too much in cash and bonds for long periods. Short-term volatility can be very tough to live through, but what can be even tougher is maybe cutting your lifestyle in half in 20 or 30 years because you took on too much benchmark risk and your long-term returns are too low. Really great investors, almost to a person, have hardened themselves to normal volatility for just this reason. (And yes, volatility is normal. Read more in Chapter 3 of my 2011 book, *Markets Never Forget*.)

Benchmark risk doesn't apply only to stocks versus bonds. You take on benchmark risk by becoming too heavily weighted in any category relative to the benchmark. Think of the investors who got killed in the Tech bubble crash. If your benchmark was 30% Technology in 1999 (about the S&P 500's weight then) and you were one of many who let their Tech allocation creep up to 50% or 60% (or 80% or 90%) of your overall holdings, you adopted tremendous benchmark risk. With such a big relative overweight, your portfolio had to crumble relative to the market as Tech imploded. This happened to many, many folks without their ever knowing what hit them. What hit them? A lack of risk control by failing to control benchmark risk! When you focus on benchmark risk, the risk of something like Tech going crazy on you is ever present in your foresight. Must be!

Anytime there's an asset bubble that nails investors hard, investors look for scapegoats. It's natural! They blame greedy bankers, stupid central bankers, stupider politicians. Maybe any or all of them are to blame, maybe not. But none of them are responsible for your portfolio decisions. Folks who let a part of their portfolio get out of whack and then get whacked bigger than they should after that part implodes should blame, first and foremost, their own overconfidence that led them to take such massive benchmark risk.

Overconfidence can cause benchmark risk in the other direction, too. Heavy underweighting or divesting entirely of a benchmark sector can hurt just as much as being a crazed over-investor. This would be all the folks who said in 1995 they would never own Tech because they didn't understand it. It isn't so hard to understand. And from there, over the next five years, Tech did great, and not owning it at all seriously hurt. Making that decision—saying I won't own something that is a huge part of the world and one easily learned with a little effort—is a little like saying, "I don't understand women, so I won't ever associate with any." Tough choice! Stupid choice! A lot of benchmark risk. A lot of lifelong opportunity cost.

Investors who either tremendously overweight or underweight any sector aren't asking Question Three. They're suffering from overconfidence (among other errors) and can't see they might be wrong about the bets they make. That was what guided me when I maintained a small position in Tech in 2000, even though I was certain I knew something others didn't about what would cause a Tech implosion. I was ready to act on my bet, but I didn't want to make it too extreme, knowing I could be wrong.

If you make a big bet against your benchmark and are wrong, you won't get the performance your benchmark would have given you without the bet. Investors overweighted in Tech in 2000 were wrong and paid the price. Investors hiding under a rock in 2003 were wrong about Tech, and the rest of the market to boot, as stocks boomed. Because they took big bets away from their benchmark and were wrong, they likely lagged big. Big benchmark lag can be very hard to make up. The remedy is simple—if you don't believe you know something others don't, just be like your benchmark. Be passive! If you believe you know something others don't, bet on it, but don't be too darned extreme— because you still may be wrong. And will be sometimes.

There is one, and only one, instance when, in my view, it can be worth risk to adopt huge benchmark risk and seriously deviate from your benchmark. But we're not ready for that—not quite. Get the Three Questions under your belt, and we'll talk about how to improve your odds of recognizing a true bear market in Chapter 8.

You may wonder how to be like your benchmark and how to know what a benchmark looks like. All major equity indexes have websites (www .standardandpoors.com and www.msci.com, for example) where the indexes are conveniently broken down into sectors and even percentage weightings. Usually, you can even find the P/E for your index, helping you decide if you want to be more value or growth oriented. Let those percentages guide you, not your overconfident Stone Age brain. Start from those weightings and make departures from there based only on what you believe you know but others don't. Bet where you can. Where you can't, be passive and benchmark-like. The benchmarks are good road maps toward long-term equity returns.

Beating the Market Is Hard—But Possible

What about beating the market? Beating the market is possible, though difficult. But more important, it needn't be an occasional lucky accident. There are those among professionals and academics who want you to believe the market is so darned efficient, if you do beat it, it was unrepeatable serendipity. They would have you believe Bill Miller, Bill Gross and Peter Lynch were simply lucky for so long. Nonsense! What did they have in common? They knew things others didn't.

You can aim to increase your success rate if you know something others don't via the Three Questions. How? Take measured amounts of benchmark risk. The idea is to outperform the market if you're right with your bets and not get hurt too badly if you're wrong. You needn't be right with every bet. And you probably won't be! You just must be more right than wrong on average—as long as you don't try to be too extreme with any bets.

Remember what you learned in Chapter 3—if you're really bullish on a sector and the sector is about 10% of your benchmark, consider making a small bet by increasing your holdings to 13% or maybe 15% of your overall assets. Heck—double the weight and make it 20% if the Three Questions have you convinced (but not overconfident) you have found something really unique. If you're right, you participate even more in a hot sector. If you're wrong, you aren't hurt too badly. Same on the flip side—if you think a sector is for the birds and it's 10% of your benchmark, don't ax your entire holding. Instead, drop it back to 5% or 7% or 8%. If you're right, you have participated less in a lousy sector. If you're wrong about the sector and it's the best per-forming one this year, you won't have missed out entirely.

You have plenty of potential decisions every year—each with a chance to make a bet. More foreign or US? More value or growth? Small-cap bias or large? Health Care or Tech? Energy, Materials, Telecom, Utilities? And what about industries and sub-industries? The list goes on. Decide where and when and how much to make a relative over- or underweight on each part of your benchmark (always limiting yourself to what you think you know others don't). You don't need an educated opinion about each and every category. Don't know how to analyze the Telecom sector? If you can't make a bet based on knowing something others don't for a category, just be benchmark-like. Telecom is 8% of your benchmark? Then hold 8% in Telecom—maybe hold 2% to 3% in a few different Telecom stocks to be diversified. Or buy a Telecom ETF. That's easy.

Get more bets right than wrong on average over your long time horizon, and that's a recipe for beating the market. As Warren Buffet used to say, this is a game where you can wait for a great pitch—the ball coming at you that you know something unique about.

If you use your benchmark, beating the market isn't the insurmountable task many believe. And if you do become great at the Three Questions, you still won't beat the market each and every year and maybe not even for two, three or four years in a row. I've had multiple periods where I lagged the market for several years because I got my bets wrong, but by controlling benchmark risk, I didn't lag by a lot, and you can make that up later. The reason so many fail longer term—including most investing professionals—is (1) they don't restrict themselves to making investing decisions based on something others don't or can't know and (2) they don't use a benchmark to control risk, and their risky bets can go haywire on them.

Some folks claim they use a benchmark and do actually check how the S&P 500 does each year. But mostly those people are more focused on maximizing return than on maximizing the odds of beating the benchmark. They aren't managing benchmark risk on an ongoing, forward-looking basis. They just use the benchmark return to tell them how well or badly they did—after the fact. Even investors who focus on relative return often use their benchmark incorrectly. If you compare their portfolios with their benchmark's sector weightings, you may find them far too heavy in their favorite sectors and light to nil in those sectors they "don't understand" or "don't like." That's why proper global benchmarking is a wonderful Question Three capital markets technology you can use right away, and it won't fade away from you no matter how many others adopt it.

Now that you know the Three Questions and can use the results to develop tools to create forecasts and remain disciplined, you're ready for some more applications of the Three Questions and ways to know something your fellow investors don't or can't. In other words, you are ready to start beating the market. Onward!

5 WHEN THERE'S NO THERE, THERE!

Johns Hopkins, My Grampa, Life Lessons and Pulling a Gertrude

This chapter expands on examples of how Question One helps uncover false myths "everyone" knows even though no one bothered to fact-check. But first, pardon me as I digress while getting personal before we start on these examples.

Like many of you, my paternal grandfather was very important in my youth. My mother's father passed away before I was born. But my father's father—I idolized him from before I can remember. I was his favorite. We were playful pals until he passed on when I was eight. I still keep pictures of him all around wherever I sit. He was my hero. I wanted to be a doctor, just like him. For no other reason than I idolized him. I didn't learn until later I didn't like any of the parts of doctoring—particularly blood. Yes, I appreciate we need doctoring; I just don't want to be the one doing it.

But Grampa did a superbly cool thing. Arthur L. Fisher was in the third graduating class of Johns Hopkins School of Medicine, graduating and becoming Arthur L. Fisher, MD in 1900. By definition, he started at Hopkins before it had graduated its first full class and well before it built its reputation. He was a pioneer, doing something before others knew how to do it—on a very different scale, a similar leap of faith Bill Gates would make starting Microsoft. After all, there were computers and software before Bill Gates. He just changed everything with a pioneering vision. In medicine, Johns Hopkins changed everything.

Hopkins, by any real standard, was the first modern American medical school, accomplishing myriad firsts from the get-go that eventually became included in the standard mix. For example, it required what we today would call a pre-med technical education—pretty much something other medical schools didn't do then. (My Grampa's undergraduate degree was in chemistry from UC Berkeley.) Hopkins was also first to emphasize early on what we now call interning—working with real patients, overseen and mentored in the craft by journeymen doctors—real, practical, supervised experience. Back then, overwhelmingly most doctors were licensed with no patient experience at all.

Also, Hopkins admitted women from the very first class, in every class—beyond unusual then. In the coming decades, Hopkins defined modern medicine for America. Before Hopkins, an American who wanted to be a really good doctor went to Europe to study. Even after Hopkins, this was standard practice for a while, and my grandfather did European post-doctoral work to gain his specialty in orthopedics (again, specialties didn't really exist then). But Hopkins was the early US model for how a school would combine creating state-of-the-art medical science with the disciplined craft of medicine.

Even what didn't come from Hopkins often came from Hopkins. For example, Rockefeller University, which has had a huge imprint on medicine, started in 1901 as Rockefeller Institute for Medical Research. It was conceived by John Rockefeller's vision and philanthropy, but the legendary William Welch at Hopkins guided its origination from Baltimore. Rockefeller knew, and was advised by others, there was simply none other than Welch for that job. My grandfather was there, in Baltimore, at Hopkins, doing pre-institute postdoctoral research under Welch between 1900 and 1902, funded by John Rockefeller as Welch was starting the Rockefeller Institute. My Grampa, funded by John Rockefeller. I have that in handwritten letters from Welch that are treasures. Grampa may have been the first person to receive a scholarship in medicine funded by Rockefeller. Hopkins actually has in its archives some of my grandfather's original handwritten research from those years. Hopkins was the very yeast in which grew the explosion of America's early twentieth century medical successes.

While idolizing my grandfather in the 1950s, I had no clue he had been at the epicenter of an amazing and early American example of transformational evolution. In that regard, as I've evolved through a more recent transformation of capital markets science and technology, I've held Hopkins in my mind as one long-term model of how science and technology were built correctly in America and wedded to craft, in a world when few thought about such a possibility.

Where am I going with all this? Well, one of those very first women in that early Hopkins world, going to school with my Grampa, was a woman who dropped out and later became an international literary figure: Gertrude Stein. Toying with science from her youth, like my grandfather, she came from German-Jewish origins. (My family's paternal origins come from Buttenheim, Germany, the same town Levi Strauss came from. In fact, my great-grandfather, Philip I. Fisher, was Strauss's chief accountant until he retired in 1906.) Like Grampa, Stein was born in America. She was raised in Oakland, California. German-American Jews were pretty cliquish back then. One year behind Grampa at Hopkins, both from the Bay Area, in a world of tiny classes and few women, they naturally knew each other and associated.

There are several lessons we can learn from Gertrude Stein. When I first heard about Ms. Stein, I had no idea my grandfather knew and went to school with her. What I heard was her infamous line about Oakland, California, on the east side of the Bay from where I was raised—"There is no there, there." Disparaging line! Maybe her most famous. Cuts to the bone. From 1902 on, she did everything she could to separate herself from her youth in pedestrian Oakland. Of course, there is a there, there. Still, her point "there is no" is a famous literary reminder of Question One. She was asking the right question even if she got the wrong answer. Is there or is there not a there, there? You can ask that about everything. That is my Gertrude Stein corollary of investing.

One fact few know about Gertrude is she had a wealthy father. Her time at Hopkins and, in fact, her later literary career were all funded with income provided by daddy's estate. But daddies die, and she had no interest in worldly realities. Fortunately, she had a caring brother, Michael, who was a great investor and very good to her and took care of her money all her life so she could live life in an otherwise artsy and economically nonproductive way until late in her life, when her works finally started to catch on and make money—primarily her most famous work, *The Autobiography of Alice B. Toklas*. I wanted to give you the top 10 investment lessons from Gertrude Stein's life but at best could only fathom six. Sorry, Grampa!

The Six Investment Life Lessons of Gertrude Stein

One: A rich daddy and a fat inheritance is a great career if you can land it early enough. Stein made a life of it. Marrying into it is ok, too. If you've got that, maybe you don't need this book. (For more ways to get rich, see my 2008 book, *The Ten Roads to Riches*.)

Two: If you've got a great investor for a sibling like Stein's brother, Michael—one you really trust—who will take care of your money for the rest of your life, no matter what silly and embarrassing things you do, you needn't read this book. You've wasted your time so far. Go to France and fritter if you want. No one can stop you.

Three: Gertrude could have benefited from Question Three. Don't let your mind blindside you into doing something stupid. She dropped out of Hopkins in the midst of a world-changing transformation and seemingly never, ever knew it or saw it around her. What in the dickens was her brain doing to blindside her? The people creating the Hopkins reality were way cooler than her early 1900s Parisian artisto pals. Somehow, Stein saw life backward. But then again, so do so many investors because they can't use Question Three. The Hopkins folks saved lives and changed modern medicine and modern life forever (we get to that soon when we talk bird flu), which is way cooler than anything Gertrude's friends did. (Except maybe her buddy Ernest Hemingway. I'll admit he was pretty cool—for a while. Finally, as an alcoholic, he killed himself, and that isn't too cool.)

Four: If you start something, finish it. Why not? Don't drop out when you've still got lessons ahead. Only Bill Gates and Michael Dell can pull off stuff like that—dropping out—and you're not them or you wouldn't be reading this book. Had Stein stayed in Hopkins and graduated, she would have known a reality that changed the world in ways her fictional, artistic world couldn't fathom. It takes a long time to learn capital markets and build capital markets science and technology. Don't drop out as a freshman or sophomore because you don't know enough yet. Right now, you're halfway through this book. Finish it. If you want to drop it, you can always do that later just like she could have.

Five: When thinking stock market, remember what Ms. Stein didn't get—science is vastly more important than art, hands down. Folks say things like, "Markets are part science and part art." Think capital markets science. Markets are really part science and part making mistakes. Learn something never known before. Imagine you're at Hopkins in 1900 and your goal is to help learn what's never been known before. It's what others don't know that you profit from, not fictional works you create. If you want to do art, go to Paris and be an artist. If you want to do markets, be a scientist of capital markets.

The Number One All-Time Most Important
Gertrude Stein Life Lesson

Six: Is there, or is there not, a there, there? This is basically a restatement of Question One. And who would think Gertrude Stein would, in a different phraseology, make Question One a world-famous statement I knew long before I ever thought about being a money manager?

Skip Oakland—Think Bird Flu

I'm no expert on social or cultural issues—or art. So I don't really get Gertrude Stein's dissing Oakland. It's a real place with many of the same qualities permeating America. And America is the coolest place ever. If you don't get that, you don't quite fathom the full beneficence, grandeur and tolerance of capitalism, which, through creative destruction, has offered unparalleled contributions to humanity during decades of American growth. No place has ever done capitalism as well as America on a sustained basis; so if Oakland is representative of the great unwashed of America, more power to Oakland.

But I am an expert on asking Question One, and all the rest is for the birds. For example, when I first wrote this book in 2006, many folks were anxious about bird flu. Some for health reasons and others for stock market reasons. The fear was a huge bird flu pandemic would cause stocks to implode. Readers in 2012 likely won't remember just how strong and widespread the fear was—but in 2006, it was nonstop fodder for media headlines and punditry.

My normal response when a big fear is grabbing headlines like that is, if I'm in front of a big group, I ask folks to raise their hands if they've heard of the fear. Usually, most raise a hand. Then I describe how anything widely discussed you likely needn't worry about relative to markets because markets are discounters of all known information and anything so widely known must be about nearly fully discounted. Then I ask if they've known about the fear for some long time, like a year or so, and they nod affirmatively. And per Chapter 2, I remind them old arguments don't have power over markets the way new ones do because older ones are more fully discounted.

Then someone disagrees, saying that would be fine if it were financial, but something big from the nonfinancial real world, like a huge chunk of people dying from bird flu causing survivors to become paralyzed with fear—then maybe the discounting effect wouldn't work.

So, I offer two examples. The first they envision easily: What happens if bird flu never becomes a pandemic? They can easily see that wouldn't be something to fear—and actually something to embrace. Just like when Y2K had been widely and long feared, stocks actually boomed hugely in the run-up to the actual event. So many being afraid of it beforehand means when markets see it as a nonevent, sentiment (and therefore demand) improves, helping stocks. Few fight me there.

Then I give the second example. I ask have we ever had a huge pandemic before? If so, where, when and what happened to markets then? And after? Gertrude was trained to be a scientist. She would know how to do this. It's such a simple, straightforward "is there a there, there" question most people can't go there. But you can.

The best example is the 1918 global flu. If you don't know the background of this tragic pandemic, the biggest single killer in history, I suggest a great and easy read on the topic, *The Great Influenza* by John M. Barry (Penguin Books, 2004). It even has some added commentary on more recent bird flu scares. Great book! I'll not recount the 1918 flu in any detail. But, simply said, in a much smaller global population than today, it wiped out about 100 million people in less than 24 months—devastating the Western world. It seemingly started in the heartland of America at the height of World War I, when the world wasn't well able to organize against anything. If you read Barry's book, you will also witness the wall of force that was Hopkins Med's impact on this pandemic. It details how the fight against disease in those days could only come from the minds created at Hopkins. You can read about William Welch, a host of others and John Rockefeller, but you won't read about Gertrude Stein.

To get a Gertrude, just ask yourself, "Was there a there, there?" relative to the stock market. What happened? Throughout 1918, with the exception of a few small corrections (which are normal and should be expected), the stock market was gangbusters. It had a small correction late in 1918—but that's it. And all through 1919 as the flu progressed, the market went through the roof. A stock market bust during or after a massive flu pandemic? Didn't happen! There was no there, there. The market did great in the midst of the biggest pandemic of all time.

Admittedly, the market took a pretty good whack in 1917 stemming from war news, so some air had been deflated from the market before the pandemic arrived. Still, the pandemic could disrupt life but not the market, even without having a long time to discount fully into pricing such as we have had with intermittently surfacing bird flu fears. There is no there, there. Now let's look at a slicker version of pulling a Gertrude.

In the Center Ring—Oil Versus Stocks

As investors, we seem compelled to assign causality where none exists, creating the basis for false investing "truisms." As our Stone Age brains try to establish order in a disorderly world, we data-mine, look for data confirming our biases, ignore contradictory evidence and commit other cognitive errors. Unfortunately, this trend of taking two otherwise unrelated events and creating hysteria by purporting causality shows no sign of stopping. Hence the need for Question One.

Recall, your goal in asking Question One is to prove or debunk the factors behind your decisions. When you discover a baseless myth with Question One, you haven't just avoided another investing mistake. You may have a basis for a market bet. If everyone is fretting over something they believe will surely cause stocks to drop or rise and you can disprove the connection, you can bet against the consensus and win more often than not. You have found something where the outcome they expect simply won't happen.

An excellent example, and frequently a popular cause for panic, is the high price of oil. Investors presume when oil prices are high, that's a negative for stocks. Few disagree: If oil's price keeps rising, stocks must suffer. You hear it in the media consistently by an unending barrage of TV wags—so this is a great Question One candidate.

Oil as a cause for hysteria isn't new. It cycles in and out every few years or so. In the 1970s, we had disco, Jimmy Carter and oil embargoes. In the 1980s, we had power suits, Charlie Sheen in *Wall Street* and an oil crash. In the early 1990s and again more recently, we had a few wars with what some would say was the sole intention of stealing all the oil from a benignly quirky (and now dispatched) Mesopotamian despot. Personally, I don't understand this contention that we only go to war to "steal oil." If we really wanted to steal oil, we'd invade Canada and Mexico. We get double the amount of oil and petroleum products from Canada than we do from Saudi Arabia.[1] Mexico and Saudi Arabia frequently flip-flop as our second biggest source.[2]

America's miserable record at stealing oil aside, oil is regularly high on investors' freak-out list. A primary worry is our reliance on so finite a commodity. The media often reports our oil will run out in our immediate future. To the chagrin of the entire population of Berkeley, California (Gertrude's hometown neighbor!), that won't happen—not anytime soon.

Oil is indeed finite. But we keep finding more of that elusive sludge. A fact few people appreciate: We're aware of vastly more oil reserves now than we were in the 1970s. Yes, we were supposed to run out of oil a long, long time ago. That oil didn't magically regenerate—the oil companies invested in technology and better ways of finding and getting to newly discovered oil fields. Will we find more reserves? Yes! Will we run out of oil one day? No. Not in your life.

We Just Don't Know

You don't believe me, but we have no way of knowing what the total supply is now or any time—and never did. Oil firms haven't explored unendingly because once they get a big enough stockpile of reserves, more exploration isn't cost effective. And besides them, no one else will do the searching. Waves of exploration come and go over the decades and will continue. Every generation thinks not much more can be found, and every generation finds more. Once the price gets high enough and reserves low enough, they start searching and find more. What's more, they innovate new, cleaner and cheaper ways to find and get at oil previously thought unrecoverable. And that will continue in the future. And no one believes it until it happens. How much oil can we find? Who knows? We can all speculate on how much. But that's all it is—speculation. And it doesn't matter all that much.

One big supply-side problem isn't oil in the ground but refineries, or the lack thereof. The NIMBYs in Congress have made certain no material, new refinery has been built on US soil since 1976.[3] Our refinery capacity can't pace our demand, even if oil were infinitely available. When something unexpected happens, like a natural disaster in the Gulf Coast temporarily knocking out a significant chunk of refining capability or popular uprisings in the Middle East as we had in early 2011, petroleum gas prices tend to rise. With more domestic refineries, we could better and more flexibly deal with national disasters, wars, senatorial idiocy (sorry for being redundant) and other supply disruptions.

Those predicting doomsday insist no matter how efficient we get, we cannot escape oil's depletion. At a price, they're certainly wrong. In the short term, that can't be proved. In the long term, it will be. Maybe folks most fearful oil will soon run out skipped Econ 101 the day supply and demand were taught. Oil is a freely traded open-market commodity. The only two things in this entire universe determining oil's price are supply and demand. Not George W. Bush. Not Halliburton. Not oil executives. Supply and demand.

Our elected officials don't seem to believe in supply and demand, so they occasionally decide to "cure us" of our "oil addiction" by proposing to artificially raise oil's price through taxes. Only a poli-tic can cook up such a stupid idea. Quite naturally, as supply dwindles and demand continues unabated, oil's price will rise. We don't need taxes or regulations or anything else for that. And it's not because oil companies are evil or greedy—it's because that's how a free market works.

In the long term, if the poli-tics don't intensify their meddling, the market will price in any dwindling supply. Oil prices will rise to where either a replacement energy source will alleviate the supply pressure or demand will start dropping or some combination of the two. What definitely won't happen is one day you go to the pump and—surprise, surprise—no more oil! While oil is becoming prohibitively expensive, a replacement will come along to power our vehicles and laptops. What that is, I don't know. But it will happen. Maybe hydrogen, solar or nuclear power. Remember, the early steam engine innovators certainly didn't envision Volvos running on gasoline any more than you foresee whatever the next innovation is.

Necessity is often the mother of invention. Seriously! We will never get to the last barrel of oil and say, "Oh, well. It was fun while it lasted," and as a society don potato sacks and wander into the wilderness to spontaneously take up subsistence living with resurrected *Whole Earth Catalogs*. In 2110, the gas-powered SUV will seem as quaint to our great-great-grandchildren as the steam locomotive seems to us.

Lurking behind these oil histrionics is the direct ripple effect folks think high oil prices have on the economy and stock market—right here and now. This concern is misplaced and easy to disprove. Higher oil prices sometimes coincide with weaker markets, sometimes stronger. But the one provably isn't a direct cause of the other.

Folks also mistakenly think higher oil prices cause inflation, economic stagnation and worse. My guess is this stems from many folks misremembering the late 1970s. Ask the Three Questions. Did high oil prices in the late 1970s cause the inflation and stagnation? Recall, in 1979 we were in the midst of a staring contest with the new Iranian regime led by fervent religious fundamentalists. Enraged at slights—real or imagined, but probably imagined—from "the Great Satan," Iranian students took 66 American hostages, 52 of whom were held for 444 days. That capped off a decade of sanctions and OPEC embargoes that helped drive gasoline prices up and created long lines at the pump, even rationing.

Before you think you're dizzy with déjà vu seeing today's Iranian problems, recall during most of the 1970s, we had frightfully horrendous inflationary monetary policy to go with our bell bottoms. Driven by endless money creation in and outside America, runaway inflation did its best to dampen an already lackluster economy, which in turn led to high prices of all types, *including* oil, long-term interest rates and everything else—as well as high US unemployment rates. Times weren't so rosy, economically speaking, mostly due to poor governance. High oil prices didn't cause those problems. Oil was high as a *result* of those problems. It's critical to not reverse cause and effect.

Colorado, Canada and China Have It in Common—Not "C"

Let's flip this on its head and ask a Question One: Is a high oil price so bad? First, at some price, we will seek alternatives for economic reasons. And we already are! Look at the fracking boom taking place in North America. We have massive oil and gas reserves in shale rock and tar sands under Colorado, Utah, Wyoming, North Dakota and Canada. All of this together dwarfs many times over the amount of known reserves in all of Saudi Arabia. Developing all this is just a matter of price. We can debate exactly what price it takes but not that it's just a matter of price. But as it happens, the threat of oil embargoes won't have nearly the potency we've feared. After a certain price, vastly more shale and tar sand reserves will open up. Technology will keep improving, too, so while the initial innovation of new technologies is pricey, with broader use and Moore's law, those technologies eventually get cheaper—and so too does the energy we extract, helped along with the increase in supply. This is simple economics, and yet I'm amazed at how few folks in the world accept it.

You have a choice. Do you want oil's price up or down? Outside a few temporary supply disturbances like Gulf Coast hurricanes, the price has been driven largely by demand growth from an expanding economy—not just in America, but around the world, including India and China. Higher oil prices in recent years are overall a symptom of a growing global economy, not an unhealthy one. Yet people cower at the impact China's future growth may have on energy demand and prices and how that may hurt us. China has more energy under it in the form of coal than the total of all its energy needs until many decades from now. As with the shale in North America, it's simply a matter of price when coal substitutes for oil there. In fact, it's on coal, not oil, that China bases its future energy needs—for what should be obvious reasons.

Unless we discover a massive new oil field or radical new technology, we should generally expect oil prices to stay firm for some time or even rise. Price spikes can happen, but outside of those, higher oil prices shouldn't much hurt us. First, despite what you may have heard, we're less dependent on oil today than ever. Figure 5.1 shows energy intensity has steadily dropped over the last 30 years.

Why? Our GDP's composition has greatly changed. Two of the larger sectors—Information Technology and Financials—are much less energy intensive than manufacturing and agriculture, both of which have dwindled in relative size. All this means we've gotten much more efficient and less dependent on oil per dollar of output since the groovy 1970s. If energy prices remain high and get higher, we will get still more efficient—future growth will make oil even less important because we're growing most in non–energy intensive industries.

Believe the Stock Market, Not Me—Stocks and Oil Prices Don't Correlate

A primary investor concern is oil and stocks have an inverse relationship. People believe when oil prices rise, stocks fall and vice versa. Investors worry about oil wars, dwindling supply, environmental devastation and their

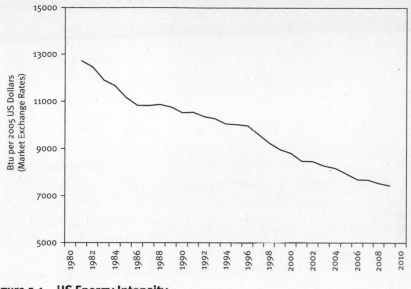

Figure 5.1 US Energy Intensity
Source: **US Energy Information Administration.**

neighbors negligently driving huge SUVs. They're sure all this will drive up oil's price and drive down stocks. Nobody wants that. There is plenty of support for this view—you can see it endlessly in media headlines: "Oil Prices Weigh on Stocks!" "Stocks Fall as Oil Rises!" Try a Google search to see how often articles claim an inverse relationship between oil and stocks.

It seems commonsensical. Higher oil prices lead to higher gas prices, which means folks have less money to spend on other things—like groceries and plane tickets and tube socks. Firms making and distributing groceries, plane tickets and tube socks must suffer because Joe Sixpack is stubbornly wearing holey socks and refusing to fly to resort destinations, so revenues fall, scaring stockholders. Soon Joe changes his last name to Fivepack. Oil rises, stocks fall—end of story. Everyone knows. Not Gertrude. She would ask if there is a there, there. Is it true oil and stocks have an inverse relationship— do rising oil prices drive stock prices down? Both prices exist all the time. If there is a there, there, we can measure it.

We supply the data for you in Figure 5.2, but if you want to test it on your own, you can download historical S&P 500 data from Yahoo! Finance (or elsewhere). Historic oil prices can be found at the Energy Information Administration's (EIA) website. Figure 5.2 graphs historic oil prices against the S&P 500 from 1982 to 2011. You can see overall there isn't much of a

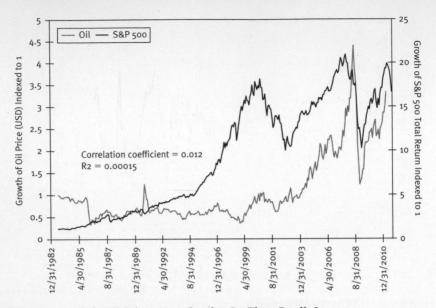

Figure 5.2   High Oil Prices Hurt Stocks. Do They Really?
Sources: Global Financial Data, Inc., S&P 500 Total Return Index, West Texas Intermediate Oil Price (US$/Barrel) from 12/31/1982 to 09/30/2011.

there, there, other than they both seem to rise over time. That shouldn't be too shocking, given most prices tend to rise over time with inflation.

Unscientifically, the chart doesn't look too convincing—like Chapter 1's high P/E scatter plot. For a more conclusive answer, we need the correlation coefficient (see Appendix A). If the variables both rise and fall at the same time and by the same amount, then the correlation coefficient is 1, meaning a one-to-one relationship. If they're strongly *negatively* correlated—one zigs when the other zags, like we think oil and stocks do—the coefficient will be close to –1. The closer the coefficient is to 0, the less the variables correlate at all.

Fact: Oil and stocks have a correlation coefficient of 0.012—effectively no correlation. To know how much the two variables may impact each other, you create the R-squared from Appendix A. (Remember, R-squared shows the relative *relatedness* of two variables.) Here, the R-squared is 0.00015. That means you can blame only 0.015% of stocks' jumping around on oil price movements. Nothing. Here's another way to see this since the prices of oil and stocks move around so much and sometimes, over short spurts, one may impact the other. Figure 5.3 shows a one-year monthly rolling correlation between oil and the S&P 500.

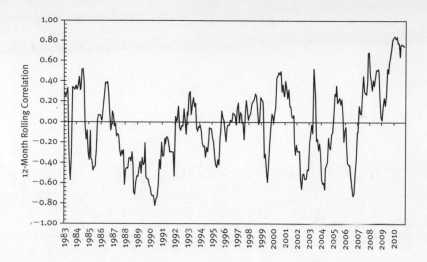

Figure 5.3   Oil Versus S&P 500: One-Year Monthly Rolling Correlation
Sources: Global Financial Data, Inc., S&P 500 Total Return Index, West Texas Intermediate Oil Price (US$/Barrel) from 12/31/1982 to 09/30/2011.

Figure 5.3 clearly shows peaks and valleys of correlation. You see troughs of negative correlation in the early 1990s following the 1990–1991 recession. You see increasing correlation as both oil and stocks rose following the 2009 global stock market bottom. In general, all these peaks and troughs were short-lived and all rotated around a mean of nonexistent correlation.

Yet another way to see this is the five-year rolling R-squared, showing how much impact the variables may have on one another (as in Figure 5.4). From late 1992 to early 1994, over 20% of the movement in stock prices could be attributed to oil, and that was an unusual high point—and right then no one noticed. You didn't notice. There was a bit of a there, there, briefly, and we all pretty much missed it. Before that and ever since, oil hasn't had much power to move stocks. Hasn't been a there, there. Not up, and not down. Not at all. Still, people think there is. Isn't that cool! And you, me and Gertrude know.

You may be pretty satisfied now in knowing oil's price movements don't impact stocks much. But remember, if something is true in America, it must be true in most places or it isn't really true. Whenever possible, test your conclusions in foreign markets for verification. If something only works here, then it might be something unique to some domestic situation (like the election cycles) or a fluke. Even Gertrude thought outside of America, even if she didn't get that America was a better place to live. Figure 5.5 is an illustration of the relationship between oil and stock prices in Britain.

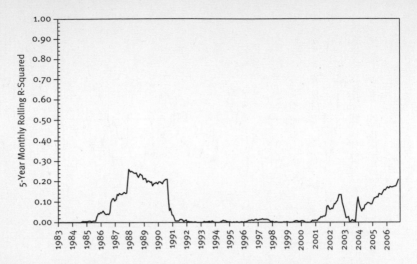

Figure 5.4   Oil Versus S&P 500: Five-Year Monthly Rolling R-Squared
Sources: Global Financial Data, Inc., S&P 500 Total Return Index, West Texas Intermediate Oil Price (US$/Barrel) from 12/31/1982 to 09/30/2011.

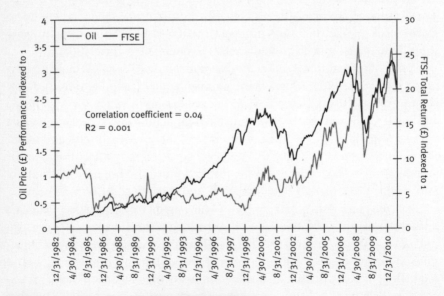

Figure 5.5   Oil Prices and the FTSE All-Share
Sources: Global Financial Data, Inc., FTSE All-Share Total Return Index, West Texas Intermediate Oil Price (£/Barrel) from 12/31/1982 to 09/30/2011.

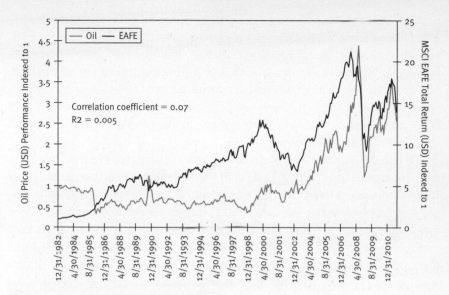

Figure 5.6   Oil Prices and MCSI EAFE
Sources: **Global Financial Data, Inc., MSCI EAFE Total Return Index, West Texas Intermediate Oil Price (US$/Barrel) from 12/31/1982 to 09/30/2011.**

In Britain, you get very similar results. The correlation coefficient is 0.04, and the R-squared is 0.001. Pretty much no correlation, and yet the Brits panic about high oil prices driving stocks down just like Americans. In fact, my gut says they worry more (and I spend lots of time studying Britain).

Then, comparing oil prices to an all-foreign stock index shows, globally, oil doesn't much impact stock prices either. In Figure 5.6, the correlation coefficient is 0.07 with an R-squared of 0.005. No impact—none! Yet your fellow investors can't or won't see there is no correlation over time—positive or negative—no there, there.

I Can Confirm It's Confirmation Bias

This is compelling evidence against a particularly pervasive myth. So why does it have such sticking power? Enter Question Three. The way your brain is messing you up is *confirmation bias* and *illusion of validity.* Our brains often like to cling to instances confirming our prior biases and common sense and ignore instances contradicting them. Gertrude suffered confirmation bias her whole life. That's how she saw Parisians as better than boring Americans whether in Oakland or at Johns Hopkins in Baltimore. She saw confirmation of what she wanted to see. Most folks do. When was the last time you saw a headline reading, "Oil Was Up, Pushing Up Stocks!" Never, because that isn't a good news story. When oil is up, the chance of stocks being down is measurably and provably pretty much a coin flip. But that isn't how our brains remember it. And that certainly isn't how our newspapers want us to see it. They and we remember instances confirming our biases—focusing only on the days when oil and stocks move in opposite directions. My writing this book and teaching you or reporters how to do simple correlations won't change our human confirmation bias.

When the opposite is true and oil and stocks rise or fall together, investors may excuse this by *reframing*. Instead of the daily prices of oil and stocks, they insist some other arbitrary time frame matters. They reframe the issue claiming you can't look at just one day—it takes longer periods (like one week, three months or a year) or particularly extreme examples. (Of course, then they don't prove it.) Still, the daily moves obeying their bias confirm the myth in their minds, while contradictory evidence necessitates a longer or different observation period or scale not actually accounted for. Apples and oranges.

Some claim oil being up doesn't drive stocks down that same day; instead, you must allow for a time lag—another reframe. They say this, but they don't check it out. I've looked. I've yet to see a time lag providing for any material correlation. I don't believe it exists (must work overseas, too). When testing for any number of time lags—3 days, 1 week, 2.5 weeks, 7 months, 9.82 months—the results were similar. No matter what arbitrary lag you pick, oil and stock price movements don't correlate enough for any sane soul to bet on.

Insisting on a "time lag" is just another way of data mining, reframing and submitting to your confirmation bias. It shows what good Stone Age cognitive-error generators humans are. Data-mine all you want, but you won't find a credible link between oil and stock prices. Or maybe I'm wrong, and you will—more power to you—you're better than I am, and I accept that. Let me know when you find it. But I'll bet you don't. I'll bet there are many more readers of this book (not you—those other readers) who will simply presume I'm wrong and never lift a finger to run correlations on their own.

This is a great example of a myth debunked without expensive tools or complicated equations. Recall, if your analysis must be convoluted or complicated to prove your hypothesis, it's probably false. Let me give you some more gas on this one.

The Gas-Pump Quiz

My suggestion for mitigating oil price hysteria is requiring every consumer to pass a little quiz before filling their tanks. You must get three of the following four correct to drive your car:

1. Crude oil, the primary component of the gasoline powering most cars, is a:
   a. Tool of the devil
   b. Conspiracy cooked up in Texas
   c. Commodity
   d. Primary cause of global warming
2. Oil prices are determined by:
   a. An evil conspiracy
   b. Halliburton
   c. Supply and demand
   d. a & b
3. The US government could *immediately* lower gas prices by:
   a. Reducing regulation
   b. Reducing taxes
   c. Sending Dick Cheney bird hunting—with Shell's CEO
   d. a & b
4. The number-one exporter of oil to the United States is:
   a. Iraq, but don't tell them because we steal it
   b. Saudi Arabia
   c. Halliburton
   d. Canada

Never fear, my test won't be instituted. (And really, it's another form of regulation, so at heart, I'm opposed.) But, meanwhile, you have another game-able bet. Whenever most folks freak out, predicting stock prices must drop because of rising oil prices, you know that outcome is far from guaranteed. First, because the concern is likely priced and, second, because there's no consistent correlation worth betting on.

Anything the French Can Do We Can Do Better

But if you want to see $20/barrel oil again, it's easy. It's certain! Technically, it's trivial. Just remember, the French get half their energy needs right now from nuclear power and have for a long time.

If America, Britain, Japan and China all somehow announced a cooperative treaty to build their nuclear capacity over 10 years such that these big four energy consumers got as much of their energy from nuclear as the French do right now, the price of Texas crude would implode toward $20 faster than you can say "Remember the Alamo." It's a no-brainer. Berkeleyites wouldn't fantasize about punishing rich oilmen because it would have just happened already.

We haven't built a nuclear power plant in America since 1974. Been scared of nuclear! Those political and social decisions are long-standing and hard to shake but certainly are political decisions nonetheless. Even as I say "nuclear," I can see many now gray-haired, 1970s eco-combatants cringing in their Birkenstocks at the thought of allowing America to do what the French have done all along. Remember your Gertrude. Is there a there, there? The French have been living safely with nuclear in abundance for decades. And if the French can do it, we can do it better.

Some may point to the March 2011 Tohoku earthquake and Japanese tragedy as evidence we can't do nuclear safely. Except the tragedy rather proves we can. The damaged Fukushima Daiichi reactor was built to sustain a massive earthquake—and did! The fifth-largest ever recorded. The damage was caused not by the quake but the massive tsunami taking out the power grid. Except, even before the tsunami, later models of the same reactor were improved to withstand such deluges.

Nuclear is incredibly efficient, green (yes, green) and safe (yes, safe). Go nuclear, and suddenly, fears of finite energy sources and being energy dependent on the Middle East evaporate. Effectively, there'd be no reason for oil to ever "run out." I don't know about Gertrude on this, but my Grampa would like that—he loved his touring car for exploring the Sierras.

Sell in May Because the January Effect Will Dampen Your Santa Claus Rally Unless There Is a Witching Effect

Another popular myth—or set of myths—is what I'll lump together under the category "Sell in May." Sell in May comes from the old saw, "Sell in May, go away"—which is supposed to mean summers have lackluster returns. These kinds of myths include all the month-of-the-year, day-of-the-week, holiday myths and so on. Santa Claus rallies. The October effect. Monday effect. Friday effect. The summer rally. Triple Witching. The month-end effect. The third-Thursday-during-a-waxing-moon effect. The second-Tuesday-each-month-of-baseball-season effect. Ok, you got me again. I made those last two up, but they don't sound much sillier than the others.

Investors usually don't believe all these all at once. They believe some and not others. But they don't check to verify validity. "Who would believe in a Friday effect? That's silly," one investor may say while preparing for the Santa Claus rally. You may instinctually know these are so much hogwash. Yet the media loves reminding us of them and telling us the market did thus-and-such on Friday, so we know this, that and the other should happen on Monday.

There are a fair number of published studies—some in scholarly journals that should know better and others described in popular media—showing from time X to Y, if you bought on day A and sold on day C, you would beat the market. Invariably, if you vary the beginning and end dates—or look overseas—the effect vanishes completely, showing the signs of a planned or unintentional data mine.

Perhaps the most popular recent myth is "sell in May, go away" because it's been on a roll, like someone flipping four out of five heads. It's been around for decades, and its popularity comes and goes with its luck. At one point, it may even have made some seeming economic sense. Eons ago, summers were marked by a slight slowdown in US business tied to farming cycles and, later, vacation cycles. Even now, much of Europe basically checks out during warmer months.

But does it hold true now, if it ever did? It was never a real stock market cycle. It's silly and demonstrably false. In an age of instant, wireless, 24/7 communication, is it possible there is a routine arbitrage lethargy during summer months? Many perfectly respectable investors believe wholeheartedly summer months are bad for stocks. This is another easy one to test with Question One. Table 5.1 shows market returns for June through August, along with the total return for each year, starting in 1926.

In Table 5.1, the average total return for the June to August period is 4.4%—making the returns positive on average and beating cash or bonds. Of course, the market itself is generally positive more often than negative. *Note:* There have been plenty of times when summer months were very strong. That it's markedly more positive than negative tells you the "sell in May, go away" strategy is a money loser. Some investors instead will say "sell in May" really means the summer *half* of the year is inferior to the winter half—May to October yields lesser returns than November to April. Sheesh—how much of a data mine do you want? On average, May to October has yielded a bit less than the winter half but is still positive. What does that tell you? You want to sit in cash and yield much less? There is no economic reason why one set of six months should be better than another. Why May to October? Why not "sell in July, so you won't cry"?

This isn't like the oil versus stocks myth where there is a 50/50 chance of the two variables confirming an investor's previously formed bias (though believers in this myth are certainly guilty of both illusion of validity and confirmation bias, too). If a given summer is positive, "sell in May" fans will simply say you should use longer observation periods (or shorter specific ones). What they miss is the cold, hard truth that the market is obviously positive more often than negative during the summer months. No fancy analysis to

Table 5.1   Sell in May and Go Away?

Year	Summer	Whole Year	Year	Summer	Whole Year
	Return (June–August)	Return (January–December)		Return (June–August)	Return (January–December)
1926	12.4%	11.7%	1969	−6.9%	−8.5%
1927	11.6%	37.7%	1970	7.6%	4.0%
1928	5.5%	43.8%	1971	0.2%	14.3%
1929	28.8%	−8.5%	1972	2.3%	18.9%
1930	−11.7%	−25.0%	1973	0.1%	−14.8%
1931	8.0%	−43.5%	1974	−16.4%	−26.5%
1932	91.6%	−8.4%	1975	−3.7%	37.3%
1933	16.2%	54.4%	1976	3.7%	23.7%
1934	−3.7%	−1.5%	1977	1.8%	−7.4%
1935	19.3%	47.7%	1978	7.6%	6.4%
1936	12.1%	32.8%	1979	11.8%	18.4%
1937	−0.1%	−35.3%	1980	11.4%	32.3%
1938	31.9%	33.2%	1981	−6.2%	−5.1%
1939	−2.4%	−0.9%	1982	8.5%	21.5%
1940	15.7%	−10.1%	1983	2.3%	22.5%
1941	12.1%	−11.8%	1984	12.0%	6.2%
1942	7.8%	21.1%	1985	0.5%	31.6%
1943	−1.3%	25.8%	1986	3.1%	18.6%
1944	5.1%	19.7%	1987	14.5%	5.2%
1945	4.5%	36.5%	1988	0.7%	16.6%
1946	−12.3%	−8.2%	1989	10.5%	31.7%
1947	7.3%	5.2%	1990	−9.9%	−3.1%
1948	−3.0%	5.1%	1991	2.2%	30.5%
1949	9.2%	18.1%	1992	0.4%	7.6%
1950	−0.2%	30.6%	1993	3.7%	10.1%
1951	10.1%	24.6%	1994	4.9%	1.3%

(continued)

Table 5.1 (Continued)

Year	Summer Return (June–August)	Whole Year Return (January–December)	Year	Summer Return (June–August)	Whole Year Return (January–December)
1952	6.5%	18.5%	1995	6.0%	37.6%
1953	−3.6%	−1.1%	1996	−2.0%	23.0%
1954	3.4%	52.4%	1997	6.5%	33.4%
1955	15.0%	31.5%	1998	−11.9%	28.6%
1956	6.1%	6.6%	1999	1.7%	21.0%
1957	−3.8%	−10.8%	2000	7.1%	−9.1%
1958	9.3%	43.3%	2001	−9.4%	−11.9%
1959	2.3%	11.9%	2002	−13.8%	−22.1%
1960	2.9%	0.5%	2003	5.1%	28.7%
1961	3.0%	26.8%	2004	−1.0%	10.9%
1962	0.0%	−8.8%	2005	2.9%	4.9%
1963	3.2%	22.7%	2006	3.2%	15.8%
1964	2.6%	16.4%	2007	−3.3%	5.5%
1965	−0.6%	12.4%	2008	−7.9%	−37.0%
1966	−9.7%	−10.1%	2009	11.7%	26.5%
1967	5.9%	23.9%	2010	−3.2%	15.1%
1968	0.9%	11.0%	Average	4.4%	11.8%

Sources: Global Financial Data, Inc., S&P 500 total returns.

figure that out. Of course, by definition, you will have negative summers. That is true for every season and every month.

What about other seasonal myths—ones cautioning us about certain days, months, holidays and so on? Is there any truth to any of them? No. They all fall apart under statistical analysis. Remember, based on Question Two, if something seems to have correlation, you must show it working overseas as well and be able to demonstrate the fundamental underlying economics of why it should work. You can't do that with any of these seasonal myths.

Let's say the Monday effect, to pick on just one, is real. In a way it is. The Monday effect tells us Monday will continue Friday's trend. If Friday is positive, Monday will be, too; if Friday is negative, expect a down Monday. This obviously contradicts another popular myth—the "weekend effect," which purports stock prices fall over the weekend. But never mind. For now, just consider the Monday effect actually works. It does if you account for it wrong. On years when the market is up, Friday and Monday and every other day are more likely to be positive than negative.

So in those years, a Friday, any Friday—positive or negative—tends to lead to a positive Monday. And since there are more positive than negative Fridays in bull market years, the scheme works. In bear market years, Fridays and Mondays and every other day tend to be more negative than positive. Any Friday in a bear market year is more likely followed by a down Monday than an up Monday—and the same is true for every other day of the week. So it works.

But this is just seeing what you want to see because in a bull market year, betting a down Friday leads to a down Monday loses money heavily. In bear markets, betting an up Friday leads to an up Monday also loses money. The fact the market is up about two-thirds of the time on average makes any day followed by any day more likely to be up than down and makes the basic principle work—if you account for it wrong—but still be a misleading and money-losing strategy.

There is no good statistical evidence to support any of these myths. Table 5.2 illustrates the average monthly total returns for the S&P 500 since 1926. All the average returns are positive save a modestly negative (on average) September because—say it with me—the market is positive more often than negative. Were there any truth to seasonally related myths, some month (or months) would blow away the others. Some months look, on average, marginally better than others—but remember this is an average and takes into account the market's volatile nature and the random nature of luck. Obviously, you can't expect a 1.66% return each April and a 1.06% return each November. Averaging this in the past tells you nothing about what may happen in the future because those numbers include past random luck, which may be different than future random luck. This demonstrates there is no credence to any of the sentimental myths regarding days, months, seasons and so forth. All any month in a year can tell you is when to change your clocks or plant your corn.

Many of these myths, in my view, were propagated by someone, once upon a time, wanting to make some money off commissions by getting investors to trade too often—making a good living off transaction fees. I'm sure some advisors advocate these things out of well-intentioned but wrongheaded

Table 5.2   S&P 500 Average Monthly Returns

1926–2010	Monthly Average Returns
January	1.43%
February	0.09%
March	0.79%
April	1.66%
May	0.29%
June	1.07%
July	1.94%
August	1.23%
September	−0.64%
October	0.49%
November	1.06%
December	1.80%

Sources: Global Financial Data, Inc., S&P 500 total returns from 12/31/1925 to 12/31/2010.

analysis. If you're solicited to make a stock transaction because of an alleged impending seasonally related move, simply ask for supporting documentation. You may find someone who will send you a "research report" from his firm or elsewhere "detailing" the seasonally related move. It won't include the raw data. It will be based on averages over a set time period confirming the bias and won't be adjusted for the market's normal tendency to be up more than down. But you can get the raw data. You can get them off the Internet. You've got your Excel spreadsheet. And you can run Question One to see if there is a there, there and answer it for yourself without him. The fact is, when you do, there is no there, there.

Time for Some Homework

Now that you've seen a few examples and can calculate a correlation coefficient and an R-squared, you can begin testing myths on your own. (Also, check on the difference between arithmetic averages and annualized averages in Appendix E.) Getting started is easy—just ask Question One about something. Anything! Start with those things you are most confident need no testing. No one will think you're crazy. Even if they do, it won't hurt. You know what else doesn't hurt? Making fewer mistakes over time. Tell that to your poker group if they laugh at you.

Here are a few investing beliefs for you to practice Question One on—right now! You may believe some, all or none of these, but in general, they are widely believed and easy to check and therefore debunk:

- Plenty of investors believe a high unemployment number is bad for stocks, low unemployment better. Is it true? I'd tell you there's no correlation either way, but it's easy to check for yourself (find unemployment numbers at the Bureau of Labor Statistics, www.bls.gov).
- While you're at it, you can check if unemployment numbers—high or low—impact GDP growth. Most investors will tell you high unemployment spells doom for GDP. I'd tell you growth begets jobs, not the other way around. But check it and see!
- The VIX (the Chicago Board Options Exchange [CBOE] Volatility Index) is a popular negative indicator for the S&P 500. As they say, "When the VIX is high, it's time to buy!" Really? Run some correlations, and I bet you'll find the VIX is statistically worthless.
- High dividend yields have long been thought to be predictive of good stock returns and low dividend yields of poor returns. Find historic dividend yields on the Internet to see if you should bet on this myth. (*Hint:* You shouldn't.)
- Pundits and professionals wail over low consumer confidence numbers and their impact on GDP and the stock market. Is it warranted? I'd tell you there's no there here, there or anywhere with consumer confidence numbers. Check two consumer confidence indexes published by the Conference Board (http://www.conference-board.org/data/consumerconfidence.cfm) and the University of Michigan (http://www.sca.isr.umich.edu/) to see if you can prove me wrong.

You'll be a pro at doing Question Ones in no time. But the real fun of using Question One is when you can discover a myth so widely, passionately and irrevocably held, no one dares breathe even a whisper of dissent. That is where you can find investor beliefs so wrong, the complete reverse is true. Let's find some now.

6

NO, IT'S JUST THE OPPOSITE

When You Are Wrong—Really, Really, Really Wrong

Chapter 5 expanded on how Question One helps uncover false myths "everyone" knows, even though no one bothered to fact-check. More exciting, you can find myths so broadly, irreversibly and passionately held, the exact reverse ends up being true. Where mythology is so really, really, really, really wrong, it's actually backward—like our example of federal budget deficits leading to great stock market returns instead of disaster. You link a Question One to a Question Two and learn the exact reverse of common mythology is a bet-able truth. We'll demonstrate a few of those in this chapter to show you how you can do it on your own. Just start with anything people are intensely righteous about. You may be labeled a heretic by acquaintances, but so what? (It's not your business what people think about you, remember?) One reason so many investors fail is they fear asking questions that make them seem like crackpots. Don't fear being seen as a crackpot—fear making bets based on possible fabrications.

When Debt Is Good!

Let's begin by exploring a topic sure to unite just about everyone, regardless of creed, in an appalled uproar.

Debt.

In Chapter 1, I showed how the universally deplored federal budget deficit historically hasn't led to poor stock returns—rather to good ones. I showed you the data—the *what*—but not the *how* and *why*. For that, you must understand debt and deficits better—know something others don't and see how they're used, abused and misconstrued. (As I update this in 2011, many will be particularly sensitive about debt because of the 2008 credit crisis and the eurozone debt woes that came to light starting in 2010. But nothing fundamentally has changed about the economics of leverage—though the fear of debt may be greater or smaller from time to time.)

From infancy, we're taught debt is bad, more debt is worse and loads of debt is downright immoral. In fact, for many centuries, collecting interest on a loan was considered a sin throughout Christianity—leaving money lending to seemingly shadowy social fringes. Never accused of being the life of the party, Cato the Elder equated usury with murder. Early Christianity, Judaism and Islam all prohibited lending with interest. (Jews weren't permitted to charge interest to other Jews, while Shariah law prohibits charging interest to this day.)

Investors perceive our debt and budget deficit to be a massive economic drain because eventually someone will pay it back—creating a presumed stranglehold on our children, our children's children, their children, their pets, the future aliens who colonize those great-great-great-grandchildren and the cockroaches that overthrow them all—living, debt-laden, in a *Mad Max* post-World-War-III-style world where there's no Mel Gibson to save us. All because of debt!

Everyone knows we're over-indebted. You read it everywhere—and it's rarely (if ever) challenged. And everyone agrees someone must pay it back. And when that happens, it will be heinous. Stocks can't rise into that, right? Let's ask Question One and see. Is it true debt is bad for the economy and stock market? Are we really over-indebted to the point of difficulty?

For this question, you must know how much debt we really have, properly, in scale. Then you must ask a question so basic no one ever asks it (but you will, very soon).

But first, some scaling. As I update this in 2011, the US has about $9 trillion in federal debt held by the public.[1] (I don't count intra-agency debt because that's money the government effectively owes back to itself. What matters is what the government owes other people.)

Nine trillion is a lot of anything in absolute terms. For perspective, just one trillion is 1,000 billions. And just 1 billion is hard for our Stone Age information processors to conceive. For example, a billion hours ago, our ancestors were in the literal Stone Age. A billion minutes ago, Jesus lived. So $9 trillion seems overwhelming.

But is it bad? Most people think so. But remember Chapter 3's bunnies and Hummers? You must think relatively and consider scale whenever you see big numbers. For that, you need an accurate picture of the US hard asset balance sheet (see Table 6.1).

Unless you're a client of my firm, you've probably never seen a balance sheet for America presented this way. (Though all these data are publicly available, my guess is people just don't think to do this.) It's built just like a business balance sheet totaling all US assets and liabilities—including public and private debts. Adding up the left side, the asset line items give the United States approximately $129 trillion in total assets. (Nine trillion immediately feels smaller, doesn't it? Scaling!) Moving to the right side (the liabilities side), we have $64 trillion in total debt outstanding. As with any balance sheet, subtract the

Table 6.1   Aggregate Hard Asset Balance Sheet of the United States

Assets	(billions)	Liabilities	(billions)
Cash & equivalents	$12,333	Home mortgages	$9,988
Public stocks*	13,510	Credit cards & auto loans	2,404
Other corporate stock	17,191	Non-corporate business debt	3,462
Non-corporate businesses	10,203	Non-financial corporate debt	7,293
Fixed income	43,361	Financial sector debt	14,171
Total Financial Assets	96,597	Savings/checking accounts	14,687
		Federal government debt	9,646
Residential real estate	18,117	State & local government debt	2,445
Other real estate	14,248	**Total Debt**	64,096
Real estate§	32,365		
		Net Worth	64,866
Total Assets	$128,962	**Total Liabilities & Net Worth**	$128,962
US Income (GDP)	15,010		

* Market value as of March 31, 2011.
§ Excludes government-owned real estate.
Sources: Standard & Poor's, Federal Reserve Flow of Funds Accounts (3Q 2010).
Note: Other assets and liabilities considered one-for-one offsets excluded. Examples of such items are life insurance policies and reserves, consumer durables like a sofa or dishwasher and pension obligations and benefits.

liabilities from the assets and you get America's net worth of about $65 trillion. (*Note:* Our balance sheet doesn't address assets and liabilities that are contractual one-for-one offsets, like life insurance policies and reserves and pension obligations and benefits. Since they perfectly offset each other, they don't impact our analysis, nor do off-balance sheet obligations like Medicare and Social Security—ones easily later politically eliminated by a vote of poli-tics.)

What Is the Right Amount of Debt for a Society to Have?

But a better question—the real killer question, a Question Two—is: What is the *right* amount of debt for society to have? And how would you know it was the right amount? This is a question I've never heard asked in public or commented on—ever. It's a Newtonian-like question because at its roots are heretofore unthinkable fundamentals. What is the right amount of debt of all types for a society to have? Most folks presume less debt is better and the best amount is none.

But we know that must be silly. Look at corporations. They generally use debt to finance their activities prudently—do it all the time. They do it to maximize their net worth over time by achieving a higher return on assets than their borrowing costs. Having no debt isn't optimal, so what is optimal? How would you figure it out? It would be an amount where having more debt would be bad but having less debt would also be bad—that is, just the right amount. No one ever thinks to ask what that level is because their confirmation bias leads them to presume less debt is always better. Maybe you do, too, but you can benefit by asking Question One to see if you could be wrong. Because if you've been wrong about this, you're in vast company.

To find a "correct" level of debt (and what the "incorrect" level is), we must revisit basic economics and finance theory where we learned debt by itself isn't bad, immoral or a sign of character weakness. Debt is obviously a right and necessary tool of capitalism. And we've already defined capitalism as inherently good. An early lesson of corporate finance is how to calculate an optimal capital structure for a firm or the right mix of debt and equity to maintain on a corporate balance sheet. If you're a CFO, you calculate the optimal capital structure for your company to capture maximum return on investment. Though this is different for different firms, and even varies sector to sector, the right debt level is almost never zero. Most firms can't maximize profit without leverage. Therefore, having no debt isn't optimal for a society. So, again, how much?

Borrowing—whether you're a CEO running a $100 billion behemoth or a mom running a five-person household—is good if the after-tax cost of borrowing (the interest rate) is sufficiently lower than the conservatively estimated expected rate of return on a contemplated investment. Most easily agree with that. The spread between the two, quite simply, is profit. An optimal debt-to-equity ratio is achieved when the incremental borrowing cost just equals the incremental return on investment from those funds.

The "just equals" part makes some nervous. But if I told you our widget firm had a 15% return on investment from widgetry and a borrowing cost of 6% pretax (say, 4% after tax), you wouldn't be upset if we borrowed money and added on to our widget plant. You know we would make money on the spread, and you'd like that. But still—"just equals" is scary.

Did you take microeconomics in school? If not, bear with me for a few sentences because the next few lines are for those who did. If you did, you recall in economic theory, profit maximization occurs when marginal costs equal marginal revenue (sales). (You can get that from any introductory micro-economics text. I'm not saying anything racy here.) One marginal cost may be interest costs from borrowing. Via what they taught you in school, when the marginal cost of borrowing just barely exceeded the marginal return gener-ated from the activity in which the borrowed funds were used, optimization did occur. Because we would have borrowed all we could use to profit by—being maximally efficient—and no more!

The "Right" Amount of Debt

The right amount of debt for society to have is that amount where marginal borrowing costs of all kinds equal marginal return on assets of all kinds. This is very simple, purely rational and straight from economic theory. So extend that. If a society's return on assets is very high compared to its borrowing costs, it could borrow more money, invest it and get the return on assets to make its citizenry richer. For those still hung up on morality and debt, a richer citizenry is moral. A poorer citizenry is immoral. Got that?

When it comes right down to it—whether more debt is good or bad or less debt is better or worse—it's all about the return on assets. If return is high relative to borrowing costs, more debt is good, less debt is bad. If the reverse is true—if return on assets is lower than marginal borrowing costs—less debt is in order. So how do we know if the United States has the right level of debt? Simple—by looking at our return on assets relative to borrowing costs. How do you do that?

To figure our borrowing costs, look at the liabilities side of our balance sheet again. You know approximately what the interest rates are on the vari-ous types of debt. (As I update in 2011, interest rates are even *lower* than they were when I originally wrote this!) The interest on home mortgages for the most part is tax deductible, so that cost is lower than you think, but it hovers around 4% right now for 30-year money[2]; after tax is maybe half that. Credit cards have higher interest rates, but credit card debt as a percent of overall debt is much lower than many think. When you average in auto loans (which are still basically interest-free), the rate on aggregate consumer debt isn't so high. We've discussed corporate borrowing rates in this book as well as federal debt. And intuitively, you know state and municipal debt, being tax-free, are lower rates still. Looking at all of the debt together, it's safe to assume our average interest rate for all our debts is about 3% to 4%. Give or take. And after tax it is lower, maybe 2%. Something like that.

Surprise!

What is really important is the US return on assets, but how do we figure that? Just like a corporation does! Take our total income (GDP) and divide by our total assets. Based on the data in Table 6.1, GDP is about $15 trillion. GDP is the right number to use because it's our national income, and someone receives and benefits from every bit of it. Our income is our "return"—in many ways no different than the income a family or corporation gets, which is how they calculate their return. When we have more income, people are overall better off (which is the goal). More income for more people—that's more moral. And while you don't think about it this way, GDP is an after-tax number, too—taxes wash out because your income tax is still included in GDP. It's just the part our government gets. So dividing our GDP by our total assets gives us a return on assets of 12%. (That's as of 2011. Interestingly, it was also 12% when I first wrote this in 2006—Americans are good at producing a decent return on assets.)

Quite obviously, our return on assets is much higher than our after-tax borrowing cost of about 2% to 3%. So the way a good CFO would consider it, we're not over-indebted, we're *under-indebted*. And if our guess as to the average borrowing rate is off a bit or GDP or total assets is a little off because government accounting is inherently sketchy—it doesn't really matter much because however wrong we are, our borrowing rate is still tiny compared to our return on assets.

First, a 12% return on assets is impressive—very! Second, though this will be harder for readers in 2012 to believe than it was for 2006 readers, we're nowhere near over-indebted.

To get to that point where our return on assets about equals our borrowing cost, we'd need to borrow and invest a lot more—maybe two or three times more. If we borrowed a lot more, eventually that would put pressure on interest rates, driving them up. And if we buy enough more assets, we would eventually engage in ever more marginal activities and our return on assets must eventually fall. But before we get to that point, overall societally, we must acquire much more in assets producing a higher level of absolute income. And borrowing more to invest and produce more income is exactly how you move to optimization in economic theory.

We maximize profit and wealth for our citizenry when we do, and until we do, we're under-indebted. My guess is this goes against everything most readers have ever been taught. My point isn't to advocate for more debt. Rather, I want you to see that nearly everyone fears we are over-indebted when, applying basic economics and finance theory, it's easy to see we are very, very far from that point.

Is More Debt Bad . . . or Good?

This is the ultimate Question One. No one has bothered to ask if we have too little debt. And they don't because consensus mythology is so overwhelmingly pro-debt reduction. It's like some kind of sociological religion where questioning the mythology makes you a heretic. But flipping Question One on its head is about the most fun you can have in finance. Let's get really perverse: Is more federal debt actually good for our economy and stock market? How about this question: If we're under-indebted, how much more debt should we have, and what could we do with it? That is the Question Two kicker part that, when answered, lets you fathom something others can't fathom. To see this, we start thinking from a corporate view and then move through individuals to government debt.

One consideration firms look at is their *debt-to-equity* level. Optimal debt-to-equity levels will differ from industry to industry and even firm to firm. Going back to Table 6.1, the US has a debt-to-equity ratio of about 99% (debt divided by net worth). But is that high or low? Problematic or not?

Look at it this way. Time Warner, a perfectly fine, well-run firm, has a debt-to-equity ratio of 350%. Deere & Co, one of America's oldest firms, has debt to equity of 348%. Marriott's debt to equity is 722%! Sunoco's is 270%, Kellogg's is 264%, Lockheed Martin's is 269%, Boeing's is 207%.[3] I could rattle off many, many more.

You know all these firms. They aren't fly-by-night. They are long-standing firms and some of America's largest. They have much huger debt-to-equity ratios than our nation as a whole and aren't in some way doomed. These firms may not be at their optimal debt-to-equity levels, but near as I can tell, they aren't approaching disaster and manage to have decent earnings over time— even with their relatively big debt loads. That's not to say the US should have a debt-to-equity ratio so high. Rather, that you shouldn't automatically assume 99% is bad or wrong.

You may say, "I'm ok with corporate debt in theory. And I have no problem if Boeing borrows to build a plant to make money or if corporations in general do—they're rational about their usage of it—but not for idiotic consumers or, worse by far, the idiotic government."

What you aren't ok with is a heroin addict ringing up credit card debt to finance more heroin and buying Pink Floyd songs on iTunes—squandering meager borrowed funds on drugs and foolery. What an idiot! Still, many of you are more ok with the heroin addict's iPod debt than our federal government's debt—because you feel the heroin addict is basically smarter, more disciplined and a better spender than the federal government. As far as total governmental debt goes, you hate your local municipality's debt but see it as less stupid than your state and your state as less stupid than the federal government. (Unless you live in California—then you see the state as more stupid.)

To see the government's and heroin addict's debt better, let's start with corporate debt again. Suppose you're CEO of an average-quality corporation with a medium-grade Standard & Poor's credit rating of BBB. In mid-2011, your company could borrow 10-year money for about 4.6%.[4] To afford this debt while generating additional income, you need a return on assets better than your net after-tax borrowing cost. Suppose you have a 33% corporate tax rate. Then your 4.6% borrowing cost is 3% after tax. If you don't believe you can beat 3% a year over the long term, you shouldn't be CEO in the first place and your board should fire you.

So if you can build a plant or launch a product or otherwise do anything yielding maybe a 12% return—but anything markedly higher than 3%—your shareholders (and your customers and employees—in other words, everyone including the general citizenry) will like you better if you borrow more and invest to create wealth. Borrowing then is good for everyone and moral and right.

Here's a good example of debt and corporate morality. Assume you're CEO and your stock has a P/E of 16, which is an earnings yield (E/P, the reverse of the P/E) of 6.25%. Recall, that's after tax because the P/E was after tax. If you can borrow at 3% after tax and buy back your own stock, reducing available supply, you boost your earnings per share, capturing the 3.25% spread as profit—getting free money for your shareholders. Done right, it's effectively a no-lose trade as long as your earnings aren't about to fall otherwise. And if you're the CEO, who would know that better than you? (Again, you should be fired if you can't do that.) It's the moral thing to do.

But maybe not! Maybe you have higher uses for borrowed money because you can build a plant making widgets yielding 15%. More power to you.

Do it—instead of buying back your stock. Or do both. You are borrowing responsibly—and possibly should keep borrowing more—as long as you have abundant opportunities to make ready profit at high returns materially exceeding your borrowing costs. That's rational and shouldn't have the mental sting normally associated with debt in our society.

Using debt in these ways provides capital for research, development and making acquisitions; increases shareholder value; and improves long-term prospects for the firm—we all understand that. The company in turn provides better goods and services for a more competitive price, which benefits the consumer. And let's not forget the employees who receive better salaries, health care and other benefits because of the growth involved. It's beautiful!

Multiplier Effects and the Heroin-Addicted iPod Borrower

Let's shift to the heroin-addicted iPod borrower and the similarly stupid government. For readers who took a college economics class, you may recall when a bank makes a loan, it increases the quantity of money—it's effectively just like printing money from thin air. Simply said, every loan has a "multiplier" effect. In America, money newly created through a new loan gets spent—changes hands—on average about six times in the first 12 months of its existence. Economists call how fast existing money changes hands *velocity*.

So pretend there is a banker stupid enough to lend money to a known heroin addict. The addict is tired of his old iPod and wants to borrow to upgrade it and buy more heroin. (Very dumb.) The banker lends to him (presumably charging him a higher rate than someone more responsible, like you). The addict buys some heroin from his drug dealer and the iPod from his iPod dealer. The money has changed hands stupidly. Now, the iPod dealer is rational and normal. He got some of that addict's money and spends some on sales tax, some replenishing his inventory from Apple—which is pretty normal, and Apple likes it—and some feeding his family in normal ways, not stupidly at all. That's the second spend—the money is spent four more times on average before the first year is out, and every time after that first stupid spend by the addict, it's spent pretty darned normally—boringly so by normal, rational people and corporations. Said another way: After the stupid first spend, the next five spends end up being very average.

Then there was the money borrowed and spent on the drug dealer. Here there is no sales tax for obvious reasons. This dealer isn't so terribly stupid or he would already be in jail. So this smarter-than-your-average drug dealer spends his new money doing what the iPod dealer did—inventory (which never shows up in GDP accounting, for similarly obvious reasons) and supporting his family in normal ways. For example, he buys clothes at the clothes store, but then the clothes store spends it again in normal ways. And he perhaps buys some produce from the local hippie organic farmers, who spend it in fairly normal ways—maybe at the tie-dye T-shirt store. Maybe the drug dealer even has some druggie employees, so he pays for employee salaries and health insurance premiums. And this all gets re-spent afterward pretty normally—about four more times in the first year.

When a loan is made to a person, even a heroin-addicted iPod borrower, the multiplier effect means the money gets passed on and is spent pretty normally after the first stupid spend. When someone (or some corporation—or anyone!) spends money, they can only pass it on to a few different types of recipients: a corporation/business entity, another person, a government or a charity. That's it. Of course, people don't normally borrow money to give to charities, but it happens. The government does it all the time! But the charity then takes the money and spends it on baby formula, light bulbs, liability insurance, job training or something—anything! And still, it ends up being spent pretty normally after the first spend.

So when the heroin-addicted iPod borrower borrows money and spends, it isn't as good as when GE does. But after the first spend, the other spends are pretty much the same—identical in their normality. If you and I borrow personally and spend, it's only slightly smarter on average than the six spends by the heroin-addicted iPod borrower (maybe a part of one-sixth smarter) and only slightly stupider than when GE borrows to put in a plant for profit—the only thing different is the first spend, or maybe just part of it. Only the first spend! Ditto when the idiotic government borrows.

Just my opinion, but I do think our various governments are inherently stupid spenders on average. That doesn't make the outcome of their stupid spending necessarily bad. Not as good as if GE were doing the spending—to be sure—but still not bad because of the next five normal spends. Mind you, if the government could be a smarter spender, that would be better than being a stupider spender. But I assert even with the government being a stupider spender, it's overall good, not bad, because just one out of six spends is stupid and the rest are average. The initial stupid spend by the government generates only a little less economic activity and income than when the first spend is optimally smart and efficient.

Whether they spend it on $500 hammers, bridges, dams and roads or hard liquor for heroin-addicted iPod borrowers who would much prefer heroin—no matter how stupid—still, it can be spent only a few ways. It's either spent on government employees (people); on vendors, which are typically corporations but sometimes are people; or in transfer payments to people, corporations, charities or another government entity. Think about that.

The only other thing they can do is spend it overseas—which isn't very different in effect than when you take a foreign vacation and spend there. That may take money out of America, but if you're thinking globally like you should, you know it contributes to the global economy. And when they spend it on another government entity, like when the federal government gives money to your state who gives money to your county, the same thing happens. All the county can do is the same thing—spend on people, business entities, charities or other stupid governments. There are no other choices. Then the recipients re-spend the money five times, normally and averagely.

So if a society is technically under-indebted, meaning it has a very high return on assets compared to its borrowing costs as we do here in America, then more borrowing isn't automatically bad and can in fact be good, even if the first spend is more stupid than normal—even very stupid—even completely stupid. Why? More money being spent, exchanged, invested, whatever it is, no matter how smart or how stupid the first spend, eventually ends up being spent, exchanged and invested in a way that over time benefits the economy, providing more wealth for more people.

It also explains why stock returns have been materially *better* following peaks in budget deficits and much worse after surpluses, as shown in Chapter 1's Table 1.2. Recall, following deficit peaks—shown as relative troughs on Figure 1.6—markets averaged 16.7% after 12 months and 27.1% cumulatively 36 months later. Surpluses and even peaks where we've gotten close to a balanced budget have had much worse results—stocks fall an average –1.2% after 12 months and rise a mere 8.8% cumulatively after 36 months. You should prefer the higher returns. But maybe not. Maybe you're addicted to heroin!

Why do stocks do better on the deficits? One major reason: In years we run a deficit, we're adding debt while being under-indebted—getting closer to our optimal debt level. Hence, future income and wealth should be higher, and the market knows that and prices it in. In years when we run a surplus, we're reducing debt when we're under-indebted and moving farther away from optimality—going backward. The market knows that, too, and prices it in, and the market does badly.

Remember always: If it's true federal budget deficit peaks signal good times for US stocks, then it must be true in most other Western developed capitalistic places. And it is. High budget deficits have led to good stock returns and surpluses to poor returns on average in other developed economies, as shown in Figure 6.1. Deficits bring them closer to their optimal capital structure, and surpluses take them farther away.

UK High Points — Subsequent FTSE All-Share Returns

Date		1 year	2 year	3 year
1971	Annualized	7.04%	−13.09%	−28.32%
	Cumulative	7.04%	−24.47%	−63.17%
1989	Annualized	8.24%	12.32%	7.17%
	Cumulative	8.24%	26.17%	23.09%
2000	Annualized	−15.70%	−15.02%	−1.09%
	Cumulative	−15.70%	−27.79%	−3.24%
Average Annualized		−0.1%	−5.3%	−7.4%
Average Cumulative		−0.1%	−8.7%	−14.4%

UK Low Points — Subsequent FTSE All-Share Returns

Date		1 year	2 year	3 year
1976	Annualized	68.24%	39.36%	32.51%
	Cumulative	68.24%	94.23%	132.66%
1993	Annualized	−0.16%	10.65%	16.42%
	Cumulative	−0.16%	22.43%	57.78%
2000	Annualized	−15.70%	−15.02%	−1.09%
	Cumulative	−15.70%	−27.79%	−3.24%
Average Annualized		17.5%	11.7%	15.9%
Average Cumulative		17.5%	29.6%	62.4%

Germany High Points — Subsequent DAX Returns

Date		1 year	2 year	3 year
1969	Annualized	−20.55%	−1.55%	4.88%
	Cumulative	−20.55%	−3.07%	15.35%
1977	Annualized	27.09%	10.77%	3.88%
	Cumulative	27.09%	22.70%	12.14%
1989	Annualized	−3.27%	−0.19%	−4.45%
	Cumulative	−3.27%	−0.39%	−12.77%
2000	Annualized	−23.04%	−25.93%	−3.32%
	Cumulative	−23.04%	−45.13%	−9.64%
2007	Annualized	−45.09%	−16.24%	–
	Cumulative	−45.09%	−29.84%	–
Average Annualized		−13.0%	−6.6%	0.2%
Average Cumulative		−13.0%	−11.1%	1.3%

Germany Low Points — Subsequent DAX Returns

Date		1 year	2 year	3 year
1976	Annualized	15.88%	22.23%	5.88%
	Cumulative	15.88%	49.40%	18.70%
1993	Annualized	5.89%	16.06%	19.62%
	Cumulative	5.89%	34.69%	71.17%
2000	Annualized	13.45%	17.45%	9.64%
	Cumulative	13.45%	37.95%	31.78%
1995	Annualized	12.84%	17.53%	19.36%
	Cumulative	12.84%	38.14%	70.07%
2003	Annualized	17.86%	14.56%	21.98%
	Cumulative	17.86%	31.25%	81.48%
Average Annualized		13.2%	17.6%	15.3%
Average Cumulative		13.2%	38.3%	54.6%

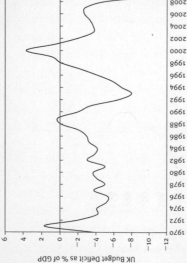

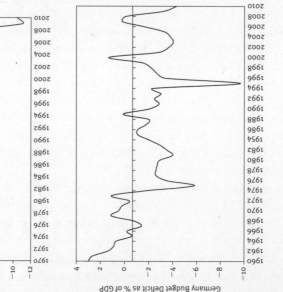

Figure 6.1 Budget Deficits Are Good for Stocks—Globally
Sources: Thomson Reuters, Office of National Statistics.

Not the Dow Again! EEK!

Let's consider this yet another way and return to our original question: Is debt bad? Our federal debt is the cumulative result of running budget deficits. Our state and municipal debt is similar if accounted for similarly. Let's start with the stupidest, biggest and dumbest government, Uncle Sam, and why intuitively its deficits and, hence, debt have led to good stock returns and its surpluses worse returns. Simply think of Uncle Sam as a corporation using leverage to spur growth.

Figure 6.2 shows net public federal government debt outstanding divided by GDP going back in time. Today, such debt accounts for 62% of GDP.

That the debt level is high relative to recent history won't surprise many readers. But we've had periods of much higher debt—like the period from 1943 to 1950. Some may say, "But that was war-related debt." Fine, except debt doesn't care about the reasoning behind it. Debt is debt—it must be serviced no matter if you see it as morally right (fighting Nazis) or morally ambiguous (stimulus). And recall, the period following the period of elevated debt isn't remembered as being dreadful. The 1950s are generally remembered as (and were) a period of fine economic growth and innovation. (Read more in my 2011 book, *Markets Never Forget*.)

Flip that on its head. Have you ever heard people talk about the famous 17 years when the stock market did so terribly from 1965 through 1981? People

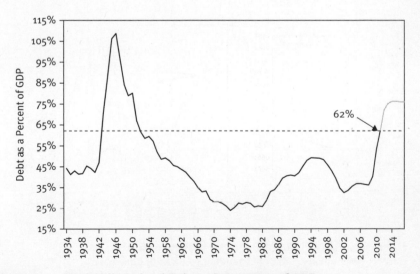

Figure 6.2   Net Public Federal Debt as Percentage of GDP
Sources: **Thomson Reuters, Treasury Direct, Congressional Budget Office, May 2011 Release.**

commonly claim the market was flat overall from 1965 through 1981. But that's because they're using the highly flawed Dow Jones Industrials Average (covered in Chapter 4 as a completely misleading index in terms of economic reality) to measure returns. If you use the S&P 500 as a reasonable proxy for America, average annual returns were 6.3%, total return, over those years[5]— below average for sure, but still positive and not at all disastrous! Even so, for most investors it was a long—almost two-decades long—period of below-average

A Long History of Big Debt

For something to be true in the US, it must be true elsewhere. And debt not being disastrous *is* true elsewhere. Figure 6.3 shows the much longer history of UK debt—back to 1700! At points, the UK has had vastly more debt as a percent of GDP without long-term harm. In fact, from about 1750 to 1850, the UK had debt in excess of 100% of GDP—peaking above 250%. This was a period when the UK was a global economic leader and leading the charge in industrial innovation. Debt wasn't disastrous for it then, and it's not automatically disastrous for the US now.

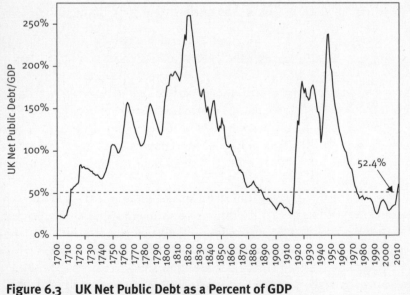

Figure 6.3   UK Net Public Debt as a Percent of GDP
Source: HM Treasury, UKpublicspending.co.uk as of June 2011.
Includes budget projections through 2011.

returns. Partly that was because more of the returns came from dividends than appreciation, and it sure felt like the market went nowhere.

Well, those grindingly below-average returns are exactly when we completed the process of getting our debt as a percent of GDP down to its lowest level of your life. Reducing debt relative to the size of the economy didn't ensure better stock returns.

Has America ever had no government debt at all? Many people think debt is a twentieth-century creation. But, no, we've always had debt except once, in the mid-1830s, when Andrew Jackson paid it off with gold garnered from Western land sales. (For a chronicling of that mishap, I refer you to my 1987 book, *The Wall Street Waltz*.) Jackson's pay-down was disastrous, leading to the infamous Panic of 1837 and the Depression of 1837 to 1843—one of the three biggest, longest and worst Depressions and stock market crashes in US history (the others being those starting 1873 and 1929). The history of paying down debt isn't stock market or economy friendly because it goes the wrong way when we're under-indebted.

Does Someone Need to Pay Back This Debt? No

Still, some detractors shake their heads and worry we are greedily enriching ourselves now to the detriment of future generations who, they fear, must pay it all down one day.

Ask another Question One here: Is it true we must pay down the debt? Look at what happened before when we have. Not good! If we can afford our debt (we can) and we get a good return on assets (we do), there is no need to ever waste cash flow on reducing debt service. We simply roll over the old debt, and as we grow bigger, we add more. The answers to our Questions here are: Debt isn't bad for the stock market or the economy. In fact, it's just the opposite. Debt, used responsibly, is good, right and important, and we have yet to reach our optimal debt level. Federal debt in America shouldn't be feared or demonized.

Now, don't get me wrong. I'm all for smaller government—and I don't like government spending at all. I'd like to see government spending as a percent of GDP shrink markedly. I already told you I think governments are pretty stupid spenders. I'm actually pretty anti-government at basically every turn, but decidedly not because it would reduce our debt! I'm anti-government because I see government as largely anti-capitalistic in most things it does and to me, all good things come from capitalism ultimately. So reducing government activity reduces anti-capitalistic activity and, in that sense, is good in my view. Feel free to disagree.

Let's Trade This Deficit for That One

So maybe the debt and budget deficit aren't the demons many fear them to be. But there are other headline-making, panic-inducing deficits giving investors frights—like the current account and trade deficits. Let's dispense with the current account deficit here and now. It's by and large comprised of the trade deficit. When folks tell you they're worried about it, they mean they're mostly worried about the trade deficit. What's more, the current account deficit is always, and by definition, perfectly offset by the capital account *surplus*. It balances! Has to. Anyone exercised about the current deficit is telling you more of what they don't know than what they do.

As for the US trade deficit, it hit $500 billion in 2011![6] (EGAD! Huge number!) Freaks folks out—particularly those fearful of a weak dollar. Disapproval of the trade deficit and a desire to reverse it are exceptionally widely and passionately held. You don't read anywhere that you shouldn't worry about it at all. That is always a great time for a Question One. Is it true trade deficits are bad for our economy, stock market and dollar? While we're at it, throw in a Question Two: Is it possible the trade deficit might be something good rather than bad? If so, how?

Again, here is an investing concern bred seemingly from common-sense analysis, confirmation bias and an inability to scale (all errors combatable via Question Three). A trade deficit seems to signal we spend more on imports than we earn on exports and are bleeding money. Some see it like a gigantic zero sum game—if you have more minuses than pluses, you lose. By that logic, a trade deficit is bad for the economy because it's unsustainable and bankrupting. If America were a gigantic hardware store, a sustained trade deficit could be bad. If everyone acts nuts, the money bolts out the door (nyuk, nyuk). You want your hardware store to sell more stuff (nuts, bolts, drill bits) than it buys (computers, employee time, Cheetos for the employee break room), else the hardware store would bolt to bankrupt.

Nonetheless, folks who think this way make several cognitive errors. First, as a general remedy, think globally. If you do, trade deficit concerns disappear. Why? No one worries whether Montana runs a trade deficit with the rest of America. Or California or New York for that matter. It's impossible for the whole world to run a trade deficit or surplus-trade balances. Among developed nations, trade deficits and surpluses aren't materially more important to the overall level of global stocks than the trade balance between Montana and New York.

One key point in seeing this clearly is the US and developed foreign markets with which we have deficits behave similarly. They tend to rise and fall together. Sometimes America does better. Sometimes other countries do. And that is true of countries with similar deficits and ones with surpluses. We have a big trade deficit, current account deficit, budget deficit and debt. Some countries have none of those. Some run huge surpluses. If deficits are bad and surpluses good, the US stock market and varying foreign markets should be zigzagging all over the map. The United States would be down big when foreign is flat or up big. But it's not so.

Look at Figure 6.4, which shows US and foreign stocks since 1973 (when we have good data for the EAFE). It shows US and foreign markets moving— not identically—but certainly in the same direction and sometimes the same darned magnitude.

Think of the logic of this for a second. Once you get in your bones the US market may lead or lag the rest of the developed world but doesn't go a markedly different direction, you know trade balances don't matter to the global stock market. They just can't. If the deficits mattered, and we have a big deficit to the rest of the world, then why are our stock markets more correlated than not? If a US trade deficit is bad for America and American stocks, then, by default, a surplus should be good for America and American stocks. Fair enough? If a trade surplus is good for America and American stocks, then a trade surplus in another Western nation should be good for that country and its stocks. That means an American trade deficit (implying a foreign trade

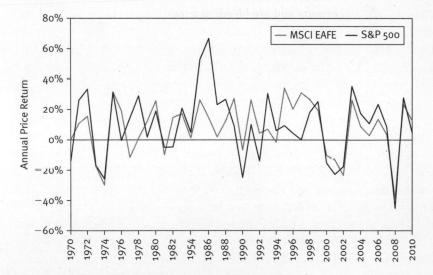

Figure 6.4   US and Foreign Stock Market Movement
Sources: Global Financial Data, Inc. and Thomson Reuters, MSCI EAFE and S&P 500 price return from 12/31/1973 to 12/31/2010.

surplus) should be good for foreign stocks. And US stocks are just about 50% of total developed world stocks—so the two offset each other perfectly with no overall effect on global stocks. Make sense? People talk as if that's so. But if it were, US and non-US stocks would be negatively correlated, not positively.

That still assumes a trade deficit is bad for US stocks, a point I'm unwilling to concede. I'm still on Question One. The logic falls apart as soon as you get to global markets. We can all agree that, globally, trade balances. To argue cogently a US trade deficit causes the global market to fall, you must argue trade deficits are *more* negative than trade surpluses are positive. To date, no one has ever expressed such a notion publicly, much less the theoretical economic justification for such a notion. No one even thinks that far. They simply stop at "the sky is falling" before getting to the notion the world can't have a trade surplus or deficit.

So ask the question: Is our trade deficit, in fact, bad for US stocks and our economy? First, we should scale—trade balances involve big numbers. Figure 6.5 shows the US trade balance back to 1980 as a percent of GDP along with trade balances of the UK, Germany and Japan.

The United States has run a trade deficit the entire time—at times bigger as a percent of GDP, at times smaller.

It's currently about 3.4%.[7] Now, a better question: Is that trade deficit too big and bad for our economy and stock market? Or do a Question Two: Is a big trade deficit a symptom of a healthy economy and a sound financial system and not an indicator of future financial ruin?

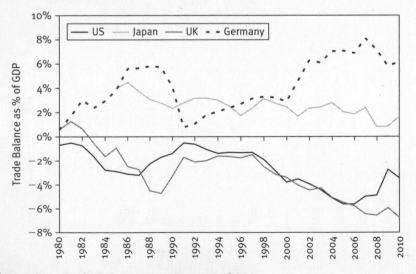

Figure 6.5   Trade Balances as a Percent of GDP
Sources: US Census Bureau, Foreign Trade Division, Thomson Reuters.

Yes, our trade deficit has gotten remarkably wider since 1980. Yet even including the 2007 to 2009 recession, the United States also had a fine, healthy economy overall, growing nearly the entire time. Since we've been running a trade deficit consistently starting in 1980, we've enjoyed average annualized GDP growth of 5.8% (nominal) and annualized market returns of 11.3%.[8] Hard to argue that's very terrible.

Still, critics make several arguments. First, they say it hasn't hurt us *yet*, but things haven't yet come home to roost and will soon. Well, fine, but at what level of trade deficit or cumulative trade deficit does that occur? To date, I've never heard such a trigger point articulated—nor, even more important, articulated with an underlying fundamental argument as to why that is where a trigger point should be. Second, some may concede the trade deficit hasn't done enough damage to make our growth negative or nonexistent—but they ask, "How do we know what our growth *would have been* without the trade deficit? We might have had even *more* growth were it not for this damaging deficit."

For example, consider Britain. Its markets have done well. Its currency has been stronger than ours. In fact, the pound sterling has arguably been the world's strongest major developed currency in recent decades. Surely this is the proof in the pudding (the Brits love their pudding) that our trade deficits have hurt us relative to them.

The UK is actually a good litmus test for many of our own economic conditions because the UK has been in almost exactly the same economic situation in the same proportions in terms of deficits, trade balance—everything. Look at Figure 6.5 again. The UK has run a trade deficit since the early 1980s in almost exactly the same size relative to its economy. The current trade deficit (accounted for the same way as ours) is about 6.8% of GDP[9]—bigger now than ours, but for most of the period, the two have been quite similar.

And its economy and markets have been overall strong just like ours. The British stock market has averaged an annualized 11.9% return since they started running a trade deficit in 1980, and the economy has also been healthy, annualizing 5.4%—near identical to the US.[10]

The UK has had a similar-size trade deficit but a stronger currency. What gives? What does that tell you about trade deficits? It tells you they don't impact currencies. If the pound sterling has been strong, and trade deficits impact currencies, how can the UK trade deficit, which is comparable to ours, be good for the pound sterling but ours be bad for the dollar? Critics may say, "That's just this year's deficit." Look at Figure 6.5 again. You see the progression is similar. You simply can't argue the size of our trade deficit relative to our economy is too big and causing the greenback to fall here while arguing the Brits' almost exact same-size trade deficit relative to their economy now and cumulatively over time has somehow allowed the pound to be strong. Is something else causing the relative strength or weakness of our currencies? Sure—but that is for Chapter 7. This litmus test is never contemplated by grumpy trade deficit bears.

Let's Play the "Which Country Do You Want to Be?" Game

Think about this yet another way. If a trade deficit is bad and a trade surplus is good, we can settle the question just by looking at examples of developed countries with big deficits and big surpluses. Without analyzing anything further than which country you'd rather be, look at Figure 6.5. Would you rather be the US and UK with big and growing trade deficits but robust GDP and strong market returns over the past 30-plus years? Or would you rather be a country with a steady surplus?

How about those clever Germans—responsible for driving machines *par excellence* and punctual trains? They've had a surplus steadily since 1980. Yet Germany's economy has annualized 4.5% and its stocks 9.4%.[11] Data from Japan on its visible trade balance start in 1985—but they've had a surplus ever since. During that period, its economy annualized 5.7% and stocks 5.4%.[12] For all their "economically superior" surpluses, their economic growth rates are in line with big-deficit US and UK (Germany's rate is slightly lower). And Germany's stock returns are fine but still lower than the US and UK, and Japan's are much lower.

So who do you want to be? Would you rather be the countries with the trade deficits and the better market returns? Or do you want to boast a trade surplus and poorer returns? All but the irrational would opt for the deficit and better returns. And a trade surplus sure isn't an economic panacea. In fact, our trade deficit is a symptom of our economic vigor and rapid growth, not a political problem to be tackled.

Mercantilists Are Darned Near as Bad as Commies

The real problem isn't the US trade deficit. The real problem is the trade surpluses in Germany and Japan and many European nations. Why do they have them, and why is it a problem? Before capitalism evolved in America and Britain as a dominant economic theory, mercantilism preceded it. People forget about mercantilism. Find a basic economic history text and read about it. My personal favorite fast read on this is Douglas C. North's, *Growth and Welfare in America's Past* (Prentice Hall, 1966), but from his references, you can find many other sources.

Real capitalism first reared its head just as America was birthing. Recall Adam Smith's legendary *The Wealth of Nations*, the seminal book on capitalism, was published in the year of our nation's birth.

Mercantilism operated then to a more extreme extent but much as Japan and Germany do now. Those countries deploy government-based economic throttles to purposefully create trade surpluses on the theory surpluses should help their economies. They think just like those who think our trade deficits are bad. They think trade surpluses help and deficits hurt, so they purposefully manufacture trade surpluses by constricting consumption governmentally and pushing exports.

But forcing policy through an economy to create anything at the expense of freer markets and purer capitalism leads to suboptimization and slower growth. Always! Why? To maximize growth, you must let capitalism run wild. Positively amok! That is the basic economic lesson of the past 200 years. Deficit bears are too clever by half with their views of good and bad and can't get the beneficence of Adam Smith's invisible hand. They want to interfere—with a policy hand that gets in the way and simply stifles growth. Bet on capitalism and growth, not on mercantilism and trade surpluses. Our growth creates the capital flows sustaining our trade deficits; as long as we continue to grow rapidly, our current account and trade deficits will remain high and we will remain happy. If our growth slows or ends, our trade deficit will, too. That is all there is to it.

So, in using Question One with a Question Two follow-up, we've learned debt, a budget deficit and a trade deficit aren't the negatives most people would have you believe. When you hear drumbeats warning of market decline and, worse, because of a "too large" or "unsustainable" deficit or debt or both, know that fear of a falsehood is bullish. Keep that in mind because deficits and debt frequently recycle as reasons for bearishness.

You should fear any effort to force a reversal in these deficits à la mercantilism—usually from senators. And you should fear surpluses. Repeat after me, "I would prefer not to see budget and trade surpluses in America. I would prefer to see rapid growth and deficits." Say that at your next cocktail party and someone may throw a drink in your face. First, that reaction tells you this truth still has power and legs. Second, hey, free drink!

The New Gold Standard

For another Question One myth and reverse truth, consider William Jennings Bryan. Remember him? The Populist with the booming voice and his famous "Cross of Gold" speech and his indifferently supported campaign to move to a silver standard as 1900 approached? (Read more about him in Appendix F.)

America abandoned the gold standard (again) in 1971, but a new standard has arisen—the widespread belief gold is the ultimate portfolio hedge. The belief cycles in and out of fashion, but when it's in, you endlessly hear that when gold is up, stocks are down, and vice versa. Gold is pitched as a good hedge against downside volatility. A long-held derivative theory is gold will protect you when capitalism inevitably fails. Something like that.

Folks also sometimes say gold is a good inflation indicator. Rising gold prices should signal bad news all around for stock investors because stock prices will drop and rising inflation will stagnate growth. But is it true? The love affair with gold comes and goes but naturally intensifies if gold prices do well for a while.

The Golden Hedge

The gold hedge belief, like many entrenched investor beliefs, appeals to our common sense. Gold is a commodity—it has weight and heft you can see and feel, and you can take possession of it. Stocks are slips of paper—nowadays, barely even that—just bits of data in a wireless cloud. It seemingly makes sense two such different asset classes might behave differently. And because of prior long history of the government pegging currency value to gold, both here and globally, there is sentimental value in owning gold.

But is it right? The more I hear old, long-held governmental policies paralleling our faith in gold, the more skeptical I get—particularly when I remember gold standards started during mercantilism's reign.

Use Question One: Is it true gold makes a good hedge? If gold is a great hedge, it should be negatively correlated to stocks. Think short and long term. For example, as I was writing this book in mid-2006, stocks had just gone through a pretty normal global stock market correction. If gold were a proper hedge, it should have continued to rise as stock prices dropped—or at worst, remained flat. Figure 6.6 shows the price of gold and the S&P 500 from the beginning of the year to mid-2006.

Gold wasn't doing what hedgers expected. Over this period, gold correlated strongly with the stock market, not the reverse. The market fell sharply, and so did gold. If you hoped to protect yourself against downside volatility with gold, you were instead getting it double. It moved with the market and was (and still is) just about as volatile as the market. Then, too, think about 2009 and 2010. Stocks rose, and gold did, too! Positively correlated direction-wise during much of that period. And when stocks fell in global corrections in both 2010 and 2011, gold didn't consistently keep rising—it corrected some, too.

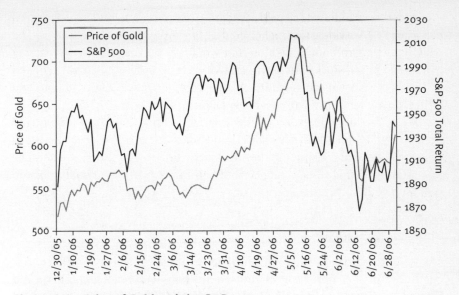

Figure 6.6   Price of Gold and the S&P 500
Source: Global Financial Data, Inc.

Thinking short term is a fun exercise but not really useful looking forward. If gold isn't reliable as a consistent security hedge, could it make sense as a long-term investment? Figure 6.7 shows growth of a dollar in gold, US stocks and the 10-year US Treasury since gold started trading truly freely, when post–Bretton Woods controls were finally dropped in 1973. In this period, $1 invested in gold became $16.04. It became $21.58 in Treasurys and $37.76 in US stocks. And that's including the run gold had in recent years as I update in 2011.

Gold may continue climbing, or it may not—but the odds are you aren't well served using gold as a hedge or as a long-term investment if any kind of growth is your goal. To do well with gold, you must be good at in-and-outing. If that's your plan, you should ask yourself: If you're not good at in-and-outing stocks, why will you be with gold? The answer, as with all other things, comes down to the question: Do you know something others don't about gold? (For more on why gold is the ultimate timing issue, see my 2010 book, *Debunkery*.)

Gold, Inflation and 206 Years of the Long Bond

Gold could serve a useful purpose if its price can tell us something about where inflation is headed. Plenty of folks believe higher gold prices mean runaway inflation is ahead.

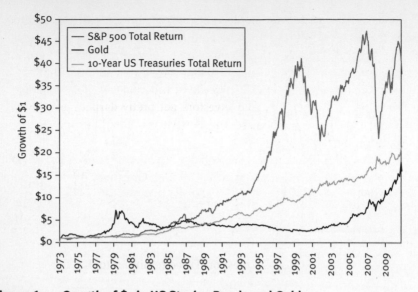

Figure 6.7   Growth of $1 in US Stocks, Bonds and Gold
Sources: Global Financial Data, Inc., Gold Bullion price per Troy ounce (US$/ounce),
S&P 500 total return, US 10-Year Government Bond Index total return, monthly returns
from 11/30/1973 to 09/30/2011.

Except Question One shows us this is a myth, too. Inflation is a monetary phenomenon relating to how much money is sloshing around the economy. Inflation occurs when there's too much excess supply (supply being controlled by central bank actions) relative to the amount of goods sold in an economy, chasing prices of those goods higher. Some degree of inflation is normal and good. Few fear very low inflation rates and everyone fears high ones.

Runaway inflation, such as in the 1970s, is a problem—one many readers will remember clearly. It's easiest to think about runaway inflation on the extreme end. Recall Germany's Weimar years in the early 1920s. The central bank was so loose, printing so much money, money became worthless. Germans burned money as fuel because crates of their valueless cash couldn't buy coal or even wood. And before too long, the Nazis took over, so you know hyperinflation isn't so good. But low inflation levels aren't scary. Which would you prefer—modest inflation or modest deflation? Probably inflation, though statistically they are two edges of the same sword. Deflation, made by creating less new money than new goods or services, causes prices to drop and can lead to problems, including folks delaying economic activity, which can cause a big economic slowdown, massive unemployment, etc. No fun.

So what does all this have to do with gold? Nothing. Gold is a commodity and is traded on a free and open market. Inflation is a monetary phenomenon, as Milton Friedman once famously said, "Always and everywhere." Just because, over time, gold has appreciated at roughly the rate of inflation, you shouldn't conclude gold can tell you where inflation will go. It should tell you over long time periods, gold investors get pretty darned low returns—which is what Figure 6.7 showed and is what you should intuitively expect from most industrial commodities.

So, if in addition to not being a good bet as a long-term investment, gold's not a good indicator for inflation, what is? Use Question Two. This one is really simple.

What Is It? What Isn't It?

This Question Two requires a Question Three reminder to think globally. But first, let's think about what inflation is and isn't—quite literally. It isn't what's happening to your cost of living, which people often confuse with inflation. Inflation is an averaging of prices of all types of newly produced goods and services, whether you buy them or not. It isn't about the price of gold or any other commodity. It isn't about the cost of used cars, although used car prices may be impacted by inflation. It isn't reflective of wages, although wages are part of what it's about. It is an averaging of all goods and services produced and, in that regard, is simply a reflection of the change in the value of money to buy the average item.

Maybe some prices are going up a lot and some a little—some down a little, and maybe some down a lot. Gasoline up a lot. Health care up a lot. Electronic gadgets down a lot. Brokerage commissions down a little (a service). Shoe prices down a little. In a perfect world of 0% inflation (correctly calculated), it isn't true all prices would remain flat and unchanged. No, in such a world, about half the prices would be rising, half the prices falling—all at a variety of speeds.

Older Americans who pay for lots of health care and their grandchildren's private school and college educations often presume inflation is rampant and our inflation indexes are massively off and understate inflation. That's confusing what they buy with inflation. I'll not defend the inflation indexes because my view is pretty much all government economic indicators are very inaccurate. But whether the Consumer Price Index reflects inflation correctly or not has nothing to do with whether the items you buy are reflective of the average items produced and, therefore, reflective of inflation. They aren't. Few people experience an average experience. Consumer buying habits are very diverse.

It would be bizarre for a very young person to buy a similar basket of goods as an elderly couple—or a middle-aged one.

Take this further. In 1900, most of what you might buy was made in America. In today's more global world, much of it comes from here, there or anywhere. And much of what is made in America is only partly made in America. Today, higher prices on one type of good from one country may be wholly or partly offset by lower prices on another type from another country. Today, inflation takes on global aspects. During the past 20 years, we saw some American inflation while Japan and much of Asia felt deflation because they created more goods than they created money, and the type of goods they created were often prone to falling prices. But still, within their deflation, some prices would rise, others would fall and others would go down even more.

Inflation as a concept is always an averaging. Japanese deflation then, including the prices of goods created there and sold to America, helped keep American inflation down to lower levels than it would have been otherwise via substitution. At one level, we partly exported inflation to them and they partly exported deflation to us, and each partially offset the other.

So if what you buy isn't necessarily reflective of inflation, then what America averages isn't necessarily totally reflective of inflation. One way to think better about inflation is to try to see it globally. Thinking globally, you worry less because globalization can mitigate country-specific inflation effects. Global competition leads to ever-increased specialization of labor and technology, and short-term excess production capacity in one country offsets shortages elsewhere. American prices for many goods and services subject to foreign competition are actually falling. Everyday items from tube socks to toys to cars to sundries are cheaper today than just a few years ago, adjusted for inflation. This is a lost story because rising oil prices make for better television. The media had consumers so focused on the higher price of crude and steel they didn't notice the cars they were fueling up were actually cheaper. A cheaper car is as much (or more) a good thing as higher gas prices an annoying thing.

But is there something that can signal if inflation is rising? Well, it can't be your buying habits. It can't be Montana's buying habits. It really shouldn't even be America's buying habits. What it should be is something measuring the value of money spanning the whole wide global world because that is what inflation is all about. Use Question Two to ponder: What is a good measure of the value of money? What is the price of money today? What is its price tomorrow?

Well, we know for a fact we can borrow money today so we can have it tomorrow. We know what the rent is for that borrowing. In the long term, the price of renting money is what we otherwise call long-term interest rates.

The 10-year Treasury bond rate, for example, is one way to measure the cost of renting long-term money in America.

From a lender's view, money rental is very vulnerable to the ravages of accelerating inflation. Lenders want to be paid for higher inflation and higher inflation risk by getting a higher interest rate. America may not exactly be experiencing the world's buying habits, but global long-term rates react to global long-term inflation fears. Therefore, global long-term rates are most sensitive to changing inflation expectations. For this, I refer you back to Chapter 2 where we introduced to you the concept of global short- and long-term interest rates. The global long-term rate is a perfect way to see if global inflation is rearing its ugly head or not.

As of this writing, it quite clearly isn't. Globally, long-term rates are very low. Historically so! (And as I update in 2011, lower than when I first wrote in 2006.) If inflation were rising as a problem, global long-term interest rates would likely rise. If it is falling as a problem, global rates typically reflect that.

Remember, the global interest rate is the price of renting money. Figure 6.8 shows the global free market measuring precisely the problem of concern—the total global or country-based value of money. This chart is updated as far as possible into 2011. Euro rates ticked up tied to debt-related fears there, which doesn't surprise you. Even so, overall, they're not much

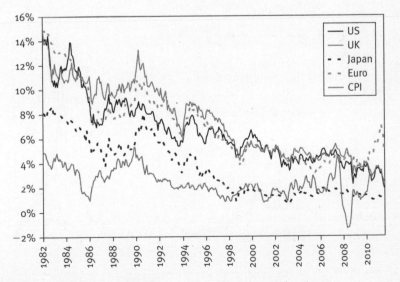

Figure 6.8 Global Long Bonds
Sources: Global Financial Data, Inc., US 10-Year Bond Constant Maturity Yield, UK 10-Year Government Bond Yield, Japan 10-Year Government Bond Yield, Eurozone 10-Year Government Bond Yield, G7 Consumer Price Index from 1/31/1982 to 09/30/2011.

higher now than they were in the mid-1990s. Outside the eurozone, rates globally are very low.

That global long-term rates have been benign in recent years tells you markets don't fear inflation rearing its head in a materially increasing way. You just fathomed something most can't fathom. More important, we can see historically the long bond has been sensitive to inflation concerns and is a good measure.

Why has inflation—and, therefore, long-term rates—steadily if somewhat irregularly fallen over the past 30 years? Beginning in the 1980s, central banks steadily gained the upper hand against the 1970s war on inflation with help from free trade and globalization. This in turn caused global long rates to fall from historically elevated levels.

Maybe you don't remember it that way. Figure 6.8 certainly makes it look like all the 10-year rate has done over the long term is fall—with a little wiggle en route. How could that be predictive about inflation at all? What's more, in recent years, professional forecasters have tended to believe this (now 30-year) downward trend will reverse. Except, flipping back to Chapter 4, you know the professionals keep getting their long-term bond forecasts wrong as well.

Figure 6.9—showing US long-term interest rates way back to 1800— puts long-term rates into perspective. First, investors tend to talk about today's

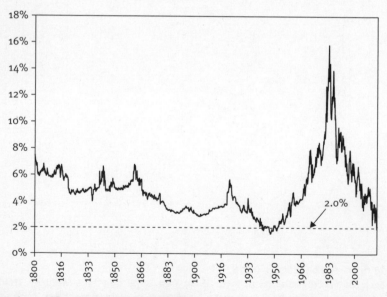

Figure 6.9   US 10-Year Treasury Yield
Sources: Global Financial Data, Inc., USA 10-Year Bond Constant Maturity Yield.[13]

10-year Treasury rate as "historically low." And it is pretty low—as I update in 2011, the 10-year US Treasury yield is 2%. But here's another way to look at it. Maybe the long bond rate during the 1970s was "freakishly high"! Investors may be frustrated they can no longer buy Treasury bonds with a 13% coupon as they did when they were young in the 1970s, but they fail to remember the economy was stagnating and inflation wiped out even super-high coupon payments. Save your 1970s nostalgia for the Bee Gees. (Ok, I take that back.)

Second, the long-term interest rate spike clearly correlates with the onset of and recovery from horrid monetary mismanagement and resulting 1970s hyperinflation. Why? Because the long bond is traded on a free and open market and accurately represents the market's true inflation expectation. Don't focus on short rates—remember, they are controlled by the monopoly that is the central bank. Long bond interest rates aren't controlled at all; instead, they are perfectly free-market set. And that reflects the market's expectation for the quality of the job central banks are doing and is a great (though not perfect) indicator, at least for right now, of where the market is pricing future inflation risk.

Now that you're getting the hang of asking Question One and debunking myths, you can move on to finding new or ignored patterns that will give you a basis for market bets using Question Two. More examples in Chapter 7.

7

SHOCKING
BUT TRUE

Supply and Demand . . . and That's It

This book is partly about how to know something others don't—by processing information others find unfathomable and creating capital markets technology to do that. If information can't be processed well by our brains one way, reframe it in another more useful way, like our P/E-to-E/P flip. Or cut it in half and look at it anew. Or ask: "What does it correlate to?"

The news is full of useful information, if you can use Question Two to connect the dots. Just be creative and ask, "I wonder if that could mean anything? Wouldn't that be nuts?" One phenomenon that pops up occasionally is increased merger and acquisition activity. It's normal for mergers and acquisitions to increase in an economic expansion. Firms with improved balance sheets awash with cash look to acquire additional valuable market share, parallel product lines, vertical integration, new core competencies, new product categories or just simply diversify. In one way, this is unremarkable and mundane.

But can it mean anything for the stock market? Conventionally, market lore says merger manias lead to poor stock market results. Partly that is because mergers happen after the economy has been improving for a while—and after that, at some time, comes another recession. So it's easy to see why folks see merger manias leading to bad times. Look at the late-1990s mergers coinciding with the Tech IPO craze. After a wave of deals like the Time Warner takeover of AOL, we were rewarded with a severe bear market and recession.

185

It makes sense takeovers should backfire often. After all, sellers (knowing the business inside out) usually know more about what they sell than buyers (being outsiders) know about what they buy. So shouldn't it be true buyers fare less well than sellers—arguing for lower prices later when reality sets in and the buyer and its shareholders realize they've been fleeced?

I made this point in my second book, *The Wall Street Waltz*. And I was wrong. Historically, there is some validity to the argument, but I put too much emphasis on some time periods and not enough on others. My conclusions were too dependent on takeovers of the 1920s and late 1960s. There was a lot of unintentional data-mining and confirmation bias in what I said then. Now I'd say I was wrong then, and the whole thing is very 50/50. It depends on the nature of the deals involved, and half are this way and half that way—and it varies with time.

Cash, Stock or Hybrid?

There was a crucial difference in how most of those 1990s mergers as well as the 1920s and late 1960s deals were structured compared to the post-2002 deals. The bulk of corporate mergers taking place in 2003, 2004, 2005 and 2006 were mostly transacted in cash, whereas those done in those three earlier periods were transacted mainly in stock. In the one, an acquirer pays earnest money for the shares of the acquiree; in the other, the acquirer simply issues newly created shares to fund the takeover. Question Two: Is there a difference between the two and their potential impact on the stock market? What can you see differently about this situation others don't see? What can you fathom that is unfathomable to most?

When Company A buys Company B for cash, it exchanges the cash for Company B's shares and then simply destroys those shares. After the deal, there are the same number of Company A's shares as before the deal and no shares of Company B. Company A now has its earnings and Company B's earnings, so Company A's earnings per share rise. Very simple!

This assumes on an annual basis Company B is profitable and its earnings exceed the interest payments Company A must pay to borrow the money to buy Company B. But otherwise, the acquisition is immediately *accretive* to earnings—shares are destroyed and, all else being equal, the acquirer's earnings per share rise immediately. The supply of equity outstanding in this case is reduced as the acquired company's stock is destroyed. Let me say that again. Cash-based acquisitions reduce the supply of equity outstanding. If demand remains constant and supply shrinks, prices should rise. Cash-based acquisitions tend to be bullish.

Takeovers transacted wholly in stock are different. Afterward, usually the acquirer's earnings per share fall because more shares are dumped on the market, diluting value. See it this way: Firm A is worth X. Firm B is worth Y. To acquire Firm B, Firm A must bid up B's price. Perhaps Firm A bids Firm B up by 25% to 1.25Y. That extra 25% is paid for by increasing the supply of stock of Firm A—newly created, never-before-existing shares. Firm A issues enough new shares to cover all of the prior value of Firm B plus enough newly created shares to cover the 25% markup. So, there are more real share equivalents after the deal than before.

Now, if Firm B has a higher P/E than Firm A at 1.25Y, Firm A's earnings per share fall when the deal is done. This is most of the deals in the 1920s, late 1960s and 1990s. It is the AOL-Time Warner deal. These increase supply of equity, are dilutive and make earnings per share fall.

There is a third type of deal—Firm A buys Firm B partly for cash and partly for newly created shares. Hybrids deals are common, having some of the qualities of both, but usually are more cash-like than a pure equity deal. Why? In these deals, usually the acquirer can't borrow enough cash to take over all of Company B, so it borrows what it can and issues shares to make up the difference. Usually these are bigger deals.

Suppose Firm A is worth $10 billion and B is worth $20 billion. A buys B. The smaller A swallowing the bigger B may frighten lenders. Maybe lenders will lend Firm A only $14 billion to buy B—exactly why doesn't matter for this example. Before the deal there were $30 billion of equities outstanding representing A and B together ($10+$20=$30). To buy Firm B, Firm A bids B up 20% to be worth $24 billion. It uses the $14 billion it borrowed and issues another $10 billion of its own newly created shares to total the $24 billion it needs. At the end of the deal, there are $20 billion of equities—down from $30 billion before the deal. The supply of equity shrank by $10 billion— not by as much as if it had financed the whole thing with debt—but the equity supply shrank nonetheless. Almost always, a stock and cash deal reduces the supply of equity and should be accretive to earnings—just not as much as pure cash deals.

These aren't radically new ideas. Anyone who took accounting or perhaps Economics 101 in college (meaning lots of folks) should know the difference between accretive and dilutive. What's more, you can easily monitor which firms are doing takeovers and which ones are dilutive or accretive. In our über-regulated business world, we get plenty of notice when a company launches a merger, acquisition, IPO, new stock issue, a global plot to steal oil—you name it. We know when the mergers are taking place, for how much and in what form.

Merger manias financed by newly created shares increase the supply of equity and are, all else being equal, a bearish factor. Merger manias transacted for cash destroy stock supply—reduced supply is a bullish factor. But few people see the difference.

What Really Makes Stock Prices Move

Before tackling what you can know about the impact of cash mergers on the stock market, we must delve into what really drives stock prices. This combines Question One and Question Two. There are countless myths regarding what people think causes price movements you can debunk with Question One. But Question Two—What can you fathom about what causes stock prices to move that others cannot fathom?—is easy. Way too easy for humans to want to fathom.

There are just two factors in this whole, wide, wonderful and whacky world driving stock prices. Always and everywhere, stock prices are derived by shifts in supply and demand. I've said so throughout the book, but sometimes the easiest concepts are the toughest for human minds to accept. Supply and demand are commonly known concepts, but few investors make the cognitive leap to securities pricing. Most folks who took college economics forgot about supply and demand as fast as possible after finishing finals and never thought about securities prices in terms of supply and demand. Folks with PhDs in economics were trained, but usually not in securities prices and decades later don't think in terms of supply and demand for securities.

Myriad research reports, newsletters and media reporting tell you where the author(s) sees the market going but almost never based on analysis of supply and demand shifts. Your news anchor, poli-tic, stockbroker or tennis partner may tell you it's any number of economic or technical indicators, pop-culture concerns, political conspiracies or self-fulfilling prophecies driving stock prices. Go to your favorite finance website and you'll see:

Interest Rates Buoy Stocks
Jobless Report Drives Stocks Down
Oil Scares Spook Stocks

You never hear a talking head say, "Supply of stocks remained relatively stable today, but demand increased for reasons we can only guess about, causing stock prices to rise." It's boring! Supply and demand of stocks as a storyline doesn't sell advertising or influence you to a particular side in a political, social or economic feud. There is no reason media would be so understated.

These two dueling pressures set prices of all we buy. Seeming pressures, such as increased regulation or an alien space invasion, are just more forces on supply and demand—an alien invasion likely decreases demand for equities, and increased securities regulation likely decreases supply of equities. Myriad things can impact both supply and demand pressures—but, ultimately, it always comes back to supply and demand.

Supply and demand shifts explain why people eagerly pay extraordinary amounts for an original Beatles vinyl, an original Le Corbusier chair or a limited edition Star Wars poster—if those things float your boat. However, no one pays up for plain old paper clips. First, there are billions of paper clips floating neglected in office desk trays everywhere. Second, if you run short and don't feel like running to your local Office Depot, you can use a binder clip or even a rubber band. That's called *substitution*. Things with easy substitutes never command premium pricing like those that can't be replaced. Third, paper clips are easy to make. Unless Andy Warhol bent a particular paper clip into a reasonable rendering of Marilyn Monroe, a paper clip won't fetch a premium.

In college economics, you probably learned supply and demand are both about eagerness. Eagerness is emotional. Demand describes how emotionally eager consumers are to buy something at varying prices. Typically, but not always, at higher prices, consumers want less of something than at lower prices. Makes sense! Alternatively, supply is a concept depicting how eager suppliers are to generate output of some good or service at varying prices. Generally, but not always, suppliers want to produce more of something at higher prices than at lower prices. If the price is low enough, they won't want to produce at all.

It starts getting interesting when either producers or consumers become more eager to supply or consume at the same prices. If producers become more eager to supply—meaning supply increases—but consumers aren't any more eager to consume, the market floods with supply and prices drop. You may say, "Why would suppliers ever do that?" Maybe new technology cuts their costs and prods their eagerness—sort of like Moore's Law pushed the semiconductor learning curve to lower prices for decades, making electronics firms ever more eager to make more at lower prices. On the flip side, if consumers become more eager—meaning demand rises—but producers don't step up supply to match increased demand, prices rise. Straightforward.

Eagerness to buy or eagerness to supply can shift for psychological reasons deriving from any number of factors. After all, eagerness is an emotion, and emotion is psychological. And markets are psychological. All this you would have heard in any economics class—nothing remotely controversial here.

But supply and demand are a little different when it comes to securities in several ways. Unless you did very unusual work in graduate school, you probably never saw any college study of supply and demand for equities. Demand for equities is about the eagerness to own or not own existing securities. Do we want to own GE stock more than we want to own a bond or an Andy Warhol Marilyn Monroe paper clip? Has that changed for some reason? How do we feel about owning GE stock versus Pfizer?

The aggregate emotion of demand for equities can shift within the bandwidth of our human emotion very quickly and freely, in just the same way tempers can flare or a movie can suddenly make you cry or laugh. Witness this by watching the volume of daily shares traded. In our super-connected world, people can become worked up and decide to buy or sell and, within moments, complete a transaction. If their eagerness waxes or wanes, they can nearly instantaneously act in massive volume. They can completely reverse course hours, days or months later if they are so emotionally inclined.

Demand can shift fast, but only as far as people can become emotionally eager or uneager. See it like this—you can only be as angry as you get or as happy as you get, and you can quickly swing from one extreme to the other in the right circumstances but, at the extreme, only as far as you go personally. Someone else might get a lot angrier than you do or a lot more giddy. Maybe you suffer depression. Some people do. Others don't—ever. Maybe you're very steady-rolling—maybe too much so, and your spouse complains about that. We vary a lot individually, but overall, as a group, we're average. For people as a whole, total demand shifts only within the average bandwidth of our aggregate emotion, although it can do that quickly—nearly instantaneously. Think how much emotion shifted in the hours after 9/11. Hence, demand has a tremendously powerful effect on pricing in the short term because it can shift so fast. It has less power in the long term because it can shift only within our overall average emotional bandwidth and not farther. It can only go so far.

Think of this differently. It's hard for you to keep your emotions at extreme levels for long. This is why most folks can't stay extremely angry or giddy very long. It's just like that super party when you were 23 on a warm summer night with the right friends—it was just perfect—and you felt perfect. But the next day you felt tired. Things scar some of us sometimes, and as individuals, we never get over them. As we live life, those things change us. But newly changed—for good or bad—we only get so high or low. Altogether, when we get very angry or very ecstatic, we tend not to stay that way too long because there is too much energy exerted in staying away from our emotional norm.

So shifts in demand tend to be forceful, fast, not too far and then revert to the mean with time. This is part of why demand shifts impact short-term pricing so much more than long-term pricing.

Shifts in supply are different. In the short run, the actual supply of securities is almost completely fixed as it takes time and effort and a cooperative multiplicity of players to create new shares or destroy existing ones. Think about how long it takes for IPOs or mergers—or even just a debt offering—to evolve and the amount of advance notice the companies are legally required to give the public. An increase in supply technically means increased eagerness to supply equities. But initial eagerness is dampened early on because no one is actually sure if the deal can be pulled off. There is no assurance all the necessary pieces will come together for that offering—a process that will take many months if it happens at all. You can't be overly eager about something you know may not happen. Eagerness on a deal grows over the time period in which the deal is successfully pursued.

Take a new stock or debt offering. When a company decides to issue stock or debt, it first must find an investment banker to manage the process. That alone takes time, particularly if it creates a competition among several investment banking firms, which is common. At this point, the potential issuer doesn't know what the deal might look like, if it will go through with it, if it *can* go through with it or even when it can happen should it be willing and able to do it. The investment banker will require freshly audited financials from a major auditing firm—typically, one of the "Big Four"—also taking time. Then, in an equally uncertain process in a debt offering, the investment banker works with the issuer to secure an adequate rating from the three main rating agencies: Moody's, Standard & Poor's and Fitch. Also in parallel, it starts the filing process with regulators who must approve the offering—from the Securities and Exchange Commission (SEC) federally down to the state regulators in every state where the issue is to be sold (or the appropriate regulator overseas, such as the Financial Services Authority [FSA] in Britain). Then it markets the deal, which takes another few months. It's only toward the end of that process the issuer has any real sense of how eager it can be to offer the securities or not.

Maybe by the time all this is done, the market has faded. Maybe it's fading throughout the marketing process. Maybe a similar competitor got to market two months ahead of you, beating you to the punch and sapping demand in your category of offering. Plenty of deals get pulled at the last minute. Think how depressing that can be.

Under the best of circumstances, when the stars align, offerings are never a speedy, painless process—allowing you to assume supply is pretty well fixed in the short term. Conversely, no matter what anyone would have you believe, no one has any way to predict supply in the far-distant future. (Read more on this in Chapter 6 of my 2011 book, *Markets Never Forget*.) This is among the reasons why long-term mechanical forecasting notions are usually way, way wide of the mark. No one knows what whacky things may happen to the creation or destruction of equity supply 5 to 20 years from now. If you hear someone forecasting stocks to be a good or bad investment over the next 10 or 20 years, you're dealing with someone who is telling you more about what they don't know about how capital markets work than what they do know.

Stock prices 10 years out will be determined more by what happens to supply seven, eight and nine years from now than anything else. As I write, no one has any capital markets technology or know-how allowing them to predict such a thing. In general, stocks are more positive than negative. Beyond that generality, no one should make a forecast for more than 12 to 24 months ahead. Said alternatively, shifts in demand are often more powerful in the short term, and shifts in supply are regularly more powerful in the long term. Sometimes you can foresee shifts in demand others don't see— justifying a 12- to 24-month forecast. But longer than that, you're just peering into fog. In the very long term, demand will bounce from very low to very high many times, but supply, subject to fundamental forces, can be almost infinitely bullish or bearish if the right conditions exist to increase new supply or destroy it.

The Three Drivers of Stock Demand

Because supply of securities is relatively fixed over the short term, your focus in most times should be measuring demand. Figure out the direction of demand, and you've figured out how to make a short-term forecast. (Usually— sometimes you must account for supply; we get to that later.) That's something your fellow investors probably aren't seeing clearly and something you can know they typically don't. And they won't just because I wrote this book. Set aside everything else—what you hear in the media, what you hear from friends, what so-called experts tell you about technical or fundamental investing—and focus on what impacts demand. For this, the Three Questions are handy. There are three broad forces at play impacting investor demand— economic, political and sentiment.

Economic Drivers

Phenomena like GDP growth, corporate earnings, technological innovations, budget deficits, monetary conditions and the like are economic drivers. For example, if GDP is growing at a fast clip and corporate earnings are beating expectations, people usually feel more positive about the economic future and more inclined to take on equity risk (unless they think everything is too good, so it must get worse—which happens sometimes). If the economy is in recession and CEOs are being perp-walked to the curb, investors will likely be overall less keen on the stock market.

Investors get in trouble here because either they or their information source misinterprets economic news. What's more, investors focus on known information. If a surprisingly good GDP report comes out, it's too late for you to act on it. The market moves ahead of or simultaneously to news—good and bad—but not after it's widely disseminated. What economic releases can do is help you paint a more accurate picture of current (or just past) economic conditions. From there, you must make your own forward-looking estimate about how these drivers may shift and how that is likely to impact demand, for better or worse.

Political Drivers

Elections, shifts in political control implying new future legislation impacting the tax code and the like are examples of political drivers. Recall from Chapter 2, the threat of material new legislation, particularly any threatening property rights, may cause loss aversion and fear of political muggings. Politics have more impact on market risk aversion than even their narcissistic little brains can fathom.

Generally, capital markets fear change, which is why the presidential-term-cycle capital markets technology works. The market is never sure if a poli-tic is a zealot, a phony, a genuine phony or just a moron. Usually the best thing, politically, is gridlock, as we saw in the mid- to late 1990s, because it implies little change. The markets doing so well from the November 1994 election into 2000 with perfect gridlock isn't coincidence. The market wasn't worried about much legislation getting passed by a Republican Congress with a tiny majority and a Democratic president embroiled in multiple scandals and obsessed by polling numbers.

A Question One political myth you already know you can make a market bet on is the belief (by many) tax cuts lead to budget deficits, which are bad for the economy. The op-ed pages and media commentaries are full of otherwise rational people advancing their political agenda by making you believe tax cut-based deficits rob the government of desperately needed capital to run the government correctly, which leads to recession, bear markets, high unemployment and dashed hopes. Nonsense. Those folks don't understand what we covered in Chapter 6—deficits have generally and measurably resulted in zippier GDP growth and strong stock market returns. Most important, the government doesn't run anything very correctly—regardless of whether you have a Democratic or Republican Congress or administration. Or as President Ford once said, "If the government made beer, it would be 50 bucks a six-pack and taste bad."

Investor Sentiment

The third driver, investor sentiment, is pure emotion. Sentiment is constantly moving—weekly, daily, even second to second. It's everything else that impacts investors' feelings. In many ways, it isn't any more complicated than that party we mentioned earlier. It got you feeling great. The next morning you didn't feel great. The day after that you'll likely feel better. It is partly that we can't sustain our emotions at extremes for long, as mentioned earlier. But we can artificially push them there temporarily.

That Wall of Worry

When headlines are most dour and your friends and colleagues are bemoaning how terrible things are, you can be confident they will feel better later and sentiment will improve at some point. Those who were most worried and sold their stocks low with hindsight bias gradually regain confidence and begin buying again. An initial reaction to higher prices is glee. You get pulled back to the middle of your emotional bandwidth by fear of heights. New, higher prices scare people. Since they didn't expect stocks to rise as much as they did, they now fear they may fall. Since investors fear losses more than they enjoy prospects of gains, this creates rising anxiety. This is the proverbial "wall of worry" bull markets climb. The higher it goes, the more angst those who didn't predict it feel. Since they didn't see why it should go up, they can't see why it shouldn't go down. Since they hate losses much more than they like gains, the fear of downside dominates.

A good illustration of this is the first-year returns following a bear market. When people assume they face the most market risk, they miss out on a

Table 7.1   Stock Market Returns Following Bear Markets

Bear Market Bottom	S&P 500 12-Month Returns from Bottom
06/01/1932	120.9%
04/28/1942	53.7%
06/13/1949	42.0%
10/22/1957	31.0%
06/26/1962	32.7%
10/7/1966	32.9%
05/26/1970	43.7%
10/03/1974	38.0%
08/12/1982	58.3%
12/04/1987	21.4%
10/11/1990	29.1%
10/09/2002	33.7%
03/09/2009	68.6%
Average	46.6%

Source: Global Financial Data, Inc., S&P 500 price returns.

remarkably low-risk period. First-year returns following true bear markets are super above average, as shown in Table 7.1

The reason the bell curves in Chapter 4 worked for equities is they were a good measure of sentiment. The bell curves showed where sentiment was at a point in time, not where it was going. If you know and accept that, you can game the future direction. For example, in the late 1990s, the forecasting consensus wasn't bullish enough. Markets came in high because demand was too low and had to move higher. The bell curves were a good capital markets technology innovation for measuring investor sentiment.

Supply: How It Works

Supply is like an unending accordion that can be expanded or contracted continuously. Other than what the market can bear, there is no limit to how many shares may be issued in IPOs or reissues or how much debt can be raised if underlying economics justify it. Or how many shares can be bought back and destroyed through stock buy-backs or cash-based takeovers.

When there is sufficient incentive to flood the market with new supply, prices will eventually drop, overpowering any demand. This is how it works. Take a hot sector, like Tech in the late 1990s. As prices appreciate rapidly, everyone wants in on the action. Suppose Firm A makes a novel product and has a total private market value of $1 billion. It floats a hot offering at a high price, raising lots of money while giving up very little control of the company—it raises $250 million but gives up only 20% of the company. The prior existing 80% of shares remain privately held. Effectively, that values Firm A before the money at $1 billion. With the money, the deal is completed at $1.25 billion. The founders and other shareholders who initially had private stock of questionable liquidity now have a public security with a daily price making them multimillionaires. They're happy. The investment bankers are thrilled with their 7% of the $250 million—$17.5 million in fees!

Eager observers watch the post-offering price rise and hope the market can handle an offering from another similar outfit. So they find an entrepreneur and venture capital and create privately held Firm B, which is a Firm A look-alike. They get their investment banker to take Firm B public to get in on the cheap money. Maybe they have just a plan and no revenue, like many of the 1990s dot-coms. If B's offering goes well, someone else will attempt it with Firms C, D, E, F and so on.

Firm A now realizes, as the high-quality, granddaddy of this product line, it can raise more capital with more newly created shares. It senses it can garner premium valuations over the group of inexperienced newbies. This time, it raises another $350 million but gives up only 17.5% of Firm A in newly created shares. Now Firm A is valued at $2 billion.

Now Company X, a mature, boring firm worth $100 billion, decides it can't take the risk of not being in on the hot new product category. It initiates a hostile takeover bid to acquire Company A for $3 billion, paid for with new Company X stock. Company A shares disappear and are replaced with new Company X shares worth $1 billion more than the $2 billion Company A previously had been selling for. Again, Company A shareholders get rewarded, but, suddenly, there are a lot more newly created shares. Earnings are the same as before. This, like most stock mergers, was dilutive to earnings. It's the same amount of earnings but many more shares. All the IPOs and new issues start flooding the market with shares in the hot category. Eventually, supply drowns demand and prices roll over. If demand drops, prices implode.

Just as they did when the Tech market crashed close on the heels of the Tech-IPO craze in March 2000.[1] Demand fell all the way to the market's ultimate global double bottom in 2002 and 2003.[2] The scapegoats were many for the Tech bubble. People blamed Tech companies for being overvalued. (A term that is often over-abused—companies are worth what people pay for them at a point in time.) Greedy CEOs got their share of blame, too. Corporate accounting rules were deemed too lax or not expansive enough.

The reality was the Tech bubble burst because the market was inundated with supply, and demand couldn't keep pace and then fell. That is the most apt explanation. Some would blame investment bankers, but that isn't fair or appropriate—no matter how you feel about them. Investment bankers simply respond to investor eagerness for more supply (demand). The real culprits were investors' overconfident brains, letting them run rampant and over-allocate to a sector. Investors were too eager—demand was too high. Absent their demand, investment bankers and issuers can't flood the market with supply.

You should pretty much always be wary about excessive euphoria regarding IPOs in the latest "hot sector." Every time we see a hot sector—throughout the entire history of investing—investors claim, "It's different this time." It's never really different this time—just the niggly details. There is never anything different about an inundation of supply surpassing demand and causing prices to drop. (For more evidence of how it's never different this time, see the reprint in Appendix G of my March 6, 2000, *Forbes* column, "1980 Revisited," calling the top of the Tech bubble because of parallels to the 1980 Energy bubble.)

Merger Mania

Supply of stock can increase infinitely (which wouldn't be so good for stock prices in the long term) but may also be reduced when a company, thinking its stock is too cheap, uses cash to repurchase its own shares. Through stock buybacks, as discussed in Chapter 6, and cash-based takeovers, as discussed earlier, supply can be destroyed nearly infinitely. Using Question Two, we know cash-based merger manias can be followed by good stock market returns. If demand remains the same (or even greater) but supply is reduced, prices should rise, all else being equal.

How does knowing this Question Two truth help you? Simply keep in mind the difference between equity-based (dilutive) and cash (accretive) mergers. Are there a lot of IPOs hitting the market and on average more equity-based mergers taking place? That's a potentially bearish concern. Not the only factor to consider—but one among others that should shape your forward-looking assessment. Conversely, lots of cash mergers probably present a little-noticed bullish surprise—news most investors don't process correctly because they don't know how.

Knowing increased cash-takeover activity is a positive factor can help you shape better forward-looking expectations. But does that provide additional insight into which sectors you should overweight and which individual stocks you may want to buy? Absolutely! Look at the sectors where the mergers are occurring and work your way, top down, to a good buy-out target. If you're right on a few of your buy-out targets, you get a nice price bump if (and when) the merger is announced. It's easy, free money.

Riding the M&A Wave

You can ride the M&A wave by finding stocks ripe to be taken over. Acquisition premiums paid to shareholders of buy-outs often yield large increases in share prices. Good buy-out targets are likely to have some or all of the following characteristics:

- Low valuations
- High free cash flow
- Strong balance sheets
- Quality brand names
- Regional strength
- High relative market share
- Smaller in size
- Strong distribution networks
- No concentrated controlling shareholders

The good news is you can check for those attributes by reading share-holder reports—available for free on corporate websites. Here are just two examples (stocks I identified as buy-out targets in *Forbes*) showing how to look for and apply these attributes.

I wrote about MBNA in my May 9, 2005, *Forbes* column.[3] MBNA was the world's largest credit card company, issuing familiar cards like Visa, MasterCard and American Express, with a successful strategy of focusing on affinity groups like associations and financial institutions. If you had one of those cards, it was probably issued by MBNA, whether you knew it or not. Besides credit cards, it had strong business in consumer and home equity loans. It had all the qualities of a perfect takeover target—strong brand name, healthy balance sheets—plus, valued at 12 times trailing earnings, it looked darned cheap. Bank of

America thought so, too. It announced its intention to buy MBNA on June 30, 2005, and MBNA ended the day up 24%.[4] Had you bought on the day I recommended it, you would have been up a very nice 30%.[5]

CP Ships was a great takeover candidate I wrote about in my April 18, 2005, *Forbes* column.[6] Though this container shipper was domiciled in Britain, 80% of its business activity focused on North America. With a fleet of 80 ships, it was the leader in most of its routes. In 2005, this little British stock was overlooked because shipping is a cyclical business. But it's also a growth business, and this stock looked cheap at 13 times 2005 earnings and $3.7 billion in very real revenue. The Germans at TUI AG—a massive, well-diversified tourism and shipping company—expanded their shipping business quickly and cheaply by announcing a merger with CP Ships on August 22, 2005. CP Ships shareholders got a nice 8%[7] boost that day. However, had you bought when I recommended it, you would have been up 56%.[8]

Categorically, you know the bulk of cash-based deals will occur with stocks that are cheap in terms of having a high earnings yield compared to the acquirer's pretax cost of long-term borrowing. Suppose the average company borrowing rate (the BBB 10-year bond rate) is 6% and the average corporate tax rate is 33%. The after-tax average cost of borrowing is therefore 4%. Takeover targets will tend to have earnings yields greater than 4% after they've been marked up with a maybe 25% pricing premium. Hence, most takeover targets will have an earnings yield above 5% before the deal is announced, translating to a P/E below 20. To get the acquirer's earnings per share to rise the most from the deal, the higher the earnings yield, the better. Most cash-based takeovers will tend to be value stocks with lower P/Es (high earnings yields). Seek those kinds of stocks to capitalize on cash-merger mania.

No One Stock Style Is Always Better—Period!

Supply and demand being the only determinants of stock pricing—and the potential to create or destroy new shares being nearly infinite—is why no correctly calculated index, size, style, country or category is better for all time. (Remember our graphs in Chapter 4?) While collectors of a particular category type (small-cap value, large-cap growth, Japan, biotech) believe the category they like is permanently better, it isn't and can't be.

But when an equity category collector tells you his or her category is permanently better—and many believe this—you're being told what the teller doesn't understand about markets. Supply creation is infinitely elastic if given enough time in the right circumstances. And demand bounces constantly in the short to intermediate term. There is no evidence supply of any equity category is capped, can't be bought back and destroyed or is in anyway predictable in the long term. Consider this: If there is demand for a category, the investment bankers will meet it—they don't care about investor perception about a particular category needing to be superior over time.

For example, plenty of folks are diehard adherents to small-cap value. I'll give you a simple tip. Whenever big-cap growth does lousy, small-cap value does well—they are polar style opposites. Saying one does well is the same as saying the other does badly. You can always find investors firmly convinced small-cap value is permanently better.

I started doing small-cap value stocks three decades ago, long before the word small-cap value existed. My first book, *Super Stocks* (published in 1984), was about price-to-sales ratios—specifically how to use PSRs to find small-cap value stocks others couldn't find. Even then the term *small-cap value* didn't exist. The term evolved in the mid-1980s on the heels of that earlier period as small-cap value stocks did well. A period much like the past six years.

In 1989, when Callan Associates, a major consulting firm to institutions (primarily defined benefit pension plans), introduced the very first small-cap value peer group for institutional investors to use in calibrating how well or badly a given manager did, only 12 of us were included in that initial group. They couldn't find any other pure-play small-cap value managers. That was how primitive this category was not quite 20 years ago.

Today, my firm still manages money in the category for large defined benefit pension plans, endowments and foundations. It's a perfectly valid part of the market to include in a much broader portfolio (which all these institutional investors have). But the category has times when it shines and times it doesn't. Folks forget that—including many who should know better.

I'm not arguing against owning small-cap value or for owning big-cap or the market as a whole. I'm saying there are painfully long stretches when things seeming to work in the very long term don't actually work. And these times are too long to not drive everyone, including you, nuts. For periods of 5, 10 or 20 years, it will be shifts in supply determining most of the return of the market and of the market's subsets. In the very long term (and lots of subsets thereof), all major categories, correctly calculated, should have very similar returns. Falling in perpetual perma-love with some category won't guarantee you perma-superior future return.

Weak Dollar, Strong Dollar—What Does It Matter?

Can what you know about supply and demand be applied largely to any freely traded security category? Sure. We can apply it to the dollar and

discover still more unnoticed Question Two investing truths (while dispel-
ling more myths).

The poor US dollar can never catch a break. When it's weak, folks uniformly believe it will lead to our economic undoing. Views down this line are
near religious in their conviction. In 2010, there was nonstop talk about the
dollar being replaced as the world's go-to reserve currency. (Folks who say this
almost never have a workable solution for what should replace it.)

Investors forget: In the late 1990s, we were all concerned a too-strong
dollar would keep foreigners from wanting to trade with us, leading to our
economic undoing. Following that logic, what doesn't lead to our economic
undoing? Maybe there is an optimal exchange rate with every other world currency we should aspire to achieve. I don't know what that exchange rate would
be or how we'd endeavor to maintain it in a free market. And I'll take a free
market over a government jigger any day of the week or year of my life.
But investors must think such a state of jiggering perfection exists because
they love to complain about the dollar and its direction leading us to hell.

Here's a Question Two: Does a weak or strong dollar even matter? But
first we have to hit Question One: What do you believe about what causes currency prices to move that's wrong? Let's hit on some popular myths.

Myth Number One: The Budget Deficit Will
Cause the US Dollar to Fall

Budget deficits are periodically a favorite patsy for a weak dollar. (Again—the
assumption is a weak dollar is bad and a strong dollar is good.) This belief
runs something like this—foreigners fear our inability to put our fiscal house
in order, thus creating less dollar demand.

First, as covered in Chapter 6, a federal budget deficit in the US isn't automatically bad for the economy or the stock market. Rather, historically, there's
no evidence a big budget deficit has led to bad times, and in fact, the reverse
seems true. As showed in Chapter 1, periods following peaks in the federal
budget deficit were followed by positive stock markets, whereas budget surpluses were followed by less rosy conditions.

Second, exchange rates are monetary phenomena while budget deficits
are fiscal—wholly unrelated. One doesn't beget the other. There's no connective
mechanism. Yes, if the central bank monetized the debt created by the deficit
(as it arguably did with two rounds of quantitative easing following the 2008
credit crisis), it would create new money that might weaken the dollar down
the road. But why not just focus directly on the money creation because it's the
money creation that does the do? Money creation can weaken the dollar
whether there's a deficit or not.

Third, the US ran big budget deficits throughout the 1980s and early 1990s. During many of these periods, like 1992 through 1993, the dollar soared. Today, the British are running a budget deficit. If a budget deficit is bad for the US dollar, why isn't it bad for the sterling? The truth is, no major Western country's budget deficit or surplus has any relationship to the relative strength of its currency.

Myth Number Two: Currencies Are Determined by Trade Balances, Foreign Policy, International Popularity, Etc.

As covered in Chapter 6, you can't argue our trade deficit is bad for the dollar but Britain's (or anyone else's) is good for its strong currency. Trade deficits are never "paid back." Per Chapter 6, this is a mercantilist view and about 250 years behind the times. We live in a world where Apple imports memory chips and other components manufactured dirt cheap overseas, creating a trade deficit. But Apple turns around and sells the latest iPod creation (to heroin addicts and normal people) at a hefty profit margin, increasing its earnings per share, which in turn increases shareholder value. The mercantilists' heads would explode if they tried to contemplate a world where trade deficits coexist with increased wealth for everyone. But that is our world, and it's beautiful.

Tied to this is the myth foreigners are "propping up" our dollar. This is often referred to as "being dependent on the kindness of foreigners." I simply have no evidence of foreigners behaving this way. Why would a foreigner act any differently than you? When you're investing, do you place your money where you think it's likeliest to make money, or do you invest where you think it will do the most good for the world? Where the world needs the most propping?

Foreigners aren't propping up anything in America. Mercantilists think foreigners "prop till they drop." Those who think correctly know they "invest where they think best." They invest here because they think they will get a better return for their money than other alternatives. If they didn't think this was the case, they would invest elsewhere. No other rational explanation.

Finally, Myth Number Three: A Weak Dollar Is Bad for Stocks

If you're holding foreign securities during a time when the dollar falls, your foreign securities may seem to net a higher return. The reverse is true as well—stocks domiciled in a country with a relatively weaker currency may seem to perform not as well at exchange time. Don't forget, to invest globally, you needn't trade your dollars for euros, yen or ringgit. Buying foreign

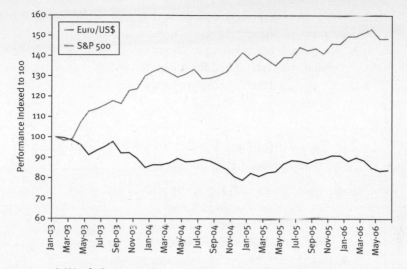

Figure 7.1   A Weak Currency Doesn't Mean a Weak Stock Market Return: US
Source: Thomson Reuters.

ordinaries (stocks in foreign countries in the local currency) can be an ordeal for individual investors—you may have to establish a custodian account in that country. Skip the hassle. If you're an American, trade in American depositary receipts (ADRs)—foreign stocks traded in gringo dollars. Plus, over the long run, because currencies are so cyclical, the currency effect nets out to be close to zero anyway.

But what can the dollar tell us about where the stock market is going? It can make some sense that a strong US dollar might help US stocks—and vice versa. We can check to see if the facts support this theory. If the dollar is weak, then stock returns would similarly be weak. But as we can see in Figure 7.1, stock returns can be strong—very strong—even as the dollar is weakening.

And that is something true in the US and around the globe. Currencies don't dictate the direction of the stock market, or vice versa (see Figure 7.2).

There is no basis for thinking a strong dollar leads to good stock returns or vice versa. The dollar isn't predictive of US stock performance, global stock performance, Polish stock performance—none of them. Weak or strong, by itself, you shouldn't fret currencies.

Let's bring in Question Three and think about the dollar the way we thought about the US trade deficit and our stock market versus the rest of the world. When the global stock market explodes upward, you know the US market probably will too, right? They're positively correlated. If the global stock market implodes, you know the US probably will be down, too.

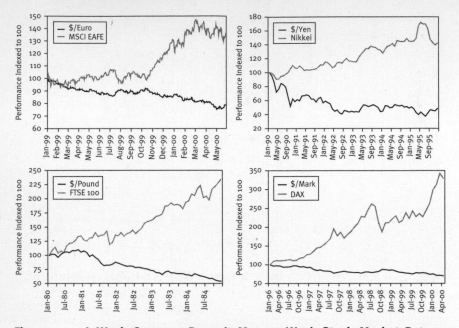

Figure 7.2   A Weak Currency Doesn't Mean a Weak Stock Market Return: Global
Source: Thomson Reuters.

Sometimes America goes up more than the world, and other times it falls more. But they tend to go the same direction when there is any material direction. And the US is about half the world stock market, give or take, depending on when you measure. So, if the falling dollar is supposedly bad for US stocks, shouldn't the rising non-dollar currencies be good for non-US stocks? Yes! Because they are an equal offset.

But there can't be a global falling currency, only global inflation. Likewise, there can't be a global trade deficit, yet people act as if the negative is more powerful than the positive, though they never explicitly state this. Yuck! Mercantilists! (Although, despite their never saying this, there is some behavioralist basis for it—in the concept of myopic loss aversion.)

Said another way, the US (as I update in 2011) is about 23% of global GDP, making the rest of the world 77%. If a falling dollar is bad for the US economy, shouldn't a rising non-dollar be good for the other 77% and more than offset the deteriorating US economy with improvements to the non-US economy? Alas, no one thinks globally much, so they can't quite get themselves to see it this way. These mercantilists aren't stuck in the 1960s; they're stuck in the 1690s.

Yes, Supply and Demand Determine Currency Prices, Too

Different currencies are simply flavors of money identified by their issuers (central banks) and their banking systems. Because they're commodities traded on free and open markets, they derive their relative value in the same way as other assets—by supply and demand.

An exchange rate reflects the value of one currency quoted in another currency's terms. It's entirely relative and has no absolute meaning otherwise. Each particular exchange rate is driven by a complex combination of the supply and demand characteristics of each of the two currencies. Relative increases in demand or decreases in supply will drive one currency's exchange rate up versus another and vice versa.

Currency Supply

The base supply of a currency is determined solely by the issuing central bank, expedited by banks operating under it. It has a monopoly on the creation or destruction of its currency. Central banks desire relatively stable prices with moderate monetary growth, which in turn should yield relatively low inflation rates. If they act responsibly, major currencies should have fairly stable exchange rates in the long run—though volatility is normal over shorter periods.

However, an irresponsible central bank or a government taking control of its country's central bank can undermine its country's position as a major, developed country. Like in Germany's Weimar years. That was arguably a singular example in modern history as they completely wiped out the German currency in the early 1920s due to excessive money creation, leading to hyperinflation. Developing countries, like Brazil in the early 1990s, often don't have independent central banks and can experience much longer directional currency moves, almost always on the weakening side. But big countries have reasonably disciplined and independent central banks, like our Fed, and typically don't experience permanent, unidirectional currency moves.

Over the long run, just like with stocks, supply determines relative currency strength or weakness. When a central bank allows excessive money creation relative to real economic requirements, the excess supply depresses the currency price and boosts inflation. More money for the same amount of assets decreases the currency's store of value. The reverse is true if the central bank is too restrictive in creating money—but too strong a currency isn't a goal either. There's absolutely nothing investors can do about the monopolistic central banking system, besides hoping it won't make too many mistakes, nor is there any way to predict the long-term direction of supply.

Fortunately, our central bankers have gotten better in recent years. The Fed was an unmitigated disaster between 1929 and 1932 as it shrank the quantity of money by 30% at the worst possible time, making the Great Depression vastly worse than necessary and arguably causing it. That was its low point, to be sure. Since then, the Fed hasn't always been great, but, on average, it has been getting better.

Traditionally, former Fed chairmen were derided for their many mistakes at mismanaging the economy. William McChesney Martin, Jr., Arthur Burns, G. William Miller—they were all criticized widely and wildly after their time. Before he became chairman, Burns criticized Martin nearly endlessly. Martin ran the Fed from 1951 to 1970, giving Burns plenty of time to attack him. Burns claimed Martin knew better than to make the mistakes he did.

Martin later claimed when you became head of the Fed, you took a little pill making you forget everything you ever knew, and the effect lasted just as long as you were head of the Fed. After becoming head of the Fed and coming under attack himself, Burns claimed he took "Martin's little pill." (To people under 50, this was a play on a famous health aid called "Carter's Little Liver Pill"—which had nothing to do with being good for your liver—its name was changed to Carter's Little Pill and is, in fact, a laxative.)

They were all criticized. And rightly so as they all made many mistakes—but fewer as the decades went on and they learned from prior mistakes.

Paul Volcker was the first Fed head not roundly criticized later—although Volcker forced the 1980 and 1982 recessions in the name of breaking inflation's back. Some would say that was too heavy-handed, but overall, he did a better job than any prior Fed head. Greenspan was next and did better still because he was capable and could learn further and more. Their predecessors were assuredly not idiots (though Miller might have been politically, but he is another story altogether)—they were just doing the best they could, stabbing in the dark based on largely untested theory with, by today's standards, very primitive data-collection capabilities and vastly inferior electronic analytical capability. Only with the onset of improved technology and 24/7 instant information could Fed heads test theories and check for correlations (i.e., do Question Ones) before deploying policy to horrific results. And they could react faster and learn from prior mistakes. As a result, we've seen fewer egregious policy errors in recent decades.

Errors still happen—like when Greenspan created way too much money in 1999 in fear of potential Y2K problems, flaming the economy. Then he sucked it back out in 2000 after Y2K proved unproblematic—helping make the 1999 and 2000 boom-bust bigger than otherwise. But mistakes are made less routinely and massively than in the pre-Volcker era. Greenspan's worst mistakes were pretty good compared to the best of earlier decades.

The same has been going on overseas. My guess is, as central bankers benefit from future improved information flows and accumulated lessons of the past, on average, they keep making mistakes but the mistakes are fewer and not as bad. As major developed nations' central bankers tend to make fewer dumb errors, intermediate-term currency volatility may decline somewhat from historical levels.

Currency Demand

Demand for currency is determined by several factors. Principal among them is the amount of economic activity conducted in that currency (e.g., a grocery store in Dallas uses dollars, not yen). The more economic activity using a particular currency, the more demand for that currency. Another important money demand source is the "store of value." If investors believe assets denominated in a currency will hold or grow in value versus other assets in different currencies, demand for that currency grows.

Short-term (from minutes to months) factors impacting demand include when a senior government or central bank official *jawbones* (speaks favorably or unfavorably about a currency or interest rates), which can push short-term sentiment and shift demand—but usually only fleetingly—moving currency markets for a few minutes up to perhaps a month.

Also, discretionary central bank *open market operations*—when a central bank buys one currency in exchange for another—can have a short-term impact. But no one bank has a big enough balance sheet to overwhelm all the other factors impacting the currency market by simply exchanging currency.

Even frequently demonized "speculators" can have some small and fleeting impact on demand and the relative prices of currencies, but speculators have an even smaller impact than central banks because their balance sheets are so much smaller. Decades ago, George Soros did take down the Bank of England—down hard—but only because in that earlier era, it had put itself in a position to be taken down. And Soros is widely quoted as saying the same could never happen these days. Further dissipating the impact of speculators is the fact they generally don't act in any organized fashion. Speculators speculate on different currencies going in different directions, and, to some extent, they cancel each other's impact.

Like stock movements, currency movements are exceedingly fickle in the very short term. You shouldn't care much about what a currency does from day to day or even month to month anyway (unless you're betting on currencies—which has all the same qualities of betting on any other commodity).

What Really Drives Currency Demand

Time for another Question Two: What can you see driving currencies and demand for them others can't? There are a few obvious factors contributing to short-term shifts in supply and demand for currencies. First, nondiscretionary central bank operations. When a country pegs its currency to another currency (the Chinese yuan to the US dollar, for example), the pegging central bank must either buy or sell the other currency to maintain the relationship. Second, when one country's economy grows faster than another, the demand for its currency increases because more transactions take place in that currency. Both of these are easy to fathom—you don't need Question Two for them. But what else could drive currencies? What can you fathom?

Each and every day, speculators make bets on exchange rates through what is called a *carry trade*. A carry trade works thusly: You borrow short-term money in one currency, convert it to another currency and buy a short-term bond (though you might choose to make a longer-term bet with a longer-term bond) in the new currency. The idea is to borrow at a lower interest rate and buy a bond yielding a higher rate on the presumption the higher-yielding rate won't fall enough to reverse the interest rate spread during the period you hold the bond. Done right, the difference between the two rates is free money. (Everyone likes free money.)

The key is to borrow in a currency you think won't appreciate markedly against the higher interest rate currency where you will park the money—a great Question Two. Since you're selling the borrowed currency and buying the currency you lend into, if many people do this all at once, it tends to make the acquired currency appreciate. Then you get not only the interest rate spread but also the appreciation on the currency. Icing on the cake. Very attractive.

It would be completely irrational to borrow at a higher interest rate and buy a bond with a lower interest rate. That is the reverse of free money. So, if Country A's short-term rate is lower than Country B's, investors are more likely to borrow at Country A's lower rate and invest at Country B's higher rate, putting downward-selling pressure on A's currency and upward-buying

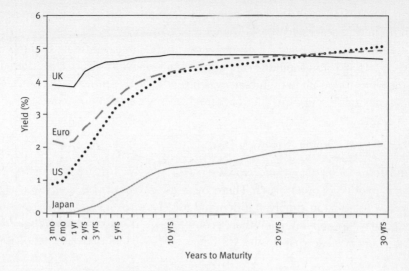

Figure 7.3   Global Yield Curves, January 1, 2004
Source: **Bloomberg Finance, L.P.**

pressure on B's currency. Currency prices then become a bit of a self-fulfilling prophesy, as carry trades take place in huge volumes daily.

In theory, it makes sense, but let's scope some actual scenarios to see if this is correct. Figure 7.3 shows the yield curves for the US, the UK, Japan and the eurozone at the beginning of 2004. At the short end of the curve, the US curve is well below the UK's and the eurozone's yet still above Japan's. It so happens the dollar was weak that entire year. Investors were borrowing in America and investing in short-term instruments abroad, contributing further to a weak relative dollar. If you borrowed in America at a 1% six-month rate and lent into euroland at above a 2% rate, you picked up the 1% spread as free and easy money as long as the euro didn't fall in value. Since lots of people did it all at once, they sold dollars and bought euros, pushing the dollar down and the euro up. The opportunity was even more extreme if you lent in Britain, which is the reason the pound sterling was so strong.

In 2005, after multiple fed fund rate raises, the short end of the US yield curve had risen above Germany's and Japan's and was closing a lot of the gap with the United Kingdom. The dollar strengthened considerably during 2005 against pretty much every major world currency, as the carry trades started going in the other direction. Effectively, as the Fed raised short rates, it choked off the carry trades that had been holding the dollar down (see Figure 7.4).

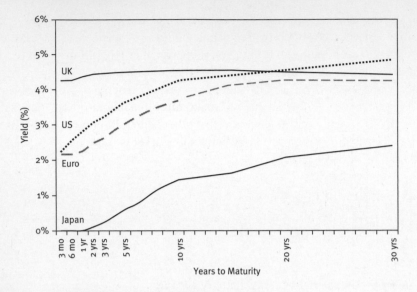

Figure 7.4   Global Yield Curves, January 1, 2005
Source: Bloomberg Finance, L.P.

With some exceptions within developed Western nations, countries with higher short-term interest rates that keep moving higher tend to have the stronger currencies. Countries with low short-term interest rates that remain unexpectedly low tend to have weaker currencies. This pattern is compelling and makes sound economic sense due to carry trade activity. Another way to say that is: Demand for a currency increases and the price with it when appropriately moving yield curve differentials between countries pay people to be more eager to own a given currency.

This is why the British pound sterling for a long time was so strong relative to the US dollar (and many other currencies)—Britain kept its interest rates higher than everyone else's. Pretty simple! As the Fed paid up in 2005, people stopped borrowing in US dollars, selling and investing overseas, and instead started doing the reverse—borrowing overseas and buying dollars—then the dollar strengthened. Demand for currency, more than not, increases when central banks pay people to demand more of their currency—which relates to them adjusting their supply. What I'm telling you isn't unknown, but few notice it, and fewer still believe it, which is why it will have legs for some years. You can use this information to discount strong currency sentiment based on myths we debunked earlier in this chapter. And you can use it for a rational basis for a market bet.

Investors talk about supply and demand and know intuitively supply and demand drive prices but just aren't applying these concepts to the securities, bonds and commodities they buy. And if they do, they typically aren't thinking about supply or demand correctly. Now that you know securities pricing is always and everywhere a result of supply and demand, you can focus your energy on what counts and start to make more reliable 12-month forecasts. And that is something you can know that others don't. But how can you make a forecast? And how can you know what the market is more likely to do? For that, we move to Chapter 8.

8

THE GREAT HUMILIATOR AND YOUR STONE AGE BRAIN

That Predictable Market

Presume at every turn, the market is actually out to get you. I'm not being paranoid—it's true. I don't call the market The Great Humiliator (TGH) for nothing. Think of it as a dangerous predatory, living, instinctual beast doing anything and everything to abjectly humiliate you out of every last penny possible. Just knowing and accepting that is the first step to getting the whip hand of TGH. Your goal is to engage TGH without ending up too humiliated. In the next chapter, we talk about how to create a strategy to increase the odds you reach your long-term goals, but first, let's talk about exactly how to use the Questions to see clearly how the market operates so you can cease being humiliated.

TGH headfakes you by moving in disorderly patterns. We know the market historically has averaged about 10% yearly over long time periods.[1] So is it reasonable to expect about 10% absolute returns each and every year? No way. Since 1926, there have been relatively few years the stock market has actually returned something close to the long-term average. Normal market years are anything but average. This is an easy Question One truth shown in Table 8.1.

Not only are returns wildly variable, but it's a global truth. Think globally and check elsewhere. In the UK, TGH goes by Ye Olde Humiliatour (YOH), as shown in Table 8.2. (In Germany, TGH is Der Grosse Demütiger.) Returns should continue to be wildly variable year to year.

Table 8.1 Average Returns Aren't Normal. Normal Returns Are Extreme—US

S&P 500 Annual Return Range			Occurrences Since 1926	Frequency	
>		40%	5	5.9%	Big Returns (37.6% of the time)
30%	to	40%	13	15.3%	
20%	to	30%	14	16.5%	
10%	to	20%	17	20.0%	Average Returns (34.1% of the time)
0%	to	10%	12	14.1%	
−10%	to	0%	12	14.1%	Negative Returns (28.2% of the time)
−20%	to	−10%	6	7.1%	
−30%	to	−20%	3	3.5%	
−40%	to	−30%	2	2.4%	
<		−40%	1	1.2%	
Total Occurrences			85		
Simple Average			11.8%		
Annualized Average			9.8%		

Source: Global Financial Data, Inc., S&P 500 total returns from 12/31/1925 to 12/31/2010.

From this disorder, your brain doesn't neatly notice the market doing one of only four things in any given year. Those four market scenarios are:

1. The market can be up a lot.
2. The market can be up a little.
3. The market can be down a little.
4. The market can be down a lot.

Markets can do myriad things in short spurts in a seemingly disordered way. But it really does just one of the four things in the course of the year.

These four conditions simply simplify possible outcomes and help you see more clearly and make more disciplined decisions. They also provide a way for you to assert self-control over your behavior—note, I said behavior, not skill—and are the essence of asking yourself Question Three.

Your brain, working with TGH, tries to persuade you the market will do any number of things. But all you must focus on is whether you think it likeliest the

Table 8.2   Average Returns Aren't Normal. Normal Returns Are Extreme—UK

UK FTSE Annual Return Range			Occurrences Since 1926	Frequency	
	›	40%	7	8.2%	Big Returns (34.1% of the time)
30%	to	40%	7	8.2%	
20%	to	30%	15	17.6%	
10%	to	20%	19	22.4%	Average Returns (41.2% of the time)
0%	to	10%	16	18.8%	
−10%	to	0%	12	14.1%	Negative Returns (24.7% of the time)
−20%	to	−10%	5	5.9%	
−30%	to	−20%	3	3.5%	
−40%	to	−30%	0	0.0%	
	‹	−40%	1	1.2%	
Total Occurrences			85		
Simple Average			12.9%		
Annualized Average			10.5%		

Source: Global Financial Data, UK FTSE total returns from 12/31/1925 to 12/31/2010.

market will end up a lot, up a little, down a little or down a lot—looking out about a year. Everything in between is TGH distracting you. Four things! Is it nudging up or down a little, or is it a meltdown or melt-up? (Investors almost never think about a melt-up, but it's as important as a meltdown.)

Direction, Not Magnitude

Focusing on these four market conditions helps you make the key decisions having the most impact on your portfolio—the asset allocation decisions. The four conditions are a framework for guiding your *behavior* and keeping your brain from leading you astray.

Also, what's most important about your forecast is getting market direction right, not magnitude. Why? Because getting the market direction right keeps you on the right side of the market more often than not.

Also, if you expect up a lot, up a little, or yes, even down a little, you want to be maximally exposed to equities (as dictated by your benchmark). It doesn't matter if you think the market will return 8% or 88%. Either way, if your goal is longer-term growth, your major asset allocation decision should be maximal equities. Your sector weights might be impacted by an up-a-lot versus an up-a-little forecast, but even if you get all of that wrong and still make the decision to stay fully invested in equities and are right, you should enjoy the return you get from getting the asset allocation right. This is all about getting the horse before the cart and not vice versa.

You may rebel at remaining maximally exposed to stocks in expectation of a down-a-little year. Should you try to avoid down-a-little downside by shifting to cash? In my view, only if you're supremely confident (and not overconfident) you know things others don't. Otherwise, you're too likely wrong for what is only a little benefit. Trying to avoid a down-a-little year is the perfect example of a brain overcome by overconfidence. Even if you expect down a little, my view is you should focus on relative return. Beating the market is beating the market, even if your absolute return is negative.

If you think the market will be down a little and want to move heavily away from stocks, ask Question Three. First, you may be suffering from myopic loss aversion, and you should try accumulating some regret. Second, recall you may be wrong and the market might be up a little or a lot instead. The difference between up 5% and down 5% in a year can be just a psychological wiggle toward year-end based on serendipity. But even if you're right and the market is down a little, the transaction fees you incur selling your stocks or funds, ensuing tax bills on your gains and inherent timing errors outing and inning can seriously reduce any benefit you might gain by skipping a down-a-little move.

Then ask, if you get out, will you know when to get back in? Will you time it right? Probably not and certainly not perfectly! If you're really looking for market-like returns (and if you're reading this book, my guess is you are), remember the long-term market average includes negative years. In the course of your long investing time horizon, you will experience periodic downside. You should expect it. Downside is intensely painful to live through but is part of the reality of the long slog that is investing in equities with an aim of getting market-like returns. Renew your faith in capitalism. Grit your teeth and know better times are ahead.

Also, many presume they'd prefer a portfolio that's up when the market is down, but a portfolio like that likely lags when the market is up. If the market is positive more often than negative (which it is), and you have a portfolio running counter to the market or cutting off the downside at the expense of upside, you won't average out to be happy.

Recall always: When you go to cash, you adopt massive benchmark risk. You become completely unlike your benchmark. And just think what happens if you're really, really wrong and there is a melt-up. You incurred transaction costs, paid taxes and lost maybe 25% relatively or more, which comes to about 1% a year over the next 25 years—very hard to make up. This is exactly what people do at the bottom of major bear markets when they choose to remain out so they can wait "for things to become clearer." In exchange for avoiding a down-a-little possibility, they forsake an up-a-lot market. In my mind, for long-term investors wanting market-like return, there's no error more damaging.

Look Out Below!

As for the fourth scenario, the down-a-lot scenario, it's the only time, in my view, it's appropriate to take on massive benchmark risk by moving heavily away from equities—going to cash or another defensive posture. Then, and only then, should you focus more on absolute return instead of relative return and try to beat the market by a lot. But if you're right, you get relative return, too. If you are very confident the likeliest outcome is the market being down huge 20% or more—maybe 35%, 40% or even 50%—then it can make sense to try for cash or bond-like returns. Getting a cash-like return doesn't sound like much, but if you are correct and the market is down a lot, you have blown the market away on a relative basis.

This should be rare and prompted only by something you are supremely confident you know that most others don't. It shouldn't be done by gut feel, by fear or by your neighbor's opinion. The Three Questions should figure in largely here. And the benefits can be huge. If for 30 years, you simply invested in a passive index fund, but just once in those years you sidestepped a 25% drop while getting a 5% cash-and-bond return—over the 30 years, you would do 1% per year better than the market. In the process, you would have beaten more than 90% of all professional investors based on only one correct bet. Getting defensive successfully even just once or a couple of times, even if you don't do it perfectly, can provide you with a major and lasting performance boost.

At a bull market peak, there is endless advice saying you should never turn bearish and you should never "time the market," and that people who do are destined to miss the big returns of bull markets. In 2000, this advice was rampant. That is simply TGH sucking you into the bear market as it moves disorderly down a path few will fathom. Make no mistake; the rewards from occasionally seeing a bear market correctly are big enough to justify building your bear market muscle—knowing you use it exceptionally rarely.

After bear markets, the heroes are those who did "time the market" and turn bearish. Many of them will have been bearish way too early—often for years before the bull market peak—having been a "perma bear" (stopped clocks who often have miserable long-term relative returns but are short-term media heroes nonetheless). Alternately villainizing then making heroes of those who went defensive is TGH at its finest as it teases investors' brains to keep looking backward instead of forward. The key is to keep the bear market timing skill for long periods of time when it's never used—dry powder for the rare day you need it.

I've turned defensive only three times—mid-1987, mid-1990 and late 2000. I was very lucky each time. The next time, I'll probably screw it up. (Reminding myself of that is one way of reducing overconfidence.) Avoiding a big slice of those bear markets is a huge piece of what built my career. When you avoid a slice of a full-fledged bear market, you simply buy years of excess return. If you went into the bull market peak slightly lagging the market, one successful bypass of a chunk of a bear market catches you up and moves you ahead. It's hard keeping a skill set you use only a few times in your investing life honed and available. Most folks won't, which is why you should. They want to hone the skills they use daily, not once a decade.

GETTING IT WRONG

I wrote "the next time I'll probably screw it up" late in 2006 (this book was originally published in 2007), and as it turned out, I did not correctly foresee the 2008 bear market. Am I disappointed? Yes. Am I surprised? No. As I wrote here, seeing bear markets correctly is very tough. Making the decision to get defensive and move heavily away from equities is also tough—the toughest and possibly riskiest move a money manager can make from a relative return standpoint.

In my 2010 book, *Debunkery,* I write more on why, for long-term growth-oriented investors, being fully exposed to a bear market feels bad but shouldn't derail you from achieving long-term objectives. This is hard for most investors to get—but if you want long-term growth, that is just going to come with market-like volatility and periods of being down. Even down huge. Knowing that can help you avoid making knee-jerk decisions in response to downside volatility that can have much longer-term repercussions.

Building a Defensive Portolio

Suppose you use your Three Questions and are confident the most likely market scenario over the next year (or so) is down a lot—a true bear market. What do you do? What should a defensive portfolio look like? It depends.

You may hate hearing that, I know, but it's true. Different bear markets are different. In some bear markets, some sectors survive swimmingly, but you won't know which until it is on you—and maybe not even then.

In sustained bear markets, if you forecast them well, a mostly cash portfolio can make the most sense. Liquidity is key—markets move fast as bull markets begin, so you need to be prepared to get back in. If you're illiquid or you ease your way back into the market, you're likely to miss the big bang off the bottom. You can use money markets and short-term government bills. You probably don't want to buy anything with a long maturity unless it can be sold instantly. Be defensive but liquid.

Market Neutral

As an example, during the 2000 to 2002 bear market, I wanted a portfolio that acted cash-like but with better-than-cash returns. I wanted to be immunized against downside volatility and to be very liquid so I could quickly get back into the market. I wanted tax efficiency. And I wanted to take advantage of knowing something others didn't by overweighting certain sectors and underweighting others. Since I expected Tech to be weak and had dedicated significant resources to that call, I wanted to get some juice from it. To do that, I had to be market neutral—own equities with sector exposure but no net exposure to owning equities. What does that mean?

I created what I called a "synthetic cash" portfolio encompassing all those goals. My asset allocation during that time added up to 130% of my real portfolio. (See Figure 8.1.) Here's how.

First, I had 30% in huge, blue-chip, defensive European and US stocks—big drugs, banks and consumer staples. Anything that was considered "defensive," so cyclicals were out. I wanted companies with inelastic demand for their products, not elastic, since during bear markets folks tend to dial back their discretionary spending. A lot of these were super-cap stocks bought in the late 1990s with capital gains I didn't have to realize because I didn't have to sell them. Effectively, you can think of it this way: When the time comes to create synthetic cash, sell what you can that doesn't involve a capital gain, and then do the index shorting (mentioned shortly) to ensure you don't lose capital from the bear market decline.

Next, I had about 38% in liquid US government bonds (not too risky).

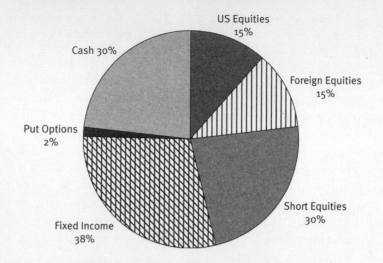

Figure 8.1   Hypothetical Defensive Portfolio Allocation
Note: **For illustrative purposes only. Not to be interpreted as a forecast.**

I had 2% in index puts against the S&P 500. I bought puts expiring about a year out. Index puts are a classic dream—they're relatively cheap insurance with relatively low premiums at the right time (market tops) and very expensive insurance at the wrong times (market bottoms). Index puts are just like casualty insurance where the casualty is the index dropping big. The puts would pay off handsomely if that happened and simply expire worthless if it didn't. I had little to lose with such a small position. A 2% loss, if they didn't pay off, would largely be covered by my bond income. But the portfolio would get considerable juice if the bet paid off. Every time the stocks sagged the puts soared in value.

Then with 30%, I sold short the Nasdaq 100 and the Russell 2000 (20% and 10% respectively), took the proceeds and held it in cash—another 30%. (30% + 38% + 2% + 30% + 30% = 130%. That's how I had 130%.) My bet was the combination of the Nasdaq and Russell would drop more than the stocks I held. So I borrowed the indexes and sold them short with the hope when they dropped, I could buy them back at a lower price, and the difference was all profit—and bigger than the losses I had on my stocks that fell. Instead of reinvesting the proceeds from shorting the indexes, I held the cash in the event I was wrong. But even the cash earned some income.

This time I wasn't wrong, and the market fell a lot during those bear market years. This portfolio fared very well in those conditions. The Nasdaq 100 short did a lot better than the Russell 2000, but together they worked just fine, rising in value as the stocks I held fell. I don't know how I'll construct my next bear market portfolio, but next time, based on the conditions then, I'll likely try to create contemporary synthetic cash that is nonvolatile, liquid, tax efficient and still allows for some stock and sector picking.

Anatomy of a Bubble

As mentioned previously, I did fine foreseeing the three bear markets in 1987, 1990 and 2000 and missed the one in 2008.

I'll address 2008 in a bit, but what led me to forecast the Tech sector–led bear market in March 2000 were worrisome realities I felt others were missing. Seeing something dreadful others miss is the basis of a successful bear hunt.

Pros were too bearish, expecting negative or single-digit returns, in 1996, 1997, 1998 and 1999 as US stocks exceeded 20% each and every year. The consensus finally turned strongly bullish in 2000, as measured by my senti-ment-based bell curves (which, you recall, were still little utilized then and therefore still had considerable power), agreeing the market would break the 10% mark. (The 2000 bell curve is shown again in Figure 8.2.)

I knew I could rule out anything under the consensus bell—from flat to up 20%. I was left with the possibility of an up-a-lot year and two holes on the bearish side, either down a little or a lot. I wouldn't turn bearish just to be a contrarian. But I was concerned about an inverting yield curve because no one talked about it. As you know, inverted yield curves are fairly reliable predictors of bear markets and recessions (if few notice them)—and it was happening globally. But no one was talking about it, so there was no fear of it. By contrast, in 1998, the financial press couldn't stop clamoring about an inverted US yield curve even when the yield curve didn't get past flat. But in 2000, no. (They talked about it in 2005, probably because no one talked about it as it happened in 2000—and, of course, in 2005 there was no recession or bear market.) Bond yields were also very high compared to earnings yields (see Figure 1.5 in Chapter 1). There had been a lot of equity-based takeovers. The only really bullish feature was it was the fourth year of the president's term.

And there certainly wasn't fear, period. *Business Week*'s January 2000 cover story lauded "The New Economy."[2] The premise was not only sky-high Tech valuations were here to stay, but they'd soon be mimicked in other indus-tries and globally. But *Business Week* wasn't the only one. I could find little bearish sentiment (except the cadre of perma-bears). Just a year earlier, Y2K was supposed to be the end of all life as we knew it. Two years earlier, the Russian ruble crisis and the bankruptcy of a second-tier hedge fund were

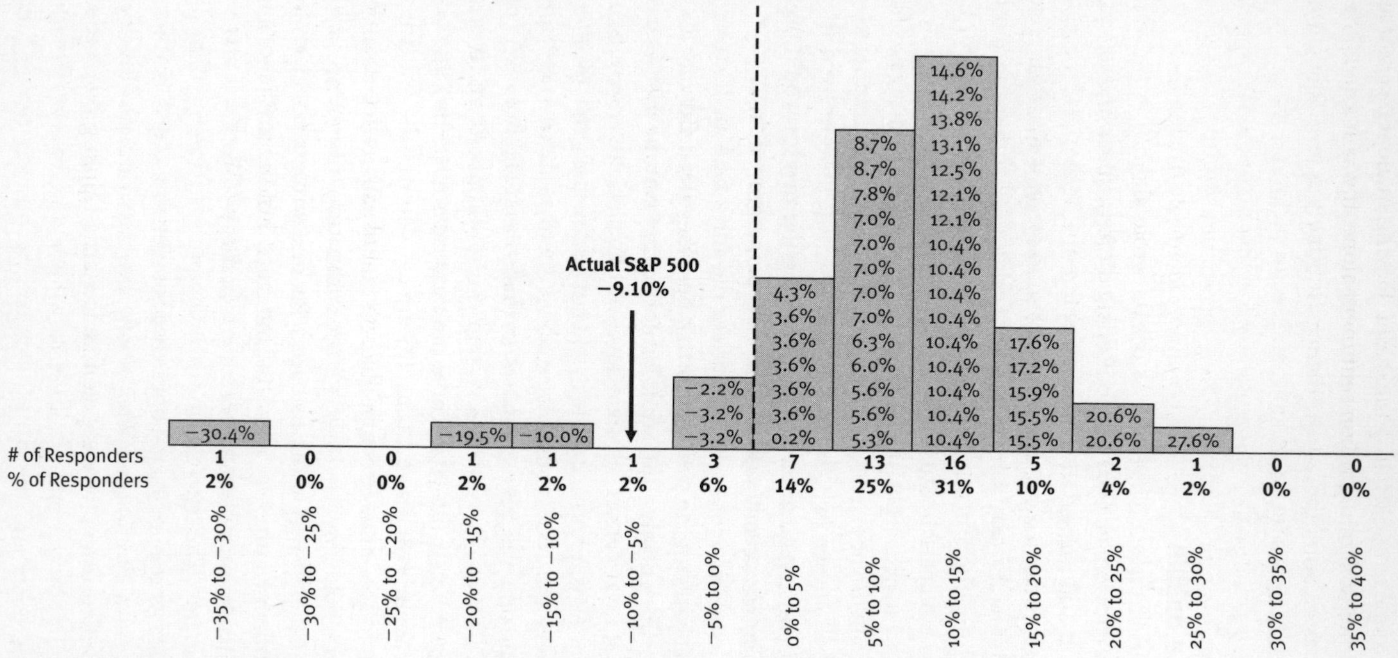

Figure 8.2 The Sentiment Bell Curve Shifts to the Right (S&P 500 Forecast 2000)
Source: BusinessWeek.

widely feared capable of crippling the world. Having made it through all that, folks opted for optimism. Based on sentiment alone, it was reasonable to contemplate the benefit of a defensive posture. But that is a long step from actually turning bearish.

There was something fundamentally worse that no one saw. After years of Tech IPOs, stock supply was in my view threatening to drown demand. The late 1990s Tech boom was measurably almost identical structurally to the 1980 supply-demand imbalance in Energy stocks. I wrote about it in my March 6, 2000, *Forbes* column entitled "1980 Revisited" (reprinted in Appendix G). That the article was published mere days before the Tech and US market top was pure luck—I had no idea this particular market call would be so timely.

Bubble Trouble—It's Always a New Paradigm

I'm hesitant to use the word *bubble* since it's bandied about so much by so many who understand bubbles so little. Bubbles are much more often forecasted than they ever truly appear.

And when a true bubble is inflating, it's often overlooked. Before they burst, real bubbles are often seen as a "new paradigm," a "new era," fundamentally different from the past, where the old rules no longer apply, where you get great returns with little or no risk because "it's different this time." (Read more in my 2011 book, *Markets Never Forget*, about the danger of believing "it's different this time.") Before Japan's bubble started bursting in 1990, it was seen as having superior businessmen with whom the West couldn't compete. When Tech was a bubble it was, "The New Economy." But when something is called a bubble that hasn't actually burst yet, it means the price has gone up a lot, and a lot of people fear it will go back down. (This is our heights framework again.) That fear is often already in the market, minimizing risk by its mere presence.

When something is really a bubble, it's not usually called a bubble, and people don't fear it. In the years 1997, 1998 and 1999, there was no national press coverage of Tech as a bubble. Tony Perkins wrote a book late in 1999 describing Internet stocks as a bubble, but it got little notice. My *Forbes* column calling Tech a bubble was one of the first appearances of that word in national print associated with Tech.

And what I saw in early 2000 was eerily similar to what I had witnessed and later measured without having actually forecasted it in the Energy sector in 1980—a real bubble with the potential to start a rippling, fierce, sector-led bear market.

Think back to 1980 and how unstoppable the Energy sector seemed. Thanks to 1970s global central bank monetary mismanagement, inflation was soaring and commodities booming. OPEC was powerful while the Iran-Iraq War was raging. Oil was $33 a barrel, and the consensus was forecasting $100 a barrel in four years. No one was calling for oil prices to fall. Just so, in early 2000, the consensus foresaw Internet users tripling globally in four years, and most folks were heralding "The New Economy," saying things like: Earnings don't matter. It's a new paradigm. It's clicks, not bricks!

There were abundant Energy-to-Tech parallels—in March 2000, the 30 largest US companies represented 49% of the US stock market's value—and half of those were Tech stocks.[3] Rewind to 1980, and the 30 largest US stocks made up a third of the US market's value, and half of those were Energy. The relative valuation multiples compared to the whole market for Energy in 1980 were similar to those for Tech in 2000. Too many parallels—all unnoticed seemingly by anyone—so I could fathom an outcome not dissimilar to 1980's.

Another key overlooked parallel was the number of IPOs as a percent of all stocks—swelling supply. The Energy bubble also featured an IPO boom then a stock-price bust. I started with the notion a flood of Tech-stock supply might topple prices. Table 8.3 demonstrates the rapid increase of stock supply in both sectors through respective IPO booms in the late 1970s and late 1990s. In 1980, nearly half of the increase in value of all new and existing US companies came from the Energy sector. In 1999, nearly all of the increase came from the Technology sector.

Also, note the similarities between the percentages of new Tech stocks relative to all new stocks and all US stocks in 1999 to those of 1980's Energy bubble. And, the price-to-book value of each sector was trading at roughly twice the market multiple. Who would remember today that in 1980 Energy stocks were priced like growth stocks? Scary times. The key is few saw or mentioned it.

Now look at the relative weights of these two sectors in Table 8.4. The top three tables show Energy relative to the S&P 500 during the bubble and after the crash in 1979, 1980 and 1981; the bottom three show Tech during 1998, 1999 and 2000.

At its 1980 peak, Energy was 28% of the US market. But Tech's explosion was more remarkable—growing from 5% in 1992 to just over 30% in 1999. The way I saw it, Tech had further to fall. But it didn't need to fall much further to create the same major bear market Energy created between 1980 and the summer of 1982. Both of these observations weighed heavily in my decision to call a peak in the Tech market in 2000.

Table 8.3   The Making of Two Bubbles

US Energy stocks	12/31/79	12/31/80	Change	US Technology stocks	12/31/98	12/29/99	Change
# of Energy Companies	229	301	72	# of Companies	1460	1652	192
Value of Energy Companies (000's)	$189,795	$324,629	$134,833	Value (000's)	$2,307,384	$4,930,559	$2,623,175

All US Stocks	12/31/79	12/31/80	Change	All US Stocks	12/31/98	12/29/99	Change
# of Companies	4291	4417	126	# of Companies	8656	8785	129
Value (000's)	$1,024,832	$1,325,489	$300,656	Value (000's)	$12,881,072	$15,748,729	$2,867,657

New Energy Companies as a % of Total New Companies	20.3%	New Technology Companies as a % of Total New Companies	21.2%
New Energy Companies as a % of Total Companies	1.7%	New Technology Companies as a % of Total Companies	2.2%
Increase in Energy Value Relative to Total Market Value	44.8%	Increase in Technology Value Relative to Total Market Value	91.5%
Price/Book of Energy Stocks	2.6x	Price/Book of Technology Stocks	13.9x
Price/Book of S&P 500	1.3x	Price/Book of S&P 500	5.6x
Energy/S&P 500 P/B Ratio	2:1	Tech/S&P 500 P/B Ratio	2.5:1

Source: **Standard & Poor's Research Insight.**

Table 8.4   A Brief History of Sector Bubbles: S&P 500
Economic Sector Weights

December 1979		December 1980		December 1981	
Basic Materials	9.64%	Basic Materials	8.88%	Basic Materials	8.58%
Capital Goods	10.28%	Capital Goods	10.82%	Capital Goods	10.03%
Communication Service	6.05%	Communication Service	4.62%	Communication Service	6.53%
Consumer Staples	10.90%	Consumer Staples	9.23%	Consumer Staples	10.58%
Consumer Cyclicals	9.86%	Consumer Cyclicals	8.00%	Consumer Cyclicals	8.84%
Energy	22.34%	Energy	27.93%	Energy	22.80%
Financials	5.79%	Financials	5.34%	Financials	6.01%
Health Care	6.42%	Health Care	6.54%	Health Care	7.42%
Technology	10.86%	Technology	10.69%	Technology	10.33%
Transportation	2.17%	Transportation	2.89%	Transportation	2.95%
Utilities	5.70%	Utilities	5.07%	Utilities	5.92%
	100.00%		100.00%		100.00%

December 1998		December 1999		December 2000	
Basic Materials	3.11%	Basic Materials	2.09%	Basic Materials	2.41%
Capital Goods	8.07%	Capital Goods	8.40%	Capital Goods	9.01%
Communication Service	8.33%	Communication Service	7.93%	Communication Service	5.47%
Consumer Staples	14.89%	Consumer Staples	10.88%	Consumer Staples	11.35%
Consumer Cyclicals	9.13%	Consumer Cyclicals	9.14%	Consumer Cyclicals	7.56%
Energy	6.22%	Energy	5.43%	Energy	6.45%
Financials	15.59%	Financials	13.20%	Financials	17.22%
Health Care	12.07%	Health Care	9.05%	Health Care	14.10%
Technology	18.54%	Technology	30.02%	Technology	21.85%
Transportation	0.93%	Transportation	0.70%	Transportation	0.67%
Utilities	3.11%	Utilities	2.28%	Utilities	3.91%
	100.00%		100.00%		100.00%

Source: **Standard & Poor's Research Insight, Thomson Reuters.**

In some ways, I could fathom Tech being worse than the Energy bubble. In 1980, none of the 50 largest Energy stocks were an IPO of just a few years before, say 1978 or 1979. The 1978 to 1980 IPOs, though many, were smaller. In 2000, 11 of the 50 largest stocks were IPOs in 1998 and 1999. That increased risk, in my view.

Was I certain Tech would implode and the market drop? No, but it was logical. First, all the ugly parallels to 1980 seemed invisible to everyone. Second, you had to wonder who was left to buy who hadn't done so. Who was left as fresh fodder for TGH? Based on sentiment, the yield curve, the budget surpluses, equity-based takeovers and Energy parallels, I was content to eliminate possibilities of an up-a-lot or up-a-little scenario for 2000. Then again, down a lot seemed unlikely, too. As I knew from looking at 1981, it took a long time for the oil meltdown to ripple out through other sectors. A sector bubble bursting doesn't normally ripple to other sectors fast. So my presumption was Tech would start down and be down a lot. But it would take time to drag down the rest of the market. So for a major market meltdown, we would be waiting longer. Finally, I knew bull markets die with a whimper, not with a bang—bull markets don't normally have a dramatic spiking top, but roll over slowly. Around the 2000 peak, there was over a 10-month period where the world stock market never got out of a 9% bandwidth (see Figure 8.3).

Note again Tech started 2000 as 30% of the total S&P 500. If a 30% sector is down 39%, as Nasdaq was in 2000, and everything else is flat, then the

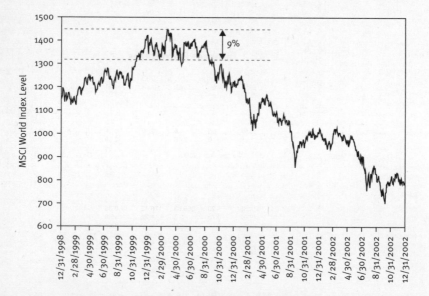

Figure 8.3   Bull Markets Die With a Whimper, Not a Bang
Source: **Thomson Reuters.**

whole market should be down 11.7%. But the S&P was down only 9% in 2000.[4] So technically, the rest of the market—the non-Tech part—was up a hair. The sector breakdown hadn't yet rippled out to take down the rest of the market with it.

But throughout 2000, my view was the Tech sector continued deteriorating. I could see new Tech companies burning feverishly through their cash, just as new Energy companies had in 1980—almost identical proportions. We could measure how many would run out of cash if they didn't get back to the public market to raise more money—implying either company implosion or yet more new stock supply; either had to be bad, looking forward.

For a gauge, we calculated the *burn rate* for as many new Tech stocks as we could find data. Burn rate measures how fast a firm will run out of cash in the absence of new cash. To measure burn rate, we compared cash and net losses through the second quarter of 2000 (it being September when we last did this). Assuming these firms found no further outside funding, we divided current cash by second quarter net loss to get the burn rate.

In all, we found 223 material publicly traded companies so short on cash if they didn't pull off a new stock offering very fast, they would be a quaint memory. Table 8.5 shows the 25 worst offenders. In just one quarter, the aggregate market cap of companies fitting this mold jumped from $140 billion to over $312 billion—not from the prices rising, but because so many were increasingly close to hitting the wall, and no one was counting. The market was flooding with stock supply from profitless companies. With the IPO market

Table 8.5   Internet Burn Rates

	Ticker	Company	Market Cap	Total Debt	Q1 Cash	Q2 Cash	Q4 1999	Net Income Q1 2000	Q2 2000	Burn Rate
1	ONEM	ONEMAIN.COM INC	282.12	30.45	17.06	1.42	-32.73	-39.84	-35.88	0.04
2	FLAS	FLASHNET COMMUNICATIONS INC	52.3	8.61	0.23	-	-11.42	-4.96	-	0.05
3	GENI	GENESISINTERMEDIA.COM INC	86.98	33.15	0.35	0.41	-6.66	-5.13	-7.34	0.06
4	HCOM	HOMECOM COMMUNICATIONS INC	8.14	0.48	0.08	-	-2.3	-1.49	-	0.06
5	3EFAX	EFAX.COM INC	16.07	1.5	1.6	0.18	-10.14	-5.38	-2.56	0.07
6	CLAI	CLAIMSNET.COM INC	23.19	0	2.49	-	-2.39	-1.93	-9.31	0.27
7	NETZ	NETZEE INC	120.52	16.22	1.33	5.41	-18.85	-15.67	-17.77	0.3
8	LUMT	LUMINANT WORLDWIDE CORP	235.83	6.79	9.44	-	-24.47	-29.65	-29.12	0.32
9	3ESYN	ESYNCH CORP	83.41	0.11	0.5	-	-2.14	-1.49	-	0.33
10	RMII	RMI NET INC	66.39	3.78	3.26	-	-12.24	-7.4	-8.41	0.39
11	DGV	DIGITAL LAVA INC	26.88	0.27	2.59	0.68	-2.25	-1.54	-1.74	0.39
12	ECMV	E COM VENTURES INC	22.18	54.42	2.91	-	-0.13	-6.62	-	0.44
13	ZDZ	ZDNET	135.59	0	0.02	1.21	2.05	-1.57	-2.64	0.46
14	MRCH	MARCHFIRST INC	2679.63	20	369.83	176.43	8.36	-117.33	-374.45	0.47
15	GEEK	INTERNET AMERICA INC	48.92	0.73	3.3	1.72	-0.9	-1.58	-3.27	0.53
16	ROWE	ROWECOM INC	51.25	6.96	9.29	10.13	-1.61	-15	-19.16	0.53
17	PRGY	PRODIGY COMMUN CORP -CL A	677.28	109.36	21.13	20.73	-29.76	-34.91	-38.95	0.53
18	WAVO	WAVO CORP	22.19	3.37	10.23	4.77	-14.42	-3.51	-8.91	0.54
19	ELTX	ELTRAX SYS INC	150.96	17.7	14.2	-	-1.66	-5.24	-26.34	0.54
20	KANA	KANA COMMUNICATIONS	5575.49	1.72	35.67	162.84	-	-14.45	-284.94	0.57
21	ATHM	AT HOME CORP	7578.71	873.23	502.28	388.73	-723.01	-676.52	-668.26	0.58
22	PILL	PROXYMED INC	30.88	1.75	7.91	7.38	-	-5.72	-10.48	0.7
23	AHWY	AUDIOHIGHWAY.COM	14.36	0.46	8.34	3.47	-5.86	-4.01	-4.78	0.73
24	BFLY	BLUEFLY INC	10.77	2.87	3.91	3.93	-5.69	-5.67	-5.3	0.74
25	ELIX	ELECTRIC LIGHTWAVE -CL A	941.85	710.4	25.99	-	-35.02	-35.14	-34.96	0.74

Source: **Standard & Poor's Research Insight.**

soured, pretty much all these companies were gone 12 months later. The bubble had only just begun to burst.

(Putting together this table is pretty straightforward, should you ever want to measure burn rates yourself. All of the information we detailed is publicly available. You just need a fast Internet hookup and a sector you suspect.)

Most unsettling was no one noticed the parallels between the Tech fervor and the last sector bubble 20 years earlier. I wasn't the only financial practitioner to have witnessed the Energy crash—by any means. I wasn't the world's only person with access to the data for comparison. There were lots of folks who should have seen this before me. But I couldn't see them seeing it anywhere, which was scary. Around the campfire, they were peering a different direction.

Nothing had yet changed to alleviate the cash-starved supply flood of Tech IPOs and secondaries. In my view, as 2000 ended, supply had finally likely drowned demand. Dot-com after dot-com ran out of cash. This had to ripple out of being a sector-specific phenomenon—the rest of the global market would start pricing in the supply glut. If there had been even a little fear in the market about Tech or the yield curve or anything, I could have seen the market being down just a little again in 2001. When most everyone has no fear is the best time to get really fearful. The wonderful mantra attributed to Mr. Buffett is: "You should be greedy when others are fearful and fearful when others are greedy." I could fathom at the end of 2000 there simply being no buying pressure in 2001 to keep the market from being down a lot.

As 2000 faded, with the Nasdaq down 39%, the S&P 500 down 9% for the year and investors and professional forecasters still bullish, I finally concluded the time was nigh to turn fully bearish. Not just bearish to Tech, but overall bearish.

Sympathy Selling

Often (though not always) in a bear market, some sector goes bad first. Selling ripples to other sectors in a process I call *sympathy selling*. It works like this. Suppose you were a generic Tech mutual fund. You own little dot-coms and big established Tech giants. Out of nowhere, as some of your dot-com holdings implode, you get simultaneous redemptions. You must sell something to get the cash to cover redemptions. What do you sell? You can't sell the little dot-coms getting hammered so badly—they aren't that liquid, and you hope they'll bounce back—so you sell your Intel, Microsoft and Oracle because you can—big and liquid stocks. And that selling hits those stocks. But this is also happening to all the other generic Tech funds. But then some growth stock funds own Tech, drug stocks, consumer products companies and whatever else. As Intel, Microsoft and Oracle get hit, that fund manager must sell something else to cover his redemptions, so he reaches out and sells Merck and Procter & Gamble. This ripples from fund to fund having the most impact where the process started but eventually rippling far enough to hit not all, but most of the market. From 2000 to 2003, the only parts of the market that escaped were the small, steep discount value stocks—exactly the reverse of where the damage began with high-end growth Tech stocks. (And by the way, this sympathy selling was evident in 2008 into 2009 as the damage done in the Finance sector rippled out to other sectors.)

So in 2000, I cut my Tech holdings, and at the end of the year I got completely defensive and stayed that way for 18 months.

Some Basic Bear Rules

Why 18 months, you ask? While bull market durations vary considerably, most bear markets last about a year to 18 months on the outside. Very few in modern history last fully two years or longer. If you're making a defensive move, you probably shouldn't bet on one lasting so long. The longer a bear market runs, the more likely you're waiting too long to get back in. The 2000 to 2002 bear market was unusual—longer in duration than the 2008 bear market! The 2008 bear market was huge in terms of magnitude, though the 2000 to 2002 one had big magnitude, too. That we had two big bear markets in a row likely make many think bear markets are normally that long or steep—an example of *recency bias* and a cognitive error. If you are betting the next bear market lasts much more than 18 months, you are basing that bet on a historical outlier—and you must have strong, fundamental reasons not based on fear or emotions backing up that view. Then, too, if you remain bearish for longer than that, you may miss out on the rocket-like ride that is almost always the beginning of the next bull run. Missing that can be very costly.

Further, if you get out successfully and time proves your success, your Stone Age brain may fear exposing you to losses—which could keep you out until *after* that initial next bull market rocket ride. Staying may feel more comfortable—it lets you feel right longer, particularly if you convince yourself the start of the rocket ride isn't real. Your brain wants to accumulate pride for having gotten out successfully. Switching back to bullish means you might be wrong, and if you are, people will ridicule you, and our antiquated brains hate that.

Bear markets rarely last as long as your brain wants to think they do once you've gotten out successfully. You hear plenty of rhetoric about "cyclical bulls within long-term secular bears," which is supposed to mean positive years are blips in an overall downward super-cycle, but history is decidedly clear here—stocks rise much more than fall, and true secular bear markets just don't exist, not the way many think. (Read more on the fallacy of hunting for secular bear markets in *Markets Never Forget*.)

Understanding the nature of bear markets makes it clear why it's good to define, in advance, a reentry time frame. Historically, only about a third of bear market losses occur in the first two-thirds of the bear market duration—or what I call my "Two-Thirds, One-Third Rule." (Mind you, none of these rules are binding, and all should be accompanied by other fundamental reasons for making any broad asset allocation changes.) It's a gross generalization, but about two-thirds of the losses don't happen until the back of the bear. The 1973 to 1974 bear market was a good example, as Figure 8.4 shows.

You won't time your reentry perfectly (I sure didn't in 2002)—expect that now. The back of bear markets being brutal is TGH's way of humiliating you out of the initial rocket-surge of a new bull market.

The flip side of this rule is: The start of bear markets isn't steep. It's later they get steep. For the first 10% to 20% of the duration after the peak, the market slips slowly. Per Figure 8.3, 2000 was a perfect example. This isn't true for all countries—small countries can have very steep drops off the peak. But for America, the total foreign market and the world as a whole, it's very true. So when looking for a major bear market, you needn't try to forecast it before it

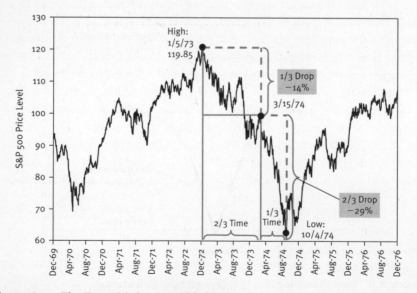

Figure 8.4   The Two-Thirds, One-Third Rule
Source: Thomson Reuters.

peaks—which is near impossible to do. It's easier to see a peak after something has happened than beforehand when nothing has actually happened.

At market bottoms, the reverse is almost always true. While bull market tops don't spike top, bear market bottoms do V-bottom or sometimes W-bottom. Think about the bottom like a V (or a W—if there is a double bottom)—like Figure 8.5. If you successfully get defensive sometime after the peak, does it matter which side of the V you get back in on? Not really. You still end up in about the same place, no matter whether you get in on the left side of the V or the right (adjusted for a little interest lost from getting in too early).

TGH wants you to wallow in loss aversion and hindsight bias, waiting to get back in until the market has rallied materially. Exiting at the right time takes guts—*if* you can forecast the bear correctly (which is devilishly tough). Getting back in is equally agonizing. The 18-month rule can help provide discipline and self-control.

If you want to exceed the 18-month rule, fine. But create your own limit beforehand, whether 20 or 22 months or whatever, and stick to it. One way to combine my rule with yours is to take the 18 months and see where you are. If after 18 months you believe you still know something others don't as to why the market should keep going lower, let it go lower. If it isn't lower a month later, force yourself back in. If it is lower, let it keep falling, but if it gets back up

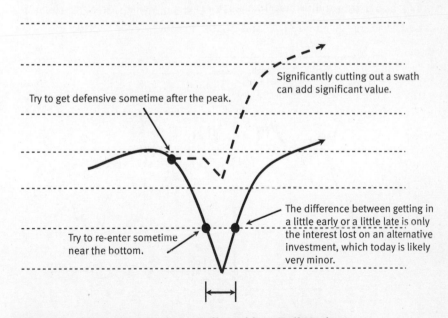

Figure 8.5   Every Bear Market Is Followed by a Bull Market
Note: **For illustrative purposes only. Not drawn to scale. Not to be interpreted as a forecast.**

to where it was after 18 months, then force yourself back in—that would be one way to force some discipline. You're just on the same place on the other side of the V. Take your unruly brain out of the picture.

Here's another reason you needn't time the start of a bear perfectly. Every US and global bear market we've looked at, except two, had an average monthly decline, top to bottom, ranging between 1.25% and 3%, but 2% is a fair enough average—1973 to 1974 is a good example again (see Figure 8.6). The exceptions are 1987, which was so short-lived in duration, and 2008. That bear market—the biggest since the Great Depression—had steeper average monthly losses thanks to a precipitous drop in roughly the final third after Lehman Brothers collapsed, making it another exception.

The purpose of this particular rule is to prevent yourself from bailing on what may be normal volatility. If you suspect you're experiencing a bear, be patient and watch. If you see a market decline exceeding the 2% average, wait for it to bounce back before getting out. You may simply be experiencing a correction. But with a typical bear market, you'll soon see a short-lived pull-back to higher prices within that 2%-per-month range off the top and have a better chance to get out. Patience is a virtue here.

Joe Goodman was a wise man and longtime-running *Forbes* columnist. (I surpassed him to become the fourth-longest running columnist in August 2007.) To my thinking, he was the best columnist *Forbes* ever had. He advised readers in the 1940s and 1950s to never call a peak too soon.

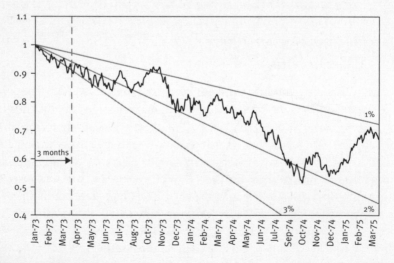

Figure 8.6 The 2% Rule
Source: **Thomson Reuters.**

He advocated waiting three months after you suspect a peak has happened before calling a bear.

Again, none of these are hard and fast rules to be blindly adhered to. Rather, they are meant to help instill some discipline and keep you from pulling the rip cord too soon on a correction and then watching a bull market soaring still higher. And if you see any of these "rules" or a combination of them, in my view, you still must see something fundamentally and hugely bad few others see to justify getting defensive.

Never a Dull Moment

If you are a long-term growth-oriented investor and take one thing away from this book, it should be that you shouldn't take forecasting a bear market lightly. The world is a scary place—but that has always been true. That big, scary events happen (and happen a lot) isn't sufficient to cause a bear market.

As investors, we misremember past events and our reactions to them (*hindsight bias*), so we think we handled them better than we did. But history is rife with major events, and stocks have overall risen with volatility through it all. Table 8.6 details some major historic events and the subsequent global stock return. It may surprise you how resilient stocks have been.

Look at the list of historic events in Table 8.6 and try to remember—honestly—what you felt during, say, the Cuban Missile Crisis (if you were around). Or when JFK was shot. Or when the American embassy in Iran was seized. Or Y2K's approach. Don't let hysteria scare you heavily out of stocks at what may be an inappropriate time. That is just what TGH wants.

When Bulls Cross-Dress

TGH will try fooling you into thinking every bull market is really a bear market in disguise. TGH conspires so a new bull market comes dressed in all the trappings of a "secular bear" market. Bull markets are unabashed cross-dressers. I've never seen a bull market that didn't come to the party wearing a full-on bear suit. Unfortunately, most investors aren't looking for cross-dressers. All they know is, way late into the party— WHAMMO! They've missed out on the first 50% up-leg of a bull market because TGH had their minds warped.

Arm yourself against TGH by knowing how to tell a cross-dresser from the real deal—a correction from a bear market. The major differences are magnitude and duration. A correction is a short-term, 10% to 20%, scary global downturn—but sometimes can be a bit more. It's typically short, sharp and comes from nowhere with a spike top and a fantastic story leading you to

Table 8.6   Never a Dull Moment

Year	Events	Global Stock Returns
1934	Depression; First margin requirement; Hitler declares himself Führer of Germany	2.6%
1935	Spanish Civil War; Italy invades northern Africa; Hitler rejects Treaty of Versailles; Social Security created by law	22.8%
1936	Hitler occupies Rhineland	19.3%
1937	Monetary policy tightened; Capital spending and industrial production decline severely; Recession	−16.9%
1938	World war clouds gather; Wall Street scandals uncovered	5.6%
1939	War in Europe dominates headlines; Germany and Italy sign 10-year military pact	−1.4%
1940	France falls to Hitler; Battle of Britain; US institutes the draft	3.5%
1941	Germany invades USSR; Pearl Harbor; US declares war on Japan, Italy and Germany	18.7%
1942	Wartime price controls; Battle of Midway	1.2%
1943	Meat and cheese rationed in the US; FDR freezes prices and wages	19.9%
1944	Consumer goods shortages; Allies invade Normandy; Bretton Woods system established	−10.2%
1945	FDR dies; Postwar recession predicted; Invasion of Iwo Jima; Atom bomb dropped in Japan	11.0%
1946	Employment Act of 1946 passed; Steel and shipyard workers strike	−15.1%
1947	Cold War begins	3.2%
1948	Berlin blockade; US government seizes railroads to avert strike; Israel founded	−5.7%
1949	Russia explodes atom bomb; Communists win in China	05.4%
1950	Korean War; McCarthy and the Red Scare	25.5%
1951	Excess profits tax	22.4%
1952	US seizes steel mills to avert strike; Top federal income tax bracket is 92%	15.8%
1953	Soviet Union explodes H-bomb; Economists predict depression in 1954	4.8%

Table 8.6   (Continued)

Year	Events	Global Stock Returns
1954	Dow tops 300—common belief that market is too high	49.8%
1955	Eisenhower falls ill	24.7%
1956	Egypt seizes Suez Canal	6.6%
1957	Russia launches Sputnik; Treasury Secretary Humphrey warns of depression and President Eisenhower agrees	−6.0%
1958	Recession	34.5%
1959	Castro seizes power in Cuba	23.3%
1960	Soviet Union downs U-2 spy plane; Castro seizes US oil refineries	3.5%
1961	Bay of Pigs invasion fails; Green Berets sent to Vietnam; Berlin Wall erected	20.8%
1962	Cuban Missile Crisis—threat of global destruction; JFK cracks down on steel prices, scaring Wall Street	−6.2%
1963	South Vietnam government overthrown; JFK assassinated	15.4%
1964	Gulf of Tonkin; Race riots in New York	11.2%
1965	Civil rights marches; Rumor of LBJ heart attack; Treasury warns of gold speculation	9.8%
1966	Vietnam War escalates—US bombs Hanoi	−10.1%
1967	Race riots in Newark and Detroit; LBJ signs huge defense spending bill; Six-Day War	21.3%
1968	*USS Pueblo* seized; Tet Offensive; Martin Luther King and Robert Kennedy assassinated	13.9%
1969	Money tightens—markets fall; Prime rate at record high	−3.9%
1970	US invades Cambodia—Vietnam War spreads; Money supply declines; Bankruptcy of Penn Central	−3.1%
1971	Wage price freeze; US ends Bretton Woods system of exchange rates—ends gold standard	18.4%
1972	Largest US trade deficit in history; US mines Vietnamese ports; Nixon visits Red China	22.5%
1973	Energy crisis—Arab oil embargo; Watergate scandal; Yom Kippur War; Vice President Agnew resigns	−15.2%
1974	Steepest market drop in four decades; Nixon resigns; Yen devalued; Franklin National Bank collapses	−25.5%

(continued)

Table 8.6   (Continued)

Year	Events	Global Stock Returns
1975	New York City bankrupt; Clouded economic picture	32.8%
1976	Economic recovery slows; OPEC raises oil prices	13.4%
1977	Steep market slump; Social Security taxes raised	0.7%
1978	Rising interest rates	16.5%
1979	Oil prices skyrocket; Three Mile Island nuclear disaster; Iran seizes US embassy	11.0%
1980	All-time high interest rates; Health hazards in New York (Love Canal); Carter halts grain exports to Soviet Union	25.7%
1981	Steep recession begins; Reagan shot; Energy sector begins collapse; AIDS identified for first time	−4.8%
1982	Worst recession in 40 years—profits plummet, unemployment spikes	9.7%
1983	US invades Grenada; US embassy in Beirut bombed; WPPSS biggest muni bond default in history	21.9%
1984	Record federal deficit; FDIC bailout of Continental Illinois; AT&T declared monopoly—broken up	4.7%
1985	US and Soviet arms race begins; Ohio banks closed to stop run; US becomes largest debtor nation	40.6%
1986	US bombs Libya; Boesky pleads guilty to insider trading; *Challenger* explodes; Chernobyl; Tax reform act passed	41.9%
1987	Record-setting, single-day market decline; Iran-Contra investigation blames Reagan	16.2%
1988	First Republic Bank fails; Noriega indicted by US; Pan Am 103 bombing	23.3%
1989	Savings & Loan bailout begins; Tiananmen Square; SF earthquake; US troops deploy in Panama; Berlin Wall falls; Japanese buy Rockefeller Center	16.6%
1990	Iraq invades Kuwait—sets stage for Gulf War; Consumer confidence plummets; Unemployment rises	−17.0%
1991	Recession; US begins air war in Iraq; Unemployment rises to 7%; Soviet Union collapses	18.3%
1992	Unemployment continues to rise; Economic fears; Monetary supply tightened; Bitter election contest	−5.2%

(*continued*)

Table 8.6   (Continued)

Year	Events	Global Stock Returns
1993	Tax increase; Economic recovery uncertain—fears of double-dip recession	22.5%
1994	Attempted nationalized health care; Republican revolution in midterm elections	5.1%
1995	Weak dollar panic; Oklahoma City bombing	20.7%
1996	Fears of inflation; Conflict in former Yugoslav republics; Fed chair Alan Greenspan gives "irrational exuberance" speech	13.5%
1997	Tech mini crash in October and Pacific Rim crisis	15.8%
1998	Russian ruble crisis; "Asian flu"; Long-Term Capital Management debacle	24.3%
1999	Y2K paranoia and correction; Graham-Leach-Bliley passed (removes aspects of 1933 Glass-Steagall)	24.9%
2000	Dot-com bubble begins to burst; Contested presidential election (Bush v. Gore, hanging chads)	−13.2%
2001	Recession; September 11th terrorist attacks; Tax cuts; US conflict in Afghanistan begins	−16.8%
2002	Corporate accounting scandals; Terrorism fears; Tensions with Iraq; Sarbanes-Oxley passed; Brazil narrowly averts default	−19.9%
2003	Mutual fund scandals; Conflict in Iraq; SARS	33.1%
2004	Fears of a weak dollar and US triple deficits; Indian Ocean earthquake and tsunami kills 200,000+	14.7%
2005	Tension with North Korea and Iran over nuclear weapons; Hurricane Katrina; Oil price spikes to $70	9.5%
2006	North Korea testing nuclear weapons; Fear of housing bubble; Continued war in Iraq; New Fed chair fear (Bernanke)	20.1%
2007	Oil prices at all-time high; Fallout of subprime securitizations force US banks to raise capital; Rise of sovereign wealth funds	9.0%
2008	Global financial panic; Steepest calendar-year stock market declines since 1930s	−40.7%
2009	Massive fiscal stimulus plans passed globally; Global central bank interest rates at historic lows; Major debate on US health care	30.0%

(*continued*)

Table 8.6   (Continued)

Year	Events	Global Stock Returns
2010	PIIGS sovereign debt scares; Double-dip recession fears; May "Flash Crash"; Democrats lose House majority; Health Care reform passed; Financial reform passed; Basel III banking reform passed	11.8%
2011	Arab Spring; Japanese earthquake and tsunami; Continuing PIIGS sovereign debt concerns; Bin Laden killed; US downgrade	−5.5%

Note: Returns from 1970 to 2011 reflect the Morgan Stanley Capital International (MSCI) World Index, which measures the performance of selected stocks in 24 developed countries and is presented inclusive of dividends and withholding taxes. Returns before 1970 are provided by Global Financial Data, Inc. and simulate how a world index, inclusive of dividends, would have performed had it been calculated back to 1934.
Sources: Global Financial Data, Inc., Thomson Reuters.

believe more downside is ahead. It's usually over just as fast and rockets higher returning to new highs about as fast as it fell—but while stocks are falling, it can feel like it's going on forever.

You may think 20%, just like mid-1998, is quite a lot and officially qualifies for a bear market, but the operative words here are "short and sharp"—right off the cliff, defying our 2% rule. Corrections are common in bull markets (one every year or two on average) and devilishly tough to time—you shouldn't try because they down-and-up so fast. To time these successfully, you must be right on *both* ends. Odds are you'll miss either a good exit or reentry point or both. Don't bother. (No one—and I mean no one—in the history of asset management, with all of the tens of thousands of practitioners, has ever made a successful long-term practice of timing short-term downturns. If it were possible, at least one person would have done it by now. But no one has. And if you could, you wouldn't be reading this book.)

Similar to a down-a-little scenario, any benefit you get by being super lucky and accurately timing a correction can get eaten up by transaction costs and taxes.

When Bears Cross-Dress

But a bear market's beginning feels nothing like a correction. It feels fine, usually. A bull market top won't announce itself with a sudden price drop.

There is no announcement effect (except 1987, the exception to the rule—even 2008 wasn't like that). Instead of a bull in a bear suit, you get a bear in a bull suit. As stated earlier, bull markets have grinding, rolling, whimpering tops and a relative absence of bearish sentiment (other than perma-bears). You won't hear a bang. You likely won't "feel" like you are about to experience a prolonged downturn. In fact, you might "feel" like your diversified portfolio is boring and you should place big bets on individual stocks or spectacular sectors to boost returns.

Historically, if markets have been positive 72% of the time,[5] and some of those negative years were only down a little, you're looking at very few years of the truly scary, bearish, down-a-lot type. They happen. They hurt. But if you want long-term equity-like returns or thereabouts, you likely are exposed to that downside. And when it happens, it can be easy to believe stocks will only ever do lousy going forward—but history, fundamentals and the power of profit motive (and human nature) all argue against that.

Another way to see this is if you're bearish much more than three or four times in two decades, you're likely overdoing it. Recall as human beings, we normally exert more effort to avoid pain than achieve gain. Remember that. If your brain keeps telling you a bear is always impending, your brain is wrong. Successful bearishness requires being virtually alone. You must act alone, without others. But if you have the Three Questions, you're never really alone.

Getting in Too Early

Making a successful bear market call is only half the battle. If you get defensive on the stock market, you still must decide when to get back in. Our Stone Age brains make deciding when to "re-equitize" as fraught with peril as deciding to get out. Just as you can't rely on a fixed set of indicators to get out, there's no magical way to know when to get back in.

After my Tech bubble and bear market call, my firm and I decided to get bullish again in May 2002. In hindsight, too early because broad markets didn't bottom until October 2002. I didn't expect to time the bottom perfectly, but getting in the market just in time for TGH to throw a precipitous drop at you is never fun.

Why did my firm and I decide to get back in the market that May? Following are key reasons. And despite being wrong and too early, these were rational, disciplined decisions driven by the Three Questions:

- According to my 18-month rule, I was committed to re-equitizing by June 2002. I was not comfortable with missing equity exposure for longer than that period for clients expecting equity-like return.

- The consensus was bearish for the first time since the bear market started. Therefore, I thought down a lot was the least likely condition over the next 12 months. As it turns out, 12 months later, the global market was down—but basically down a little. It remains impossible, in my view, to ever know with certainty where the market is moving in the next few months. This time, even though I was right the market wouldn't be down a lot a year out, it was down a lot almost immediately. I stepped into a hole. No one likes negative returns, but I wanted to remain equitized in the expectation of the first three scenarios.
- Bear market investment products were proliferating, such as mutual funds specifically designed to do well in down markets. Bear market newsletters were then wildly popular and their writers considered rational sages.
- Major sources of bad news were widely known and, in my view, discounted into pricing, their "surprise" power having largely dissipated over the previous two and a half years, including recession, earnings deterioration and potential bankruptcies, terrorist attacks and the impending war, accounting scandals (Enron, WorldCom) and the rest.
- At the time, it looked as though a double bottom had formed between September 2001 (just following the terror attacks in New York, Washington, DC, and the skies over Pennsylvania) and May 2002 lows.
- Monetary conditions were generally favorable. Broad money growth was greater than the inflation rate, short-term liquidity was on the rise and we had a steep US and global yield curve. Most important, few noticed.
- For the first time, foreign markets were acting stronger than America's, signaling a potential shift and possible end to the global bear (although this would fade away again until returning with a vengeance in 2003).
- A piece of capital markets technology we developed, the *Run Strength Indicator*, showed the market was vastly oversold and ready to move up. Unfortunately, all the data we had built it on were from post–World War II, smaller global bear markets, and on its first real-time maiden voyage, it didn't adequately reflect reality.

The Run Strength Indicator

The Run Strength Indicator was a measure of sentiment fatigue. It's another example of capital markets technology my firm developed using Question Two and a way to measure short-term sentiment that is a major driver of stock demand—and a big part of determining stock prices in the short term. It was a complicated algorithm combining many factors that basically offered hope of knowing when a market move—up or down—was simply too fatigued to continue. Giving it an indexed number of 0 to 100, we had observed when a variety of different equity indexes all fell below 20, a strong rally followed.

Conversely, when it rose above 80, an extreme overbought condition existed, and prices usually fell. We back-tested this, and it stood up well.

In May 2002, the indicator fell to extreme lows, far below 20—seemingly signaling an extremely oversold condition. We witnessed this on most major indexes. This condition hadn't been seen in decades and might not be seen again for decades. To not use it when we did would mean we probably wouldn't any time soon either. But it had never been used real time before. While we back-tested it extensively, we hadn't been able to test it in relevant, real-time conditions. But time was of the essence.

By late June, we knew the indicator clearly hadn't been working right as a timing mechanism. In hindsight, we can see sentiment can (and did) get very much worse. Effectively, the Run Strength Indicator simply wasn't up to measuring something as extreme as that bear market, reflecting instead more normal bear markets.

Still, all the other rules applied, so we had no reason to turn and get back out. I accumulated regret and learned some good lessons (a small way to get back at TGH).

Creating capital markets technology for infrequent extreme phenomena requires using old, historic data that are comparable. But will those data be clean? I already knew, but better learned through this process, that old data are pretty consistently corrupt in ways hard to know. This experience really put through my forehead the need to be sure the old data are good. As a result, we have yet more stringent and exacting ways to confirm old data to make sure we're basing assumptions off as close to reality as we can get. The more extreme and infrequent, the more you must be sure. Clean data are next to godly data and also next to impossible.

Here's another important lesson I learned. I learned to listen more to my clients—but in a different way from what you might think. When we got reinvested in May 2002, we noticed virtually none of our clients thought that a bad idea. They were eerily complacent about the decision to take their assets from entirely cash and synthetic cash to fully exposed to stocks. When we got out of Tech, that was widely seen as a missed opportunity—and of course, in retrospect, it wasn't. But very often, investors want to do exactly the wrong thing at precisely the wrong time.

But in May 2002, we thought then our client base wasn't representative of the rest of the world. Since we had avoided most of the downside in the bear market, we subsequently thought they had heavy confidence in us and therefore didn't fear stocks. We found out within a month that couldn't have been true as the market fell—many clients let us know they didn't enjoy that.

As a result, we have built redundant technology aimed at measuring the same thing in our client base, real time, moving forward. Our client base is big enough to be representative of American high net worth investors as a whole—and hence, a great laboratory for testing sentiment. If our clients don't feel the fear, it's probably not broadly out there. Today we can measure daily incoming call volume of clients and calibrate it and aggregate the degree to which our client base is feeling fear or extreme optimism, which is on its own a valuable sentiment tool.

Of course, I missed other things. I didn't see the Sarbanes-Oxley legislation coming at us in July 2002, which was and remains a negative. I underestimated the degree to which society would temporarily adopt the "all CEOs are crooks" mentality late in 2002 that both led to Sarbanes-Oxley and seemingly was also partly fueled by it. For example, by July, rumors were rampant in and out of the media Jack Welch was a bad guy and GE would be the next Enron. If GE could go bad, then everything could go bad. All that was just sentiment, but I didn't see it coming. But seeing the sentiment twists of the last stages of a bull or bear market is both difficult and often done wrong. And this time, I was simply too early and wrong. Getting in too early was a big mistake to make, but as long as you're right more than wrong, even if you are really wrong from time to time, you can still beat the market in the long term, which is what the game really is about. When I was back in, I was still moving with the market.

Not Getting Out

As I update this book, I have yet another "wrong call" that has given me the opportunity to keep learning. As I've said throughout this book, investing isn't a craft. It's a nonstop query session—but also an endless learning session.

I missed the 2008 call because, in many ways, that bear market had many features inconsistent with most past bear markets. Its top was utterly devoid of euphoric or even optimistic sentiment—unusual for the bear markets I'd seen or measured before. To me, the early stages were classically characteristic of a correction. And indeed, in my view, it might have been nothing more than a correction—had it not been for the deleterious impact of the Financial Accounting Standards Board rule 157 (fair-value accounting).

In short, this rule caused banks to value illiquid (or near-illiquid) assets using standards that simply didn't make sense. It forced banks into a near-self-perpetuating cycle of asset write-downs that basically obliterated their balance sheets, forcing them to sell other assets to comply with (fairly arbitrary) capital ratios. This forced a number of even large institutions to the brink—which didn't help investor sentiment at all. Further, the bear market started in late 2007—about when the rule went into practice—and ended in March 2009, when it became clear the rule would likely be suspended or killed. (And it has, in fact, since been killed.) My view is that's no coincidence.

Then, too, the government's response to financial firm weakness in 2008 was incredibly haphazard. Some firms were pushed into arranged marriages (like JP Morgan and Bear Stearns), some nationalized (like AIG and Fannie and Freddie) and some were simply left to die (Lehman). There was seemingly no rhyme or reason to how each situation was addressed—and markets don't like uncertainty.

My view is, without FAS 157 and then the haphazard government response, 2008 would have seen a big correction or even a smallish bear market. Then again, I might be wrong about that, and there'd be no way to know. My point is, if you aim to get long-term equity-like growth, you always face the risk of getting walloped, hard, by TGH. All you can do is learn what you can and keep investing by looking forward, not back.

A key lesson from the 2008 bear market was even small accounting or regulatory rule changes can have an outsized impact—so we built into my firm the muscle to review changes and analyze what future impact they may have. It was a hard lesson to learn, but investing is a nonstop query session—some lessons will be easier, some harder.

(For those interested in reading more on the 2008 credit crisis and how it evolved, I highly recommend *Senseless Panic*, by William Isaac, former chairman of the FDIC.)

The 70/30 Rule

I've been wrong quite a bit in my career. I'll be wrong again. I know it and expect it. That's all part of investing. And yet, CXO Advisory Group, an independent website ranking market prognosticators, has consistently ranked me among the most accurate long-term public forecasters anywhere based on my *Forbes* columns starting in 2000. (My *Forbes* columns are a good but not perfect proxy for the market strategies my firm deploys for our clients.)

How can it rank me so highly? As I've said in these pages, in investing, your aim shouldn't be perfection—that's impossible. Your aim should be to increase the odds you're right more than wrong. As I write in 2011, CXO gives me an accuracy percentage of 63% (you can find its "guru grades"—its terminology, not mine—at www.cxoadvisory.com). It doesn't have anyone right now at 70%. Just being right 51% is enough to give you an edge over the market—70% makes you an all-time legend. But that still means super-legends must be comfortable being wrong 30% of the time. If I could simply sign a contract to be right in the market 70% of the time and wrong 30%, I'd sign the contract, put down my money and never bet beyond that again. You might still get some market bets pretty astoundingly wrong, but over time, being right more than wrong wins out over pretty much everything.

What Causes a Bear Market?

There's simply no single answer to the question: What causes a bear market? It might be monetary conditions, yield curve shifts, surpluses, a sector implosion, excess demand reverting or bad legislation impacting property rights. But it likely won't be what it was last time. Two bear markets in a row rarely start with the same causes because most investors are always fighting the last war and are prepared for what took them down last time.

Maybe you suspect a bear market will start because the bull market has run on too long. Question One—is there a "right" time a bull market needs to last? No! There is no "right" length for a bull market. As bull markets run longer than average in duration, there is normally a steady stream of folks who say a bull market must end because it's too old. (Read more on this phenomenon in *Markets Never Forget*.) That isn't right. They all end for their own reasons and will end eventually—but age isn't among them. People started saying the 1990s bull market was too old in 1994, only about six years too soon. "Irrational exuberance" was first uttered in 1996—again, way too early. Bull markets can die at any age.

Use your Questions to test some of these. Find a few of your favorite indicators and see if they've reliably led to bear markets before. You will find there is no fundamental indicator on its own, no technical indicator on its own, no single silver bullet, no nothing on its own perfectly predicting when a bear market will start. Nor can you have a "feeling" indicating when you should get out. I hear from far too many investors (even professionals) they "have a funny feeling" about the market going one direction or the other they "can't explain," but they "just know." That's TGH. If it isn't, take an aspirin and an antacid and get over it. Then take Question Three for this one because that's what you really need. If you believe you've been right about a "funny feeling" in the past, you may have been. Luck happens. But you're also suffering hindsight bias and forgetting times you had "funny feelings" that were completely wrong.

Osama Bin Laden, Katrina and Foghorn Leghorn Walk Into a Bar

Some may say, "But we live in a different world now. A terrorist attack would break the market, right?" That's a fair question. The tragic attacks on September 11,

2001, came two-thirds of the way through a material preexisting bear market and a recession—possibly stalling off market resurgence (though we have no way to measure if that's true or not). So pull a Question One. Is it true September 11 had a lasting, devastating impact on the market?

The US stock market closed that day and stayed closed until September 17 when trading resumed. The S&P 500 nosedived when the market opened—down 11.6% by September 21.[6] But amazingly, in only 19 days, the US market was trading above September 10 levels. And it remained above those levels for months. We remember this differently because long before the attack, the global economy was in a recession and bear market. Did the attack exacerbate the situation? Maybe! But, again, the market retreaded the steep fall and stayed above pre-9/11 levels for months. Note the higher period included all those fears in the fall of 2001 about anthrax. Remember anthrax? The market moved higher right through it without interruption, lifting to prices steadily higher than on September 10.

As always, think globally to see how more recent terrorist attacks on Western nations have impacted the stock market in Figure 8.7.

On March 10, 2004, al Qaeda took credit for a massive train bombing in Madrid. The Spanish referred to the event as "Our 9/11"—a devastating national tragedy. And yet the S&P 500 dropped 1.5% that day and traded at pre-attack levels five trading sessions later. On July 7, 2005, al Qaeda bombed the London Underground, and the S&P 500 was positive that day. The market was indifferent to the attack.

Terror attacks have since continued, and markets largely shrug them off—continuing whatever trend they were on anyway. Whether all future attacks have already been discounted or not is debatable. But since 9/11, there has been no market panic to terror anywhere. How can investors be so blasé about terrorism? This is a new, terrible and very real threat to us wherever we live, work, travel and defend ourselves and our friends. Or is it? We have had previous terror attacks here in the US and on US interests. There was the *USS Cole* bombing in 2000. And the Khobar Towers were bombed in 1996. And that first attack on the Twin Towers in 1993. And the attack on the Marine barracks in Lebanon in 1983. And Pan Am Flight 103. And the entire history of Israel. And the Irish Republican Army in Britain. The British lived with terrorism on their soil seemingly forever, and their markets did fine then. World War I was sparked by a terrorist act. There were the Barbary pirates and Tripoli. You get what I am saying. Terrorism isn't new, devastating as it is at a human level. But we are resilient, and so are our markets. Figure 8.8 shows a number of terror attacks in recent history and the time the markets took to recover.

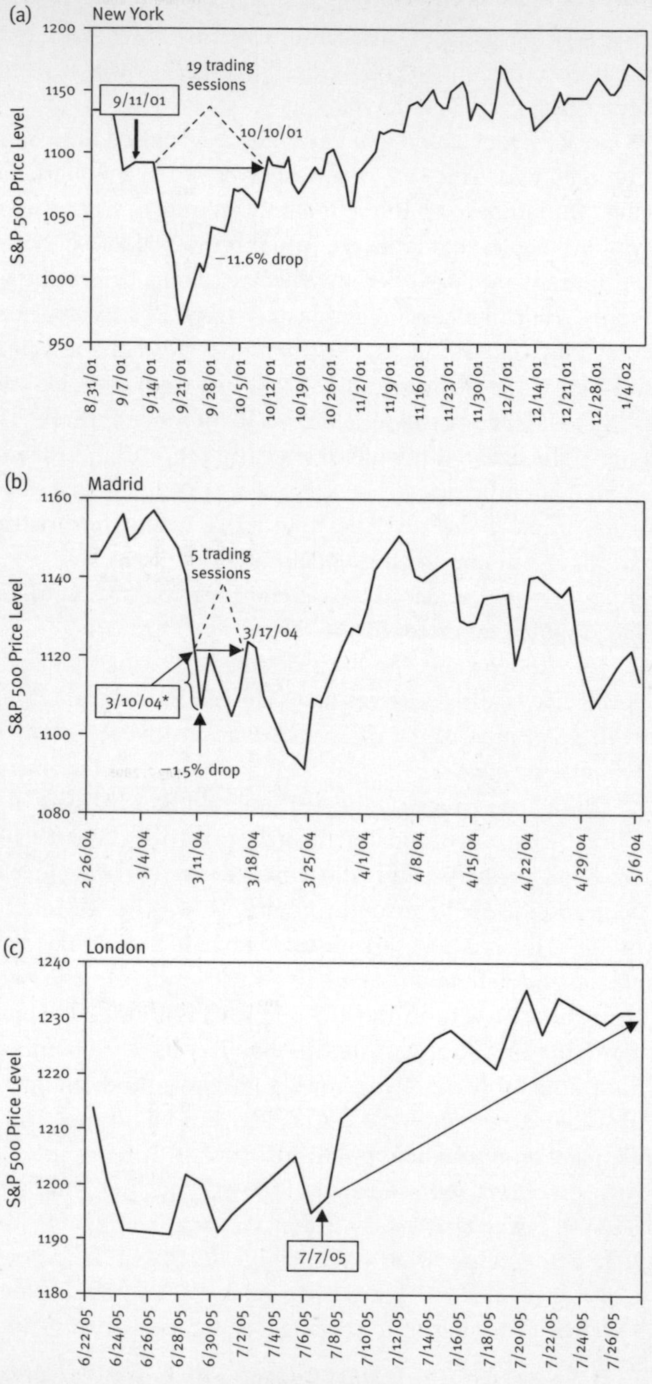

Figure 8.7 Have No Fear: The Market Doesn't
***Source:* Thomson Reuters.**

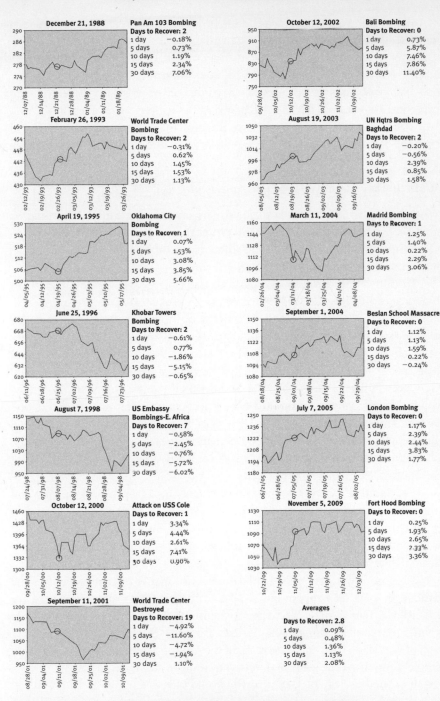

Figure 8.8   Have No Fear: The Market Doesn't—Historical Perspective
Source: Global Financial Data, Inc., S&P 500 price return.

But would a large terror attack now break the market? First, ask if another terrorist attack would surprise you. You may be more surprised—knock on wood—we've yet to experience another major American attack (as of this writing still in 2011). Put yourself back to September 10, 2001. No one fathomed 19 thugs armed only with box cutters would perpetrate a coordinated attack using planes and their passengers as bombs. That what happened would happen seemed unthinkable.

Today, it would take a lot to have a major market-moving surprise—and even the biggest terror attack in recent history had limited direct market impact.

What If They Destroyed a Major American City?

What if terrorists destroyed a major American city? Certainly, that would be terrible. But how big would the market impact be? Again, it might be less than you might think, and the way you know is partly by looking at the market impact of Hurricane Katrina on New Orleans.

In 2005, New Orleans and parts of the Gulf Coast were obliterated by Hurricanes Katrina and Rita. Much of the Gulf of Mexico's oil-refining capability came to a screeching halt. Hundreds of thousands in Texas, Louisiana and Mississippi were homeless or displaced. Businesses closed; employees were jobless. And yet the day Katrina hit Louisiana, August 29, 2005, the market rose 0.6%.[7] A pretty normal day given the flooding and ensuing chaos. And GDP growth for Q4 2005 was 2.1%, and the S&P 500 was up 2.1%.[8] Not blow-your-socks-off growth, but not the economic Armageddon many pundits predicted. Think about it this way: US stocks were up 2.1% in Q4 2005, and global stocks were up 3.1%—so the US market, even post-Katrina, was not too far off from the world.[9] Of course, maybe stocks would have risen more without Katrina. But who can prove that?

Yet, shouldn't GDP have been hurt hugely based on work stoppage and disruption of refining in the Gulf? New Orleans was decimated. That is a great Question Two to explore. Let's flip this one on its head: Why shouldn't GDP and stock returns be healthy following such a major natural disaster? Scale it, like always!

Suppose every person in Louisiana was suddenly unemployed after the two storms. Didn't happen, but suppose the worst-case scenario. There are 4.5 million Louisianans. Louisiana's income per capita is historically only about three-fourths as high as America's average.[10] So think about the population of Louisiana instead as about 1% of the United States' population. If every single person in the state of Louisiana stopped contributing to GDP as a result of the hurricanes, GDP growth would have been shaved by about 1%, one time. For one year, instead of maybe 4% growth, we would have gotten 3%, then moved on normally.

I don't mean to say Louisianans aren't productive people and important—but you shouldn't be surprised there was little impact on the overall economy's growth. America is huge. Louisiana is too small to impact America's GDP much. Then remember it's a global market and global economy, and America is only 23% of global GDP, so the impact on global growth would be smaller still.[11] Simple scaling.

Remember Grampa Fisher?

We also have history to use conveniently. The first thing I did when Katrina struck was pull out my stock charts and history books to remind myself of the natural disaster that devastated my hometown. When the 1906 fire and earthquake leveled San Francisco on April 18, 1906, little was left. Grampa Fisher (see Chapter 5) had to put off his wedding to my grandmother until later that year. They and their families lived with most of the rest of the city in tent camps in Golden Gate Park. My grandfather's medical practice was on hold for months as he devoted himself to pro bono work for those injured by the tragedy.

But the market didn't buckle. The US market dropped a hair in April, which might have happened anyway and might have been caused by other things (I don't really know) but was higher again in May and June and didn't implode that year. The major buckle was the next year, 1907, with a New York–based banking panic and the market dropping 49%, peak to trough.[12] But San Francisco in 1906 was more important to America than New Orleans in 2005. San Francisco's demise not causing the market to implode in 1906 was a pretty good guideline from history to tell you not to worry about Katrina too much from a stock market perspective. And to tell you not to worry about markets too much if the terrorists, heaven forbid, ever do succeed at causing real havoc in an American city.

You can use the Questions and this methodology to attack other presumably "bearish" events, such as outbreaks of SARS, the bird flu, Ebola, hanta virus, anthrax, chicken pox, etc. Just as SARS was a big 2003 health scare (now long forgotten), in 2005 and 2006, concerns about bird flu morphing to a human-transmittable form were rampant—and again, markets were fine.

Use your Questions to test if any geopolitical event, natural disaster, health crisis, anything we all worry about, plan for, fret about and hear on the news is inherently likely to move the market materially. You will find none of these events is a silver bullet for predicting bear markets.

Now that you have Question Three tools for recognizing the likely direction of the market and can understand what a real bear market does (and doesn't) generally look like, you are ready to build a real strategy to serve you your entire life. Read on.

9 PUTTING IT ALL TOGETHER

Stick With Your Strategy and Stick It to Him

As Chapter 3 hinted, one tool to stay disciplined with the Three Questions and keep your scurrilous brain in check and not be humiliated by TGH is having a comprehensive strategy driving decisions. Just using the Three Questions is great! But a strategy provides a basis and framework from which you can ask the Three Questions and make small (or big) bets keeping you on the path toward your goals.

Maybe you think you already have a pretty good strategy. Fair enough—but many investors who believe they have a strategy may confuse tactics with strategy. For example, some investors want market-like returns with low fees, so they may want a "strategy" of buying no-load mutual funds. That is a philosophy, not a strategy. Operating that way without a strategy, 30 years later, you may not have paid any load fees! But you also may not have gotten decent returns.

Another tactic many investors (including many professionals) use, believing it is a strategy, is rigid adherence to a static asset allocation—i.e., fixed percentages of stocks, bonds and cash. Static asset allocation may be a fine self-control mechanism for people who otherwise lack self-control, just like having someone else prepare all your meals can control your weight if you can't hack it on your own. But static asset allocation ensures you can't take advantage of the Three Questions when opportunity knocks.

Investors also use stop losses and dollar-cost averaging (both self-control mechanisms and also provably losing strategies I detail in Appendix H), buy and sell options and covered calls (another losing proposition in Appendix I), short here, go double-long there—all believing they have a strategy that works, not realizing they may just be spinning their wheels with tactics. Some fine. Some not. But all tactics. A gaggle of fancy but ineffectual tactics do not a strategy make.

There's nothing wrong with deploying a particular appropriate tactic (emphasis on appropriate, i.e., not stop losses) at a given time. But it's no more a strategy than a hammer is a blueprint for a home. What's more, what's the point of using tactics if you don't know something others don't? You want the hammer only when it's the right tactic to accomplish the strategy. You're far better off using the Questions to figure out something others don't know and using that knowledge to get ahead, rather than possibly losing your money in a slow trickle through tricky investment tactics without a strategy.

A strategy is a plan guiding your every decision. It keeps you disciplined when you're tempted to stray. The market simply isn't intuitive—one reason so many fail at it. Usually, what's right feels wrong, and what feels wrong often is right. This is why you need the Questions and a strategy to keep your brain in line.

Before you begin thinking about a strategy, let's establish a few ground rules about what you can hope to achieve. Ask anyone what their investing goals are, and you'll find a plethora of answers. Think of your own goals. Can you describe them simply in a sentence or two? If it takes 10 pages with accompanying visuals, you may not have as clear a strategy as you think. No, it should be fairly straightforward and specific to you.

For example, have you ever been asked by a financial adviser to rank your level of "risk tolerance"? Your inquirer may have had you fill out a questionnaire to determine what kind of investor you are. But very often, such check-the-box surveys best reflect how you feel *that day*. What's more, you may be asked if you fit in certain broad-but-undefined categories like "growth," "aggressive growth," "growth and income," etc. Maybe you were asked to pick from a selection of colorful pie graphs or rank yourself on a scale of 1 to 7, or 1 to 10, or 1 to 37.

The problem I find in this method is, first, what's growth to one person is aggressive to someone else is conservative to someone else. What's more, feelings investors have can change! The same folks who filled out questionnaires in 1999 saying they were highly risk tolerant and sought 20% returns year after year were saying they were risk averse in 2002 and 2003 and merely wanted low, safe, absolute returns. Nothing about their long-term goals and needs may have changed materially, just the way they felt about recent market action. And if they make changes to their long-term strategy based on how they feel about recent market action, they could be making a costly mistake—one that may not materialize until too far down the road to do much about it.

Sometimes, as an individual investor, it can be hard to determine if your own self-assessment of risk tolerance is driven by your actual long-term goals or if it's influenced by what you've read recently, what has happened to you recently, who you're talking to and what you think they're supposed to say in response to such questions.

Then, too, investors' responses may differ depending on whether they're with their spouse and offspring or not. It's a lot easier for a guy to fancy a pirate's lifestyle buccaneering the South Seas for adventure and booty when he's alone watching a pirate movie than when he's with his wife.

As Meir Statman and I demonstrated in a scholarly article titled "The Mean Variance Optimization Puzzle: Security Portfolios and Food Portfolios,"[1] risk is multifaceted and virtually impossible to fully comprehend in any moment for anyone. Your brain deals with investing risk just like it does with food and diet. Eaters and investors want at least six things at once—in both investing and their next meal. The risk they feel at any time is tied to whichever of those things they're not getting, without regard for how they would feel if they didn't get the things they *are* getting. It's tough for your brain to put it all together at once—it fixates on what it isn't getting, and to you, that's risk.

I won't fully rehash that article here. But investors not only want return, of course, they want to keep up with the Joneses, or not to suffer from excess opportunity cost. This is why the person who envisions he only wants 10% a year actually feels angst when the market is up 35% and he is only up 20%. To him, that's risk. Investors also fear volatility and see it as risk. It is. Finance theory has been excessive in portraying volatility as the risk measure. But it's just *one* risk and preys more on some than others. Of course, investors want pricing. Different investors want the pricing differently, but they feel risk if it becomes inconsistent with their sense of what it should be. They want packaging. Packaging ripples into all the other risks but includes presentation, ease of use and part of the sense of confidence implying safety and less risk that is basic to all marketing. They want prestige. Prestige can mean many things, including branding (appealing to that sense of uniqueness), a general sense of safety or lack of risk from perceived quality and a sense of higher social order than others. Another way to think of this is "bragging rights"—i.e., "I got in on Google's IPO, and you didn't." But if you take the prestige away suddenly, it feels like risk to them.

Then they want order preference. Few appreciate how important order preference is to everyone, but you can see it two ways in diet. One is why people eat breakfast foods in the morning and dinner foods at night—why not switch them around? Same calories, and yet people largely obey order even when no one is looking. The second is how people don't experiment with the foods they combine. Why not try putting salad dressing in your coffee and cream on your salad or even your steak to see how it would taste? Might be better! You don't try because it violates order preference. And if you tried that in public at a restaurant, the people with whom you dined wouldn't dine with you again. They would think you were a nut.

My point is, at any moment, the risk you notice and fret is associated with what you're *not* getting. And it's near impossible to make your brain realize all the other things that you *are* getting and how you would feel—how you would experience the risk—about not getting some combination of them.

Growth—Or Income—Or Both

You're a unique, wonderful person, I have no doubt; however, you're probably unique just about like most everyone else. You're not statistically unique. In a statistical sense, being unique is to be way, way out the end of the bell curve on some set of attributes. If you're really unique, you're technically quite weird. Most folks like to think of themselves as unique but don't like to see themselves as weirdos. As such, if you're a long-term investor, you probably share similar investing goals with a fair-size chunk of humanity. What's more, when boiled down, investing goals can fit into three basic categories:

1. Maximize terminal value
2. Cash flow
3. Some combination of the two

Maximize Terminal Value

If maximizing terminal value is your goal, you're looking to grow your portfolio to fund retirement, to purchase something now or in the future (a first or second home, a college education, a boat, etc.) or to pass to loved ones or a favorite charity. You might also think of this goal as "growth."

But "maximizing terminal value" doesn't necessarily mean increasing your pot of money. You might need to stretch your money enough to satisfy cash flow needs (the next goal). For example, a common response when asking someone what the primary purpose of his or her money is, is that it's to take care of him or her and the spouse for the remainder of their lives. That may involve growing their total money or simply stretching it. But it's probably the most common single case among investors everywhere.

Cash Flow

Many investors need their money to provide "income" to cover living expenses—now or in the future. In an extreme example, some folks might be very happy if Daddy simply died and left a guaranteed income stream and they had no say in the investments and not necessarily any knowledge of how the assets are invested. Just like Gertrude Stein. Party time!

Of course, the party-time inheritor isn't really concerned with "income" as that term is technically defined by industry wonks. What he/she wants is predictable and secure *cash flow*.

Cash flow is the better way to think about this. Finance theory is clear we should be agnostic about our preferences for type of cash flow on a real, tax- and risk-adjusted basis. For example, after tax, it doesn't much matter if our cash flow comes from dividends (which may be risky or not) or capital gains (which may be risky or not). Income streams are neither better nor worse for generating total return than capital gains. We should care about *total return* after adjusting for tax and risk—otherwise, how the cash flow comes is unimportant.

Terminal value or cash flow or some combination of the two—that's about it! (Although there is a very wide variety of subsets falling under these headings, such as, "I want to leave as much as I can after I die to the Save the Seals League," which means maximizing terminal value, in this case, for the purpose of charity.) Sound fair? For example, an investor who is 50 may see the primary purpose of his money as taking care of him (or her) and a spouse for the rest of their lives—but they have a secondary purpose of leaving a certain amount to their offspring and more to charity. They want to maximize the likelihood of that being done successfully by maximizing their terminal value at the end of their lives. Doing so allows the cash flow they need to support their lifestyle while leaving a present for the kids (and maybe the seals). That seals it for them. Most long-term investors are somewhere on the scale of needing terminal value, cash flow or both.

What About Capital Preservation?

There is yet a fourth possible goal—true capital preservation. True capital preservation means taking absolutely no risk to preserve the nominal value of your assets. In my experience, capital preservation as a long-term goal is more rare than folks think. It would apply if you know you already have much more money than you'll ever need, and you are confident inflation won't erode your purchasing power—i.e., you have no desire for more, and your primary purpose is to minimize your worry or hassle factor. Then it can make sense. But for folks investing for the long haul, my experience tells me that's rarely the case.

On a shorter-term basis, capital preservation can make sense! Some folks might be saving for the down payment on a home in six months. It makes sense then to preserve the cash needed for that home in a low-risk instrument like a CD. For a near-term goal like that, you want to avoid the inherently higher volatility of stocks. But generally, if you bought this book, you're not stashing the bulk of your cash under the mattress and have some longer-term purpose for your money.

Capital preservation is the polar opposite of growth. You often hear investors hankering for—and you may hear some investment professionals offering up—"capital preservation and growth." Sounds great! Who doesn't want to preserve capital *and* grow it? But it's like a fat-free steak. The two goals combined just aren't possible.

Why? To get some growth, you must take some volatility risk—to some varying degree. Capital preservation is the *absence* of volatility risk. The notion of combining the two implies riskless return, which is impossible.

GROWTH WITH NO VOLATILITY? MORE DANGEROUS THAN YOU THINK

Readers in 2012 will doubtless remember the sad fallout from the Madoff and Stanford Ponzi scandals. Both of these gentlemen (allegedly, in Stanford's case, who still awaits trial) marketed big returns with limited risk and little year-to-year return variability. Unfortunately, as their clients found out, such a thing is impossible. (Read more in my 2009 book, *How to Smell a Rat,* which details signs that can help you avoid becoming a financial Ponzi victim.)

Now, if your goal is growth, and 20 years from now your account has doubled two or three times (which isn't outrageous to expect if you benchmark against an equity index), you have effectively grown your account *and* preserved your initial capital to boot. However, during those 20 years, your account was up and down with the market. You got growth while enduring volatility and other risks. But you had a long time frame, and, at the end of the day, you got your equity-like return. But if your goal is really, truly, true capital preservation, 20 years from now, you'll still have your initial capital and nothing else.

If someone in the finance world offers you "capital preservation and growth," know they may be either incompetent or ill intended—either way, dangerous.

Make no mistake. Most investors need some degree of growth or they wouldn't bother with stocks, bonds or anything involving risk in the first place. If your goal is to never lose a dime over any period—true capital preservation—you should have saved what you paid for this book and stashed it instead under your mattress. Of course, even if your goal is avoiding all monetary loss, the mattress stash isn't the best bet because of inflation's long-term effect. *Inflation risk* is the weak underbelly of those seeking capital preservation. How do you really preserve capital without risk if inflation ignites? It really is hard, if not impossible, to avoid all risk.

Four Rules That Count

So—terminal value or cash flow or both? But how do you achieve those goals? And how do you start aiming to be right more often than wrong? Just as you don't need advanced scholarship or apprenticeship to learn to use the Questions, building a strategy can be as easy as following four rules my firm employs every day in managing money:

Rule Number One: Select an appropriate benchmark.

Rule Number Two: Analyze the benchmark's components and assign expected risk and return.

Rule Number Three: Blend non-correlated or negatively correlated securities to moderate risk relative to expected return.

Rule Number Four: Always remember you can be wrong, so don't stray from the first three rules.

Let's examine these four rules more closely.

Rule Number One: Select an Appropriate Benchmark

You know the benchmark is vital to success. You know what a benchmark should be (well constructed) and what it shouldn't be (price-weighted like the Dow). As important, your benchmark should be **appropriate for you**. It will dictate how much volatility you're likely to experience, your return expectation, even to some extent what ends up in your portfolio. It's your road map, your measuring stick. You shouldn't change it, not soon, unless something really radical happens to you, changing the primary purpose of your money. Something materially impacting your time horizon one way or another—like your spouse passing away, which could shorten your expected time horizon, or you remarry a younger spouse, which could lengthen it. Or something materially impacting your goals—like something changes about how much future cash flow you'll need. So it's crucial you select the right benchmark for you.

Your benchmark can be all equity (as we discussed), all fixed income or a blend of the two. Picking a benchmark—deciding if you need an all-equity, blended or even an all–fixed income benchmark—depends primarily on four things. Throw the nonsense "risk tolerance" survey baloney out the window. The four factors for figuring which benchmark is appropriate for you are: (1) your time horizon, (2) how much cash flow you need and when, (3) your return expectations and (4) any other portfolio-specific needs unique to you. For example, you're a senior executive for Big Company X and therefore can't own their stock. Or you don't want to own so-called sin stocks (tobacco, gambling, whatever you choose). Or you have weird but strong-felt views, like you hate the French or don't want to own stocks that produce you-name-it—tofu—whatever.

RISK-TOLERANCE BALONEY?

Since I first wrote this book, now six years ago, a few folks have criticized the line: "Throw the nonsense 'risk tolerance' baloney out the window." For folks doing a surface read (i.e., not reading the many pages leading up, or any of the pages that followed), they presume that means I don't think risk tolerance matters. They are incorrect. Risk tolerance does matter. Very much! In fact, this entire chapter (and, indeed, the entire book) is basically about risk tolerance and determining the appropriate amount of risk to take to increase the likelihood of achieving an investor's goals!

What I believed then (and believe now) is "baloney" is the idea there is some kind of check-the-box survey that can correctly assess the amount of risk someone can tolerate. Instead, understanding what amount of risk is appropriate to increase the likelihood of reaching investors' long-term goals requires a deeper understanding of their time horizons, goals, cash flow needs and any other factors unique to them that may impact portfolio strategy. That means doing an in-depth discovery process and then periodically revisiting the time horizon, goals, needs, etc., to ensure the strategy remains appropriate.

In my view, you can't accurately determine someone's tolerance for risk and build an appropriate strategy by asking them to tick a few boxes at one point in time.

The First Determinant: Time Horizon

Your time horizon may be your life expectancy but could be longer. Unless you hate your spouse, you should consider his or her life expectancy as well, which may extend your time horizon. If you like your kids and want to leave something behind for them, that also extends your time horizon. Simply put, your time horizon is how long you need your assets to last. Your time horizon is decidedly not how long it is until you retire or plan to start taking distributions. Far too many investors think wrongly about time horizon; they aren't using Questions One and Two to see this clearly.

COOKIE-CUTTER TIME HORIZON

The financial services industry in some part has promoted wrong thinking about time horizon, in my view. You've probably heard the old adage: "Take 100 (or 120), subtract your age, and that's the percentage you should have in stocks." This presumes the *only* factor that matters is your age! But there are myriad other factors that should be considered. I address time horizon further in Chapter 4 of my 2010 book, *Debunkery*.

You very often hear people say something like, "I'm retiring, so I must become conservative, and I can't take risk." But suppose you're a 65-year-old man, and your wife is 60 and likely to live to 90 (very common). Then you may have a 30-year time horizon that includes a third of her whole life! If you move heavily away from stocks, history says she's likelier to suffer aged poverty. Now, if you really hate her, then aged poverty is a pretty good idea. My guess, though, is that's not the intention of most people reading this book.

You may have some reasonable date in mind for when you plan to start living off your assets, but the money still needs to work your whole life or beyond, or you or your loved ones will suffer. That whole period is your time horizon.

You might have a shorter time horizon for some reason—maybe you're a 32-year-old who needs every penny to pay for that first home in three years. But in most cases, investors tend to grossly underestimate their time horizons. Because both my parents lived well into their 90s, it's easy for me to envision long time horizons. It's late in life people need their money because there are so many comforts that benefit the aged that aren't covered by any form of health insurance.

Stocks or Bonds? The 896% Question

If your time horizon is over 20 years—and if you're reading this book, it probably is—an all-equity benchmark may be most appropriate for you. Not guaranteed, because you must also consider cash flow needs and other factors. But over long time periods, stocks are by far the best-performing liquid asset class historically, and the likelihood stocks outperform bonds is great. Since 1926 through year-end 2010, there have been 66 20-year rolling time periods. In 64 of them stocks have outperformed bonds by a wide margin.[2] That's 97% of the time. In return for investing in stocks over a 20-year period, folks got an average return of 896% compared to 245% for bonds. During the two 20-year periods when bonds beat stocks, bonds returned an average 262% and stocks 243%—bonds outperformed by a 1.1-to-1 margin.[3] Not much—and stocks were still positive. Over history, it's been better to take on the odds and get the superior return.

Over even longer periods, there's simply been no contest. Measuring 30-year rolling periods, on average, stocks have returned 2,473% and bonds 532%—stocks beat bonds by a 4.6-to-1 margin on average. And bonds have never beat stocks over 30 years.[4]

You may feel as though I'm banging an equity drum. I am a big fan of stocks because of their superior longer-term returns (and lots of other reasons—recall that I pray at the altar of Capitalism's multitudinous blessings, and you can't have Capitalism without stocks), and I do believe folks frequently underestimate the proportion of stocks they should have in their benchmark. However, there are times when stocks do lousy—in a bear market—and avoiding a down-a-lot world through cash holdings can be a great tactic. But it's not a strategy.

The Second Determinant: Cash Flow

After determining time horizon, next consider cash flow needs. But it's not as easy as saying, "If you need 3% cash flow, you should have X% fixed income in your benchmark. If you need 4%, you need Y%." You must weigh such considerations against your other objectives and the likelihood of long-term survival of the assets.

Said another way: Two couples with identical time horizons, similar size portfolios and identical cash flow needs as a percent of their portfolio may well need very different benchmarks. Just because they are different people with different long-term objectives.

For a couple who needs 4% cash flow, a 100% equity benchmark may be appropriate if they are equally (or more) focused on growing their portfolio.

The other couple may care much more about just the cash flow— doesn't want to leave anything to kids or grandkids. They just need their portfolio to stretch enough to cover the cash flow. For them, a bigger allocation of fixed income in their benchmark may be appropriate.

Still, even with a blended benchmark—60% equity and 40% fixed income or 70%/30% or whatever—there may come a time when you should boost your cash to 100% to be defensive temporarily, and you shouldn't get lulled into a false sense of security with a blended benchmark. Your benchmark is your road map but not necessarily what you own all the time. In a major bear market, you'll still lose money with a rigid fixed allocation. Sometimes you need a detour. Or a dividend!

Homegrown Dividends

Another reason investors hit a panic button at or near retirement and believe they should plow all of their hard-earned assets into bonds and high-dividend-paying stocks is they may think they need the coupon payments and dividends for income. They believe if they kick off a decent percentage in income, they can sit back and let the portfolio provide for retirement. As mentioned earlier, this confuses *income* with *cash flow*.

Use Question One for this myth (and it is a myth). Is it true a portfolio stacked with bonds and high-dividend stocks will provide income throughout retirement? Maybe! Maybe you're worth $10 million and want only $50,000 a year. Maybe you don't need your assets to grow so your income doesn't get degraded by inflation. Maybe it doesn't matter much if you see your assets diminished through reinvestment risk or if the high-dividend-paying stocks tank in value.

But most folks reading this probably can't afford to have their assets stagnate or decrease significantly throughout retirement. What happens when you reinvest a maturing 6% bond from 2001, and the only thing you can buy in 2011 that isn't risky yields 1.5%? And how about when that dandy utility stock paying an 8% dividend depreciates 40% in price? That company likely slashes its dividend—a rational thing to do. Then, too, a lower percent of a lower market value is probably not what you were banking on. And what about inflation?

It's simply not true coupon payments and dividends are a surefire "safe" way to garner income from your portfolio. But how else do you get cash? If you have an all-equity benchmark and you need cash flow, you don't want to sell stock to provide cash for yourself. Do you?

Well, why the heck not? What's it there for? This is a Question Two solution I've come up with for maintaining growth while providing cash flow from portfolios, and I call it *homegrown dividends*.

Let's say you have a million-dollar portfolio, and you take $40,000 a year in even monthly distributions of $3,333 a month—give or take. You should keep about twice that much in cash in your portfolio at all times so you don't rush to sell a nitpicky number of stocks each month. Then you can be tactical about what you sell and when. But you're always looking to prune back, planning for distributions a month or two out. You can sell down stocks to use as a tax loss to offset gains you might realize. You can pare back overweighted positions. You'll probably always have some dividend-paying stocks to add some cash, but that is a derivative of picking the right kinds. Homegrown dividends are tax efficient, cheap to raise and keep you fully and appropriately invested.

The Third Determinant: Return Expectation

The third factor in selecting an appropriate benchmark is return expectation. If you're 50 and want to retire in five years and need $500,000 a year in cash flow to maintain your lifestyle and have $2 million total saved in your portfolio, you're in for a caught-with-your-pants-down rude awakening. Your return expectations are gonzo high. Unless you anticipate a windfall on the order of $10 million (or so) sometime in the in-your-dreams future, plan instead on taking $80,000 a year or less and get over it. Or keep working. Start figuring out a way to explain this to your wife (or husband) now.

But imagine an investor, call her Jane, who has a reliable income source lined up for her retirement (a pension, perhaps, with some rental income). She doesn't need her assets to grow to provide for her and her husband. Jane intends to leave her money to her kids but doesn't really care about maximizing terminal value. Instead, she is nervous about volatility and looking for that sleep-at-night factor.

For her, an all-equity benchmark may still be appropriate. Maybe not. You'd need to know more about her—but don't automatically rule out any options yet.

Why? Because Jane has a long time horizon and needs no income. I'd want to understand more of what she thinks volatility is and how that would impact her. And I'd want to more deeply understand her goals. And what is it that's keeping her from sleeping at night, exactly? What makes investors sleep at night can differ radically. As stated earlier, few investors envision their future risk orientation correctly. If you base a long-term strategy solely on how you feel *right now* and ignore all other factors, you could be making a major mistake. Will Jane feel differently in three months, nine months or a few years? And, 20 years from now, will Jane find she *really* can't sleep at night because she avoided stocks too heavily and now has much less of a portfolio cushion than she envisioned? You have to consider that among the other factors that influence a benchmark decision.

The Fourth Determinant: Individual Peculiarity

Just because most investors have similar goals and aren't as unique as they think doesn't mean they're not peculiar. This isn't about "being uncomfortable" with foreign investing, Health Care stocks, Tech, Emerging Markets or whatever because that could be more stubbornness than peculiarity. This is about having strong feelings about a particular company or a narrow sector deriving from personal belief, peculiarity or some other situation unique to you. And it's ok to create a customized benchmark reflecting your own weird idiosyncrasies.

You may simply want to never, ever own a French stock. Or the stock of a firm making tobacco products. Or a firm making tofu (ugh!). Or maybe you work for publicly traded firm ABC and can't own its stock. Whatever! It's fine to have a customized benchmark that is the World ex-France. Or the World ex-France and ex-tofu. Or ex-ABC. All fine reasons, and all should be considered as you select your benchmark.

Since all major categories should have similar long-term returns, the degree of return variation caused by those slight variances from a vastly bigger and maybe global benchmark won't be enough to count. And they'll make you feel better about what you're doing so you're more likely to keep doing it. There are no investors who have had a bad investing history having otherwise done portfolio management right because they chose to create their own customized benchmark that was the World ex-Iowa (for those of you who divorced someone from there once. Still, were I you, I'd rather get my revenge on the Iowans by buying Iowa stocks too cheap).

Whatever it is, you may have strong enough personal feelings to warrant a particular benchmark free from some offending stock or microsector. But watch if you start having feelings about whole sectors because that might be driven more by loss aversion and hindsight bias than your own individual freakiness. Plenty of investors decided they had developed a severe allergic reaction to Tech post-2002. That is a cognitive error, not a peculiarity.

So, the amount of risk appropriate for your long-term goals should be driven primarily by (1) time horizon, (2) income needs, (3) return expectation and (4) extreme individual peculiarities. Jane may consider herself risk averse now, but in 1999, did she consider herself aggressive and overweight to Tech stocks? She might feel differently again, depending on what the stock market has done in the near and immediate past. That can be a dangerous way to build a long-term strategy. Feelings can change fast. What typically don't change much, not without a major event, are how long your assets must last and how much cash flow you will take. And, of course, if you're morally opposed to tobacco now, you probably will be in the future, too. That won't go up in smoke.

I'm not saying you must have an all-equity benchmark if it will cause (or exacerbate) ulcers. I'm just saying the cause of the ulcers may be something else. Explore it a bit before committing to a benchmark, long term.

Heat Chasing—To Shift or Not to Shift

Choose your benchmark carefully because once selected, it's yours for a very long time—maybe the entire life of your assets. Superficial benchmark shifting is a recipe for disaster. Let's call benchmark shifting what it really is—heat chasing. When someone shifted their benchmark from the Nasdaq in 1999 to the Russell 2000 Value Index in 2005, you know they were matching their benchmark to what had been hot—simple heat chasing. People chasing heat forget about transaction costs and taxes and invariably in-and-out relatively backward—lagging the market by going into what used to work instead of what is likely to work moving forward.

You now know all well-constructed benchmarks should get to about the same place over the very long term. If you get the urge to switch benchmarks, check yourself and ask Question Three. Benchmark switching can be the direct result of regret shunning and pride accumulation, possibly some order preference and overconfidence to boot. Don't give in. If you switch, you may end up chasing heat and missing returns altogether. Only heartache and harm come from it.

There are two good exceptions to this rule—only two. One is if something happens to drastically change the primary purposes of your money, including your time horizon. This is the 75-year-old in bad health from a short-lived family with a 70-year-old wife in good health from a long-lived family where the wife dies unexpectedly in a car crash. No kids, no charity and his time horizon just collapsed. That's a good justification for switching to a benchmark more appropriate for a new shorter and sadder time horizon. Or the other way around: Maybe late in life you remarry a younger or healthier person, extending your time horizon. It would be ok to switch to a more appropriate benchmark then, too. Included here would also be a change to cash flow needs. Maybe later in life you discover you need more cash flow from your portfolio. Or less! Either one would warrant a reexamination of the benchmark.

The second reason to switch benchmarks, beyond a change in the fundamentals of your life, is if a future benchmark is created reflecting the same universe as your current benchmark—but the new one is somehow better constructed.

This is purely tactical. Here is an example: The MSCI World Index is an excellent, broad benchmark, but it doesn't include Emerging Markets, restricting itself to developed markets. Then MSCI created the ACWI. Same construction but broader. That should be better for the whole world.

Should you use one over the other? In my mind, it isn't a big deal one way or the other, and I'm prone to not switching—it's hard to argue the one is drastically superior to the other. If you're currently using the MSCI World, the time to switch would be when ACWI was older, after a period when Emerging Markets had done lousy for years.

The whole World-versus-ACWI issue is sort of like choosing either the northern 80/90 route or the southern 70/44/40 route to motor across America. Either is an ok benchmark and gets from East to West Coast just fine. But if there were a new world index—improved and drastically more reflective of the whole world stock market—that would justify switching, too. What I want you to see is it takes something pretty material to justify a benchmark switch.

Rule Number Two: Analyze the Benchmark's Components, Assign Expected Risk and Return

The second rule of portfolio management helps determine what exactly belongs in your portfolio, how much and when. Your benchmark, particularly if you use a broad one, will be made up of different components, as discussed in Chapter 4. The Nasdaq is fairly easy—do you think Tech will do well this year or not? But unless you seek an exceedingly bumpy ride, we've already established you probably shouldn't use Nasdaq as your benchmark.

No matter which benchmark you pick, it's your guide for building your portfolio. If your benchmark is about 60% US stocks, your starting point for your portfolio should be about 60% US stocks—unless you've used the Questions to know something others don't. (If you have, you might at a point in time own no stocks at all.) If your benchmark is about 10% Energy, you should be about 10% Energy if you don't know something others don't. (But if you think you know something others don't, you might own no Energy, 5% Energy or be double weight at 20% Energy because you have the basis for a bet.) Your aim is to perform similarly to your benchmark if you don't know something others don't and better than the benchmark if you do believe you know something. Of course, the more you know that others don't, the bigger you might make your bets, and the more dissimilar you might be to your benchmark. (If you can't recall how the heck to tell what "components" are in your benchmark, flip back to Chapter 4.)

Nervous about doing it right? Don't be. If you have less than $200,000 or so to invest, you will probably and primarily be buying funds anyway. There are plenty of index funds that can get you the exposure you need. For example, if the S&P 500 is your benchmark, you're covered beautifully with an S&P 500 index fund. Using the MSCI World or ACWI as your benchmark? Check www.msci.com for the approximate weight of the United States relative to the world (it's been fluctuating around 50/50). Buy the aforementioned S&P 500 index fund with half your dough and an MSCI EAFE (Europe, Australia, Far East) index fund with the other half. Want to beat the market? It's harder to do if you have fewer choices to make, as you will with funds. This is why a broad benchmark with lots of components gives you more market-beating opportunities. You can use your Three Questions to make foreign versus US bets. And you can use other ETFs to make bets on sectors or styles without ever owning individual stocks, which is hard to do with a smaller portfolio.

If you're richer, you can and should buy individual stocks. The more money you have, the higher the proportion that should be in underlying stocks because, in large volume, stocks are cheaper to own than anything including mutual funds, ETFs or any other form of equity. One benefit of stocks is they're cheap to buy and pretty much free to hold. But whether ETFs or individual stocks, start paying attention to individual sectors and subsectors now. All this information is also on the index's webpage. For example, your components and their weights will look something like Table 9.1, where we have listed the percentage weights of countries and sectors in the MSCI World Index as of September 30, 2011.

You should check back periodically to ensure nothing has gotten out of whack. Don't feel compelled to rebalance if your portfolio or the benchmark has shifted a few percentage points here and there. Don't sweat the small stuff. Think about rebalancing once or twice a year unless there is a major sector or country move or you come upon something in between where suddenly you know something others don't. You'll make fewer mistakes and pay fewer fees. Trading too often is a byproduct of overconfidence (thinking you have the basis for a bet when you don't).

With benchmark components in hand, move on to assigning expected risk and return. Suppose you're using the ACWI. It's made up of 45 countries, including America.[5] Which countries should perform well this year, and which should lag? Use the Three Questions to see if you can find something that might make you favor one country or region more, another less.

The same goes for sectors. Use the Three Questions to decide if what you know about current economic, political and sentiment drivers favors one sector more than another. (Also, if you want more of a primer on analyzing sectors, I recommend the *Fisher Investments On* series, published by Wiley.)

Table 9.1   MSCI World Index Weights—Sectors and Countries

Sector	Weight
Energy	10.9%
Materials	7.3%
Industrials	10.7%
Consumer Discretionary	10.4%
Consumer Staples	11.1%
Health Care	10.5%
Financials	18.1%
Information Technology	12.2%
Telecommunication Services	4.6%
Utilities	4.2%

Country	Weight
Austria	0.1%
Australia	3.7%
Belgium	0.4%
Canada	5.2%
Switzerland	3.8%
Germany	3.4%
Denmark	0.4%
Spain	1.5%
Finland	0.4%
France	4.0%
Greece	0.1%
Hong Kong	1.2%
Ireland	0.1%
Italy	1.0%
Israel	0.3%
Japan	10.1%
Netherlands	1.1%
Norway	0.4%
New Zealand	0.1%
Portugal	0.1%
Sweden	1.3%
Singapore	0.8%
United Kingdom	9.7%
United States	50.9%

Source: Thomson Reuters, as of 09/30/2011.

The object is to make bets that are right more often than wrong while managing risk relative to the benchmark. Correlate the size of your bet according to how confident (but not overconfident) you are. Yes, a bigger over- or underweight has the potential to pay off big *if you're right*. But big bets can just as easily go the other way.

If Technology is 20% of your benchmark, and you're really, *really* confident it will hugely outperform, maybe you double that weight—to 40%. But that's a huge overweight—maybe as big as you ever want to go. Remember you must take that weight away from something (or somethings) else. If you're right, that's a big win for you—this time. But if you're wrong and Tech tanks, you may have taken weight away from something that performed better—dinging yourself twice. Are you prepared to handle that? Use your benchmark as a leash to keep your bets in line with how confident you are.

What if you can't find something others don't know, and you don't feel comfortable making a particular forecast for a country or sector? Just be neutral. The idea is to be right more often than wrong, not lucky and right some and unlucky and wrong more.

Rule Number Three: Blend Non-Correlated or Negatively Correlated Securities to Moderate Risk Relative to Expected Return

Most investors, even new investors, understand intuitively diversification helps reduce risk. Remember the poor Enron employees with their 401(k)'s all or mostly in Enron stock? Huge stock-related losses can be avoided through diversification. Companies go bankrupt for many reasons. Stocks implode for even more reasons. The CEO may have done nothing wrong—just couldn't compete with fire-breathing competitors. The stock of a perfectly healthy firm can tank for no seeming reason—with no forewarning. This is why no one stock should make up too much of your holdings.

My father was a lifelong advocate of concentrated portfolios. Warren Buffett has always been an advocate of concentrated portfolios. Yet I say to you the only basis for a concentrated portfolio is near-infinite faith you know a lot others don't know. That won't allow for overconfidence. You must be certain you're not overconfident. If you don't really know a lot others don't know, concentrating portfolios is simply an exercise in overconfidence and increased risk. Stick to the general guideline of never owning more than 5% of one stock.

Owning less than 5% of one stock doesn't mean in just one account. If you have a 401(k), an IRA and a taxable brokerage account, make sure you keep single stock ownership to less than 5% across all of your accounts.

THE 5% RULE?

In my 2010 book, *Debunkery*, I clarify this rule a bit more. The 5% rule applies if you're buying publicly traded stocks. But many super-rich founder-CEOs got that way by plowing everything into one stock—the firm they founded, own and operate. The entrepreneur road to riches can be insanely lucrative, but it is a very rocky road. (Read more on that topic in my 2008 book, *The Ten Roads to Riches*.)

You've heard the saying, "You must concentrate to get wealth, diversify to protect wealth." Those who got rich on 1, 2 or 10 stocks are, very likely, insanely fortunate. Yes, with one stock you can experience thrilling upside. You can also experience crushing downside. Note the guy who gets lucky and wins this way likely accumulates pride and assumes he is smart. His wife and kids will know better and the more so for his success. (Of course, by this I don't mean owning one stock that is a firm you started and control. That's how Bill Gates and any number of other super-rich people got their riches—they started and built a firm, nothing else, and along the way got phenomenally rich. I'm talking about being concentrated in one or a few stocks you don't control.)

The Magic of Diversification

Since no one equity type outperforms all of the time (which you can test for yourself again using Question One), diversification helps spread risk among countries, industries and companies.

Though there are really many types of risk, standard finance theory defines *risk* as volatility measured by the *standard deviation* or *variance* of returns. Most investors think when the market is up, it's good and when it's down, it's volatile. But volatility is a dual-edged sword and ever present. Your question should be: Is this category or stock more or less volatile than its peers? Diversification reduces the volatility of your overall holdings and therefore reduces risk. Modern portfolio analysis has shown even a random mix of investments is less volatile than putting everything in a single category.

Make sure your portfolio has elements behaving differently in different market scenarios—which happens naturally if you have a broad enough benchmark and obey it. Each sector or country in your benchmark moves differently than the others. Maybe a bit differently, maybe very differently—but different all the same. If you follow Rule Number Three and keep those sectors and countries that have low or negative correlation in your portfolio at all times, even if you suspect they won't be your portfolio MVP, you'll reduce overall volatility.

A good example is Technology and Health Care: These two sectors often have a short-term negative correlation—one is up when the other is down. Notice in Figure 9.1 the performance of the two in 2000 is nearly a mirror image.

Rule Number Three, blending dissimilar elements, is about managing risk relative to return. The standard deviation, which is a risk measure, for each sector during the time period was 3.5% for Tech and 2.5% for Health Care. But if you had half your portfolio in each sector (not a good idea, but pretend for illustration's sake), your standard deviation, and therefore your volatility risk, was actually 2.0%.[6] You got lower risk simply by holding two differing kinds of stocks which, over this time period, had a negative correlation.

Then again, maybe you used the Three Questions to develop a strong confidence one would best the other. By all means, overweight the one and underweight the other. Rule Number Two helps you—just be sure to include all your benchmark's components and you should have a well-blended portfolio.

But having reverse-correlated positions in your portfolio is like paying an insurance premium against being wrong. This doesn't just work for components with negative correlations. Finance theory is clear: having any

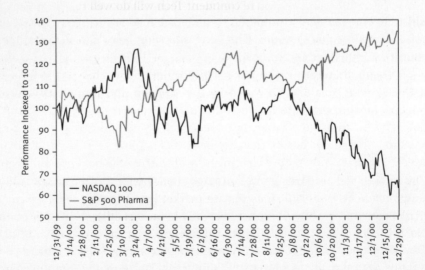

Figure 9.1   Drugs Versus Tech
Source: Thomson Reuters.

blend of dissimilar categories—whether they have negative, low or no correlation—should improve return over time while lowering risk. (Use Question One to test it out. Take any two, four or six stocks from different categories and test over long periods.)

Rule Number Four: Always Remember You Can Be Wrong, So Don't Stray From the First Three Rules

Rule Number Four, possibly the most important rule, is about controlling your behavior. It's a way to ensure including Question Three—always. Without this rule, you can be carried away by cognitive errors. Rule Four forces you to accumulate regret and shun pride. With Rule Four, you reduce the risk of being overconfident. Anytime you're tempted to disregard the first three rules and make a decision not based on the Three Questions but on some herd mentality or Stone Age inclination, Rule Four keeps you in line. With every decision you make, regardless of how confident you are, you can always be wrong. Once you accept that, you're less likely to do something too crippling.

Rule Four forces you to use your benchmark like a leash for a puppy in training. With a short leash, your pup can't get in too much trouble. The same dog on a long leash can dig up a garden, get hit by a car or chase a stray cat across town.

For example, suppose you're confident Tech will do well this year. Tech is 15% of your benchmark. But you're not satisfied with overweighting it to 20% or even 25%. You *know* Tech will be tops. Your confidence tempts you to jettison all your Health Care stocks for an even larger Tech allocation because you know Health Care typically lags when Tech is hot. Before changing your portfolio, ask yourself, "What if I am wrong?" Are you prepared for the consequences of such a big bet?

Core Versus Counterstrategy

This rule is the primary reason I manage money with a core strategy and a counterstrategy. The core strategies are market bets I make—relative benchmark overweights—based on what I believe I know that others don't. For example, if I believe America will outperform foreign, Tech will outperform Health Care, Consumer Discretionary will outperform Consumer Staples, I make overweights relative to the benchmark in those areas. Those are my core strategies.

Then I build my planned counterstrategies. These are areas I don't expect to do well. I have them there because—what if I am wrong? Hey—I'm wrong a lot. I've been fortunate to be right more often than wrong in my career, but I know I've been wrong and will definitely be wrong again and plenty of times. Each of the counterstrategies is an area I expect to do well in the event one of my core strategies fails and does badly. If I'm wrong about Tech, Health Care will likely be a better-performing sector. Either American or foreign stocks will be the lead pony, so I don't want to miss out if I'm wrong about that. I always ask myself, "What will do really well if what I think will do well actually does badly for some reason I can't foresee?" I want some of that, too. Most investors never think this way.

Having a counterstrategy means you'll always have "down" or "laggard" stocks. If you're really right like you expect, your counterstrategy stocks *should* be down or lagging. Counterstrategy stocks being down isn't bad. They can keep you from getting killed when you're wrong. That's managing risk, which is good. One thing about my career I'm pleased with is when I've been wrong and lagged, I haven't lagged by a lot. And I haven't lagged by a lot because I've built in the counterstrategies.

Here's a practical example of core and counterstrategies, again using Tech and Health Care for consistency. Pretend you're benchmark neutral on every sector but Tech and Health Care. You're new to this Three Questions thing, so you focus on just Health Care to start. You believe you've uncovered something no one else is seeing which should make Health Care super hot. Maybe you discovered every member of Congress hit their heads over the weekend (I'd vote for that). You also know the congressmen (and women) have a vote pending Tuesday on drug regulation. They want their new pain relief medicine, and fast, so they'll do something contrary to their nature—*reduce* governmental control. As such, you believe the FDA will begin green-lighting a whole slew of insanely efficacious drugs. (I said we were pretending.) No one else sees this. Everyone else thinks congressmen with headaches are bearish because they believe it will make them groggy and stupid. But you know better! (You know they were already idiots.)

Based on your unique view, you decide to overweight Health Care. You're confident—but not insanely confident—so you decide to increase your Health Care holdings to 15% from a benchmark weight of 10%. That is a 50% overweight and constitutes your core strategy.

Now, unless you're using margin, your assets must add up to 100%, not 105%, so you must reduce holdings elsewhere. Where? Suppose Tech is also 12% of your benchmark. If drug stocks do badly, your full 12% Tech weight will soften the blow—that's a counterstrategy. But if you're *very* confident about your drug play, you could take the whole 5% out of Tech, decreasing your Tech weight from 12% to 7% and increasing the real size of your bet by minimizing how much counterstrategy you have. You still have a 7% weight, but it is a smaller counterstrategy than if you took the 5% haircut from elsewhere.

Thinking it through with the Questions, you discover most folks agree Tech is undervalued because Tech P/Es are low. Also, the dollar has been strong recently (for argument's sake) and folks expect that to continue, and from that, they think US stocks will be strong. Everyone remembers the 1990s when America led and so did Tech.

But you know low P/Es aren't automatically low risk, high return. You know a strong dollar last year doesn't mean a strong dollar this year. You also know a strong dollar doesn't make American stocks beat foreign. Noting the near-universal bullishness on Tech, you conclude you really won't need a full counterstrategy and decide to underweight Tech by the full 5%—putting your weight at 7%.

Still you have a counterstrategy that helps if your core drug strategy fails. If you're right about Health Care, you'll probably (but not necessarily) also be right about Tech, and you'll have participated more in a hot sector and less in a lame one. You beat the market, just from getting one core and one counterstrategy right (in this case by betting big and minimizing your counterstrategy).

Now, you could have been more extreme. You could have moved your Health Care weight from 10% to 22% and your Tech weight from 12% to 0%. And if it worked, you would have won huge. But you didn't. You kept that 7% in Tech.

Suppose you're wrong about your head injury theory. Congress convenes with nothing more than a few mild headaches. The poli-tics ban all pharmaceuticals except aspirin. No one expected that, so Health Care tanks, and folks flock to a "hotter" sector, like Tech. Two sector bets wrong. You've participated less in the hot sector and more in the lame one. Ugh! You lag benchmark. But not by much, because you didn't go nil in the hot sector, and you didn't grossly overweight the laggard.

It's never all that bad to lag the benchmark by a few percentage points in a single year—maybe you do 16% or 17% when the benchmark does 20%. After all, this isn't a game where slight differences in one year's performance count all that much. If you lag by a little for a few years, you can always make that up (the operative words being "lag by a little"). You have the rest of your life to be more right than wrong.

In a year when more of your core strategies are right, you meet or beat your benchmark. There have been up years when I've been wrong about most of my core strategies, but because I got the big decision right—the decision to hold stocks instead of cash or bonds—I lagged my benchmark but not too badly and not by an amount I couldn't make up later. Why? Because I never aim to beat by more than I am comfortable lagging. The counterstrategies save you from lagging too much in years you're wrong.

The only time I am ever comfortable beating the benchmark by a lot—taking on massive amounts of benchmark risk—is when I believe down a lot is by far the likeliest scenario. Then, if I forecast down a lot, I will try beating the benchmark by a lot to avoid the bulk of a bear market. It's a much riskier move than folks realize—huge benchmark risk—and must never be undertaken lightly. But over long time periods, if you beat the benchmark modestly on average and beat the occasional bear market by a lot, you put serious spread on TGH. It's the only time I want to embrace huge benchmark risk.

Finally! How to Pick Stocks That Only Win

That heading was there to fool you. I hope it worked! I don't know how to pick stocks that only rise. Many claim to. But no one does. I've never seen anyone do it. Your goals in stock selection are two things and only these two. First, find stocks that are good representations of the categories you're trying to capture, and second, find stocks you think will most likely do better than those categories. Note I didn't say, "Find stocks that will go up the most." I said, "Most likely do better than the category." Your goal is to get the attributes of the category plus a little, with "most likely" as your goal, knowing some stock picks absolutely can and will lag their categories.

Stock selection is important but amazingly, over time, has the least impact on how your portfolio performs. You may find that shocking and downright sacrilegious. Maybe you bought this book hoping to get an edge in picking stocks, and here I have spent several hundred pages talking about anything but how to pick stocks. There are several reasons—first, it just doesn't matter as much as many presume. Volumes of scholarly research have been written, and there is general consensus among academics most of your return is driven not by stock selection but by asset allocation—the decision to hold stocks, bonds or cash in any given year, and what types. Scholars quibble about how much that at most translates into. Some studies have shown more than 90% of return comes from asset allocations. Others say less. I won't quibble. "Most" is ok.

At my firm, we believe about 70% of return in the long term comes from asset allocation (stocks, bonds or cash), and about 20% comes from sub-asset allocation—those decisions regarding types of stocks to own, which bonds to own—and whether to overweight or underweight (or be benchmark-like) on foreign or domestic, value or growth, size, sectors, etc. But few finance aca-demics would disagree stock selection itself generates a small piece of your total portfolio return—it's a secondary or tertiary matter.

Think about it this way—in the late 1990s, if you used a dart to pick 30 large-cap growth stocks, you did probably pretty well. It likely didn't matter much whether you picked Merck over GlaxoSmithKline—they were large-cap growth Pharmaceuticals stocks that behaved similarly. Investors spent time hand-wringing and analyzing Merck's pipeline and Glaxo's earnings and this one's balance sheet and that one's 90-day moving average, but the effort had little additional benefit. Whether Merck or Glaxo, they did pretty much the same during the 1990s, up 552% and 534%, respectively.[7] How could you have used the Three Questions to figure out something others didn't know about Merck or Glaxo? Wouldn't it have been easier to figure out something about Health Care as a whole? Or large-cap stocks? Or growth stocks? Or the US versus the UK? Had you done that, heck, you might have decided to hold both these stocks—a perfectly fine outcome (see Figure 9.2).

Fast forward to 2000 through 2002. During these years, the best decision was to be defensive and hold largely cash and bonds. If you couldn't do that, then it was small-cap value stocks. If you did that, you did ok. If you did stock picking in any other part of the market, you were likely down big. It was the decision whether to own stocks or even the type that determined return, not stock picking.

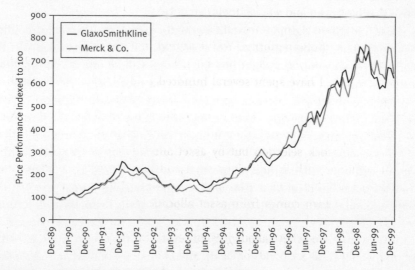

Figure 9.2   Same Sector, Similar Performance
Source: **Thomson Reuters.**

Don't get me wrong—stock selection is important. Picking the right stocks definitely adds value over time, otherwise I'd recommend everyone—even if you have vast sums to invest—buy index funds or ETFs. And like all other investing decisions, you needn't pick the best performing stocks all of the time, you just need to be right more often then wrong and let the benchmark do its work.

So where do you want to spend the majority of your investment time? On the decision that drives 70% or even 90% of your return, or on the decision responsible for about 10% of your return?

Just Tell Me How to Pick Stocks Already!

Ok! I already did that once. It was my first book, *Super Stocks*. I don't and wouldn't do it now the way I did it then, but what I did back then wasn't bad. It was fairly state of the art then. Come to think of it, there is pretty much nothing I do now like I did 25 years ago—I'd be pretty embarrassed if there were. I sure hope I know things 10 years from now that cause me to change what I'm doing now. At this point in evolution, change is the name of the game, and my goal is to keep developing new things and changing. So how would I do it now?

Here's how. It's a process of elimination.

Imagine the portfolio construction process as a funnel, like the one in Figure 9.3. Into this funnel, you pour the whole world's securities—stocks, bonds, cash, the whole gamut. The only securities that drop to the bottom are those that pass a screen at each level.

Use the Three Questions to examine the three drivers—economic, political and sentiment—to determine which market condition is most likely. In the highly likely situation you determine the market will be one of the first three scenarios (up a lot, up a little or down a little), your job is easy—you belong fully exposed to equities as dictated by your benchmark (whether that's 100%, 70%, 60%, etc.). The entire world's stocks drop through the screen to the next level.

Now you have sub-asset allocation screens. Use the Three Questions again to decide how to relatively weight countries and sectors compared to your benchmark. (Been there, done that—earlier in this book.) Here, you screen stocks based on your core and counterstrategies—what you want to overweight and underweight. In this midsection of the funnel, you determine percentage portfolio weights without thinking of a single stock name. Use some of what we've demonstrated in this book. At the end of your scientific inquiry, you'll have a simple list of countries, sectors and what you view as their appropriate percentages. Stocks drop through the next screen into a bucket based on your subasset allocation decisions, and only then are you ready for individual stock selection.

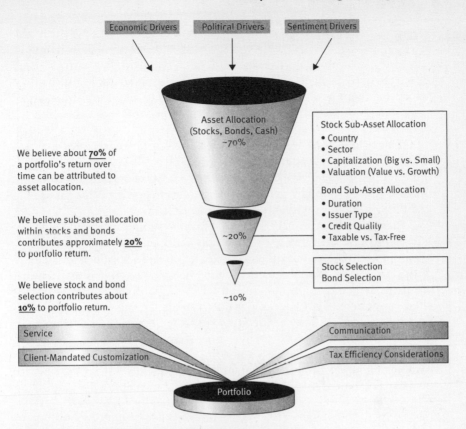

Figure 9.3 Portfolio Engineering Funnel
Note: Forward-looking return attribution is an approximation intended for illustrative purposes and should not be considered a forecast of future returns or return attribution.

Take each category, one at a time. Attacking stock selection this way is much easier and clearer. Instead of wading through the stock world, you're looking only at stocks falling in each of the specific categories you need. You're not looking at 15,000 stocks, hoping to find a handful of good ones; you're looking through 15 or 20 names per category to pick three or four stocks.

Say your higher-level decisions lead you to needing a certain percentage of US small-cap value Industrials. You need a few decent ones—as a group likely to do as well or better than the category overall. The idea is to find stocks priced relatively cheaply compared to peers. More important, you want to look for a story that, should it catch on, will drive returns. I'm not talking about what you read on the front page of the *Wall Street Journal:* I'm talking about what you can use the Three Questions to uncarth.

FORBES PICKS

As a point of trivia, I generally don't write in *Forbes* about stocks my firm selects for client portfolios. I'm not being secretive about my strategy; I just don't want to turn my clients into criminals. And I won't become one myself.

If my firm's clients were holding stocks I wrote about in *Forbes*, they could be accused of *front-running*, or I could be accused of doing it for them for pay. It would work like this: I buy for my clients then recommend it in *Forbes* strongly, getting *Forbes* readers to buy it, pushing it up, and then I sell it for my clients, taking the profit.

That would be criminal—a form of insider trading, a felony. I hate felonies. Always have! I've got a lifelong philosophy that says, "No felonies." To keep well out of the gray area and on the spic-and-span side of the law, I write about stocks that—for whatever reason—in my view are perfectly grand but we don't need for client portfolios. Because (as cited earlier herein) stock picking is only a small percentage of portfolio return, I can pick different individual stocks for *Forbes* and my clients and have both places work out just fine, thank you. There are more than enough stocks for what we need to do for clients and for *Forbes* without getting the two groups entangled in a potentially sticky way. I'll occasionally remind my readers of that in the interest of full disclosure.

Here's an example: As 2005 started, I did in fact expect US small-cap value Industrials to continue doing well. A stock I wrote about in *Forbes* at the beginning of 2005 was Flowserve (FLS).[8]

Flowserve manufactures pumps and valves for difficult liquids (corrosive ones, for example) in the chemical, petroleum and food-processing industries. Exciting, right? Who doesn't get up each day and think about pumps and valves for corrosive liquids? And how to capitalize on companies doing a spiffy job at valving and pumping? You generally don't find stocks like this looking for a needle in a valve-stack. You find them by winnowing down categories.

Why Flowserve? Why not Kennametal or Idex Corp? Also great US small-cap value industrial machinery stocks. Nothing wrong with them. But this was what I could fathom about Flowserve I felt no one else had: At the onset of 2005, investors were still hypersensitive about accounting "irregularities." In late 2004, Flowserve announced a new CFO, which can be fairly suspicious. A few days later, the chief accounting officer resigned and, just a few days after *that*, reversed his decision. Next thing you knew, Flowserve was delaying its third-quarter SEC 10-Q filing. It *seemed* fishy, and the stock behaved erratically in response. If you were a fundamental investor, this one might have scared you away because its balance sheet wasn't impressive. Even the price, at 26 times trailing earnings, seemed not so cheap.

All reasons most investors would stay away. Everybody knows potentially fishy accounting coupled with an "overpriced" stock spells trouble. But it *was* cheap. The stock sold at 60% of annual revenue. There was potential for nice gains if its profit margins improved to a normal manufacturer level. Any positive news about this firm would be pleasant upside surprise. It was priced for no good news. It was priced with the expectation of more bad news and further decline. Therefore, any good news would be bullish, and in a category that should do well, it should do well relative to its category—which is the goal.

Using Question Three, I made sure I wasn't being carried away by overconfidence or any other cognitive errors. I asked myself: "What if I'm wrong? Suppose the stock failed to deliver?" If that were the case, I would expect it to bounce around somewhere with its peers, maybe doing not quite as well. Because I expected the category to do pretty well, I thought I wouldn't be too disappointed by a laggard that everyone expected to be a laggard.

Note: I didn't fly out to Flowserve's Texas headquarters and wander around its plant in a hard hat gleaning hat tricks. I never met the CEO. I didn't hire a mole to infiltrate upper management to find out something others didn't know (which is illegal along with being ridiculous—but would make a great Bruce Willis corporate spy movie). I read what was publicly available—the same information you easily find. Then I did what I always do when I'm looking at individual stocks. I ask myself, "What is everyone else worried about?" And I toss that aside. Then I ask myself, "What can I read between the lines? What kooky thing could happen to surprise to the upside or downside? How likely is that kooky thing to happen?" Finally, like Homer Simpson, I say, "All right, brain, you don't like me, and I don't like you," and I figure out how my hardwiring, biases and ego might lead me to make a poor decision about the stock. In effect, that's it. That is how you pick stocks that always win. Just kidding. That is, in my view, how you pick stocks that, more often than not, are better than their peers.

If you had read *Forbes* and bought Flowserve at my recommendation, you would've been pretty happy. In 2005, the stock returned 44% compared to 12% for its global sector, 5% for the S&P and 9% for the global broad market.[9] Flowserve was a great stock pick—it did better than its category. Was it the best performing US small-cap industrial machinery stock? No. You might have happened upon JLG Industries, Inc. or Joy Global, Inc., returning 133% and 109%, respectively.[10] Either would have made it through the top-down selection process as well. Those two stocks might have fallen out of your funnel instead of Flowserve (or, heck, you might have decided to hold all three). But what would have made you select those? You needed to see something others could not, which is easier to do when looking at a small pool of stocks at the bottom of your funnel rather than an ocean at the top. Making the right big decisions first increases the likelihood of picking better stocks like Flowserve, JLG Industries or Joy Global from the categories you need. If you're spending hours trolling websites and CNBC to study some German small-cap value Utility stock without first considering if you even want to hold stocks or what types this year, you're likely wasting time and brainpower.

Repeat this process for all your equity categories, and you'll have a good representation of your benchmark. Know you will never pick only the best stocks consistently. Get used to it right now. You will always have a stock or three or five in your portfolio that end up dogs. The best investment managers in the world don't pick stocks that only go up.

Is it possible you manage to make the right decisions regarding subasset allocation—you pick the right size, style, country, sector, everything—but you manage to pick the one stock that misses earnings, has an accounting scandal, gets embroiled in a political melee or otherwise has peevishly poorer results than its brethren? Sure.

We've already established you should be diversified. If the Energy sector is 10% of your portfolio, you should be picking three, five or even seven different stocks there. If you pick one bad one (it will happen), you aren't hurting yourself too badly (Rule Number Four). You want three, five or seven that you see as good representatives of the category, with a likely edge over their peers. I didn't pick Flowserve because I thought it would go up so darned much. I picked it because I thought it was a good representation of a category I was bullish on and had a strong likelihood of outperforming. When you do that, some of them (like Flowserve, in this case) go up a lot more.

Focusing on diversifying among stocks you think are most likely to beat their category doesn't mean you've given up on stock picking. You haven't. But it also means you won't put it all on the line in one stock and then learn you picked badly—the stock did terribly while the category did well and didn't inject the category's effect into your portfolio. I always want primarily the effect of the category I need in my portfolio. Stock picking without a top-down approach for most investors snatches defeat from the jaws of victory eventually. Those who don't accept this often have egos bigger than brains.

What about stock picking for a small sector or category? Say you're using MSCI as your benchmark, but you want exposure to Emerging Markets.

You don't want huge benchmark risk (and holding something *not* in your benchmark exposes you to risk all the same) but you want maybe 5%. You're making a very measured, controlled relative bet (hey, good for you). You don't want to buy just one stock—that will hardly diversify your Emerging Markets category—which itself is very broad. Which one do you pick? A Zimbabwean stock? A Chilean stock? But if you buy enough stocks to diversify that small an allocation, you'll be buying odd lots and probably paying huge transaction fees. Here, you might simply find a low-cost ETF and call it a day. I'm not a fund fan for larger pools of assets (they are less efficient than individual stocks), but they can serve a purpose. After all, do you really know something others don't that justifies owning Zimbabwe versus Chile or the single stocks of East Patagonian Pepper versus the Central Cluj Transportation Authority?

When the Heck Do You Sell?

Picking stocks is only half the battle. How can you know when to sell? Just like buying a stock, a sell decision should be attacked top down. The first and easiest answer for when to sell is if you fathom the likeliest market scenario over the next year is down a lot. Then, selling most of your stocks is good—but also rare. What about in between true bear markets? How do you know when to cut and run?

The answer is: You have used the Three Questions and discovered something fundamental has changed about why you hold a stock. For example, after a fairly flat yield curve, the yield curve suddenly gets steep. You might decide to pare back your growth stocks in favor of more value stocks.

If you think firms with elastic demand (Tech, Consumer Discretionary) will do better than those with inelastic (Health Care, Consumer Staples), you can change your weights—necessitating the sale of some stocks. Or maybe you fathom some other economic, political or sentiment force impacting a certain sector or industry. For instance, you know Congress will enact yet more accounting restrictions which you (and few others) fathom will harm Financials. Or maybe, after a lengthy period of high-dividend stocks outperforming, everyone is deliriously enthusiastic about Utilities, so you somehow know it's time to underweight Utilities shifting to non-dividend-paying stocks. Mind you, this doesn't mean the stocks you sell are bad. They just don't fit what you now need as a result of using the Three Questions—you need stocks that represent your asset and sub-asset allocation decisions.

Lock and Load

What about if a stock has been up a lot? Shouldn't you sell and "lock in prof-its"? I never really understood how people "lock in profits." I think this is something people say a lot without thinking it through. Lock in profits how? The gains you take from a stock that is up don't get locked in a vault some-where. You reinvest those dollars (don't you?), and the stocks you buy with "gains" you've "locked in" aren't guaranteed to only rise. The next stock you buy may fall, erasing profits an investor thinks are "locked in," which means paying taxes on the gain from the first stock and still losing money on the second. There is no such thing as "locking in profits."

Don't sell to "lock in profits." Sell to get out, pare back a weight you need to reduce or because in your view the stock no longer is more likely to best its category whose effect you need in your portfolio.

And just because a stock is up a lot doesn't mean it can't keep rising. It happens all the time. Remember, stocks aren't serially correlated—they have a 50/50 chance of continuing in the prior direction or reversing course. Continue holding a stock that is up if the fundamentals that led you to hold the stock remain intact.

When to Sell?

What about when a stock is down a lot? Shouldn't you cut the dogs, take the loss, offset taxable gains and go your way? Maybe, maybe not.

First of all, why is it down a lot? Is it because the entire market is having a correction, and it's just doing what the market is doing? If so, it probably doesn't make sense to cut and run. Relative return is what matters, not abso-lute return (usually). Is it down because the stock's sector or category is down—either because the sector is correcting (sectors correct, too) or because it's out of favor? Is it down because the stock is part of your counterstrategy? That stock is behaving as a counterstrategy stock should—also not necessarily a reason to cut. (Focusing on one stock's performance or one sector's perfor-mance instead of how the whole portfolio is performing is order preference—a cognitive error you use Question Three to combat.) Is the stock down because some horrendous news surfaced? The CEO cooked the books, they hosted lavish Greek-themed parties on the shareholders' dime or some other rumor—believable or outrageous—surfaces?

The fact of the matter is, by the time the bad news has come out, the mar-ket may have already responded, and you've likely missed the chance to avoid the big drop. Now, you can sell at the absolute lowest and take your dough and move on, but that is buying high and selling low. And the stock where you reinvest isn't guaranteed to only go up. It might drop, too, and now you are super wrong but twice. There is still a 50/50 chance the prior direction continues—or reverses.

Don't sell as a knee-jerk reaction to a big drop. Instead, look at the company as we did when we were buying. Ignore the hype because that is past and you can't do anything about it, and look for what you can fathom that others can't. Is the "bad news" such that the company can recover from it? Is the company essentially sound?

Also, deeply consider if the bad news is correct or credible. Not to put too fine a point on it, but frequently journalists, in the rush to get the story first, don't have the story straight. Often what they report is overblown or simply wrong. They may not have a background in the firm they're reporting on. In fact, they probably don't! Something routine can easily be misinterpreted or blown up to sound ground-shaking. Or a minor infraction not material to the firm's core business may get the misinformed full-court press. Or journalists may be going on the hearsay of a disgruntled employee without doing further fact checking. Or they may overlook something truly material, because they don't deeply understand the firm's core business. Happens all the time! Journalists frequently get their news very wrong.

If the besieged firm is sound despite the hysteria, the stock may very well rebound, giving you a chance to sell at a relatively higher point later. What's more, since sentiment will be so poor about a stock that had a sudden and precipitous price drop, any good news, no matter how meager, can drive it up.

What if you're cool-headed and don't sell just because everyone else did (good for you), and you take a reasonable look at what is true about why the stock dropped suddenly? What if the bad news truly signals something rotten in Denmark, something even a big management shake-up won't help, something rotting the core business? Despite the relative low, that's still a right time to cut your losses, utter a few obloquies and know you simply can't help it when you get blindsided sometimes. This is why you diversify and never put more than you're willing to lose in any one stock.

If that makes you diabolically depressed, consider this. If you have a well-managed portfolio, you won't have much more than a few percent in any stock. If one stock gets halved tomorrow from sudden bad news, maybe you lose 1%. If you think relatively and scale (always!), you can combat order preference and focus on the overall portfolio, not the one, small, imploded position. You lost 1%. In reality, stocks rarely lose 100% of their value fast. You can experience a 10% to 20% individual stock drop, and then the overall impact is minimal. Even a massive drop in one stock should have minimal impact on a well-managed portfolio. Shake it off, accumulate regret, learn what you can for next time and move on. If something fundamental didn't occur, continue to hang on for now—but keep an eye on any such change.

Here are two examples of a single incident where my firm made two different choices on fairly similar stocks—one to sell and one to hold. (This is the *exact* example I used in 2006, but the lesson is still very valid now.)

On October 14, 2004, Eliot Spitzer, then Attorney General of New York State (before he was governor and before he was the disgraced governor), decided Hank Greenberg, then CEO of AIG, was guilty of . . . something.[11] (I believe there has never been a male member of the Greenberg family Mr. Spitzer doesn't believe is guilty of something—he's pretty much gone after all of them one way or another.)

Meanwhile, one of Greenberg's sons, Jeff, ran another huge public insurance company called Marsh & McLennan (MMC; which also owns the Putnam mutual fund family—which Spitzer attacked heavily the year before). Essentially, Spitzer claimed MMC was guilty of bid-rigging for its insurance contracts and named other insurance companies, including AIG, as being complicit. Later, Spitzer very publicly accused AIG and, indeed, Hank Greenberg of being party to the alleged misdeeds. Along the way, MMC's board, under attack from Spitzer, forced out Jeff Greenberg. Then AIG's board, also likely wary of Spitzer's force and power, forced Hank Greenberg out. Eventually, the charges against AIG were dropped, and MMC settled.

Meanwhile, Spitzer and Hank Greenberg had it out in the press, and some of Greenberg's friends got involved, including former Goldman Sachs CEO, John Whitehead, whom Spitzer may or may not have threatened with both bodily and professional harm—depending on whose version you believe.

Markets hate surprises, particularly surprises involving the AG of NY. Both stocks fell immediately on the news—AIG was down −10% on October 14, 2004, and MMC was down a big −24%.[12] What to do?

Avoiding the drop ahead of time would have been nearly impossible. There was no way to know Spitzer was planning this—not unless you had special and illegal insight into his intent. When such a market event occurs, you especially need Question Three. Sudden drops in stock prices get loss aversion working full throttle. Selling out after a big drop sometimes makes sense, sometimes is epically stupid—and you won't know which is which until later, and you won't get any appropriate cues from the market or the *New York Times*.

I was bullish on the finance sector then and insurance specifically. Everything about both stocks was right, category-wise. The only reason to sell a stock fitting my bigger portfolio themes was if something was rotten individually about it. Now, I'd met Hank Greenberg a couple of times. And while he can be abrasive at times, sort of like me, he was a phenomenal CEO for a very, very long time. Truly phenomenal, and I couldn't believe he had actually done anything very wrong because he didn't need to. (Basic rule: The most capable people don't need to break rules and won't.) On the other hand, he was 80, so he couldn't be phenomenal for long.

But I also had no idea Spitzer would later in 2005 quietly excuse Greenberg of any criminal wrongdoing (announced during Thanksgiving week, no less, where news items go to die.[13] If you want to bury a news release, announce it over Thanksgiving, Christmas, Easter or the Fourth—far fewer folks will ever see it). I knew—everyone knew—AIG was a massive company with well-diversified product lines. I understood the crime of which AIG stood accused, but I couldn't see how it would impact the long-term health of AIG overall—it wasn't a big enough crime. If it turned out something was wrong with the business group involved with the alleged bid-rigging, AIG could easily spin off the group, rout the evildoers or otherwise cut out the (alleged) cancer. I couldn't see any reason why the rest of AIG should be infected at the time. Also, there was speculation of Greenberg stepping down, and though Greenberg built AIG into what it was, at 80, his departure couldn't hurt too much. What's more, his leaving could please the market and take heat off the stock. Finally, because there was so much dour sentiment about AIG, any bad news was pretty well priced—so I could fathom any good news, no matter how weak, would be a pleasant, bullish surprise. I opted to hang onto AIG.

The story was different for MMC. MMC stood accused of flim-flammery in its main business line and core competency. The case seemed stronger. To survive, MMC would have to navigate at least one major lawsuit, with possible copycat suits from other states. It would likely do a strategic reboot, cast off a number of its upper management and generally be in a major state of disarray for months, if not years. But that was small.

The new CEO MMC brought in, Michael Cherkasky, a perfectly fine fellow, was the CEO of Kroll, a public company specializing in corporate security work that MMC bought the year before. Cherkasky was picked as CEO not because he was the optimal guy to run a big insurance firm, having extensive background and success in insurance. He didn't have that. He was picked because he had a prior background as a regulator and had worked with Eliot Spitzer before, and it was presumed Cherkasky could get along with Spitzer. To me, this was all wrong and bad. Cherkasky's prime experience as a CEO was at Kroll—a little firm, smaller than my firm. I know something for sure: I'm certainly not qualified to be CEO of something the size of MMC. Said otherwise, I'm fully as qualified to be CEO of MMC as Cherkasky was because, while I'm no insurance guy, at least I'm a financial services guy, and Cherkasky was neither an insurance nor financial services guy and hadn't been CEO of anything nearly the scale necessary to be truly qualified to run MMC's far-flung diversified operations. I knew if I couldn't run it well, he couldn't. So, my firm decided to take our double-digit loss and sell.

I'm sure many folks would, initially, view that as an odd decision. Why sell one and not the other? Aren't they cut from the same cloth? Wasn't Spitzer gunning for them both? Shouldn't we cut the dogs and buy some winners? That sounds great in theory, but we all know the stocks you buy to replace your dogs may be woofers themselves. Never sell a stock because it's down. Sell because something fundamental has changed about the reason you hold it. Think about that funnel again and the fundamental reasons, top down, why you might sell. The fundamental reason could be that you forecast a down-a-lot scenario, and you're shifting largely out of stocks. It could be you're shifting from growth to value, small to large or the reverse. Your sector outlook may have changed, and you need to move from an overweight to an underweight. Maybe you're dangerously overweighted because the stock has appreciated far beyond 2% or 3% of your total holdings. Or maybe you wake up to discover the company has done something illegal from which recovery will be either lengthy or impossible.

When Spitzer formally subpoenaed AIG in February 2005, the stock had another stomach-churning drop—over 31% to a relative low in April. Nothing had changed since October of the previous year except increased fear of Spitzer, so we hung on. Based on some larger portfolio themes, we finally sold AIG in January 2006, after it rallied 42% from its low in 2005, for a 19% net gain from October 14, 2004, when its woes began.[14] We couldn't guarantee anything else bought with the proceeds from a sale on October 14 would have been up 19%— AIG did about as well as the S&P 500 over the same time period. When we sold AIG, MMC was still down more than 3% from when the news hit and lagging its category big time. Still, I felt pretty good about not panicking and selling AIG when it was in a huge hole. (This is interesting looking back now because many feel AIG could have avoided the mess it later got into that culminated in its 2008 partial nationalization had Greenberg remained at the helm and not been chased out by a politician looking to curry favor.)

Remind yourself you aren't collecting a bunch of high-flying stocks. You aren't a stock collector. Stock collectors are hamstrung by order preference and overconfidence and focus on the two stocks that did well and forget about how their whole portfolio is doing, not to mention risk management. Your aim should absolutely not be to find the next hot stock you can brag about to your poker group (or yoga class or, worse, tofu-tasting party). Rather, you're maximizing the likelihood of beating your benchmark. You need stocks that act like the components of your benchmark. That is what this exercise is about.

With that, you have a strategy to keep you disciplined—a strategy requiring constant application of the Three Questions. Garnering market-like return when your Stone Age brain wants to cave to TGH so very badly and either hit homeruns daily or cower with a few CDs and money market funds is quite an accomplishment. But I want you to aspire to more. I want you to be disciplined with a strategy. I want you to advance the science of capital markets technology and be among those who can move down the learning curve faster. I want you to master the Three Questions and use them always. I want you to stick it to The Great Humiliator. Stick it to him hard.

CONCLUSION

Time to Say Goodbye

In concluding, allow me to get personal and address why I would write this book at all. You can blame it on the US Forest Service. I fell in love with forests as a kid. My parents lived in a suburb where their back fence was adjacent to the woods. As a kid, I was over the fence and off into a live oak forest. From my parents' home, in a world long gone, I could hitchhike up to Kings Mountain, 20 minutes out, and be in the redwoods at 2,000 feet in elevation. That's where I live and have for more than a third of a century. But as a kid, I saw myself living and working in the woods always, as a forester. I went to forestry school because I loved trees.

A summer job pulling chain for a US Forest Service survey crew convinced me I'd never, ever work for the government under any circumstances. And today, forestry is almost always either working for or with the government in one way or another or against the government. That summer taught me everything about government employment is oppressive. What I knew was that I simply didn't want to have anything to do with the government. I also knew right then, for the same reason, I'd never be a career politician because it, too, meant working for the government. Might have saved my mortal soul. Somehow I hoped I had something better to do with my life.

With no sense of what to do next, I switched majors to economics because I'd been good at it earlier.

Forests still jazz me—redwoods in particular. In fact, I'm very proud the only endowed academic chair in the whole wide world dedicated to any single tree species bears my name and is devoted to my beloved redwood. I've built and maintained a serious hobby life devoted to redwoods, including locating and excavating more than 30 pre-1920 steam-era redwood lumber mills and collecting and cataloging the artifacts. I've also compiled what I believe is the world's largest non-institutionally owned forest history library, spanning more than 3,000 volumes. But you could never get me to go to work for the government. Serious hobbies are ok, but it is important to separate what you do career-wise from what you do purely for fun.

Capital markets are fun, but they're also work. I hope the Three Questions will be profitable for you, but along the way, I also hope you liked this book and found it educational. When I first started my *Forbes* column, Jim Michaels, then the editor of *Forbes* and generally the dean of American business journalists, taught me that a column was supposed to be three things: entertaining, educating and profitable. Those are pretty good goals for much of life. But as fun as they are, markets are a great deal of work—which you can see in the large amount of data and analysis in this book. The Three Questions are a tool to let you know what you need to know to do well. But you have to apply the effort. No book can do that for you.

The opposite of a governmental employee is a worshiper of free markets and capitalism. By the time I was finished with school, I was pretty well hooked. So after school, I went to work for my father. I learned what I could from him, including that I'm not a very good employee, and struck out on my own. I was too young to know I was too young at the time to be able to succeed on my own—so I could. Over 40 years and many good whacks from TGH later, I'm still at it. Why such a long career of flagellation at the hands of TGH? Why keep going to work and dealing with all the real world's dull cares when I could retire and dedicate the rest of my life to redwoods, my cats and my wife? Why keep making very public prognostications in *Forbes* these decades, verifiable by anyone who wants to prove me wrong or attack me? Why do any of this?

Transformationalism

This is an opportunity to keep discovering and doing new things forever. The most important part of being alive at this point in history, in my view, is the ability to do the new. In Chapters 5 and 9, I spoke about my grandfather at length. When he died in 1958, he had seen amazing evolutions ranging from autos to radio, movies, antibiotics, airplanes and more. He could sit in his living room and see the president speaking to him real time in a wooden box—right there. When he was five in 1880, if he could have described to his grandfather what he would see by 1958, Isaac Fisher, my great-great grandfather, would have thought my grandfather was nuts. He would have turned to his son, Philip Isaac Fisher, and said, "Philip, what are you doing to let such crazy notions in my grandson's mind?"

But Isaac would have been wrong. My grandfather's generation saw more relative change in basic life than any other generation before or since. They were at the inflection point of the explosion—the nonlinear launching point Americans regularly underestimate, which we otherwise refer to as the American Industrial Revolution. The most singularly powerful unleashing of mental force ever. Capitalist force—the most powerful kind! Before his generation, every generation lived life almost identically to their grandparents. They might move. They might war. They might take a different career. But the basics of life changed very, very slowly in the eons before my grandfather's birth.

My father, born in 1907, saw tremendous change too—more absolute change than my grandfather did but less relative change. He saw jets, integrated circuits and the beginnings of biotech before he died in 2004. My generation has seen tremendous absolute change and will continue to—but less relative change than my father or grandfather saw. My three sons are in their mid-30s and older. They assume change is normal. Yes, now it is, but it's still very new. To wake daily as a normal person and participate in changing the world in some small part like my Grampa did as one of the pioneers at Hopkins Med or my father did in growth stock investing—that's new. That didn't happen centuries ago except for a few weird one-offs like Isaac Newton. Normal folks didn't do that. Now they do. We live in exceptional times because we can rise every day, if we choose, and participate in developing new things never before known that will be taken largely for granted by those following us.

I call this process *transformation*. Normal people now leave their field changed in their wake because of things they developed. Newton was a transformationalist before they were common. The Industrial Revolution unleashed transformationalists throughout our world—people whose imaginations knew no bounds and could fathom the unfathomable.

It happens mainly among scientists and capitalists. Julius Rosenwald was a transformationalist when he started Sears, Roebuck and Co. and changed how people envisioned retailing for 100 years. Carnegie was. Ford was. Adam Smith was when he wrote *The Wealth of Nations*. But most authors aren't—they're usually just incrementalists. Einstein certainly was, and there are a great many in science—famous and not so. More recently, Bob Noyce and Gordon Moore, cofounders of Intel, combined scientific backgrounds with business acumen to transform their little part of the world. Bill Gates is. He changed the world in ways that leveled the playing field for small businesses versus big. Chuck Schwab was. The list is long—even endless. But you need not be huge to be a transformationalist. You just have to change your little part of the world permanently so others always see it differently through your new science, knowledge, technology or vision.

Our lives—the way we live them daily—are fundamentally changed by every transformationalist. Sometimes we don't know it because we don't see it. When I endowed the Kenneth L. Fisher Chair in Redwood Forest Ecology, I did it partly because I love redwoods but also because its initial holder, Steve Sillett, is a transformationalist who is very rapidly changing the way we think about redwoods. He has no limits in his mind as to the questions that can be answered that we've never addressed. He is transforming how we know redwoods and big trees in general. I wouldn't have endowed the chair if I didn't see a transformationalist to support.

In capital markets, there's no limit to what you can do to learn and build capital markets technology that no one has ever understood before. You can be a transformationalist of capital markets. You couldn't do that 200 years ago. Today you can. Today you can wake up and work daily on asking questions simply challenging what we know—opening the vista of what we may know soon. The Three Questions are specifically for that purpose—so you, some of you who read this book, may get it in you to stretch to become a transformationalist yourself.

When I developed the PSR, I was trying to do that. When I did early work on small-cap value (before that term existed) and showed the institutional investing world how it fit in terms of variance and covariance into traditional finance theory's Markowitzian framework of mean variance optimization, I was trying to do that. I'm no Newton, no Bob Noyce. I'm no great genius by any standard. But I can ask questions. And so can you. And you may be a great genius able to fathom things I never could and become a great transformationalist.

I keep doing what I keep doing because at this point in human evolution, the most exciting and fun thing we can do is to develop the new that has never been developed before and decimate past mythologies. We will make mistakes to be sure. But we will progress for sure. You can do it as well or better than I can. If you're younger, you can do it far longer than I can. You can make a huge difference. I know most of you won't because you won't want to. But if a few of you get the idea while young or willing to ask the Questions and attempt transforming parts of finance and market theory, you can have a huge impact on the future.

The most important reason I keep pushing ahead is because I can get up every morning and address the new in my little part of the world, and maybe in 2012, I'll use the Questions and fathom a Question Two that really creates something new and shattering. Or maybe you will.

Yes, managing money is a valuable service, and doing a good job is vital in a world where so many don't. But I hold no illusions I'm saving lives like the graduates of Hopkins Med 100 years ago. I'm no capitalistic version of Mother Teresa. Yes, my firm's many clients rely on my firm's services for their well-being, and that is a pretty important undertaking—one I am honored to provide. But my firm today can do that without me. When I retire, it will carry on just as it does now because we built it with the ability to do that. The reason to get up and do it at this stage in life is for the fun of the new and different and challenging.

Another reason I do what I do? I love Capitalism. In my view, it is thus far the most holy, perfect accomplishment of humanity. Under Capitalism, all are born to opportunity. The poor become rich. The richest were mostly born not rich. Those on the *Forbes* 400 mostly fall off over time. Bill Gates was born simply upper middle class and as a youth became the richest man in America and created the biggest endowment in history. The world's great innovations and transformations and transformationalists have all come from capitalistic societies and none from elsewhere in the past 200 years. Contemporary elitist intellectuals have wrongly snubbed Capitalism since long before I was born, but they are no more right in their vision than Gertrude Stein from Chapter 5.

The stock market is pure Capitalism. The stock you buy doesn't know if you're white or black, male or female, old or young, American or French. Prices are dictated by supply and demand and nothing else. It's global, efficient, wildly volatile, always surprising, raw and beautiful. In many ways, TGH and I have a very intense love-hate relationship.

And by writing this book, I'm bringing the message to you—that Capitalism is good and the stock market is unpredictable but beatable. So what should you do now? I want you to move down that learning curve fast—hopefully faster than others—and advance capital markets science. As I've said repeatedly, you can't make market bets and win long term unless you know something others don't. I didn't share some of what I know to wow you with cute analytical tricks. It was a demonstration of applying a scientific method to the market. To show you how. The advantages I showed you will all fade away one day. Maybe some sooner than later—but all someday. Yet asking the Questions will go on forever. The only thing that will help you or me beat the market going forward is innovation. To my knowledge, while there are many books showing people investing tools—just as my first book showed my innovations like the PSR of 1984—I'm unaware of any investment book before this one, not a single one, showing you how to innovate for yourself.

So here it is. Maybe you think all this is wrong, or maybe just part of it is wrong. That's fine. I'm ok with you seeing me as wrong. But I don't want you to just think I'm wrong. I want you to prove it. If you don't believe what I've shown you, at least use the methodology to prove me wrong. Show me an R-squared, show me a cognitive error, fathom something for me scientifically I haven't fathomed—and write to tell me. But really prove me wrong. Don't just write me to tell me I'm an idiot. I won't pay attention. What you think of me is none of my business. Truly, I invite you to be skeptical about everything in this book. Get data, run an analysis, do it over long periods with different starting dates. Check it overseas to make sure you haven't found a flukey factor. Show me the data and stats, and then tell me I'm wrong.

What I don't want you to do is think I'm wrong but never prove it. That won't do you any good. It's just a waste of time. If you think I'm wrong and can show it satisfactorily with data, you haven't hurt anyone. In fact, you've just helped yourself because you've established or confirmed reality. And if you've made it to this conclusion, you must, in some small way, believe what everyone knows and accepts isn't always right. So show me how I'm wrong. I can take it! Show me the data and how you ran your analysis. Maybe you will discover a new way to stick it to TGH, and for that I salute you. But if you prove I'm wrong, you will have proved the methodology works. And in a different way, then, I'm still right—isn't that beautiful?

APPENDIX A

Causal Correlations and the Correlation Coefficient

When asking the Three Questions, you need some very basic statistical capability you can learn right here—nothing fancy. You can do wonders with a *correlation coefficient* and an *R-squared*. With these two analytical tools, you can credibly disprove, in many instances, that two events have any connection to each other. It's easy. All you need is an Internet connection and Excel.

To start, let's get some data to compare. For an easy exercise, we can see how much one stock is correlated to the market over 10 days. (Ten days isn't enough time to tell you anything about anything but will give us short columns of data to work with.)

Step 1

Go to Yahoo! Finance (http://finance.yahoo.com). (If you're Internet savvy, feel free to use whatever source you're comfortable with. Just be sure you know how to download or copy and paste into Excel.)

- Click on the link to the S&P 500, which is featured prominently—usually across the top of page.
- Click on the link for "Historical Prices"—on the left-hand side of the page.
- Select "Daily" prices, select a short time frame (use any time frame you like, just choose the same time period during Step 2—I used January 1, 2006, through January 10, 2006), and click "Get Prices." Now select "Download to Spreadsheet."
- An Excel spreadsheet will pop up with index data for the dates in question.
- Copy and paste the "Date" and the "Adjusted Close" columns into a new Excel spreadsheet page. You don't need the rest of the data for right now. Note: You'll have missing dates because of weekends and holidays. (You want the "Adjusted Close" because it's adjusted for stock splits and dividends.)

Step 2

Now go back to Yahoo! Finance and get a quote for any stock. I used General Electric (GE) because it's pretty basic. When the stock page pops up, click on the price chart and follow the same steps to get historical prices for your stock. Copy the data into the same spreadsheet, next to your S&P data. Your spreadsheet should look something like this:

	A	B	C	D
1				
2	Date	Adj. Close	Adj. Close	
3		S&P 500	GE	
4	10-Jan-06	1289.69	34.67	
5	9-Jan-06	1290.15	34.86	
6	6-Jan-06	1285.45	34.94	
7	5-Jan-06	1273.48	34.71	
8	4-Jan-06	1273.46	34.80	
9	3-Jan-06	1268.80	34.85	
10				

Not too hard, right?

Step 3

Now, don't retch when you see this—you won't need it—but technically, this is how you calculate a correlation coefficient:

$$P_{xy} = \frac{Cov(r_x, r_y)}{\sigma_x \sigma_y}$$

Don't bother figuring that out if it's been more than six months since you've taken a statistics class. Go to your Excel spreadsheet and click in any empty box. Go to your "Insert" menu and select "Function." Select the "Statistical" category. Scroll down and select "CORREL." Excel will launch a wizard to calculate the correlation coefficient for you. (Thanks, Excel!)

	Date	Adj. Close	Adj. Close
		S&P 500	**GE**
	10-Jan-06	1289.69	34.67
	9-Jan-06	1290.15	34.86
	6-Jan-06	1285.45	34.94
	5-Jan-06	1273.48	34.71
	4-Jan-06	1273.46	34.80
	3-Jan-06	1268.80	34.85
			0.028494

The wizard asks for two "Arrays." The arrays are just your columns of data. Clicking in each array box allows you to click, drag and highlight each column of data. You might have to try this a few times to get the hang of it.

Once you have your array data entered, click "OK" and, TA-DA! Correlation coefficient. And without having to do any fancy math or decipher the formula.

The correlation coefficient tells you how similarly GE behaved relative to the index over the time frame you selected (which was probably pretty small). A number close to 1.0 indicates a positive correlation (you zig, I zig). A number close to −1.0 indicates a negative correlation (you zig, I zag). A number closer to zero means there is little correlation either way (you zig, I Cleveland). Remember, when looking at short time periods, you don't have a basis for making an assumption at all.

Step 4

You aren't quite done. Now you must do something that sounds tough but isn't. To understand the relative *relatedness* of two variables, you must do a *regression analysis* and calculate the *R-squared*. It's way easier than it sounds. Simply square the correlation coefficient. (That's why they call it "R-squared.") If your correlation coefficient is 0.5, your R-squared is 0.25 (0.5 × 0.5 = 0.25). If the correlation coefficient is 0.85, the R-squared is 0.7225.

The R-squared tells you what percent of one variable's movement you can relate to (or maybe blame on) the other variable. An R-squared of 0.7225 means 72.25% of one variable's movement is caused by another (which would be an impressive find!).

You're now ready to find correlation coefficients and debunk causalities that don't exist and uncover more of what you can know that others don't.

APPENDIX B

News You Can't Use

From my July 6, 1998, Forbes *column.*

Reader Neil Bell e-mails that he is "puzzled by your lack of attention to the year 2000 problem." I write back saying I covered it in my Mar. 13, 1995, column. Reader Bell responded that I ought to look at several of the detailed Web sites showing just how serious this Y2K thing really is.

So I did and have come to the conclusion that Y2K faddists to the contrary, this thing won't seriously hurt the stock market or cause you any other major inconvenience.

My view on such things is very simple: One should be aware of all the buzz in the media, if for no other reason than to go contrary to it. If any subject has more than one Web site devoted to it, it is either wrong or already fully discounted in the marketplace. The most basic of all market notions is that the market (The Great Humiliator) is a discounter of all known information. It succeeds by making sure that whatever we all know is either wrong or is already priced into securities. Yes, listen to the buzz but never try to make money except by acting against it.

Y2K is heavily covered. Even the SEC has pronounced its fear of Y2K. So ignore it. The Great Humiliator does this stuff effortlessly. It is just like everyone's massive fear of high P/Es. In markets, it's what you don't see or know that gets you because the only thing that moves markets is surprise: There's not much surprise in anything that's all over the World Wide Web. And the most likely surprise in a high-P/E stock is from bad news, not good news, which is already in the price. In my 26-year career, now in my 15th year of doing this column, I have never, ever known this rule to let me down: The obvious never moves markets; surprises almost always do.

In 1995 I wrote this: "If you read or hear about some investment idea or significant event more than once in the media, it won't work. By the time several commentators have thought and written about it, even new news is too old."

In that spirit I say: Forget Y2K.

APPENDIX C

Greater Fools

*F*rom my October 18, 1999, Forbes *column.*

What can we learn about this year end from 1942? First: That Y2K won't hurt the stock market. It may even drive a nice rally.

What does 1942 have to do with Y2K? Well, 1942 shows how the market works, which isn't in a way that now allows a disaster from Y2K. Those who still fret Y2K's market impact don't fathom the markets, and you simply should be dismissive of them all.

There are two principles here. First, markets don't wait for known events; they move ahead of them. Second, folks who wait for events to drive prices often get trapped and trampled by stampedes.

Which was a bigger risk: Y2K in 1999 or Adolf Hitler in 1942? Yet, in 1942, long before anyone could possibly know with any certainty that we would win the war, the S&P 500 rose 20%. In 1943, it rose 26% more—in 1944, 20% more; in 1945, another 36%, before peaking early in 1946. That last year was largely driven by folks who held back cash waiting for certainty— and then threw in their money, very kindly bidding up prices for those who had bought earlier.

How did the market know to rally in 1942 and 1943, long before definitive news? It's what markets do. They decline before a war or recession or something else ugly starts. Usually, they move with a long lead. They rise long before events improve. Hence the age-old adage, "The market knows." The market is also a "discounter" of all known information. That means whatever we all know, fret, read and cluck about is well priced into markets.

It is what we don't all know, fret, read and talk about that moves markets. It isn't that those things can never be discerned. Often they can. But overwhelmingly, folks are blind and ignorant about real market movers.

For example, few can see the huge, unaccounted-for flows of foreign money pouring into America that I first told you about in 1997—that have largely driven our bull market since 1996. They just don't know it's happening. (See my columns of Oct. 20, 1997, and Mar. 22, 1999).

Y2K is the most widely hyped "disaster" in modern history. It is well documented: The only folks who aren't familiar with it are in the upper Amazon basin, rapidly fleeing the rest of humanity. I need not even define Y2K for you to know exactly what I'm referencing.

My July 6, 1998, column detailed why Y2K could not hurt the stock market. But now, with Dec. 31 so close, I'll go a step further and say that the market likely will rise as another Y2K force takes over.

There are just enough investors who do understand how markets work to potentially create a pre-year-end buying stampede. They will sense in coming weeks that a Y2K bust ran out of time and that with year end, the rigid Y2K nuts lose their reason for caution. Those sages may play the Y2Kers for great fools by getting their own money into stocks before year end. I am never sure where the market will go in the very short term, but there is more likelihood of a big pre-year-end up move than any other possibility.

So, remain 100% in equities, with 67% of that in America's 25 largest stocks. The other 33% should be in big continental European and Japanese stocks.

Forbes, October 18, 1999. Reprinted by permission of *Forbes* magazine. © Forbes, 2012.

APPENDIX D

I Hate Funds

*F*rom my August 20, 2001, Forbes *column.*

This issue, the mutual fund guide, is a great one in which to tell you this: I hate funds. So should most of you. The average *Forbes* subscriber (net worth at last count, $2.1 million) is too wealthy for funds. Funds were never meant for you. They were meant for folks with a small pool of money in search of diversification. But at a price. A big one.

For years, I've urged a global approach. I won't retread that now (see, for example, my Nov. 27, 2000, column). But foreign and global funds are expensive.

The average global no-load fund has a 1.8% annual expense ratio—for portfolio management and overhead costs. On top of that are the soft-dollar fees, which are trading commissions, over and above competitive rates, funneled to brokerages for research help they give the fund. Average soft-dollar cost to fund customers: 0.3% of assets annually. It's a fee that rips you off but is legal. The fund should pay for research from its own revenue.

Then people go haywire and hire a person or service to tell them what funds to own, because there are so many and sorting through them is confusing. The normal fee here is 1% annually. Add these three fees and you could

303

be spending 3% a year to own a global stock portfolio. At that you need real genius to come out ahead. If stocks do 10% in the long term, and if inflation averages 3%, your real return is 7%. A 3% annual fee eats up almost half of that. You wind up with bondlike returns while taking stocklike risks. That's a sucker's game.

Then comes performance. Everyone knows the average mutual fund hasn't kept pace with the market. What they don't understand is why. It isn't about stock picking. It's structural. Here's why.

Funds tend to be overweighted in small companies, underweighted in large ones. There could be a lot of reasons for this, but a big one is probably just that it's hard for the portfolio manager to justify a fat money-management fee if he owns only big, obvious stocks like General Electric and ExxonMobil. So during an era like the past decade, when big outperformed small, it was inevitable that funds would underperform the large-cap S&P 500 Index.

You can quantify this disparity. A portfolio has what's called a weighted average market capitalization. A fund 80% invested in a $10 billion market cap stock and 20% in a $100 billion market cap would have a weighted average market cap of $28 billion. For an index fund tracking the S&P 500, this calculation results in a $110 billion figure. For the average US equity fund, it's only $24 billion.

It is very restrictive for an actively managed fund to get its weighted average market cap up near $110 billion. There are, at the moment, only 15 companies with market caps above that figure. Funds own many more stocks than that.

And when small stocks beat big? Funds lose again, at least if they trade actively. Small stocks (that is, stocks of companies with market capitalizations below $5 billion) tend to have low share prices and high bid/ask spreads. If a fund goes in and out of a stock quoted at $20 bid, $20.50 offer, it will lose 2.5% to transaction costs. This is as bad as 3% fees.

So I don't like funds. The actively traded ones will cost you a bundle. The passive index funds are a lot cheaper, and of course an S&P 500 fund will track that index pretty well. But I don't like those, either. Why? Taxes. There are no tax advantages to funds, only disadvantages.

Fans of funds, including the editors of this magazine, make much of the fact that index funds are tax-efficient. That is, they have not had the habit of forcing out taxable capital gain distributions onto helpless shareholders. But they have been successful at this game in large part because they have been taking in new money over the past decade. Come a time of massive redemptions and the index funds might have to sell some of their low-cost basis shares of stock, making taxable distributions inevitable. Also note that even a tax-efficient fund can't pass capital *losses* through to shareholders. If you can use capital losses on your tax return, own shares directly.

Anyone with more than about $350,000, which is most *Forbes* readers, can do better than a fund by buying stocks. Let me put in a plug for following this column's advice. It is global. As measured by *Forbes* annually and after adjusting for phantom 1% brokerage costs, it has beaten the MSCI World, EAFE and S&P 500 for years. It costs you almost nothing. This year? I've been cashlike all year. When I turn bullish, I will be recommending stocks. Not funds.

Forbes, August 20, 2001. Reprinted by permission of *Forbes* magazine. © Forbes, 2012.

APPENDIX E

Annualized Versus Average

We often mention "annualized" returns and "annualized" averages. So what is an annualized average? And is there a difference from a plain old average?

Heck, yes.

A plain old average, or what your statistics professor would call the arithmetic average (or arithmetic mean), is different from an annualized average (called the geometric average or mean). Both types have appropriate analytical uses. But when talking about returns, always use the annualized average. Why? Because arithmetic averages don't reflect investment return reality.

For illustration's sake, use a pretend index with crazily extreme returns. In Year 1, our index rises 75%. In Year 2, it falls 40%. In Year 3, it rises 60%. You know how to calculate the arithmetic average: add 75% + (−40)% + 60% and divide by 3—an average 31.7% return.

But for the annualized average (and bear with me, because it sounds ludicrous and actually isn't hard), you must multiply 1 plus each year's return to the power of the nth root—where n is the number of years, in this case 3. Once you've got that, subtract 1—giving you an annualized average of 18.88%. You can do it easily in Excel—it should look like the formula below:

	A	B	C	D	E	F
1						
2		0.188784				
3						
4						
5						

Toolbar: Arial 10 **B** *I* <u>U</u> $ | B2 f_x =(1.75*0.6*1.6)^(1/3)-1

I multiplied 1 plus each year's return (75% becomes 1.75, −40% becomes 0.6, and so on), raised it with the caret to 1 over n (3 in this case), then subtracted 1.

We've got two very different averages—how can that be? The arithmetic mean of 31.7% and the annualized average of 18.88%. They are both technically correct, but the annualized is vastly more useful and real than the arithmetic mean.

If you invested $10,000 in the index at the start of Year 1, at the end of Year 3 you'd have $16,800—no disputing that. But if someone told you the index averaged 31.7% a year over three years, you'd expect $22,843.22. What happened to the other six grand? You aren't missing any money. The 18.88% annualized average better represents what happened to your assets. Try calculating it now—an 18.88% return on $10,000 compounded over three years gives you $16,800.

Why care? You must be able to calculate portfolio performance correctly. Say someone is selling you a mutual fund. He may say the fund averaged 19% returns over a decade, beating the benchmark average of 10%. He may be giving you a skewed arithmetic average fund return and an annualized benchmark return. The fund's higher arithmetic mean may have resulted from one or two wild years skewing the average, and the annualized return may be much lower. Always think about and ask for annualized averages.

APPENDIX F

The Wizard of Oz and an OZ of Gold

Did you know when L. Frank Baum put pen to paper to write *The Wonderful World of Oz* (published in 1900 and later immortalized in the film starring, among others, Judy Garland, Ray Bolger and Bert Lahr), he didn't intend to write a magical children's story? No. He meant it as sharp political satire and monetary allegory, involving the economic debates and political players of the 1890s.

Don't scour the movie for hidden meaning. The 1939 film was indeed intended as lighthearted fare during dark times. Instead, go back to the original text, where no one in 1900 could miss the meaning behind Dorothy's silver shoes. (Red looked better in Technicolor.) It should grab you instantly that "Oz" is an ounce of gold. Here is the story as Baum meant it.

In the 1890s and into the early part of the twentieth century, debate raged between those who supported the gold standard for our currency and those who would abandon it in favor of a bimetallic or even silver standard. After America returned to the gold standard in 1879, a period of ravaging deflation followed—prices and wages fell nationwide. A variety of policy mishaps, domestic and foreign, culminated in the Panic of 1893 and a subsequent global depression. This wasn't one of our very biggest depressions, but it wasn't insignificant, either. Though we now know there wasn't a single culprit, and American economic woes were part of a larger global trend, in America, the gold standard got its share of the blame.

Fervent support to lift the restriction on minting silver gained sudden popularity. William Jennings Bryan and his booming voice played front and center in the "free silver" movement. Critics saw this as inherently grossly inflationary. Supporters felt some inflation was in order. In popular press, the struggle was frequently framed (and greatly simplified) as a struggle between the "people" (who would benefit from a silver standard and increased inflation) and Eastern banking interests with the politicians in their pockets (who would benefit from the status quo). Incidentally, the "Common Man" versus "Big Business" is a story that still plays today. Funny how some things never change.

Baum crafted his tale against this backdrop, showing his support for the silver movement and Populist disgust for Grover Cleveland, William McKinley and their gold-standard buddies. All the characters he created would have been familiar to his turn-of-the-century audience.

Dorothy, an impoverished yet dauntless farm girl from barren Kansas (where the Populist movement began), is our Everyman. She is plucky and represents the center of America—innocent, good of heart, young, energetic and hopeful. The City of Oz signifies America itself, particularly the East and specifically Manhattan—a land blinded by and wedded to gold and the gold standard. And, of course, the Yellow Brick Road! Yellow meaning gold!

The Witch of the East was pro-gold former Democratic president Grover Cleveland, an apt villain in the Populist view because he was elected president in 1892 (the second time—remember, he was also president from 1885 to 1889, and lost to Benjamin Harrison in 1888) and was in office when the Panic of 1893 unfurled. He was also a villain because he was a Democrat supporting the gold standard, abandoning the Populists, when, in the Populist view, a Democrat should oppose the Republicans who supported the gold standard. Just as Cleveland got politically wiped out, the twister (the silver movement) drops Dorothy's house on top of the Witch of the East, leaving only the treasured silver shoes behind. Naturally, the Munchkins, living in mindless deference in an Eastern suburb of Oz, didn't understand the power of the silver shoes. The Munchkins couldn't even find Kansas on a map, provincial Easterners they were, so they sent Dorothy to see the Wizard.

She is joined first by the Scarecrow—the underestimated Western farmer who in reality is quite astute. He is kept in blissful ignorance about the silver debate because the folks from Oz think he is too simple to understand such a complex topic—that is, until Dorothy and her silver shoes liberate him.

Next up is the Tin Woodsman. Cruel Eastern interests have mechanized the common workingman and stolen his craft and, therefore, his heart. Like so many in the 1890s, this once-hearty and hale laborer is unemployed (rusted and unable to lift his ax). Finally, the Cowardly Lion joins the movement. The Lion is none other than William Jennings Bryan himself, the Democratic presidential candidate in 1896 and 1900—losing both times to William McKinley.

Bryan indeed had a commanding roar, but he was ultimately a loser and didn't have a lion's capability or courage. As the economy improved in the later 1890s, his supporters splintered. Some felt he should focus on other pressing political concerns of the day. Others preferred he continue to be the standard-bearer of the silver fight, and anything less was caving to Eastern interests. He lost courage. He didn't have a lion's heart.

The Emerald Palace, where the Wizard resides, is, of course, the White House—filled with acquiescing bureaucrats. The Wizard seems friendly and wants to help, yet he sends the four friends into the very den of the Witch of the West, who is no friend to their cause. The Wizard himself is in reality Marcus Alonzo Hanna, whom many saw as the "man behind the curtain" of McKinley's presidency. Hanna, from Ohio, was the ultimate backroom political boss of American history. He very much controlled Republican politics and, to a large extent, McKinley in the 1890s. The role of the Wizard having no real power but illusion is allegorical to politics being all about illusion.

The Wicked Witch of the West is President William McKinley, also from Ohio. How can someone from Ohio be the Wicked Witch of the West? Easy, if you're writing from Baum's point of view that everything was controlled by wicked New York City–based banking interests—then anything west of New York's Hudson River is "West." In those days, it was very common to refer to Minnesota and Wisconsin as part of the "Northwest." This is why Northwest Airlines is still based in Minnesota—same evolution of the word. We still refer to Ohio today as the Midwest. By contrast in the vernacular, the "Mideast" doesn't exist in America.

McKinley was staunchly pro-gold, pro-tariff and worse than Cleveland in the Populist view. (His annexation of Puerto Rico, Guam, the Philippines and Hawaii did little to endear him to his foes, who saw him as a greedy imperialist.) This Witch is anxious to get the silver shoes from Dorothy before she learns their true power, and tries to kill her (and the silver movement) off through a series of trials (the aforementioned annexations and Spanish-American War) meant to separate the four friends and the power they have as a united group. Glinda, the Good Witch of the South, waves her wand and resolves the foursome's problems, just as support from the South bolstered the Populist movement before it ultimately died out, and Dorothy returned to Kansas without her silver shoes.

The story is filled with more political and monetary allegory. The flying monkeys, the enslaved Winkies (nowhere to be found in MGM's version), the poppy field (golden), even the gifts the Wizard bestows on our heroes (a little liquid "courage" for the teetotaling lion—Bryan was a well-known Prohibitionist) didn't escape Baum's audience—they knew the meanings.

Don't believe me? There is a wonderful 1990 paper by Hugh Rockoff, "The 'Wizard of Oz' as a Monetary Allegory," which is available online or in your local library. Rockoff delves into more detail about the economic, monetary and political climate, along with the characters and narrative itself. Read that, and then reread Baum's classic. It will be eye-opening for you. Sometimes even your favorite childhood stories aren't what they seem to be.

Source: Hugh Rockoff, "The 'Wizard of Oz' as a Monetary Allegory," *Journal of Political Economy* 98 (August 1990): 739–760.

APPENDIX G

1980 Revisited

From my March 6, 2000, Forbes column.

Tech stocks are in a late-stage bubble. It should break later this year. I usually dislike "bubble," a word bandied about too often by extremists. But I watched a bubble like this one 19 years ago, and I have seen how it ends. Right now technology stocks are just where oil stocks were in early 1981.

Recall how unstoppable energy appeared in 1980. That was a time of high and rising inflation, booming commodity prices, OPEC's success as a cartel and the Iran-Iraq war. By late 1980, oil was $33 a barrel, with consensus forecasts of $100 four years out. No one envisioned oil's falling.

It's happening all over again. This time around it isn't oil's price that is supposed to triple in four years, but rather the population of Internet users.

Here are some other disturbing similarities. Tech's share of the S&P 500 has grown from just 6% in 1992 to 19% in 1998 and 30% in 1999. Energy's S&P weight climbed from 7% in 1972 to 22% in 1979 to 28% at year-end 1980. You know about Technology's great returns: rising 44% in 1998 and 130% in 1999. In 1979, Energy stocks were up 68%, and in 1980, 83%.

Then the bubble popped. The Energy sector's weight fell to 23% by the end of 1981, mostly in the second half of the year. Energy stocks lost 21%.

The S&P 500 lost 4.5%. In 1982, Energy stocks fell another 19%, while the S&P rose 21%. Since 1980 the Energy sector has returned 9% per year. It has lagged three points a year below the next-worst-performing S&P 500 sector. Yet energy consumption has grown steadily.

Check out America's 30 largest stocks. They represent 36% of the US market's entire value. Exactly half are Tech stocks. At year-end 1980, exactly half the 30 largest stocks were Energy stocks. Of course, if you believe in the demand for and future of technology, today's weights may make sense. But if you believe in the increasing supply of the stocks, it doesn't.

Here's another eerie similarity: Back then, Energy stocks sold at twice the S&P's average price-to-book ratio. Today, Tech sells at 2.5 times the market's price to book.

Look at initial public offerings in 1980 and now. That year was a busy one, with Energy making up 20% of the offerings. That boosted the overall number of US stocks by 2%. In 1999, Tech comprised 21% of the offerings and, again, increased total stocks by 2%. While that may not sound big, it is. Newly public companies are where the bubble breaks when they run out of cash.

Most Energy initial public offerings were formed to develop some esoteric energy technology or to drill for oil in bizarre places. They were hardly the vertically integrated giants, like Exxon, which extract, refine and sell oil. And they weren't huge: None of 1980's 50 largest Energy stocks was a 1979 or 1980 initial public offering. Eventually most went bust. But now, 11 of our 50 largest Tech stocks are 1998 or 1999 initial offerings, which means the damage will be greater if any fail.

Most new techies are as shallow in their areas as 1980's offerings were in Energy. Who has the most Internet sales? Amazon? No. Intel, selling chips to its customers, did more online business in 1999 than all the dot commies put together. Federal Express had more business on the Web than America Online and 17 times more business than Yahoo.

Most Internet stocks are merely marketing firms with no clearly defined or provable strategy. Most Net vendors have no real gross margin on sales, and that lack is a disaster waiting to happen—later this year.

As with 1980's Energy initial offerings, these new tech companies burn feverishly through cash, hoping to catch on with the public. Later this year, just as happened two decades ago, dozens will run out of cash—there are 140 now with less than 12 months' cash supply. Folks will then worry about who will run out of cash next, causing many more sound stocks to fall. Selling will run rampant in Tech from small to large, even hurting the most solid Tech stocks.

I have no clue which ones will implode first. Some will float more stock and lengthen their lease on life. But the large group of them without a viable business model are top candidates to go down hard. I don't see this immediately ahead but instead in the second half of 2000.

Last month, I forecast a flat S&P 500 in 2000, with Tech stocks down 15%. I stand by that forecast. As 2000 progresses, you should lighten your holdings in Technology, keeping the biggest and most solid companies. This is a year for moving forward with foreign equities while lowering US expectations.

Forbes, March 6, 2000. Reprinted by permission of *Forbes* magazine. © Forbes, 2012.

APPENDIX H

Popular But Problematic

Many popular tactical myths are problematic and costly, yet continue in their popularity because they appeal to our blindsided brains—they feel so right—and we typically don't know how to think them through. Sometimes these tactics (like stop losses and dollar-cost averaging) were promoted by the brokerage industry decades ago because they increased trading and hence transaction fees. Questions One and Three help you here because you can measure whether they work and see why your brain finds them appealing.

Stop Losses? More Like Stop Gains

The concept of a stop loss—even the name—is so appealing it's easy to see why this maneuver is popular. A stop loss implies setting some arbitrary percent (or dollar) amount of decline. When a stock hits that level, you sell and buy something else. For example, if you always stop losses at 15%, you will never have a stock that is down more than 15%. No disasters. No Enrons.

Sounds good. If not 15%, you can pick any other arbitrary amount, like 10%, 20%, 12.725%. Whatever! This is a control mechanism.

But stop losses don't do what investors want them to do. On average, they lose money, they don't make money. They feel good but are bad. Why? Because stocks aren't *serially correlated*—meaning when a stock moves in any given direction, the odds are 50/50 that it continues in that direction or reverses trend. There is a huge body of scholarly research based on real data proving historical price movement, by itself, has absolutely no bearing on future stock movement. Being down any given arbitrary amount tells you nothing about what the stock does next. Nothing.

If stocks were serially correlated, you could simply buy stocks that have gone up and not buy stocks that have gone down—follow the rule to cut losers and let winners run as momentum investors do. If stocks were serially correlated in the long term, momentum investors would have markedly above-average histories of performance. But it isn't so.

Even if you were adamant in wanting to use stop losses (despite my best efforts to discourage you), what level would you choose? People tend to pick round numbers like 10% and 20%. And those who use stop losses tend not to pick numbers bigger than 20% because if you believe stop losses will work, why favor 30% over 20%? In fact, why favor 20% over 15%? We could do that all the way down to 1%. Regardless, when a stock drops a given amount and hits your stop-loss level, there's a 50% chance it keeps falling and 50% it starts rising. You're trading on a coin flip.

What if you put a stop loss on individual stocks at 20%, and one drops 22% before shooting up 50%? You have a 20% loss, paid a transaction fee and face the task of replacing it. Can you guarantee what you buy next will only go up? What if the replacement stock drops again? You can keep buying 20% losers all the way to zero. History shows no stop-loss level—down 10%, 20%, 30%, 53%—leads to market-beating returns.

Another scenario. Reframe to see it clearly. Amy buys a stock at $50. It rises to $100. Sue then buys it at $100, and it falls to $80—a 20% drop from its high. Should they both sell out at $80? Or just Sue with her higher cost basis? There is no right answer because past price movement isn't indicative of future price movement.

Some propose replacing the sold stock with a similar one from the same industry. But why is that better? And if the sector begins to gain, chances are either stock would also rise. The decision to buy or sell shouldn't be driven by arbitrary price movements or targets but by the forward-looking outlook for that stock.

Some propose using stop losses without replacements so you never suffer a bear market. But then, in a normal bull market correction, stop losses tend to force the sale of most stocks at relative low points. Aren't we supposed to buy low and sell high, not the reverse? The outcome tied to an absolute stop loss is purely random. In other words, it doesn't work.

The only stop-loss certainty is increased transaction costs. In an otherwise random process, this alone makes a stop-loss strategy a money loser.

Dollar-Cost Averaging—Higher Fees, Lower Returns

Most investors accept without question that *dollar-cost averaging* (DCA)—spreading out investment additions or contributions over time—is a good strategy for reducing risk and possibly increasing return. If you add regularly to your 401(k) or other retirement saving plan, in essence, you're dollar-cost averaging.

Regularly adding to your retirement saving plan is absolutely rational. First, many investors don't have the cash flow from their paychecks readily available to fully fund their 401(k)s, 403(b)s or other plans all at once, preferring to make smaller regular contributions monthly or at other intervals. Second, many companies match contributions to a retirement saving plan, which equates to risk-free growth of your account. I'm always a fan of free money. Third, you should always max out every vehicle available for retirement saving as much as you can. But any other form of DCA is costly.

However, DCA is intuitively appealing (at first). Investors may be concerned the day they buy could be a relative high point. Spreading it out over time (so goes the thinking) reduces the risk of getting all in on a "bad" day. If you did get all in on a "bad" day, you would have a lot of regret, and people hate regret.

Something few think about, though, is when you break your money up into many little pieces, the total commissions on your total assets rise markedly, all to the broker. All else being equal, if you're not getting markedly better returns, you're dinging yourself just through increased fees.

However, data show DCA does hurts a portfolio's risk and return characteristics. Michael Rozeff at the University at Buffalo (SUNY) conducted an especially thorough study in 1990, comparing DCA with single lump-sum investments.

Using the S&P 500 as an investment choice, each calendar year from 1926 to 1990 Rozeff compared the results of a single lump-sum purchase to averaging the purchase over 12 months. The results were conclusive: In about two-thirds of the years, the lump-sum method proved more profitable than DCA with less return variability. More important, for the entire span, the lump-sum approach yielded 1.1% higher average annual returns than DCA. When applied to a portfolio of small stocks, the advantages of the lump-sum approach were even more dramatic, with an average annual return that was 3.9% greater than a DCA strategy.[1]

My firm has done its own studies more with similar conclusions recently (as I wrote about in my 2010 book *Debunkery*). Lump-sum investing works better than DCA on average because the market moves higher in the future more often than not. Not always, but enough to make DCA irrational.

Discovering DCA is an inferior strategy doesn't require fancy math or analysis, and the findings are compelling. The reason why the DCA myth persists can be dispelled with Question Three and the concept that people feel the pain of a financial loss more than twice as much as they enjoy a similar-size gain.[2] Many investors will accept an inferior strategy like DCA because it eliminates the possibility of one big mistake that could cause big regret accumulation and maybe make your spouse see you as an idiot. People think DCA reduces risk so they think it's smart. History shows DCA actually increases risk and reduces future returns. No matter what substantial gains they miss out on in the long run, most investors feel giving up profits hurts only about half as much as suffering losses.

Simply put: Dollar cost averaging doesn't work like you want it to and may only increase transaction fees. You're better off without DCA even though that feels wrong. Your feelings are your enemy here once again—always existing so TGH can use them against you even when you think you're beating him.

APPENDIX I

Covered Calls—Covering What?

Covered calls! Like stop losses, the name itself is somehow comforting. But don't be fooled.

A covered call combines a long stock position and a written call. The idea is you could can gain instant income (from the premium for writing the option), but risk is limited from the option. Ask someone who is fond of covered calls why they like them, and they usually say something like they're "safe" or "a safe way to get income." And who wouldn't want something like that? But is it true?

To know, we must consider what exactly is a covered call. We can do that by graphing the potential payouts at the exercise date (see Figure I.1). As with all option positions, the range of possible exercise profits and losses are known. The x-axis shows the stock price at the exercise date, and the y-axis shows profit or loss from this position. X indicates the strike price of the option.

So the covered call actually pays out a fixed amount for an increasing stock price (thereby limiting potential upside) but still has the stock's downside risk, less only the premium received.

This doesn't sound so appealing anymore. The fact is, this is exactly the same payout that a naked put would have (see Figure I.2). There's no

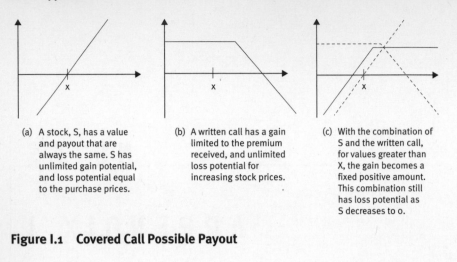

(a) A stock, S, has a value and payout that are always the same. S has unlimited gain potential, and loss potential equal to the purchase prices.

(b) A written call has a gain limited to the premium received, and unlimited loss potential for increasing stock prices.

(c) With the combination of S and the written call, for values greater than X, the gain becomes a fixed positive amount. This combination still has loss potential as S decreases to 0.

Figure I.1   Covered Call Possible Payout

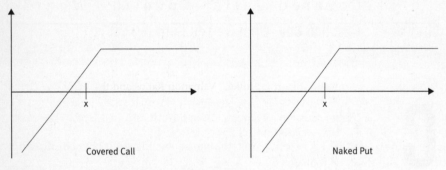

Covered Call

Naked Put

Figure I.2   Covered Calls and Naked Puts

difference. And finance theory tells us that two securities that have identical payouts are, indeed, the same security.

Many investors frown on the idea of selling a naked put, but that is really what they do with covered calls. So the perceived safety in a covered call is just that—perception.

With a naked written put and a covered call being equal, they should be viewed equally. This is another great example of investors being confused by the framework in which identical information is provided. In standard finance theory, investors are rational and never confused by frameworks, but in reality, people blindly do covered calls thinking they're safe when they would never write the naked put because to them it seems highly risky—fooled by framework.

So the next time someone wants you to invest in covered calls, you should just ask them to sell a naked put: It's the exact same thing!

NOTES

Chapter 1   Question One: What Do You Believe That Is Actually False?

1. John Y. Campbell and Robert J. Shiller, "Valuation Ratios and the Long-Run Stock Market Outlook," *Journal of Portfolio Management* (Winter 1998), pp. 11–26.
2. Kenneth L. Fisher and Meir Statman, "Cognitive Biases in Market Forecasts," *Journal of Portfolio Management* (Fall 2000), pp. 72–81.
3. See note 1.
4. See note 1.
5. See note 1.
6. If you're inclined to data and statistics, I refer you to another scholarly article Meir Statman and I did in the Summer 2006 issue of the *Journal of Investing* where we show the data for the United Kingdom, Germany and Japan.
7. Daniel Kahneman and Amos Tversky, "Prospect Theory: An Analysis of Decision Under Risk," *Econometrica*, vol. 47, no. 2 (March 1979), pp. 263–292.
8. Richard H. Thaler, Amos Tversky, Daniel Kahneman and Alan Schwartz, "The Effect of Myopia and Loss Aversion on Risk Taking: An Experimental Test," *Quarterly Journal of Economics* (May 1997), pp. 647–661.
9. Daniel Kahneman, Paul Slovic and Amos Tversky, *Judgment Under Uncertainty: Heuristics and Biases* (New York: Cambridge University Press, 1982), pp. 480–481.
10. Bloomberg Finance, L.P., Bloomberg Fair Value USD Composite (BBB), as of 12/07/2011.
11. US Census Bureau, Thomson Reuters.
12. US Bureau of Economic Analysis, as of 12/31/2010.

Chapter 2   Question Two: What Can You Fathom That Others Find Unfathomable?

1. Global Financial Data, Inc., S&P 500 total return.
2. US Department of Commerce, National Bureau of Economic Research, "The NBER's Recession Dating Procedure."
3. Thomson Reuters, S&P 500 total return from 12/31/1997 to 12/31/1998.
4. Thomson Reuters, S&P 500 total return and MSCI World net return from 12/31/2004 to 12/31/2005 and from 12/31/2005 to 12/31/2006.
5. Russell 2000, Russell 2000 Value, Russell 2000 Growth, MSCI EAFE; Barclays Aggregate, S&P/Citigroup Primary Growth, S&P/Citigroup Primary Value, S&P 500 Value from 12/31/1990 to 12/31/2010. All returns total returns except MSCI EAFE, which is net. S&P/Citigroup Primary Value index measures the performance of the value style of investing in large-cap US stocks. The index is constructed by dividing the top 80% of all US stocks in terms of market capitalization into a value index, using style. S&P/Citigroup Primary Growth index measures the performance of the growth style of investing in large-cap US stocks. The index is constructed by dividing the top 80% of all US stocks in terms of market capitalization into a growth index, using style.
6. Thomson Reuters, MSCI World Growth Index, MSCI World Value Index, all net returns from 12/31/2006 to 12/31/2011.
7. Federal Election Commission, "Appendix A: 1988–2000 Presidential General Election Percentage of Popular Vote Received by State," http://www.fec.gov/pubrec/fe2000/appa.htm.
8. See note 7.
9. "Guide to US Elections," *Congressional Quarterly* (1975), p. 271.
10. See note 9.
11. See note 9.
12. Thomson Reuters, S&P 500 total return.
13. Global Financial Data, Inc., S&P 500 total return.

Chapter 3   Question Three: What the Heck Is My Brain Doing to Blindside Me Now?

1. Investment Company Institute, Archive of Trends releases, "Net New CashFlow in Stock Mutual Funds," http://www.ici.org/stats/mf/arctrends/index.html#TopOfPage (accessed June 29, 2006).
2. See note 1.
3. Thomson Reuters, S&P 500 return from 07/17/1998, through 8/13/1998.
4. Thomson Reuters, S&P 500 total return.
5. Thomson Reuters, S&P 500 total return from 12/31/1997 to 12/31/1998.
6. Richard H. Thaler, Amos Tversky, Daniel Kahneman, and Alan Schwartz, "The Effect of Myopia and Loss Aversion on Risk Taking: An Experimental Test," *Quarterly Journal of Economics* (May 1997), pp. 647–661.

7. Gina K. Logue, "Discovery Could Change Continent's History," *Middle Tennessee Record*, vol. 14, no. 20 (April 24, 2006), pp. 8, 7.

8. Library of Congress, Bills/Resolutions, Pension Security Act of 2002, A.H.R. 3762.14.

9. Thomson Reuters, MSCI World Index net return from 12/31/2004 to 12/31/2005.

10. Thomson Reuters, Altria total return from 12/31/1999 to 12/31/2005.

11. Global Financial Data, Inc., S&P 500 total return from 12/31/1996 to 12/31/1997.

12. Standard & Poor's Research Insight, S&P 500 constituent returns 1997.

13. See note 12.

14. Brad M. Barber and Terrance Odean, "Boys Will Be Boys: Gender, Overconfidence, and Common Stock Investment," *Quarterly Journal of Economics*, vol. 116, no. 1 (February 2001), pp. 261–292.

Chapter 4   Capital Markets Technology

1. Global Financial Data, Inc., S&P 500 Index annual total returns, 1926 through 2010.

2. National Oceanic and Atmospheric Administration, National Hurricane Center, "Retired Hurricane Names 1954–2005," http://www.nhc.noaa.gov/retirednames .shtml (accessed May 11, 2006).

3. James O'Shaughnessy, *What Works on Wall Street: A Guide to the Best-Performing Investments Strategies of All Time* (New York: McGraw-Hill, 1997).

4. Kenneth L. Fisher and Meir Statman, "Investor Sentiment and Stock Returns," *Financial Analysts Journal* (March/April 2000), pp. 16–23.

5. Thomson Reuters, S&P 500 total return from 12/31/1998 to 12/31/1999.

6. Kenneth L. Fisher, "Forecasting Made Easy," *Research* (September 2002), pp. 50–54.

7. See note 4.

8. Thomson Reuters, MSCI Australia, MSCI Austria, MSCI Belgium, MSCI Canada, MSCI Denmark, MSCI Finland, MSCI France, MSCI Germany, MSCI Greece, MSCI Hong Kong, MSCI Ireland, MSCI Italy, MSCI Japan, MSCI Netherlands, MSCI New Zealand, MSCI Norway, MSCI Portugal, MSCI Singapore, MSCI Spain, MSCI Sweden, MSCI Switzerland, MSCI UK, MSCI USA, all total return indexes from 12/31/1989 to 12/31/2010.

9. Thomson Reuters, DJIA constituents as of 09/30/2011.

10. Thomson Reuters, as of 09/30/2011.

11. Thomson Reuters, as of 12/21/2011.

Chapter 5   When There's No There, There!

1. US Department of Energy, as of 12/31/2011.

2. See note 1.

3. Joe Barton, "Barton Releases Discussion Draft of Refinery Bill," U.S. House of Representatives, Committee on Energy and Commerce, http://energycommerce .house.gov/108/News/09262005_1661.htm (accessed June 20, 2006).

Chapter 6 No, It's Just the Opposite

1. Thomson Reuters, Treasury Direct, Congressional Budget Office, May 2011 release.
2. Bankrate.com, as of 12/07/2011.
3. Standard & Poor's Research Insight, Thomson Reuters, as of 09/30/2011.
4. Bloomberg Finance, L.P., Bloomberg Fair Value USD Composite (BBB), as of 12/07/2011.
5. Global Financial Data, Inc, S&P 500 total return from 12/31/1964 to 12/31/1981.
6. US Census Bureau, Foreign Trade Division; US Bureau of Economic Analysis, as of 12/31/2010.
7. US Census Bureau, Foreign Trade Division; US Bureau of Economic Analysis, as of 12/31/2010.
8. Global Financial Data, Inc., S&P 500 total return.
9. US Census Bureau, Foreign Trade Division.
10. Global Financial Data, Inc., FTSE All Share total return.
11. Global Financial Data, Inc., DAX total return.
12. Global Financial Data, Inc., Topix total return.
13. Notes: Current yields on the 6s of 1790 are used from 1800 through August 1820, and the 5s of 1821-1835 are used from September 1820 to 1834. The Federal government completely paid off its debt in the 1830s, so New York State Canal 5% bonds are used from 1835 to June 1843. US Government 5% bonds are again used from July 1843 to 1852 and 6% bonds are used from 1853 to 1865. From 1866 to June 1877, the 5/20s are used and from July 1877 to January 1895, the 4% U.S. Government Bonds of 1907 are used, and from February 1895 until September 1918, the 4% U.S. Government Bonds of 1925 are used. Where no trades were recorded during a given month, the previous month's yield was used. The source for this data is William B. Dana Co., The Financial Review, New York: William B. Dana Co. (1872-1921) which reprinted data published by The Commercial and Financial Chronicle. Beginning in 1919, the Federal Reserve Board's 10-15 year Treasury Bond index is used. 10 year bonds are used beginning in 1941.

Chapter 7 Shocking But True

1. Thomson Reuters, Nasdaq Composite Index peaked on March 10, 2000.
2. Thomson Reuters, MSCI World Index.
3. Kenneth L. Fisher, "That Wall of Worry," *Forbes* (May 9, 2005), p. 142.
4. Bloomberg Finance L.P., one-day price return of MBNA on 06/30/2005.
5. Bloomberg Finance L.P., price return of MBNA from 05/09/2005 to 06/30/2005.
6. Kenneth L. Fisher, "Surprise: America Owes Too Little," *Forbes* (April 18, 2005), p. 244.
7. See note 1, CP Ships price return on August 22, 2005.
8. See note 1, CP Ships price return from April 18, 2005, through August 22, 2005.

Chapter 8   The Great Humiliator and Your Stone Age Brain

1. Global Financial Data, Inc., as of 02/12/2012. The annualized average total return of the S&P 500 Index from 12/31/1925 to 12/31/2011 is 9.7%.
2. Michael J. Mandel, "The New Economy," *BusinessWeek*, (January 31, 2000).
3. Standard & Poor's Research Insight, top 30 stocks by market capitalization of the S&P 500 Index.
4. Global Financial Data, Inc., Nasdaq Composite Index price return and S&P 500 total return.
5. Global Financial Data, Inc., S&P 500 total return from 12/31/1925 to 12/31/2010.
6. Global Financial Data, Inc.
7. Global Financial Data, Inc., S&P 500 total return.
8. US Bureau of Economic Analysis; Thomson Reuters, S&P 500 total returns and MSCI World Index net returns from 09/30/2005 to 12/31/2005.
9. Thomson Reuters, MSCI World net return.
10. US Census Bureau, "State & County QuickFacts: Louisiana," http://quickfacts.census.gov/qfd/states/22000.html.
11. Bloomberg Finance, L.P., US GDP as of 12/31/2011.
12. Ned Davis Research, Inc., return on Dow Jones Industrial Average.

Chapter 9   Putting It All Together

1. Kenneth L. Fisher and Meir Statman, "The Mean Variance Optimization Puzzle: Security Portfolios and Food Portfolios," *Financial Analysts Journal* (July/August 1997), pp. 41–50.
2. Global Financial Data, Inc., S&P 500 total return for US stocks; USA 10-year Government Bond Total Return Index from 12/31/1925 to 12/31/2010.
3. See note 2.
4. See note 2.
5. Morgan Stanley Capital International as of September 30, 2011.
6. Thomson Reuters, technology as measured by the Nasdaq 100 Index, health care as measured by the S&P 500 Pharmaceuticals Index, which is now discontinued. Standard deviations are of each index, 50/50 portfolio and standard deviation derived by combining both tech and health care indices and rebalancing each year.
7. Thomson Reuters, Merck and GlaxoSmithKline return from 12/31/1989 to 12/31/1999.
8. Kenneth L. Fisher, "Give It Time," *Forbes* (January 31, 2005), p. 142.
9. Thomson Reuters, Flowserve return from 12/31/2004 to 12/31/2005; MSCI Industrials net return from 12/31/2004 to 12/31/2005, S&P 500 total return from 12/31/2004 to 12/31/2005, MSCI World Index net return from 12/31/2004 to 12/31/2005.
10. Thomson Reuters, JLG Industries and Joy Global return from 12/31/2004 to 12/31/2005.

11. Office of New York State Attorney General Eliot Spitzer, press release, "Investigation Reveals Widespread Corruption in Insurance Industry" (October 14, 2004).

12. Thomson Reuters, AIG and Marsh McLennan return from 10/13/2004 to 10/14/2004.

13. Ian McDonald and Leslie Scism, "AIG's ExChief Clears a Hurdle but Faces More," *Wall Street Journal* (November 25, 2005).

14. Thomson Reuters, AIG's total return from 2/11/2004 to 4/22/2005; from 4/22/2005 to 1/11 2006; and from 10/14/2004 to 1/11/2006.

Appendix H   Popular But Problematic

1. Michael S. Rozeff, "Lump-Sum Investing Versus Dollar-Averaging," *Journal of Portfolio Management* (Winter 1994), pp. 45–50.

2. Richard H. Thaler, Amos Tversky, Daniel Kahneman and Alan Schwartz, "The Effect of Myopia and Loss Aversion on Risk Taking: An Experimental Test," *Quarterly Journal of Economics* (May 1997), pp. 647–661.

ABOUT THE AUTHORS

KEN FISHER is best known for his prestigious "Portfolio Strategy" column in *Forbes* magazine, where his over 27-year tenure of high-profile calls makes him the fourth longest-running columnist in *Forbes's* 90-plus year history. He is the founder, Chairman, and CEO of Fisher Investments, an independent global money management firm managing tens of billions for individuals and institutions globally. Fisher is ranked #263 on the 2011 *Forbes* 400 list of richest Americans and #736 on the 2011 *Forbes* Global Billionaire list. In 2010, *Investment Advisor* magazine named him among the 30 most influential individuals of the last three decades. Fisher has authored numerous professional and scholarly articles, including the award-winning article, "Cognitive Biases in Market Forecasting," and has published eight previous books, including national bestsellers *The Only Three Questions That Count, The Ten Roads to Riches, How to Smell a Rat, Debunkery* and *Markets Never Forget*, all of which are published by Wiley. Fisher has been published, interviewed and/or written about in many major American, British and German finance or business periodicals. He has a weekly column in *Focus Money*, Germany's leading weekly finance and business magazine.

LARA HOFFMANS is a content manager at Fisher Investments, managing editor of MarketMinder.com, a regular contributor to Forbes.com, and coauthor of the bestsellers *The Only Three Questions That Count, The Ten Roads to Riches, How to Smell a Rat, Debunkery* and *Markets Never Forget*.

JENNIFER CHOU was a research analyst of global markets and macroeconomics at Fisher Investments. She graduated from the University of California with a BS in finance.

INDEX